THE CAMBRIDGE EDITION
OF THE CORRESPONDENCE
OF SAMUEL RICHARDSON 9

CORRESPONDENCE PRIMARILY ON *PAMELA* AND *CLARISSA*
(1732–1749)

THE CAMBRIDGE EDITION
OF THE WORKS AND CORRESPONDENCE
OF SAMUEL RICHARDSON

GENERAL EDITORS
Thomas Keymer *University of Toronto*
Peter Sabor *McGill University*

Thanks are expressed to the Social Sciences and Humanities Research Council of Canada, the Leverhulme Trust, the Chancellor Jackman Professorships Program, the Canada Research Chairs Program and Le Fonds québécois de la recherche sur la société et la culture for providing research funding towards the creation of this edition.

Advisory board
Paula R. Backscheider, †David Blewett, Margaret Anne Doody,
David Fairer, Isobel Grundy, Jocelyn Harris, John Mullan, Claude Rawson, John Richetti, Kathryn Sutherland, Janet Todd, †Howard Weinbrot

THE CAMBRIDGE EDITION
OF THE WORKS AND CORRESPONDENCE
OF SAMUEL RICHARDSON

THE WORKS

1 *Early Works*
2 *Pamela*
3 *Pamela in her Exalted Condition*
4 – 7 *Clarissa*
8 – 11 *Sir Charles Grandison*
12 *Later Works and Index*

THE CORRESPONDENCE

1 *Correspondence with Aaron Hill and the Hill Family*
2 *Correspondence with George Cheyne and Thomas Edwards*
3 *Correspondence with Sarah Wescomb, Frances Grainger and Laetitia Pilkington*
4 *Correspondence with Sarah Chapone, Hester Mulso Chapone and their Circles*
5–7 *Correspondence with Lady Bradshaigh and Lady Echlin*
8 *Correspondence with Edward Young, Johannes Stinstra, Eusebius Silvester and Lady Barbara Montagu*
9 *Correspondence Primarily on* Pamela *and* Clarissa *(1732–1749)*
10 *Correspondence Primarily on* Sir Charles Grandison *(1750–1754)*
11 *Correspondence of Richardson's Final Years (1755–1761)*
12 *Additional Letters, Appendices and General Index*

Falkirk House June 30. 1749

L. 24.

—— I will now reply to your often repeated
request of ~~my~~ giving you my Sentiments on Clarissa
Harlowe. I think taken the Work altogether it is
contrary to most books I ever read for it improves in
every page. I admire the author's being able to adapt
his language and keep up to the Spirit of each
Character the whole Way. where there are many Actors
even Skillfull hands are apt sometimes to let them
run too much into their neighbours Province: he
really does not, and each thought word and action are
natural Consequences of the Person whose Picture
he has at first presented you with. The fault I
have heard most laid to his Charge is the over
straining the Character of his principle heroine,
for that it is impossible to meet with so much
self-denial cloath'd in Mortality. I am afraid
indeed there is no such perfect Creature now existing,
but I think it is no bad Compliment to Mr Richardson
that he has given a Pattern which is censured for
being too good to imitate. I am not in the least

Henrietta Arabella Churchill to Jane Collier, 30 June 1749

SAMUEL RICHARDSON

CORRESPONDENCE PRIMARILY ON *PAMELA* AND *CLARISSA* (1732–1749)

EDITED BY
Louise Curran
University of Birmingham

George Justice
University of Tulsa

Sören Hammerschmidt
GateWay Community College

University Printing House, Cambridge CB2 8BS, United Kingdom

One Liberty Plaza, 20th Floor, New York, NY 10006, USA

477 Williamstown Road, Port Melbourne, VIC 3207, Australia

314–321, 3rd Floor, Plot 3, Splendor Forum, Jasola District Centre, New Delhi – 110025, India

103 Penang Road, #05–6/07, Visioncrest Commercial, Singapore 238467

Cambridge University Press is part of the University of Cambridge.

It furthers the University's mission by disseminating knowledge in the pursuit of education, learning, and research at the highest international levels of excellence.

www.cambridge.org
Information on this title: www.cambridge.org/9780521830355
DOI: 10.1017/9781139033145

© Cambridge University Press 2024

This publication is in copyright. Subject to statutory exception and to the provisions of relevant collective licensing agreements, no reproduction of any part may take place without the written permission of Cambridge University Press.

First published 2024

Printed in the United Kingdom by CPI Group Ltd, Croydon CR0 4YY

A catalogue record for this publication is available from the British Library.

Library of Congress Cataloging-in-Publication Data
NAMES: Richardson, Samuel, 1689–1761 author. | Curran, Louise, editor. | Justice, George, editor. | Hammerschmidt, Sören, editor.
TITLE: Correspondence primarily on Pamela and Clarissa (1732–1749) / edited by Louise Curran, George Justice, Sören Hammerschmidt.
DESCRIPTION: Cambridge ; New York, NY : Cambridge University Press, 2023. | SERIES: The Cambridge edition of the correspondence of Samuel Richardson; 9 | Includes bibliographical references and index.
IDENTIFIERS: LCCN 2023022410 | ISBN 9780521830355 (hardback) | ISBN 9781009347273 (paperback) | ISBN 9781139033145 (ebook)
SUBJECTS: LCSH: Richardson, Samuel, 1689–1761 – Correspondence. | Novelists, English – 18th century – Correspondence. | Richardson, Samuel, 1689–1761. Pamela. | Richardson, Samuel, 1689–1761. Clarissa.
CLASSIFICATION: LCC PR3666 .A4 2023 | DDC 823/.6–dc23/eng/20230628
LC record available at https://lccn.loc.gov/2023022410

ISBN 978-0-521-83035-5 Hardback

Cambridge University Press has no responsibility for the persistence or accuracy of URLs for external or third-party internet websites referred to in this publication and does not guarantee that any content on such websites is, or will remain, accurate or appropriate.

CONTENTS

General Editors' Preface *page* ix

Acknowledgements xxiii

Chronology xxv

List of Abbreviations xxxiii

General Introduction xxxv

CORRESPONDENCE PRIMARILY ON *PAMELA* AND *CLARISSA* (1732–1749) 1

Appendix: Orders and Receipts of Payment 260

Index 273

GENERAL EDITORS' PREFACE

Thanks to the editorial labours of the twentieth century, there are few major British authors of the eighteenth century – the classic period of the familiar letter as a genre – whose correspondence is not available in a standard scholarly edition. Some of the most ambitious undertakings, such as the Yale edition of James Boswell, are still in progress, and some of the most longstanding, such as the Oxford and Chicago editions of Alexander Pope and Edmund Burke respectively, now require extensive supplementation, perhaps even replacement. But there is no more anomalous case than Samuel Richardson, whose correspondence holds special interest, beyond its extraordinary scale and range, as that of a practising epistolary novelist who thought longer and harder than any contemporary about the letter as a form. Almost half of the surviving Richardson correspondence, which totals almost 1,700 letters, has never appeared in print, and barely a quarter of it is represented – with silent abridgments, conflations, and other interventions – in the early edition on which scholars have had to rely until now, Anna Laetitia Barbauld's six-volume *The Correspondence of Samuel Richardson* (1804).

The process of publication got off to a good enough start. Individual items began appearing in print within Richardson's lifetime, and in his last years he took practical steps towards preparing a selected edition. Even before the success of *Pamela* propelled him to fame in the early 1740s, a reply he wrote in humorous couplets to a guild invitation – emphatically a rhyming letter, not a verse epistle – found its way into the *Gentleman's Magazine* for January 1736. The epistolary commentaries he printed about later novels, such as his *Answer to the Letter of a Very Reverend Worthy Gentleman, Objecting to the Warmth of a Particular Scene in … Clarissa* (1749) or his *Copy of a Letter to a Lady, Who Was Solicitous for an Additional Volume to … Sir Charles Grandison* (1754), were formal versions of actual letters, written and sent in response to letters he received. Richardson also included as an appendix to *Sir Charles Grandison* extracts from his acrimonious correspondence with George Faulkner, the Dublin bookseller, about literary piracy and property. Fourteen complete or abridged letters from the poet Aaron Hill, Richardson's closest literary adviser for many years, appeared in print before this time, either in the expanded second edition of *Pamela* or, more extensively, in *The Works of the Late Aaron Hill* (1753). By 1757, when a Leipzig bookseller named Erasmus Reich approached Richardson requesting to publish a selected edition in German, he had already been at work for at least two years in sorting his correspondence

GENERAL EDITORS' PREFACE

files for family use, and he considered Reich's proposal very seriously. Surviving manuscripts are marked up for publication in his tremulous late hand, with names disguised and wordings improved, and he discussed the project with at least two correspondents, Lady Bradshaigh and Sarah Wescomb Scudamore. The following year he abandoned the idea, largely because of scruples about confidentiality. But he continued to think of the correspondence as publishable after his death, subject to permission from the writers involved, if necessary as a subscription edition to support his daughters. A venture of some such kind seems to have been in prospect in about 1780, when Richardson's nephew William issued proposals for a new edition of the novels to contain, among other addenda, 'a collection of letters written by him on moral and entertaining subjects, never before published'.[1] But the edition in question never materialized, and it was not until the death of Richardson's last surviving daughter in 1803, and the subsequent acquisition of his manuscripts by the radical bookseller Richard Phillips, that publication was at last achieved.

The edition that Barbauld prepared for Phillips has been widely criticized for its undeclared editorial freedoms. Yet Barbauld's treatment of manuscript sources was within the publishing conventions of her day, and the many small-scale changes made to punctuation and other accidentals were not her own but the work of compositors in the five printing-houses among which Phillips, in his haste to recoup his outlay, distributed production. Thanks to the researches of Barbauld's modern biographer, William McCarthy, we now know the constraints under which she produced her edition, in at most three months between receiving the original manuscripts and delivering copy to the press, and under relentless harassment from the impatient Phillips.[2] That said, it remains the case that many if not most of the 442 letters represented in Barbauld's edition are silently abridged and otherwise revised, with quite serious chronological scrambling of key correspondences (notably with Edward Young and Lady Bradshaigh), frequent misdatings elsewhere, and at least twenty-five cases in which apparently single letters in fact splice together two or more different sources; hence the total of 442 letters represented in her edition, though she appears to include only 411. Barbauld edited directly on to the manuscripts she received, many of which had already been edited by Richardson himself, and no doubt the printers worked from these originals, almost three-quarters of which later went missing. The result is that Barbauld's

---

[1] John Nichols, *Anecdotes of Bowyer* (1782), p. 157. On these abortive early attempts and the later transmission of the manuscripts, see T. C. Duncan Eaves and Ben D. Kimpel, *Samuel Richardson: A Biography* (Oxford: Clarendon Press, 1971), pp. 436–9, and Louise Curran, '"Into Whosoever Hands Our Letters Might Fall": Samuel Richardson's Correspondence and "the Public Eye"', *Eighteenth-Century Life*, 35 (2011), 51–64; also Curran, *Samuel Richardson and the Art of Letter-Writing* (Cambridge University Press, 2016).

[2] William McCarthy, 'What Did Anna Barbauld Do to Samuel Richardson's Correspondence? A Study of Her Editing', *Studies in Bibliography*, 54 (2001), 191–223.

GENERAL EDITORS' PREFACE

six-volume edition is, for all its defects, the only surviving witness for 324 letters;[3] similar uncertainties surround the text of other letters now known only from early printed sources.

Barbauld's slashing deletions in green ink can still be seen on the manuscripts that survived this process, and she was defensive about the haste of her selections. No one should find fault, she wearily declared, 'unless he had submitted to his inspection, not only the letters that are taken, but those also which are left'.[4] It was clear on all sides, however, that much more than mere chaff remained unpublished. The first supplement to Barbauld appeared in the *European Magazine and London Review*, which serialized a number of Richardson's letters to Sarah Wescomb over three volumes in 1808–9. Phillips's *Monthly Magazine* followed suit with its own selections of unpublished correspondence: first between Richardson and the poet and translator Elizabeth Carter (1813), then a lengthy, important series between Richardson and the poet Edward Young, published over a six-year period (1813–19), and finally a brief exchange between Richardson and his fellow-novelist Tobias Smollett (1819), from a somewhat longer correspondence that Barbauld had missed or ignored. Items from other correspondences, not all of them in Phillips's hands, appeared in the *Gentleman's Magazine* (1816–17), Rebecca Warner's miscellany *Original Letters* (1817), and posthumous collections of works by various writers, notably the bluestocking feminist Hester Mulso Chapone (in 1807) and the German poet Friedrich Gottlieb Klopstock (in 1821).

This process had more or less run its course by 1828, when Phillips ran into financial difficulties and was forced to sell his manuscript collection at auction. A single purchaser, William Upcott, was able to keep much of the collection together, but important parts of it were dispersed (in some cases now untraceably), and publication seems not to have been the motive for any of the buyers involved. The letters not bought by Upcott, and some he sold by private treaty before his death in 1845, are now scattered among numerous archives, many of these in England, Scotland, and the United States, with smaller collections in Germany, the Netherlands, Ireland, and Canada, and a few in private hands. The bulk of Upcott's purchase eventually found its way into the South Kensington (now the Victoria & Albert) Museum, where it has been publicly available since the death in 1876 of its last private owner, the literary journalist John Forster, as part of a much larger bequest. Catalogued as the Forster Collection, it contains about half of the surviving correspondence: some 850 letters arranged and mounted in six massive volumes (probably the work of Richard Forster Sketchley, Assistant Keeper of

---

[3] McCarthy reports that 'of the 442 letters represented in the *Correspondence*, manuscript texts are known (as of 2002) to survive for 111' ('What Did Barbauld Do', 208); seven further manuscripts of letters used by Barbauld are reported in Thomas Keymer and Peter Sabor, 'Samuel Richardson's Correspondence: Additions to Eaves and Kimpel', *N&Q*, 50 (2003), 215–18.

[4] *The Correspondence of Samuel Richardson*, ed. Anna Laetitia Barbauld, 6 vols. (London, 1804), I, vi.

xi

the Museum, whose published guide to the entire Forster Collection appeared in 1893). But although the letters were extensively consulted there and in other depositories by pioneering Richardsonians such as Clara Linklater Thomson and Austin Dobson, and by more recent generations of scholars, no significant advance was made on Barbauld's edition until 1943, when the physician George Cheyne's letters to Richardson, none of which had appeared in Barbauld, were published in a scholarly edition by Charles F. Mullett. Another substantial addition to the corpus was made in 1969, with William C. Slattery's publication of Richardson's correspondence with his Dutch translator, Johannes Stinstra: Barbauld had included three of their letters, but Slattery's edition contains twenty-three, among them Richardson's now celebrated autobiographical letter of 2 June 1753. Modern scholarly editions of letters by independently important correspondents of Richardson such as Samuel Johnson (1952, 1992–4), Tobias Smollett (1970), Edward Young (1971), Sarah and Henry Fielding (1993), Edward Moore (1996), and Charlotte Lennox (1970–1, 2012) have also made available hitherto unpublished letters, or in some cases improved texts of published letters. So too has John Carroll's pioneering *Selected Letters of Samuel Richardson* (1964), which provides lightly annotated texts of 128 letters to thirty-three different correspondents, many of them published for the first time, though often in excerpted form. For half a century, Carroll's selection, alongside Barbauld's, has been the edition cited by Richardson's critics, as well as by many other scholars of the period. More recently, Carroll and Barbauld provide the basis for Donatella Montini's *Lettere su Clarissa*, a more fully annotated selection of thirty-one letters by Richardson, published in 2009. Two and a half centuries after Erasmus Reich's original proposal for a selected edition in translation, it was in Italian, not German, that something resembling his plan came to fruition, though without adding new letters to the published corpus.

In a well-known letter to Sarah Wescomb of September 1746, Richardson celebrates 'the familiar correspondences of friendly and undesigning hearts', and extols the epistolary mode as 'indicative, generally beyond the power of disguise, of the mind of the writer'. It was for this offer of intimate access to authentic personality that the private letters of published authors were so prized in the eighteenth century, even before – as the subterfuge surrounding Pope's *Letters* of 1737 makes clear – their publication seemed fully legitimate. For the same reason, alongside the obvious value of letters as repositories of day-to-day information, they remain an indispensable resource for biographers. The six hundred or so letters by Richardson now known to survive in manuscript or early printed versions are far from conforming in every case to the ideal of artless transparency that he urged on Wescomb. Much of their fascination comes from the ways in which, as the letters of a major epistolary novelist, they reflect his self-consciousness about his chosen form, including its potential for disguise as well as disclosure. Even so, Richardson's letters exhibit a private identity unavailable from any other

GENERAL EDITORS' PREFACE

source, and one that proves, in light of his surviving correspondence as a whole, far more complex and multi-faceted than the notorious caricature that Samuel Taylor Coleridge derived from his reading of Barbauld: 'so very vile a mind – so oozy, hypocritical, praise-mad, canting, envious, concupiscent'.[5] In other contexts, Richardson was consistently reluctant to write in his own voice, to the point on several occasions of procuring prefaces to his works from other hands. Letters gave him, by contrast, a protected space for more or less direct self-expression, and those that survive provide unrivalled evidence of his personal life, his moral, social, and religious opinions, and above all his thinking about literature and the book trade, the art of fiction, and his own practice as a novelist. No other writer of the period has left such a rich, detailed, and sustained account of the composition, reception, and revision of his own works.

Inevitably, the biographical picture is not complete. No epistolary trace survives of some of Richardson's most intriguing relationships: with, for example, the unidentified high-born patron who befriended him in his apprentice years, though 'Multitudes of Letters passed between this Gentleman & me', he told Stinstra decades later (2 June 1753). His close and enduring friendship with the distinguished parliamentarian Arthur Onslow, Speaker of the House of Commons, is only indirectly glimpsed in surviving exchanges with mutual acquaintances, notably the poet and critic Thomas Edwards. Fewer than eighty traceable items are extant from the 1730s, mainly letters to Richardson from Hill and Cheyne, his most prominent friends of the period, but his own side of these correspondences is very sparse. It was not until achieving fame with *Pamela* (1740) at the age of fifty that he seems to have begun systematic efforts to preserve, copy, and file his correspondence, though these files were apparently depleted by the time they reached Barbauld, and certainly depleted further before the 1828 auction, after which more items disappeared. Like Boswell's Johnson, Richardson is a figure we witness in sometimes crushing detail for the last twenty years of his life, but one whose youth and middle age are more distantly, patchily seen. Later letters give valuable insights into otherwise irretrievable aspects of his early career, notably the famous letter to Stinstra, an epistolary memoir comparable, as an exercise in short, informal autobiography, with Laurence Sterne's 'Memoir' and David Hume's 'My Own Life'. But it is above all in Richardson's creative maturity, and at his professional peak, when his range of correspondents grew alongside his fame, that he becomes truly present – vividly, copiously so – in epistolary sources.

Yet it is not only for information about Richardson himself that the correspondence is an important resource. Thanks to his celebrity as an author, his standing and influence as a book-trade professional, and above all his unrelenting fascination with epistolary dialogue and debate, Richardson was able to draw into the circle of his correspondence numerous leading figures in the literary culture of his day.

---

[5] *Coleridge's Notebooks: A Selection*, ed. Seamus Perry (Oxford University Press, 2002), p. 82 (4–8 March 1805).

xiii

GENERAL EDITORS' PREFACE

Little now survives of the strictly professional correspondence he conducted in his capacity as a master printer, including the enormous traffic that must have arisen from the branch of work that distinguished his business, that of parliamentary printing. There are a few business exchanges with prominent trade colleagues such as Andrew Millar and William Strahan, but these are only the tip of an iceberg lost to view. Even so, from his earliest letters to Hill and Cheyne to some of his very last, notably to Catherine Lintot, granddaughter and successor of the printer Bernard Lintot, book-trade concerns are recurrently to the fore, most of all where Richardson is acting as printer for the correspondents involved, or otherwise advising them about publication matters. In this respect his correspondence ranks alongside that of the bookseller Robert Dodsley, or other storehouses like the Bowyer ledgers or Nichols's *Anecdotes*, as one of the richest and most wide-ranging sources in the period for the history of authorship and the book trade. It crucially illuminates the lives and works of the significant but now non-canonical authors to whom he was closest, whose correspondence does not otherwise exist in print. Young is the obvious exception in this category, though some new material has come to light since Henry Pettit's 1971 edition of Young's correspondence; more typical are Hill, Edwards, and Sarah Chapone, a key intermediary between Mary Astell and the bluestocking generation who is now best known for her pioneering tract *The Hardships of the English Laws in Relation to Wives* (1735).

Significant bodies of correspondence also survive involving Elizabeth Carter, the novelist Sarah Fielding, the memoirist Laetitia Pilkington, and other literary friends such as the Delanys, Patrick and Mary, and the Sheridans, Thomas and Frances, all four leading figures in the cultural life of eighteenth-century Dublin. There are also surviving caches of letters to and/or from, among other significant writers of the period, Thomas Birch, Colley Cibber, Jane Collier, Henry Fielding, David Garrick, Samuel Johnson, Charlotte Lennox, Edward Moore, Sarah Scott, Joseph Spence, and William Warburton. It is not entirely an optical illusion, as one reviews these and other names, to see Richardson as inhabiting the very centre of the period's cultural web, not least as it expanded to accommodate women writers.[6] His strenuous promotion of female authorship and learning makes the correspondence an especially important resource for the history of women and print. In 1750 Richardson sent Frances Grainger a list of thirty-six intellectually accomplished women, 'almost all of them of my intimate Acquaintances' (8 September 1750), and it was to an overlapping group that Barbauld referred when she wrote of the 'female senate' among whom *Sir Charles Grandison* was composed;[7] few of these women fail to feature in the surviving correspondence.

---

[6] See Pat Rogers, '"A Young, a Richardson, or a Johnson": Lines of Cultural Force in the Age of Richardson', in *Samuel Richardson: Tercentenary Essays*, ed. Margaret Anne Doody and Peter Sabor (Cambridge University Press, 1989), pp. 203–22, 284–7.

[7] *Correspondence*, ed. Barbauld, I, cxxiii.

xiv

GENERAL EDITORS' PREFACE

Little less attention is focused today on another category of correspondent, unknown except by virtue of their association with Richardson. Several otherwise obscure figures have become familiar points of reference for scholars, partly for their inherent interest as letter-writers, and partly for the rich evidence they provide about reading and reception. Soon after *Grandison* appeared, Richardson was approached by an obscure provincial attorney named Eusebius Silvester, whose opening letters combine discussion of the novel's philanthropic themes with a history of his own condition of impoverished virtue. Five years later, following Silvester's persistent failure to repay two generous loans, Richardson broke off relations and assembled the correspondence, with explanatory notes and connecting passages, into what he called 'a Warning Piece to Posterity' (to Silvester, 21 August 1759) – though he later altered this phrase, with his usual uncertainty about publication, to 'a Warning Piece to his Friends and Family'. Much happier was the outcome of an earlier unsolicited approach, made during the publication of *Clarissa* by an anonymous reader who, after extended games of anonymity and misdirection, at last identified herself as Lady Bradshaigh, thereafter the most cherished friend and literary adviser of Richardson's last years. Surveying the Richardson–Bradshaigh correspondence, Barbauld estimated that it was large enough to fill all six of her 1804 volumes, which indicates that much of it is now lost (as does a reference in the 1828 auction catalogue to 'many hundred letters of each', whereas 110 manuscript letters now survive).[8] Even so, this remains the lengthiest of Richardson's surviving correspondences, much of it on literary matters, and comprising in particular, as he observed when considering the Reich proposal, 'the best Commentary that cd. be written on the History of Clarissa' (to Lady Bradshaigh, 19 November 1757). Of great related interest is the correspondence that ensued with Lady Echlin, Lady Bradshaigh's Dublin-based sister, part of which concerns a wish-fulfilling alternative ending to *Clarissa* that Lady Echlin privately composed.

Other correspondences arising from the novels failed to take off, and just single letters survive from readers such as 'Philo-Paideias', 'Philaretes', and 'Philopamela', who all wrote pseudonymously to Richardson during the *Pamela* vogue. Further letters of the same kind were lost at an early stage, as in a well-known episode during the publication of *Clarissa*, when Richardson responded to two readers' letters, one accusing Clarissa of coquetry, the other of prudery, by sending 'each the other's letter for a full answer of her's. And so I lost, at setting out, two correspondents, and what was worse, my two letters, for I never could get them back, and had taken no copies' (to Lady Bradshaigh, February 1751). Normally he took greater care, and many of the manuscripts in the Forster Collection and elsewhere are not autograph or holograph letters but early copies, made not only

---

[8] *Catalogue of Manuscripts, Autograph Letters ... Also the Richardson Correspondence ... Sold by Auction by Mr. Southgate* (1828), p. 22; for other evidence from the catalogue of lost material, see Peter Sabor, '"The Job I Have Perhaps Rashly Undertaken": Publishing the Correspondence of Samuel Richardson', *Eighteenth-Century Life*, 35 (2011), 9–28 (at 17–18).

xv

GENERAL EDITORS' PREFACE

by Richardson's daughter Martha and his nephew and amanuensis William, as Barbauld reports,[9] but also by Aaron Hill's brother Gilbert, whom Richardson seems to have employed in some secretarial capacity, and perhaps also by other professional copyists. Thanks to his obsessive interest in the vagaries of reception and interpretation, and to the compelling, controversial nature of the texts themselves, three substantial archives survive of general correspondence arising from the three major novels, each with a descriptive index by Richardson himself. (Like the auction catalogue, these indexes list various intriguing items that are now missing.) At a time when literary reviewing was in its infancy and formal critical attention was rarely bestowed on novels, this body of material, which Richardson worked hard to expand by provoking his correspondents into debate, often in devil's-advocate mode, provides an unusually full and detailed archive of literary reception. In the case of the early novel, it is simply unique, not only as historical evidence of reading, but also for its traceable impact on authorial revision.

All told, in the surviving correspondence, Richardson's letters are outnumbered almost two to one by those addressed to him. Yet there is a sense in which he is always present in the correspondence, whether as writer or as addressee. Often he and his interlocutors are pitted in close discussion of one another's ideas or arguments, sometimes with extensive direct quotation, and obviously with previous items from an exchange to hand for consultation. When Sarah Wescomb complained on 23 November 1750 that Richardson had 'pulled [her previous letter] in Pieces', she merely described his standard practice, and his more robust readers responded in kind. One result is that in cases of incomplete survival, such as Richardson's debate with Hester Mulso about *Clarissa*, lost items (here, everything on his own side) can be partly reconstructed from the evidence of surviving replies. In other cases, published text can be seen to emerge from the crucible of the correspondence, as when a protracted debate between Richardson and Lady Bradshaigh, in their letters of 1750–3, over the appropriate balance of power between husband and wife feeds demonstrably into *Sir Charles Grandison*. It has only recently been noticed that an essay contributed by Richardson to Johnson's *Rambler* in 1751 began life the previous year as a letter to Frances Grainger concerning the ethics of courtship.[10]

No less interesting is the overall character conferred by these habits of conversation and debate on much of the correspondence. As each individual exchange unfolds, meaning is mutually developed and incrementally extended through a kind of epistolary dialectic, and properly resides not in any individual letter, and certainly not on any one side of a correspondence, but rather within the transaction as a whole. Not infrequently, new layers or wider circles of meaning are created when, in a practice deliberately cultivated by Richardson as a way to 'mingle

---

[9] *Correspondence*, ed. Barbauld, I, iii.
[10] John A. Dussinger, 'Samuel Richardson's Manuscript Draft of *The Rambler*, No. 97 (19 February 1751)', *N&Q*, 57 (2010), 93–9.

xvi

GENERAL EDITORS' PREFACE

minds and concerns' (to Anne Dewes, 17 August 1750), letters or whole sequences are transcribed and circulated within adjacent correspondence networks, so giving rise to further material. The sources exhibit a vigorous manuscript culture in which correspondences commingle, overlap and interact, generating fresh debate and additional writing through the mechanisms of epistolary sociability. Some writers resisted Richardson's inveterate practice of manuscript circulation, and he was admonished for it by Mary Delany; she had been 'open and free when I write to you, at all times incorrect, interlining, making blunders', she told him on 24 April 1751, and was now minded to suspend the correspondence. Other writers benefited, however. Long before reaching print in 1807, Mulso's trenchant, learned correspondence about liberty and authority in *Clarissa* was widely known, apparently in the highest political circles. Richardson even speculated that it influenced the passage of Hardwicke's Marriage Act a few years later: 'Things done in private have sometimes ... been proclaimed on the house-top', as he put it to Elizabeth Carter (17 August 1753).

These various characteristics of the surviving archive – the prominence within it of important interlocutors whose letters are otherwise inaccessible; its value as evidence of the book trade and literary culture of the mid eighteenth century, and as a capacious record of debates about major novels; the profoundly transactional or dialogic nature of the epistolary sources involved – have two main consequences. Most obviously, they dictate the publication of a full *Correspondence* in twelve volumes, as opposed to a one-sided *Letters* in four or five. They also argue strongly for the retention, albeit with necessary modifications, of a principle of organization, correspondence by correspondence, that was first established and implemented by Richardson himself. The obvious advantages of a single chronological sequence of letters notwithstanding, more would be lost than gained by fragmenting individual correspondences and scattering them across multiple volumes, which would mean as many as eight or ten respectively for key correspondents such as Bradshaigh or Young. For this reason, the Cambridge Edition observes the correspondence-specific methodology used by editors in comparable cases elsewhere, including the multi-volume Yale editions of James Boswell, Thomas Percy, and Horace Walpole. A complete calendar of the correspondence will be added in the concluding volume to facilitate retrieval by date; building on roughly 1,600 letters listed as appendix in T. C. Duncan Eaves and Ben D. Kimpel's monumental 1971 biography of Richardson, this calendar will incorporate various corrections and changed locations, the seventy-nine new findings announced at an earlier stage in the present project, and a number of more recent discoveries.[11] Other finding aids in this volume will be an index of Richardson's correspondents and a general index to the entire edition. The volume will also include Richardson's own indexes to his files of letters on *Pamela*, *Clarissa*, and *Sir Charles Grandison*; other miscellaneous

---

[11] Eaves and Kimpel, *Samuel Richardson*, pp. 620–704; Keymer and Sabor, 'Samuel Richardson's Correspondence'.

xvii

non-epistolary documents from the Forster Collection; any additional letters found during the publication of the previous volumes; posthumous correspondence about Richardson, especially that between his daughters Anne Richardson and Martha Bridgen and between Anne and her niece Sally Crowther Moodie; and an annotated transcription of the 1828 Southgate auction catalogue.

Richardson's exact organization of his files is not recoverable in detail, but the principle is clear from surviving evidence that includes apparently original foliation numbers (now overlaid on the manuscripts by later referencing sequences); prefatory sheets and connecting passages (as in the Hill and Silvester correspondences respectively); notes describing the compilation of a particular correspondence into bound books (Cheyne, Hill) and epistolary exchanges on this subject (Bradshaigh); memoranda restricting access to certain appropriate readers or categories of reader (Cheyne, Edwards). There are also original indexes in Richardson's hand, not only to the files of letters about the novels (which correspond roughly to the chronologically organized volumes of general correspondence in Volumes 9–11 of the Cambridge Edition), but also to the Edwards correspondence. Broadly speaking, Richardson's organization continues to be reflected in the Forster Collection at the Victoria & Albert Museum, and the same principle governed Barbauld's 1804 selection and the subsequent magazine editions. Inevitably, the page length of a modern volume does not always perfectly match the size of a particular correspondence. In these cases, materials have been juxtaposed or combined, either with reference to a broader social network (a volume is devoted to Sarah Chapone, her daughter-in-law, Hester Mulso Chapone, and their overlapping circles) or on grounds of thematic congruence. The correspondences with Cheyne and Edwards in Volume 2 of the Cambridge Edition are linked, for example, not only by their pronounced medical content but also by a more generally unguarded, at times frankly defamatory, character that gave unusual intensity to Richardson's anxieties about future circulation. He stopped short of burning Cheyne's letters, as Cheyne had requested, but the correspondence was not to fall 'into such Hands, as that it may be printed, or published' (note dated 11 August 1744). His cover sheet to the Edwards correspondence carries a stern instruction: 'No Extracts to be taken from it or Letters copied.'

The formidable practical difficulties posed by Richardson's letters in both their printed and their manuscript forms have often been remarked on by scholars. Eaves and Kimpel describe the many letters to and from Lady Bradshaigh for 1751, of which only printed texts in Barbauld survive, as being 'in utter confusion', and painstaking efforts have been made by John August Wood to disentangle this particular problem.[12] William McCarthy, Barbauld's biographer, remarks that the

---

[12] Eaves and Kimpel, *Samuel Richardson*, p. 657; John August Wood, 'The Chronology of the Richardson–Bradshaigh Correspondence of 1751', *Studies in Bibliography*, 33 (1980), 182–91.

GENERAL EDITORS' PREFACE

texts available to her after their various revisions by Richardson and his correspondents and heirs were already 'a thorn patch of multiple copies and different handwritings, with cross-outs and insertions enough to puzzle any would-be editor'.[13] Barbauld's interventions, and those of later owners or curators, introduce further layers of complication, but even letters untouched by later editorial markings can be hard to decipher. Richardson's hand was cramped and unsteady from an early date, and in the 1750s, from which most of the surviving correspondence dates, he frequently complains about paralysis or tremors, or about the pain and even on occasion the impossibility of writing. Parkinson's disease is usually assumed, and scientific analysis of Richardson's remains has revealed a prior condition of diffuse idiopathic skeletal hyperostosis, which 'would undoubtedly have limited extension at the wrist'.[14] Obliterations by Richardson and by some of his correspondents, especially Lady Bradshaigh, whether at the time of writing or at later stages, make matters much worse. These obliterations are sometimes heavy enough to make retrieval of the text impossible, even after protracted examination not only of the manuscripts but also of digitally enhanced photographs and scans. In other cases, problems stem from blots or tears in the manuscript causing obscurity or absence of text, and further illegibility results from the heavy cardboard mountings pasted over the extremities of letters in the unwieldy Victorian volumes of the Forster Collection. Not all the texts are quite so hard to establish as that of Richardson's first known letter to Erasmus Reich, of which only a German translation survives, in a manuscript, housed in a library in Leipzig, which was substantially damaged by allied bombing in World War II. But there is something symptomatic about this case.

In the face of all these obstacles and confusions, the aim of the Cambridge Edition is to bring order to the chaotic condition in which Richardson's massive correspondence comes down to us. It seeks to reproduce, as closely as possible, the state of the text in which each letter was sent and therefore first read. Letters are transcribed from manuscript whenever a manuscript (autograph draft, autograph letter, or contemporaneous file or letterbook copy) has survived. When a letter exists in both manuscript and a printed version, or versions, the manuscript in almost all cases takes precedence (one exception being the few cases in which the surviving manuscript is a very rough or vestigial draft and the printed version more accurately records the letter as sent and first read). The printed version may, however, contain material not in the manuscript: the manuscript may be a fragment, or the printed version may stem from a different manuscript copy. In such cases, the printed version is used together with the manuscript in an effort to recreate (though without silent conflation or other eclecticism) the letter as first

---

[13] William McCarthy, *Anna Letitia Barbauld: Voice of the Enlightenment* (Baltimore: Johns Hopkins University Press, 2008), p. 413.

[14] J. L. Scheuer and J. E. Bowman, 'The Health of the Novelist and Printer Samuel Richardson (1689–1761): A Correlation of Documentary and Skeletal Evidence', *Journal of the Royal Society of Medicine*, 87 (1994), 352–5 (at 354).

xix

GENERAL EDITORS' PREFACE

received. Printed versions are also used to supply words illegible in the manuscript. When more than one manuscript version survives, the manuscript received by a correspondent takes precedence over others, though rough drafts and transcribed copies also come into play where the original text is defective. If a letter survives in both the form of a draft by Richardson and a fair copy, by an amanuensis or a proxy, sent to a correspondent, the fair copy provides the copy-text. If the letter as received does not survive, the surviving manuscript likely to resemble it most closely is used as the copy-text.

When a printed version is used as the copy-text (because no manuscript survives), the letter is not necessarily reproduced in its existing state. In Barbauld's edition, some letters have demonstrably been conflated from different manuscript sources. In such cases, the text of the letter as originally received is reconstructed as far as possible. Where an alternative early printed version exists (such as Aaron Hill's *Works* (1753) for the Hill correspondence or the *Monthly Magazine* for the Edward Young correspondence), a hierarchy between this version and Barbauld's is established; if both were set directly from the manuscript, the earlier publication does not necessarily take precedence. Standardized headings precede each letter. These headings provide, so far as possible, the day(s) and date(s) of writing, the name of the recipient(s), the source and location of the text, a record of all extant documentary states of the letter, manuscript and printed, before 1830, the address, any endorsement (stating in whose hand, if known, or 'undetermined' if not), and the postmark (although these rarely survive).

Many of the problems posed by the texts of Richardson's correspondence resemble those of the letters and journals of Frances Burney, which also survive in a combination of manuscript material, copiously edited by various hands, and a printed edition prepared by a nineteenth-century editor, Charlotte Barrett, who made heavy use of scissors and paste in assembling her edition. Our textual policy is based, with some variations, on that in Peter Sabor's edition of *The Court Journals of Frances Burney, 1786–1791* (6 vols., Oxford University Press, 2011–), which in turn derives from Lars Troide and Stewart Cooke's *Early Journals and Letters of Fanny Burney, 1768–1783* (5 vols., McGill-Queen's University Press, 1988–2012) and Joyce Hemlow's *Journals and Letters of Fanny Burney (Madame d'Arblay), 1791–1840* (12 vols., Oxford University Press, 1972–84). While recognizing the importance of reflecting the state of the copy-text in each case, we aim to produce an edition in which fidelity to the sources is reconciled with clarity for modern readers. We also recognize that the special character of particular correspondences means that local adjustments to textual policy will be required in certain volumes; if so, these adjustments are outlined in the volume editor's introduction to the correspondence in question.

Texts are reproduced literally, for the most part, with retention of original paragraphing, punctuation, period spellings and misspellings, and neologisms (e.g. *objectible*). Richardson uses both curved and squared brackets, sometimes for distinct purposes; we have retained both forms. The original use of lower case and capitals is also generally reproduced, although beginnings of sentences and names

xx

GENERAL EDITORS' PREFACE

of people and places are always capitalized. Final periods are supplied when inadvertently omitted at the close of sentences, but not where sentences are informally separated by dashes or other punctuation or where the general practice of the writer (such as George Cheyne or Sarah Wescomb) is to use minimal punctuation. Parentheses and quotation marks are completed when required. Running marginal quotation marks are omitted. Underlinings are represented by italic type. Double and triple underlinings are designated by a footnote. Superscript letters are lowered. Obvious slips of the pen, as opposed to misspellings, are silently corrected. Obviously inadvertent omissions are supplied within {shaped} brackets. The long 's' has been modernized and the length of dashes has been regularized. Word fragments and inadvertent repetitions are omitted.

As David Fairer observes in his edition of Warton, 'obsolete abbreviations are by far the largest obstacle to the readability of a text'.[15] Like Fairer, we expand or normalize all abbreviations not in standard use today. In particular, 'y^e' and 'y^t' (where the 'y' is strictly speaking a thorn) are expanded to 'the' and 'that'. The term 'thrō' is also expanded to 'through,' and 're'd' to 'read' or 'received', with the addition of a note if the context leaves the meaning of the word ambiguous. Exceptions to the rule are the names of people, the titles of books, the direction and dateline as appearing on the manuscript, the abbreviated past participle (*criticiz'd*, etc.), and borderline cases between abbreviation and period spelling such as *cou'd*, *'tis*, and *tho'*, all of which are transcribed as they appear in the copy-text.

We have not attempted to reproduce the visual appearance of the original manuscripts in terms of layout. If, for example, a postscript is inserted at the beginning of a manuscript, for lack of space at the end, it is printed here in the normal position, with an accompanying note. Regardless of their position in the manuscripts, all salutations are printed flush left, and signatures flush right. Complimentary closes appearing on separate lines in the manuscript are run on as continuations of the last line of text, with conventional punctuation supplied when necessary. Datelines occurring at the head of the manuscript are printed flush right, and those occurring at the foot of the manuscript are printed flush left. Postscripts are printed flush left. Richardson occasionally uses hanging indents as an alternative form of paragraphing for specific purposes, and these are retained.

The following symbols are employed in the texts:

< > Text conjecturally supplied by the editor in cases of obliteration, damage, or uncertain legibility. If a word or character has been torn or cut away from the manuscript, or rendered wholly illegible by slurring, blotting, or other damage, but can still be conjectured from the context, it is printed thus: 'Lady <Bradshaigh>', 'Grandis<on>'. If a word is not certainly legible, but can be deciphered as a reasonable likelihood, the same symbol is used.

---

[15] *The Correspondence of Thomas Warton*, ed. David Fairer (Athens: University of Georgia Press, 1995), p. xlviii.

GENERAL EDITORS' PREFACE

<xxxxx *3 lines*> Three lines have been obliterated and cannot be recovered. Sometimes individual words are legible within generally obliterated passages and if so, these words are recorded.

<xxxxx *5–6 words*> Five or six words have been obliterated and cannot be recovered.

<   > Blank space left in manuscript by writer or copyist.

{ } Text supplied by the editor in cases of inadvertent omission. If a word has been omitted, it will be printed thus: 'I am now {at} Parson's Green.'

The Cambridge Edition of the Correspondence of Samuel Richardson is designed to become the uniform scholarly edition. It has extensive introductions, providing authoritative accounts of each of Richardson's sets of correspondences. Textual and explanatory notes are numbered in a single, combined sequence. This practice makes it possible (where evidence of revision needs explanation in itself, or where it clarifies interpretation of a passage) for textual and explanatory points to be discursively combined. Textual notes normally record only those substantive changes made by the letter-writer at the time of writing, whether to a draft or to the version sent; later revisions, deletions, and additions (most of which date from the later 1750s) are not recorded unless they add significant new detail or information. In recording textual changes we have taken a different approach from that of John Carroll, whose *Selected Letters* uses an elaborate system of symbols (to signal insertions, deletions, and conjectural readings) that has led to some confusion in subsequent scholarship; we have aimed instead to create a readable text, with variant readings at the foot of the page. Explanatory notes identify the numerous quotations and allusions, literary, historical, and personal. All persons named are identified, as far as possible, although exact birth, marriage, and death dates are not always available.

Standard encyclopaedias, biographical dictionaries, peerages, baronetages, knightages, school and university lists, medical registers, lists of clergy, town and city directories, army and navy lists, road guides, almanacs, and catalogues of all kinds have been used but are not specifically cited except in exceptional cases. Also consulted were a variety of online resources, including the *Oxford English Dictionary*, the *Oxford Dictionary of National Biography*, the English Short Title Catalogue, Early English Books Online, Eighteenth-Century Collections Online, Literature Online, InteLex Past Masters, the Burney Collection of Newspapers, British Literary Manuscripts Online, the British Book Trade Index, British History Online, Access to Archives, and the Electronic Enlightenment.

ACKNOWLEDGEMENTS

The co-editors are grateful to the libraries and librarians housing the letters that we have transcribed and edited. This has been a truly collaborative effort involving not only ourselves, other volume editors in the Collected Correspondence and Works of Samuel Richardson, and the general editors, but also a previous co-editor of this volume, Devoney Looser, who dropped off the project a decade ago. These acknowledgements represent Devoney's thanks as well as that of the three co-editors of this volume.

In particular, we'd like to thank Sarah Benoit in the English Department at Louisiana State University, who coordinated the student work in printing out letters from microfilm two decades ago. Melody Wells was the student who located and photocopied these letters. Mona Schulman, Mary L. Robertson, and Gayle Barkley Richardson at the Huntington Library helped not only with access but with a complicated transcription. Leslie Fields at the Pierpont Morgan Library should be recognized for extraordinary service to a breastfeeding mother! Thanks, also, to Adam Rounce for guidance on textual matters, and to Amelia Stevens Greenhalgh at the University of Birmingham for excellent research support at a crucial stage.

Our identification of Gilbert Hill and William Richardson as important amanuenses in Richardson's own compilation of his correspondence would have been incomparably more difficult without the assistance and expert advice of Christine Gerrard and Betty Schellenberg. Richard Berman, Tom Keymer, Thomas Lockwood, Michael Londry, Carolyn Woodward, and the anonymous reader for *Notes & Queries* gave incomparable support and advice in our identification of the mysterious 'Miss Churchill'. Hilary Havens worked her digital magic and helped us decipher some particularly illegible passages. Albert Rivero offered insights into Richardson's early writing and printing career. Several members of the SHARP listserv (especially Rachael Scarborough King and Eric Nils Lindquist) helped sharpen several editorial notes. Tom Mole assisted in the acquisition of crucial document images. William McCarthy shared insights into Anna Barbauld's editorial practices and marks.

We are also especially grateful for the support of librarians, archivists, and other staff at Arizona State University (James O'Donnell); Bath Record Office (Richard Meunier); Bodleian Libraries, Oxford (Oliver House); Fitzwilliam Museum (Lynda Clark, Emma Darbyshire, and Suzanne Reynolds); Haverford College

ACKNOWLEDGEMENTS

(Sarah Horowitz); Houghton Library, Harvard University (John Overholt); National Art Library, Victoria and Albert Museum (Freya Levett); National Library of Scotland (Ralph McLean); Pierpont Morgan Library (Kaitlyn Krieg); Princeton University (Brianna Cregle, Paul Needham, Gabriel Swift, and the late Rebecca Munson); Universitätsbibliothek Basel (Monika Studer); University of Missouri (James Cogswell and Ann Campion Riley); William Andrews Clark Memorial Library, UCLA (Philip Palmer and Suzanne Teichen); Wisbech and Fenland Museum; Woodson Research Center, Rice University (Rebecca Russell); and Stuart Bennett at Stuart Bennett Rare Books. Without the generosity, insight, and support of these invaluable members of the research community, the present volume would be much poorer (and potentially thinner).

Finally, we are grateful to our superlative copy-editor, Jacqueline French, and to everyone at Cambridge University Press involved with getting this volume from manuscript to print, including Bethany Johnson, Bethany Thomas, Linda Bree, and George Laver. We couldn't ask for better collaborators on the overall project or the general editors, Tom Keymer and the incomparable Peter Sabor.

CHRONOLOGY

1682
2 June   Marriage in London of SR's parents, Samuel Richardson, Sr (d. 1727), a master joiner, and Elizabeth Hall (d. 1736)

1687   Family leaves London for Derbyshire at about this time, perhaps for political reasons

1689
July–August   Born and baptized in Mackworth, near Derby, the fourth of nine children from the marriage

1695–9   Family returns to London during this period, settling in the Tower Hill district

1701–2   Probably educated at the Merchant Taylors' School, where his schoolfellows know him as '*Serious* and *Gravity*'

1706
1 July   Apprenticed to John Wilde, a printer of Aldersgate

1713
2 July   Completes apprenticeship with Wilde, where SR has become 'the Pillar of his House'

1715
13 June   Made freeman of the Stationers' Company and a citizen of London

1715–20   Works as a compositor and corrector in Wilde's business

1720   Manages the printing business of the Leake family on the corner of Blue Ball and Salisbury Courts; begins printing private bills for James Blew, a lawyer and parliamentary agent

1721   Buys 'Printing Presses and Letter Utensils of trade' from the Leakes and sets up as master printer in their former

CHRONOLOGY

| | premises, where he resides until 1736; remains in the Salisbury Court district for his entire career |
| 23 November | Marries Martha, daughter of John Wilde; five sons and a daughter from the marriage die in infancy |

1722

5 March	Granted the livery of the Stationers' Company
6 August	Three Leake apprentices turned over to SR, the first of twenty-four apprentices bound to him during his career
1722–4	Denounced to the ministry by Samuel Negus, a printer, as one of the 'disaffected printers ... Said to be High-Flyers'; continues printing Tory-Jacobite material, including the Duke of Wharton's periodical *The True Briton* (1723–4)

1725

| December | Begins printing the *Daily Journal* (to 1737), one of several newspapers and periodicals printed by SR until the mid 1740s |

1727

| 11 April | Elected to junior office as Renter Warden in the Stationers' Company |

| 1728 | Rents a second Salisbury Court house, opposite the first, for *Daily Journal* operations (to 1736) |
| September | Identified to the ministry by Edmund Curll as printer of a seditious number of *Mist's Weekly Journal* |

1730

| December | *The Infidel Convicted*, possibly by SR |

1731

23 January	Death of Martha (Wilde) Richardson
February	Becomes a junior shareholder in the Stationers' Company, purchasing progressively more senior levels of stock in 1736, 1746, and 1751
October	Incurs financial losses on the collapse of the Charitable Corporation; embroiled until mid 1733 in related legal proceedings

1733

| 3 February | Marries Elizabeth Leake (d. 1773), sister of the Bath bookseller James Leake |

xxvi

CHRONOLOGY

February	Appointed first official printer to the House of Commons (to 1761), responsible for public bills and committee reports; SR thereby becomes 'more independent of Booksellers (tho' I did much Business for them) than any other Printer'
December	*The Apprentice's Vade Mecum*
23 December	Baptism of daughter Elizabeth, d. 1734
1734	Expands business premises into a third house, in Blue Ball Court (to 1740)

1735

2 January	Baptism of daughter Mary (Polly), m. 1757 (to Philip Ditcher), d. 1783
April	*A Seasonable Examination of the Pleas and Pretensions of the Proprietors of, and Subscribers to, Play-Houses*
June	Probably begins printing the pro-ministerial *Daily Gazetteer* (to 1746)
1736	Moves to 'House of a very grand outward Appearance' on Salisbury Square, which he occupies until 1756; also rents Corney House, a tenement of Sutton Court, Chiswick, as a weekend/summer retreat (to 1738)
January	*Gentleman's Magazine* publishes a light verse epistle by SR, noting that 'the Publick is often agreeably entertain'd with his Elegant Disquisitions in Prose'
16 July	Baptism of daughter Martha (Patty), m. 1762 (to Edward Bridgen), d. 1785

1737

16 August	Baptism of daughter Anne (Nancy), d. 1803

1738

Summer	Rents large semi-rural retreat at North End, Fulham (to 1754)
October	Edits and prints updated second edition of Defoe's *Tour*; also subsequent editions of 1742, 1748, 1753, and 1761–2

1739

26 April	Baptism of son Samuel, d. 1740
10 November	Starts writing *Pamela*
20 November	*Aesop's Fables*

1740

January	Completes draft of *Pamela*, revising the text over the ensuing months

xxvii

CHRONOLOGY

29 March	*The Negotiations of Sir Thomas Roe in His Embassy to the Ottoman Porte*, edited and printed by SR for the Society for the Encouragement of Learning
17 July	Baptism of twelfth and last child, Sarah (Sally), m. 1763 (to Richard Crowther), d. 1773
6 November	*Pamela; or, Virtue Rewarded*

1741

	Expands his printing premises behind Salisbury Court
23 January	*Letters Written to and for Particular Friends*
28 May	Opening volume of John Kelly's *Pamela's Conduct in High Life*, a spurious continuation, published; SR starts planning his own authorized continuation
1 December	Elected to the Court of Assistants, ruling body of the Stationers' Company
7 December	*Pamela in Her Exalted Condition*, SR's continuation

1742

8 May	Sixth edition of *Pamela*, in octavo format and with twenty-nine engravings by Hubert Gravelot and Francis Hayman: the first simultaneous publication of both parts
May	Wins large contract to print the *Journals* of the House of Commons (to 1761)

1744

	Begins printing the *Philosophical Transactions of the Royal Society* (to 1761), one of several major projects for learned societies
June–July	Earliest references in SR's correspondence to *Clarissa*, which already exists in some form of draft
December	Sends part of the novel in manuscript to Aaron Hill; manuscript copies in various states of revision circulate among SR's friends until 1747

1746

Summer	Assists the ministry in finding shorthand experts to help prosecute Jacobite rebels
December	Hill sends SR his 'Specimen of New Clarissa', a test abridgment of the novel's opening

1747

1 December	*Clarissa*, vols. I and II

1748

28 April	*Clarissa*, vols. III and IV
5 July	William Richardson, nephew, apprenticed to SR

xxviii

CHRONOLOGY

2 August	Advertises in the *Whitehall Evening-Post* for contact with Lady Bradshaigh, who has been sending pseudonymous letters about *Clarissa*
6 December	*Clarissa*, vols. V–VII

1749

June	Prints *Answer to the Letter of a Very Reverend and Worthy Gentleman*, a defence of *Clarissa*'s fire scene, for private distribution
August	Publishes notes responding to Albrecht von Haller's critique of *Clarissa* in the *Gentleman's Magazine*
December	Prints *Meditations Collected from the Sacred Books* for private distribution

1750

6 March	First face-to-face meeting with Lady Bradshaigh, thereafter his closest literary adviser
August	Death of SR's brother Benjamin; household joined by Benjamin's 14-year-old daughter Susanna (Sukey), 'whom my Wife has in a manner adopted'

1751

January	Sections of *Sir Charles Grandison* start to circulate in manuscript among SR's friends
19 February	Publishes an essay (No. 97) on courtship and marriage in Samuel Johnson's periodical *The Rambler*, based on SR's letter of 8 September 1750 to Frances Grainger
20 April	Expanded third edition of *Clarissa*; new material separately published as *Letters and Passages Restored from the Original Manuscripts of the History of Clarissa*

1752

28 September	Fire at SR's printing house causes extensive damage and loss of stock; takes on additional Salisbury Court premises at about this time, probably as a warehouse and workmen's residence

1753

May	Begins distributing printed sheets of *Sir Charles Grandison* among friends
2 June	Writes autobiographical letter to Johannes Stinstra, his Dutch translator
30 June	Attains rank of Upper Warden in the Stationers' Company

xxix

CHRONOLOGY

August	Learns that four Dublin booksellers have stolen most of *Sir Charles Grandison* in printed sheets and plan to publish an unauthorized edition; halts printing and fires suspected employees
14 September	*The Case of Samuel Richardson, of London, Printer; with Regard to the Invasion of His Property* printed for free distribution
13 November	*Sir Charles Grandison*, vols. I–IV, simultaneously published in duodecimo ('first') and octavo ('second') editions; vols. I–VI of the piracy appear in Dublin the same month, before SR can bring out his authorized vols. V–VI
11 December	*Sir Charles Grandison*, vols. V–VI (duodecimo) and vol. V (octavo)

1754

1 February	Prints *An Address to the Public*, a further attack on the Dublin pirates and on George Faulkner, an Irish bookseller, with whom he had failed to negotiate a solution
14 March	*Sir Charles Grandison*, vol. VII (duodecimo) and vol. VI (octavo)
19 March	Revised third edition of *Sir Charles Grandison* (duodecimo)
April	Prints two commentaries on *Sir Charles Grandison*, *Answer to a Letter from a Friend* and *Copy of a Letter to a Lady*, for private distribution; the latter explains that there will be no further volumes
6 July	Becomes Master of the Stationers' Company for a one-year term
July–Oct	Rents and renovates new weekend house at Parson's Green, which his wife and daughters make their main home

1755

February	Begins writing a fragmentary 'History of Mrs. Beaumont' (partly published in 1804), possibly as the basis for a new novel
6 March	*A Collection of the Moral and Instructive Sentiments, Maxims, Cautions, and Reflexions, Contained in the Histories of Pamela, Clarissa, and Sir Charles Grandison*
5 August	William Richardson completes apprenticeship and becomes SR's overseer

CHRONOLOGY

July–Dec Builds expensive new business premises in Salisbury Court, renovating the adjoining house as a residence, which he occupies the following spring

1757

June Approached by Erasmus Reich, a Leipzig bookseller, with proposals to bring out a German edition of his selected correspondence, which he starts to prepare

1758

May Abandons the Reich project, but continues preparing letters for possible posthumous publication

August–September Revises and corrects Urania Hill Johnson's novel *Almira*, which she publishes six months after SR's death, rejecting most of the revisions

1759

May Prints Edward Young's *Conjectures on Original Composition*, composed by Young with SR's collaborative involvement

Summer William Richardson leaves SR's employment to start his own printing business

1760

28 April Revises and contributes to a translation of Marguerite de Lussan's *The Life and Heroic Actions of Balbe Berton*, printed by William Richardson

24 June Enters partnership with Catherine Lintot, heir to the printer Henry Lintot, in a law patent with monopoly rights to print books on common law

1761

March Borrows Lady Bradshaigh's annotated copies of *Pamela* and *Clarissa* to make further revisions

28 June Suffers stroke during a visit from the portraitist Joseph Highmore

4 July Dies, leaving an estate of £14,000 and bequeathing manuscripts to his daughters; buried in St Bride's, Fleet Street, beside his first wife and infant children

September William Richardson returns to Salisbury Court, taking over SR's business with a partner, Samuel Clarke

1762 Posthumous revised editions of *Pamela* and *Sir Charles Grandison*

xxxi

CHRONOLOGY

1765
March 'Six Original Letters upon Duelling' published in the *Candid Review and Literary Repository*

1771
25 January Publication of Anna Meades's *The History of Sir William Harrington, written some years since, and revised and corrected by the late Mr. Richardson*; SR's daughters contest the claim, but he had indeed advised Meades in 1757–8

1780 William Richardson issues proposals for a uniform edition of the novels, 'with corrections', but the edition does not materialize

1784 Anne Richardson and Martha Bridgen plan a new edition of *Pamela*, based on unpublished final revisions by SR, to be 're-revised' by themselves

1786
January–February Authorized 'Memoirs of Richardson', perhaps by Edward Bridgen, published in the *Universal Magazine*

1792 'New edition' of *Clarissa*, 'with the last corrections by the author', prepared with the involvement of Anne Richardson and SR's granddaughter Sarah Crowther Moodie

1801 Fourteenth edition of *Pamela*, prepared from Anne Richardson's copy, 'with numerous alterations … by the Author'

1803 Death of Anne, SR's last surviving child

1804
July *The Correspondence of Samuel Richardson*, edited, with a substantial biographical memoir, by Anna Laetitia Barbauld

1810 'New edition' of *Sir Charles Grandison*, probably from Anne Richardson's copy, 'with the last corrections by the author'; fifteenth edition of *Pamela*, with further 'numerous corrections and alterations', apparently from Anne's annotated copy of the fourteenth edition

ABBREVIATIONS

Address to the Public	Samuel Richardson, *An Address to the Public, on the Treatment Which the Editor of the History of Sir Charles Grandison Has Met with from Certain Booksellers and Printers in Dublin. Including Observations on Mr. Faulkner's Defence of Himself, Published in His Irish News-Paper of Nov. 3. 1753.* (1754), in *Grandison*, 7.424-42.
B	*The Correspondence of Samuel Richardson*, ed. Anna Laetitia Barbauld, 6 vols. (London, 1804).
BL	British Library
Battestin and Probyn	*The Correspondence of Henry and Sarah Fielding*, ed. Martin C. Battestin and Clive T. Probyn (Oxford: Clarendon Press, 1993).
Carroll	*Selected Letters of Samuel Richardson*, ed. John Carroll (Oxford: Clarendon Press, 1964).
Clarissa	Samuel Richardson, *Clarissa. Or, The History of a Young Lady*, 1st edn, 7 vols. (London, 1747-8).
CEWSR	Cambridge Edition of the Works of Samuel Richardson
Eaves and Kimpel	T. C. Duncan Eaves and Ben D. Kimpel, *Samuel Richardson: A Biography* (Oxford: Clarendon Press, 1971).
Eland	George E. Eland, *The Lobb Family from the Sixteenth Century* (Oxford University Press, 1955).
ESTC	English Short Title Catalogue
FM	Forster Collection, Victoria & Albert Museum, London
Grandison	Samuel Richardson, *The History of Sir Charles Grandison*, 1st edn, 7 vols. (London, 1753-4).
Loeb	Loeb Classical Library (Harvard University Press, 1911-).
Maslen	Keith Maslen, *Samuel Richardson of London, Printer: A Study of His Printing Based on*

xxxiii

LIST OF ABBREVIATIONS

	Ornament Use and Business Accounts (Dunedin: University of Otago, 2001).
MM	*The Monthly Magazine, or British Register* (Richard Phillips, 1796–1843).
N&Q	*Notes and Queries* (Oxford University Press, 1849–). Online edn: academic.oup.com/nq.
Nichols	John Nichols, *Literary Anecdotes of the Eighteenth Century*, 9 vols. (London, 1812–15).
ODNB	*Oxford Dictionary of National Biography* (Oxford University Press, 2018). Online edn: www.oxforddnb.com.
OED	*Oxford English Dictionary* (Oxford University Press, 2018). Online edn: www.oed.com.
Pamela	Samuel Richardson, *Pamela, or, Virtue Rewarded*, The Cambridge Edition of the Works of Samuel Richardson, ed. Alberto J. Rivero (Cambridge University Press, 2011).
Pamela II	Samuel Richardson, *Pamela in Her Exalted Condition*, The Cambridge Edition of the Works of Samuel Richardson, ed. Alberto J. Rivero (Cambridge University Press, 2012).
'Pamela' in the Marketplace	Thomas Keymer and Peter Sabor, *'Pamela' in the Marketplace: Literary Controversy and Print Culture in Eighteenth-Century Britain and Ireland* (Cambridge University Press, 2005).
Remarks	Sarah Fielding, *Remarks on Clarissa, Addressed to the Author. Occasioned by Some Critical Conversations on the Characters and Conduct of That Work. With Some Reflections on the Character and Behaviour of Prior's Emma* (1749).
SR	Samuel Richardson

GENERAL INTRODUCTION

Among prominent writers in the history of the novel, none is so closely associated with correspondence as Samuel Richardson. Not only are Richardson's great works of fiction – *Pamela* (and its sequel), *Clarissa*, and *Sir Charles Grandison* – told through letters, but they are *about* letters and the connections among human beings that letters evoke, create, preserve, and transmit.[1] This volume contains miscellaneous correspondence from 1732 to 1749. That is, the letters in this volume do not participate in any of the extended relationships Richardson conducted through letters (at least as far as we can tell from the surviving record). Those extended correspondences are published in separate volumes. What we have here are the remains of more concentrated, focused exchanges, messages that relate to Richardson's business as a printer and as a writer, occasionally with significant literary figures including Alexander Pope or Elizabeth Carter. There is no simple description of the letters in this volume, many of which directly concern the writing and publication of *Pamela*, *Pamela II*, and *Clarissa*. Some of the letters will be of little interest except to the specialist in Richardson and his circle or the literary history of eighteenth-century Britain. But many of the letters collected here are intrinsically interesting beyond the confines of the eighteenth-century literary world. There are letters about fiction and elements of fiction, about the manners and morals of eighteenth-century Britain, and about the ways in which men's and women's relationships were constructed and conducted.

If there is one word that captures the aspiration, and the fleeting effect, of the best of these letters, it might be 'immediacy'. Indeed, much of the power of Richardson's fiction stems from the narrative immediacy of the epistolary form that he adopted from previous writers and developed in what was instantly seen as a compelling new direction for writing. As Richardson himself famously described it, his novels are written 'to the moment'. They are told in the present tense, as he liked to say, bringing readers into close contact with the novels' characters and their travails. With similar immediacy – and, on occasion, prolixity – the letters contained in this volume provide a description of major elements of Richardson's life and career: his family, his work as a prominent and increasingly prosperous printer, and his new and surprising career as a writer of (extremely) popular fiction. The

---

[1] All references to *Pamela* and *Pamela II* are to the CEWSR volumes, ed. Albert J. Rivero. At the time of publication of this volume, the CEWSR volumes of *Clarissa* were not yet available.

xxxv

GENERAL INTRODUCTION

letters in this volume, therefore, show us Richardson at his most intense, his most *Richardsonian* (to use a word that came into use in 1763, shortly after his death).[2]

Many readers will be particularly interested in Richardson the novelist, and the letters in this volume provide information about *Pamela* and *Clarissa* that is invaluable to understanding Richardson's approach to writing, printing, publishing, and promoting his work. As surprising as his literary career may have been to himself and to others, Richardson embraced the role of author straightaway, and the letters careen from the fawning business correspondence of an ambitious printer to the preening self-satisfaction of a cultural sage. The miscellaneous nature of this volume, therefore, contains a broad picture of Richardson in the 1730s and especially the 1740s. There are letters that have become famous, and there are more mundane bits of writing that nevertheless show us Richardson at work.

Appropriately enough, this volume begins with the pedantic Richardson lecturing his new apprentice – nephew Thomas Verren Richardson – in 1732, well before his success as a man of letters. In enumerated paragraphs, Richardson lays out the duties of an apprentice, points that he later expanded upon in *The Apprentice's Vade Mecum* (printed by Richardson in 1733 and excerpted in the *London Magazine* of January 1734). The morality – the moralism – would become familiar to readers of *Pamela*, *Clarissa*, and *Sir Charles Grandison*: Richardson tells Thomas that his job as apprentice is to 'lighten' Richardson 'of my cares' rather 'than add to them' and that Thomas will do so through a Protestant combination of self-control and diligence. Regardless of his family relation to the master, Thomas must 'treat the journeymen with complaisance and decency, as persons who are your elders and who, by due service and years, are become freemen of London, or entitled to be so'. In this letter we see a number of traits observable throughout this volume: a tendency to prolixity, sometimes combined with self-satisfaction; a conscious attempt to bend the world's morality to the private good of a correspondent; the reuse of correspondence, whether, as in this case, in a printed work or, more typically, in letters to others; and a mixture of the personal and professional. These letters reflect the literary world of the time, a world in which authors like Alexander Pope and Samuel Johnson became central to the public's understanding of literature. At the same time, Richardson shaped the world of literature not only as an author but through his practical work as a printer, including his involvement with the Society for the Encouragement of Learning.

The authorized publication of Pope's correspondence in 1737 merely cemented a few things that had been true of the literary culture of the first four decades of the eighteenth century: correspondence was an acknowledged and popular literary genre as well as the material embodiment of information conveyed between parties for immediate purposes. Edmund Curll's 'unauthorized' editions of Pope's letters – which were actually, at least initially, clandestinely engineered

---

[2] *OED* provides a first citation from the *London Magazine* in 1763; SR had died two years earlier.

xxxvi

GENERAL INTRODUCTION

and subsequently, surreptitiously, encouraged by Pope – had sold well, reflecting not only an interest in a culture of celebrity authorship but a sense that literature could reflect human intimacy in new and compelling ways. Richardson's career as a novelist was built from his recognition of the power of correspondence, upon which foundation he constructed not only the novels that made him famous but the personal correspondence that ensured his success as a businessman as well as his value as a friend. Correspondence simultaneously connected human beings outside of social systems and hierarchies and reinforced the nature of those systems and hierarchies. Richardson was attuned to both aspects of correspondence, and his success at navigating them is reflected in the letters in this volume.

This volume contains examples of one-off letters and of short correspondences with well-known contemporaries. There is no equivalent of the Swift–Pope correspondence for Richardson. The great literary competitor/collaborator in the project of prose narrative was Henry Fielding, who – for various religious, ethical, and literary reasons – remained a rival rather than a colleague. Yet there is an admiring letter from Fielding in this collection, along with letters to and from Elizabeth Carter, Sarah Fielding, Jane Collier, and other figures important in the literary world, especially in the world of modern, moral literature. We get a picture, if only a partial one, of Richardson's involvement in the London literary scene that was growing, as the period went on, around Samuel Johnson and other writers who, like Richardson himself, saw themselves as operating in the public sphere of a widespread readership. The stilted correspondence with Pope's literary executor, William Warburton, in 1742, shows how far the literary world had developed in twenty years. The letter from Pope himself, in contrast, is easy and natural, suggesting that Warburton's pompous relaying of Pope's ideas for a sequel conveys Warburton's tone rather than Pope's own. (The idea that Pope evidently put forward – to capitalize on the 'simple nature' of Richardson's characters as a basis for passing judgements on 'high life' – would come to fruition later in the century in Frances Burney's novel *Evelina*.)

Some of the correspondence with well-known figures came about through Richardson's presumption. The letters exchanged with Elizabeth Carter are some of the most interesting in this volume. The relationship got off to a bad start: Richardson had included Carter's 'Ode to Wisdom', set to music, in *Clarissa* without asking her explicit permission though assured, he tells her, by the person who passed the ode's text on to him that he had all the authority he needed to use it. Carter was neither pleased nor amused, and she apparently sanctioned Edward Cave to publish a correct version in the *Gentleman's Magazine*. But a year later, she writes to Richardson politely of 'the very high Entertainment I have received from your Clarissa' (16 December 1748). Better yet, Carter gives her endorsement of the catastrophic ending of the novel, a point upon which much of his readership remained divided.

Even Henry Fielding, resented and suspected by Richardson since the publication of *Shamela* (1741) and *Joseph Andrews* (1742), seemed impelled to convey his appreciation for Richardson's second novel. Much of Fielding's letter is

xxxvii

GENERAL INTRODUCTION

taken up with a discussion of the thirst for authorial fame, but that is at least purported to demonstrate Fielding's disinterested approbation of the character of Clarissa as well as the conduct of the novel (Fielding had just finished reading volume V): 'What I shall say of holding up the [marriage] Licence? I will say a finer Picture was never imagined. He must be a Glorious Painter who can do it Justice on Canvas, and a most wretched one indeed who could not do much on such a Subject. The Circumstance of the Fragments is Great and Terrible; but her Letter to Lovelace is beyond any thing I have ever read.' The circles of the two authors overlapped, and some of the most interesting letters in this volume relate to Jane Collier and to Sarah Fielding, authors whom Richardson had encouraged in their own writing. Richardson certainly courted and appreciated women as correspondents, seeking their opinions on his writing and doling out his advice – and his self-justifications for what and how he wrote his own novels. As a professional author, Richardson had more in common with Sarah Fielding and Collier than with Henry Fielding: he was largely self-taught as a writer, taking advantage of his profession and his vocational training in a way that resembled Fielding's and Collier's reliance on family and on the informal type of education that women could receive. Unlike Henry Fielding, unable to avoid referring to his elite background even in a letter praising his 'rival', Richardson wrote in the day's vernacular. The correspondence in this volume, therefore, reflects not only Richardson's career as printer and novelist until shortly after the publication of *Clarissa*; it represents a dispersion of literary culture into a network of consumers who were also writers, of critics who may print their responses to the day's literary production but might also take their responses directly to an author eager to be among his readers.

Printing Correspondence

With the publication of *Pamela*, Richardson became known, and wanted to be known, as an author of literary works. But as critics and biographers have noted, by the time that his first novel exploded in popularity and turned into a full-blown 'media event' from early 1741, Richardson was already over fifty years old and had become a noted hard-working professional as a printer, a practical embodiment of the Protestant work ethic. At the same time, Richardson's work in 'the trade' gave him access to reading material that provided a rich education in various kinds of writing in English. Out of this constellation, *Pamela, Clarissa*, and *Sir Charles Grandison* emerged as books that blend the imagination and concrete reality in ways that were fundamentally new in literary history. His steady, respectable, and remunerative work as a printer insulated him from the Grub Street milieu in which Daniel Defoe and a host of other writers immortalized in Pope's *Dunciad* pursued their careers as scribblers. Yet Richardson worked as hard as any Grub Street writer in his literary creation of voluminous and ever-expanding worlds. What the correspondence in this volume related to his printing career demonstrates is his continued immersion in practical aspects of the trade even while his

xxxviii

GENERAL INTRODUCTION

professional, personal, and literary circles began to overlap and expand, establishing Richardson as a uniquely popular figure in all three of those circles.

It should therefore not be surprising that much of this volume of miscellaneous correspondence, composed and exchanged in the period in which Richardson was first publishing his imaginative writing, is taken up with his letters to and from colleagues in the printing world, mostly in London but including (and with reference to) a network of printers throughout the British Isles. Some of the correspondence related to Richardson's trade overlaps with letters about his novels. In a letter of 1 December 1748, for example, Philip Yorke, future Earl of Hardwicke, thanks Richardson (the novelist, the printer, or both?) for sending a 'Present' of the recently published *Clarissa*. With knowledge gleaned from his experience as a printer, Richardson was able to amplify the sales and reputation of Richardson the novelist. Most of the letters in this volume that can be related to his printing career, though, deal with printing as a concern separate from his career as a writer.

Richardson was held in high esteem in 'the trade'. A letter from William Strahan to Richardson (17 August 1749) puts this respect in exalted words:

> I remember your long-continued friendship for me with pleasure and gratitude. I admire your generosity, your benevolence, your sagacity, your penetration, your knowledge of human nature, and your good heart; I esteem you as my friend, my adviser, my pattern, and my benefactor; I love you as my father; and let me, even me also, call you my Nestor.

The letters from Strahan, one of the most eminent printers in London junior to Richardson, were written during Strahan's visit to his native Scotland. They continually evince love and respect for his mentor. The correspondence with Strahan and other printers demonstrates the web of personal and professional relationships comprised in the Stationers' Company. Strahan named one of his sons 'Samuel', after Richardson, as 'a living monument of your friendship'; the letter in which Strahan informs him of this naming overflows with confident friendship. Anna Laetitia Barbauld included letters from Strahan to Richardson in her 1804 edition of the *Correspondence*, probably because their explicit affection for the recipient reveals the genuine warmth with which colleagues engaged him. Barbauld's edition, like the present one, attempted to capture all elements of Richardson's character in its selection of letters.

Strahan was not the only member of the trade who had received Richardson's mentoring, which could tend towards meddling. One example comes in Richardson's letter of 30 January 1746 to Charles Ackers, printer of the *London Magazine*. Warning his colleague not to reprint a piece of gossip that had been inserted without his knowledge into the *Daily Gazetteer* of 20 January, Richardson writes, 'I have no other Motive but Such as one Printer ought to be govern'd by another.' Richardson was the printer of the *Gazetteer* and therefore stood to gain or lose in reputation by the material he helped usher into the public domain. Concerned about the 'offence to several Persons of Quality' that the piece had

GENERAL INTRODUCTION

given and the 'good deal of Trouble' it had already caused him, he tried to prevent potential harm from befalling others within his profession.

Other professional correspondence provides insight into the state of printing as a business in the 1730s and 1740s. Printers had to contend with government interference, even when the impact may have been unintended. For example, Richardson complains to Thomas Birch on 19 April 1746 that the addition of a clause (requiring that additions and corrections included in revised editions of a publication be available for separate purchase by owners of earlier editions) to the renewal of the Importation Act of 1738, then under debate in the House of Commons, would make it difficult and costly to publish some second editions – including, as it turned out, Richardson's own *Letters and Passages Restored from the Original Manuscripts of the History of Clarissa* in 1751. In the event, the particular book with which Richardson is probably concerned in this letter – Charles Yorke's *Some Considerations on the Law of Forfeiture, for High Treason* – did see a second edition later the same year. But Richardson's lobbying of Birch to try to halt the clause demonstrates the way that government and the trade were interconnected. Indeed, Richardson's own career was strongly propelled by his contract to print the *Journals* of the House of Commons in 1742. Government needed the printing press, and the printing trade responded to direct and indirect action by the government.

'The trade' was undergoing significant changes in the first half of the eighteenth century, and Richardson's place within it was complex. Richardson's main work was as a printer, supervising the physical printing of texts for a fee, usually under contract with another business – like a bookseller – or with an institution like the government. Booksellers, who had traditionally been in the business of selling books in physical locations and distributing them to other sellers and renters of printed materials (including circulating libraries), were transforming into 'publishers' who bought copyrights from authors on speculation and then managed the printing and distribution. While Richardson's government contract was critically important to his material success, he also worked with booksellers on identifying and shaping publications that might promise a worthwhile return on investments as well as with authors who wished to publish their works for themselves, 'printed for the author' in the parlance of the day. When the author was a friend, Richardson's work became complicated. A letter of 4 July 1746 to Samuel Lobb illustrates Richardson's conflicted role. He will not 'use my Friend worse than I would use a London Bookseller', and so he agrees to wait to see how much money *The Benevolence Incumbent on Us, as Men and Christians, Considered* will make through sales before charging the author. As it happened, Lobb's work (perhaps unsurprisingly) failed to earn its author enough to pay Richardson a profitable premium for printing the work, so Richardson waived the printing costs entirely. This kind of work has more recently been called 'vanity publishing', and Richardson found himself embroiled in it from time to time.

In fact, all of Richardson's own novels were 'printed for the author', too, with the added benefit that the author was also his own printer, though not his own 'publisher' – for that, he drew on colleagues in the trade like Charles Rivington,

xl

GENERAL INTRODUCTION

John Osborne, Andrew Millar, and brother-in-law James Leake. The copyright for *Pamela* was entered at the Stationers' Company on 4 November 1740 jointly by Richardson, Rivington, and Osborne and thus established Richardson's authorial claim on the text, though the publication itself created the fiction of an editor figure to try to preserve his anonymity. Rivington and Osborne were not only 'particular Friends' but colleagues eminent in the trade. They had encouraged Richardson to write *Familiar Letters* (which they published in 1741) and *Pamela*, written in a burst of creativity in 1739 and finished early in 1740. Later accounts of Richardson's authorial genius, including most prominently Edward Young's *Conjectures on Original Composition*, focus on the author's imaginative creativity, but as the letters in this volume demonstrate, Richardson the author is intrinsically connected with Richardson the successful tradesman.

A Novelist's Correspondence

In the midst of his extremely successful career as a printer, Richardson achieved eminence through the influence of his own creative writing. Much of the correspondence in this volume relates to his career as a writer from *Familiar Letters*, which provided something of a model for his novels, to *Clarissa*, Richardson's masterwork. *Pamela, or Virtue Rewarded* (and its sequel, *Pamela in Her Exalted Condition*) and *Clarissa* have been seen as critical works in the period's development of prose fiction since well before Ian Watt's *Rise of the Novel* (1957), which identified Richardson as the true creator of the genre for a generation of students and scholars. Watt bolstered his case not only through delineating a genealogy of prose fiction but also by showing readers how Richardson's mastery in depicting the daily lives of his characters lies at the heart of the novelist's craft. The earliest items in this volume of Richardson's correspondence reflect the day-to-day concerns of a businessman eager to promote the quantity and quality of his print productions. But letters in this volume also illuminate Richardson as artist, as a particular kind of writer whose career became possible through new developments in the ways that stories were produced and disseminated. His professional career, then, is linked closely to his artistic career. Richardson was not only an innovator in literary form – as was recognized in his lifetime – but a literary entrepreneur who pioneered new ways to reach new audiences and to make money out of it.

Criticism has long opposed the form of the novel practised and popularized by Richardson to the aristocratic romances of the sixteenth and seventeenth centuries. A simple contrast between the forms becomes simplistic: after all, the name Pamela stems from one of the most important earlier English prose romances, Philip Sidney's *Arcadia*. Yet Richardson's admirers themselves promulgated the distinction between the two literary forms and, predictably, supported Richardson's literary practice. 'Philo-Paideias' writes on 30 January 1741 that

> Too long have Tales obscene defil'd the Stage;
> And Novels loose deprav'd the present Age,

xli

GENERAL INTRODUCTION

> With silly, long, Romantic Stories fill'd,
> Where mad knights, woo, and the kind Princess yields

In the mock prefatory letters to *Shamela*, Fielding skewered the extravagant praise heaped on *Pamela* in reviews and puffs, but even Fielding's satire had the unintended effect of reinforcing Richardson's method in the novel by serving as its complementary (and necessary) negative. In June 1741, 'Philaretes' explicitly refers to *Shamela* as an attempt to prevent Richardson's novel from stamping out vice through a natural rendering of a 'monstrous' and therefore unnatural immorality: 'the *Rake* and the *Debaucher* as the most savage and monstrous creature in Nature'. In this and other letters, rejection of the fantastical and the immoral in favour of the putatively realistic and properly moralistic *Pamela*, then, carves out space in the market and positions Richardson's novel as something new.

Richardson was one of the first writers, and probably the first novelist, to engage with women readers who, in some cases, were writing their own literary criticism, poetry, or works of fiction in response. Other volumes in the Cambridge Edition focus on his relationships with circles of women readers. In this volume, we can see Richardson experimenting with his writing persona and the level of engagement with readers who are responding to the deep sense of immediacy created by his novels. Richardson's novels encouraged readers – men and women alike – to believe that they could be close to the author himself. Richardson was seen as a genius but also as a surprisingly approachable, occasionally cranky celebrity willing to write back, especially when the correspondent was a woman. Examples abound in this volume, from the '6 Reading Ladies' (a pseudonym for the letters' writer or writers, identifying as women from Reading 'reading' *Pamela* very carefully and with an eye to engaging the book's author) to Sarah Fielding and Collier, women of letters who were among *Clarissa*'s most perceptive and most valued early readers. Among the most interesting exchanges is the one with Elizabeth Carter, perhaps the foremost female intellectual of the mid-eighteenth century and (as we have seen) a poet whose work Richardson purloined for use in *Clarissa*.

Collier's letter to Richardson (9 July 1749) on the infamous 'fire scene' in *Clarissa* (IV, pp. 289–300) demonstrates how gender was a necessary and complicated element in Richardson's correspondence. In this scene, Lovelace has a small fire set and uses that fire as a pretext to gaze at and clasp to his breast the barely dressed Clarissa. Some readers supposedly experienced this scene as pornographic and complained of its nefarious influence. Collier wrote in strong defence of Richardson's method:

> to a female Reader, there cannot possibly be any thing inviting or inflaming in the Idea of such a Scene, unless She should shamefully avow, that She condemn'd the Behaviour of Clarissa; and then indeed might She condemn the Scene: but the Reason of a Man's blaming it as being too highly painted must be from his dwelling more strongly on the Person of the lovely Sufferer, than on her Innocence and Distress.

xlii

GENERAL INTRODUCTION

Collier's letter suggests that women were the most appropriate readers of *Clarissa*, since they alone, from their own perspectives and experiences, could fully understand not only the character of the novel's heroine but the technique with which Richardson wrote it.

In general, the letters concerned with Richardson as a novelist are markers of shifts in authorship and the understanding of literary writing during the period, shifts that Richardson's letters both reflected and brought about. In *'Pamela' in the Marketplace*, Keymer and Sabor describe the 'deluge of print' occasioned by the novel's publication (p. 1). As the letters in this and other volumes in the Cambridge Edition demonstrate, *Pamela* also unleashed a deluge of correspondence. Near the end of 1740, 'letters' – what might better be termed advertisements taking on epistolary form – began appearing publicly, puffing the forthcoming novel to build readership. The first such letter in this volume is by William Webster, published in *The Weekly Miscellany* in the form of a cover letter to himself under the pseudonym Richard Hooker, publisher of the journal, with the main letter addressed to Richardson to congratulate him on the novel. Webster praises the character of Pamela for embodying a trait Richardson had tried to inculcate in his nephew Thomas: 'A glorious Instance of Self-Denial!' This letter was republished in the prefatory materials to *Pamela*, as Richardson demonstrated a knack for promotion honed by years of working with the book trade.

As engaged and minutely invested as Richardson was as a printer and correspondent, he was equally diffident and shy (or affected to be so) as an author, at least initially and in public venues. Richardson thus wrote to the poet Mary Barber in 1741 that he 'did not design that any body should have known the Author; but those three or four Friends to whom I could not help owning it, would not let me have my own way: And I have suffer'd by it, as well in my own Mind, as in the Malice and Envy of others.' In a letter to Ralph Allen responding to his esteemed correspondent's suggestions, Richardson announced that he would leave out some of the commendatory prefatory letters on reprinting *Pamela*: 'since I cou'd not pass as the Editor only, as I once hoped to do, I wish they had never been Inserted' (8 October 1741). Nevertheless, even after *Pamela in Her Exalted Condition* was published as the true sequel in the context of a deluge of spurious continuations, unauthorized adaptations, and satiric attacks, the '6 Reading Ladies' asked the author whether the novel really was based on a true story as it had originally claimed to be. Mustering plenty of evidence as to why the story would have to be well known to a large number of people if it was documentary rather than fictional, they ask in early 1742 'whether the Story is real or feigned?' In his response, Richardson deflects the Reading ladies' question by returning on them their own objections to his anonymity when, with a flirtatious attempt at intimacy, he asks for their names and for time to inquire into the character of each of them: 'You see, Madam, what a Curiosity you have raised by *your* Curiosity.' Of course, *Pamela* – and then *Pamela in Her Exalted Condition* – was both 'real' *and* 'feigned'. The combination of those qualities, in opposition according to the 'Reading Ladies' but complementary as developed by

xliii

GENERAL INTRODUCTION

Richardson's literary technique, continued to animate Richardson's writing both for the public and in his private correspondence.

Whether he designed it or not, Richardson's authorship was known soon enough, and its very fact catapulted him into a public role. *Pamela* spurred hack writers and publishers to try their hand at sequels. Richardson at first declared that he would not be continuing his best-selling novel, but he did not expect that others, disregarding his own authorial intentions, would go ahead. Ever protective of markets for his print productions as much as of his control over the stories and morals of his fictional narratives, Richardson was compelled to pen a sequel of his own and quickly wrote to his correspondents asking for feedback on his continuation. He sent two sheets – which in octavo would have included thirty-two pages – to a number of trusted readers. Some of the responses praised Richardson's sequel, others were more circumspect. Stephen Duck, the 'thresher poet', went so far as to suggest that, by the nature of the life Pamela was to lead as the wife of Mr. B., it would be impossible for the sequel to excite the reader's attention: 'I am somewhat doubtful that these moving Incidents will be wanting in this Second Part from the very Nature of the Subject which seems too barren of Distress to excite our Pity' (14 October 1741). Nevertheless, Duck believed that *Pamela in Her Exalted Condition* might be 'useful'. Richardson fulsomely thanked those who offered praise, and he swallowed his anger at Duck and refrained from sending a reply to defend his method (through the typical contrast between his *Pamela* and the 'French Marvellous and all un-natural Machinery'), concluding sarcastically instead: 'I only beg, my dear Friend, you'll take no notice to any one, that you have seen the Sheets. Because People will be asking for your Opinion, and I am so much convinced of your Friendship, that I should suspect your Partiality in my Favour, may wound your Judgment.' Richardson's gratitude throughout this volume is paired with his thin skin and tendency to self-justification.

Scholars of literary history have noted that both highly individualistic and collaborative writing practices characterize authorship in the eighteenth century. Richardson, lauded by Edward Young as an authorial genius in *Conjectures on Original Composition*, also sought unusually extensive pre-publication criticism and collaboration. One particular letter to Charles Rivington (15 November 1740) includes attacks upon Richardson's style as 'too near the Vulgar'. Many of the people who made up Richardson's circle – those correspondents with whom Richardson shared early drafts of *Clarissa* and *Sir Charles Grandison*, considering and rejecting their advice while keeping them personally engaged during the months of composition – are included in the more focused volumes of the Cambridge Edition. It is notable that, whether he was discussing his writing with occasional correspondents of renown such as Warburton, Duck, Joseph Spence, or Edward Moore, or with anonymous writers offering detailed critiques, Richardson wanted to know what they thought and how they might correct his work. These letters support the notion of social authorship, but they also illuminate social *readership*, the way that letters emerged from a society brought together through print and the post office alike. Print and manuscript together created an intimate world defined and fuelled by literature.

xliv

GENERAL INTRODUCTION

Both in the run-up to the publication of the first volumes of *Clarissa* in December 1747 and in the aftermath of its blockbuster cultural status, Richardson solicited responses, sending work in progress to Warburton, Colley Cibber, David Garrick, and other prominent cultural figures as well as encouraging critiques from readers such as Collier, Solomon Lowe, and Philip Skelton. Although Richardson asked for corrections, he used these exchanges more significantly as occasions for defending his artistic and moral choices in writing the novel as well as a means of drawing on his extensive correspondence networks to build an audience and a reputation for himself and his writing.

Even in the midst of writing to authors about technicalities in the printing of their own works, Richardson was alluding as early as May 1746 to his being 'exceedingly taken up ... in the writing Way' (SR to Lobb, 16 May 1746). And whereas the more extended correspondences collected in their own volumes in the Cambridge Edition demonstrate the depth of consultation on *Clarissa* with close friends, we can see in this volume's miscellaneous correspondence that Richardson consulted widely as well as deeply on some of the novel's central questions. Indeed, Richardson's reliance upon pre-publication reader response resembles literary publication in an age of manuscript circulation.

One of the main questions correspondents in this volume raise relates to Lovelace and religion. Should Richardson make his villain an atheist? Indeed, the character of Lovelace animates much of the most interesting of the literary and cultural criticism contained in the letters on *Clarissa*. Playwright Edward Moore gets to the heart of an issue that has continued to provoke readers: how could the mild-mannered, Christian printer of middle-class origins have so fully imagined the highborn rake, Lovelace? 'For to have a Heart to conceive the Mischiefs of a Lovelace, and to have the smallest spark of Goodness in that Heart, is of more Merit than the whole Catalogue of Virtues in Another' (1 October 1748). Richardson pitted his correspondents against each other, evidently sharing either their letters or at least the substance of those letters to provoke arguments for one side or the other. Perhaps he really wanted to understand what his correspondents thought in order to improve the novel. But it is equally likely that he sought arguments that would end, one way or the other, in confirming the decision he had already made. In this case, Richardson had decided that Lovelace would not be an atheist. And yet in his circle of admirers there were many (including painter Joseph Highmore, who had illustrated *Pamela*) who believed that someone believing in God could not act as Lovelace does. Richardson evidently shared Highmore's views with an otherwise unidentified 'R. Smith', who directly attacks them in a letter supporting Richardson's artistic decision that Lovelace could acknowledge the existence of God yet not live up to the implications of that belief: 'How inconsistent is the Gentleman in advising Lovelace to be made an Infidel or Atheist in the same Paragraph, which concludes with proposing him to be represented as an Hypocrite!' 'Smith' signs his letter 'Elisha Brand' and may in fact have helped Richardson create the character of Elias Brand, who would come to prominence in the third edition of *Clarissa*.

xlv

GENERAL INTRODUCTION

Some of the most amusing of the letters in this volume come from anonymous readers in excruciating suspense, having read the first two printed volumes and anticipating the whole. One anonymous writer (27 December 1747) tells Richardson that he had better hurry up and publish subsequent volumes because too long a delay between instalments would mean that readers 'will have forgot it, and not care whether they ever read the others'. 'Philaretes', some months later, threatens Richardson with refusing to continue to read unless he allows Clarissa to be 'happy with Lovelace at last'. If not, 'I am determined to read no more: ... I should read the Account of her Death with as much Anguish of Mind, as I should feel at the Loss of my dearest Friend', adding: 'I know a great many Gentlemen that are of my Mind, and I believe your Book will sell very indifferently, unless you alter it in that respect.' And one anonymous correspondent simply wrote: 'As I am a well-wisher to you, and your Writings, I take this Opportunity of informing you, that you'll greatly oblige Multitudes of both Sexes, if you'll expeditiously publish the Residue of Clarissa. From Your unknown Friend & Servant' (2 September 1748). Such intense pressure, born out of readers' sense of intimacy with fictional characters and author alike and expressing their keen engagement, sometimes even identification, with some of the fictional material, is only too familiar to modern writers especially of genre fiction; the current volume helps to outline some of the early history of the phenomenon.

Richardson must have conveyed distress at the amount of complicated advice he was receiving. Joseph Spence, for one, believed that Richardson should trust himself above the views of others: 'I wish you would take up a resolution ... of neither trusting others, nor distrusting yourself, too much' (12 January 1748). Young's *Conjectures on Original Criticism* takes the form of a letter written to the author of *Sir Charles Grandison*. Young describes genius as an almost organic aspect of Richardson's character, echoing Spence's urging of Richardson to consult no one and rely only on himself when making difficult authorial decisions. It does not seem likely that Richardson would have needed Spence's advice, which would have confirmed the confidence he often expressed in his own literary instincts. At the same time, he must have been glad to hear from a correspondent who warned against the cuts that his proponents and adversaries alike had recommended. 'Upon reading the contents of the whole', Spence wrote, 'I am more and more convinced that much ought not to be parted with.'

Richardson describes the air of reality with which he tried to imbue the novel in a letter to Warburton (14 April 1748), who had provided a piece of writing used to preface volume IV of the first two editions of *Clarissa* (but dropped thereafter). This is a far cry from passing off the letters as genuine, as he had initially seemed to do with *Pamela*:

> Will you, good Sir, allow me to mention, that I could wish, that the 'Air of Genuineness' had been kept up, tho' I want not the Letters to be thought genuine; only so far kept up, I mean, as that they should not prefatically be owned not to be genuine; and this for fear of weakening

xlvi

GENERAL INTRODUCTION

their Influence where any of them are aimed to be exemplary: as well
as to avoid hurting that kind of Historical Faith, which Fiction itself is
generally read with, tho' we know it to be Fiction.

We can admire Richardson for his skill in promoting the success of *Clarissa* and
his willingness to engage with readers, well-known and anonymous. But in the
letters in this volume, we can see that the pose of an engaged and respectful correspondent could be occasionally impossible to maintain. In a letter of 23 December
1748, for example, Edward Moore includes a couple of narrow criticisms of the
ending of the novel among many lines of fulsome praise. Richardson had evidently
sent the final three volumes, recently published, to select friends for their impressions, already with an eye to another, revised version of the novel. Moore was duly
impressed – 'Upon the Whole, I have never been so interested, so entertained,
or so instructed' – and ventured to offer advice on alterations to further sharpen
the novel's salutary effects. Richardson exploded in response, going step-by-step
through Moore's questions and suggestions, all with an eye to proving Moore
wrong and the way he wrote the novel right. This is one of the longest letters in
the volume, minute in its self-justifications.

Similarly, when Solomon Lowe meekly conveyed his friend Thomas Cooper's
suggestion that a marriage between Lovelace and Clarissa would have allowed
Richardson to show off post-nuptial scenes that could exalt Clarissa and her
virtue, Richardson penned an even longer screed full of quotations from the
novel supporting Clarissa's steadfast refusal to wed her rapist, and he concluded
by admonishing Lowe that 'the Story would neither have answered my Design
… nor been my Story' (21 January 1749) if he had managed it in the way that
Cooper had suggested. Lowe reported back to Richardson the overwhelming success of his argument: try as he could to represent to them the force of Cooper's
objections, Lowe's daughters would have thought it a 'Crime' for Clarissa to have
married Lovelace. Still, Lowe conveyed Richardson's spirited rejoinder back to
Cooper, who gamely stuck to his argument. The extant copy of this letter is in
Richardson's own hand. As much as he rejected Cooper's argument, he nevertheless wanted to preserve all of the controversy: letter upon letter, writing on
top of writing, topped off by 'Mr. R. Smith's Thoughts on the preceding', which
responds to Cooper's criticisms of the novel, and with a flourish of lines supposed to have been written by Elias Brand demonstrating 'resentment against
[Clarissa's] defamers' (3 February 1749).

Familiar Correspondence

The *Oxford English Dictionary* defines 'familiar', in its eighteenth-century context,
as 'Unceremonious, as among close friends; free, casual, informal'. Richardson's
letters related to his careers as printer and writer participated in the culture of
the 'familiar letter' while instrumentally seeking to achieve his particular goals.
In this volume of miscellaneous correspondence, we get a sense of the intimacy

xlvii

GENERAL INTRODUCTION

that Richardson could reflect, and create, in his personal letters. Editors as early as Anna Laetitia Barbauld, in her 1804 *Correspondence*, recognized that Richardson's correspondence was of interest beyond his career as novelist and printer. Other volumes in the Cambridge Edition allow readers to understand the iterative nature of his deep and evolving relationships. In this volume, we get context for those individual relationships as well as gain an appreciation for the ways in which Richardson created and maintained social connections. For example, the volume of correspondence with George Cheyne provides a richly textured conversation that illuminates connections between health and writing in Richardson's life and work. That extended correspondence is contextualized in this volume by letters like that of 21 April 1743 from James Leake, brother-in-law and colleague in the world of printers, as it expands on the individual relationship between Richardson and Cheyne to show that their friendship was itself a matter of interest beyond themselves. Leake's letter combines an intensity of concrete description with abstract moralizing, making it both a very personal document and a participant in a public genre.

Richardson's correspondence often enacts friendship through business; Richardson claims to eschew form while writing within the expectations of the genre of familiar correspondence. A letter to Samuel Lobb of 16 May 1746 illustrates the complex set of expectations, intentions, and understandings that characterized epistolary friendship in the period in general and Richardson's friendships in particular. The letter begins with business: Richardson lets Lobb know that changes to one of Lobb's manuscripts would necessitate cancelling twelve pages, the expense of which Richardson would make 'as gentle to you as possible'. Then follows a tortured passage in which Richardson apologizes for not making clear to Lobb that he would *always* serve him as a printer, but that he has been absent on account of being in 'the writing Way' (he was writing *Clarissa*). And, Richardson admits, he has lost Lobb's letter and therefore does not, at the moment, possess the intimate knowledge of the other's life that their friendship requires. Richardson narrates a set of misunderstandings and then justifies discussing Lobb with brother-in-law Leake, who was a mutual friend: 'I had not complain'd ... to Mr. Leake, if I had had mere Forms in my Head. I have long, intentionally, discarded that from my Friendships.' Richardson concludes this line of argument by asserting that, 'when I presumed to think my Heart was known, I troubled not my self about it'. To confirm their close personal and familial connections, Richardson then asks questions about Lobb's family, including Lobb's son William who would himself become a correspondent of Richardson. Richardson's wife and daughters 'desire their affectionate Respects, to You, and Yours'. Finally, Richardson asks that his 'Compliments' be relayed to Lobb's 'Patron', Ralph Allen, the eminent supporter of literature and good works. The connection to Allen reminds us that these familiar friendships were conducted in the context of social rank, financial means, and reputation in the larger world. The letter's last paragraph is marred by tears in the paper. Many of the words are indecipherable. The tantalizing phrase 'But had I been a woman' is bereft of the words that might explain

xlviii

it. Richardson writes, 'Altho' my whole Heart is at your Service; yet is my Head up<xxxxx *unknown number of words*> now, and in half as many different Places.'

This is a letter of apology, a letter of business, and a letter in which Richardson's affections emerge even in the midst of carefully calibrated explanations and requests that demonstrate acute sensitivity to the 'Forms' that its writer supposedly disregards when true friendship is at stake. In this letter, as in this volume of miscellaneous correspondence as a whole, Richardson's 'Head' and 'Heart', his talents and flaws are on display – and we see the writer whose literary genius seemed to have emerged from nowhere make a self-confident assertion of the value of common morality against social structures defined by inherited norms and inherited wealth.

A Note on the Text

Richardson's correspondence regarding *Pamela* and *Clarissa* has been notably well preserved, an immediate benefit of Richardson's interest in keeping a record of exchanges with his readers and friends regarding the two novels that founded and cemented his fame as a novelist. Indeed, the absence of letters from the 1720s and the paucity of letters from the 1730s suggest that Richardson's correspondence had probably been discarded by him and his interlocutors prior to his becoming a published writer. At some point in the 1750s, he gathered many of the letters contained in this volume into two dedicated volumes, indexed and annotated them, and continued to pay considerable attention to their preservation throughout his life by copying letters himself or arranging for amanuenses to prepare such copies. As Christine Gerrard remarks in her introduction to Richardson's correspondence with the Hill family, we may have this practice of copying to thank for the preservation of a significant portion of Richardson's surviving letters.[3] The present volume, in particular, would have been considerably slimmer had it not been for Richardson's own activities in creating copies of some of his correspondence as well as for the work of Richardson's daughter Martha, his nephew William, and above all of Aaron Hill's brother Gilbert. As a result of these efforts as well as of his friends' and family's continued valuing of the correspondence, 117 of the 146 letters collected in this volume survive in manuscript.[4] The majority of these manuscript letters are now held in the Forster Collection at the Victoria and Albert

---

[3] *Correspondence with Aaron Hill and the Hill Family*, ed. Christine Gerrard (Cambridge University Press, 2013), p. xlix.

[4] Five of these manuscript letters were sent neither to SR nor by him: three were enclosures in letters to him but originally intended for other recipients (Chetwode to Courteville, 24 January 1741; Cooper to Lowe, 1 February 1749; and Collier to Cave, 19 September 1749); the other two were letters originally addressed to others but written about him or indirectly intended for him to see (<Churchill to Collier?>, 30 June 1749; and Anonymous to Rivington, 15 November 1740, respectively). The two orders of payment and nine receipts for annuities collected in the appendix are not included in this count.

xlix

GENERAL INTRODUCTION

Museum,[5] with two more clusters in the British Library and at Yale; the rest are dispersed among archives in Europe and the United States. Three of these letters survived in manuscript until relatively recently, and may continue to survive, but are now deposited in untraced private collections or lost.[6] In some cases, traces of the letters' contents survive in auction catalogues as well as in reports or transcriptions by those who had access to them at an earlier date. We have endeavoured to recover as much of these letters as possible, but reliable information is often difficult to obtain. The remaining 29 letters survive only because their texts – or at least a version thereof – were at some point published either in Barbauld's edition of Richardson's correspondence or in a periodical like the *Monthly Magazine*.[7]

Beyond the issue of textual sources, some interesting patterns emerge when we look at the frequency with which letters survive in manuscript – as an autograph or a copy – or in print as well as at the balance between letters to or from Richardson among the surviving letters. Letters written *to* Richardson, of which there are 95 in this volume, are far more frequently preserved in print (26 of them) than letters written *by* Richardson, of which we have 46 (with 3 preserved only in print). While Richardson seems to have been more conscientious about preserving letters from his correspondents than they were about preserving his letters to them – no doubt in part due to his diligent efforts to collect, catalogue, and copy – those letters' manuscripts are also far more likely to have been lost and known to us only through their print versions, possibly because their loss occurred precisely in that process of publishing which some sections of Richardson's correspondence underwent in the early nineteenth century.[8] Among the letters that do survive in manuscript – 69 *to* Richardson, 46 *from* Richardson, and five enclosures or letters otherwise entered into the correspondence – those written *by* Richardson survive more frequently as an autograph (25) compared to those sent *to* Richardson

[5] Most of the letters are collected in FM XV, 2, and FM XVI, 1, with a few more scattered across additional volumes. These are not the two volumes of correspondence on *Pamela* and *Clarissa* as Richardson arranged them – complete with an index for each and a title page for the *Pamela* letters (FM XV, ff. 1–2; FM XV, 3, ff. 3–4) – but reflect later collectors' arrangements. The letters were 'windowed in' to the FM volumes – done by cutting away a book's page except for a thin frame around the margin and pasting the letter onto that frame – which occasionally obscures or even obliterates text around the letter's edges.

[6] These are SR to Ackers, 30 January 1746; SR to Moore, 3 October 1748; and Garrick to SR, 12 December 1748.

[7] For a more detailed discussion of the publication history of SR's letters, see the 'General Editors' Preface' in this volume.

[8] For the use of manuscript letters as printer's copy and the subsequent loss of some of those manuscripts, see William McCarthy, 'What Did Anna Barbauld Do to Samuel Richardson's Correspondence? A Study of Her Editing', *Studies in Bibliography*, 54 (2001), 198–201.

GENERAL INTRODUCTION

(11 autographs).[9] In combination with the increased survival rate of Richardson's own letters in manuscript, this seems to indicate that his correspondents, and later their families and executors, were relatively quick to recognize the value of preserving Richardson's letters in their original form and in his own hand. For Richardson, on the other hand, the collecting and cataloguing of epistolary texts and their contents seems to have outranked preservation of the material letters or interest in their writers' original hands: letters collected in this volume that were written to Richardson are more likely to have survived in the form of a copy (58) than those letters that Richardson had sent to others (19). All enclosures and letters exchanged between other correspondents that eventually found their way into Richardson's hands survive as copies rather than autographs. This pattern in the survival of copies may suggest that some of his correspondents or their families recalled their letters during Richardson's lifetime, a practice not uncommon during the eighteenth century and actually documented in connection to the Richardson correspondence when Hester Mulso recalled her letters after Richardson's death.[10] Above all, the patterns of letters' survival as copies vs. autographs demonstrates Richardson's determination, especially after the publication of *Pamela*, to preserve and organize a record of all his correspondence, including the copying of his own letters: seven of the letters in this volume that were originally sent *to* Richardson, five of those *by* Richardson, and one of the enclosures survive as copies in Richardson's own hand.[11]

Finally, our close tracking of the copying of letters as well as our identification for the first time of many of the hands involved in the transcription, editing, and organization of Richardson's correspondence reveals the longstanding, indeed cross-generational, work that Richardson together with family members and friends invested in the preservation and cataloguing of the letters. By comparing the hands of copied letters to samples drawn from known autograph letters, we were able to ascertain, for example, that Gilbert Hill was responsible for transcribing the vast majority of letters in our volume that survive as copies: 47 of those sent to Richardson, 13 sent by Richardson, and two of the enclosures as well as the anonymous letter sent to Charles Rivington but indirectly meant for Richardson (15 November 1740) are in Hill's hand.[12] In addition, our comparison of hands also reveals that he played a significant role in the editorial tagging

---

[9] SR to Moore, <After 23 December 1748>, survives in two parts: a copy of the opening section in Gilbert Hill's hand and an autograph draft of the letter's later sections.

[10] B: I, cxcviii.

[11] Of particular interest in this respect are SR's correspondence with Solomon Lowe in 1749, most of which survives copied in SR's hand, and Henry Fielding's single known letter to SR (15 October 1748).

[12] We have used Gilbert Hill to SR, 17 August 1750, as a sample of Hill's hand, in which he may have advertised his skills as a copyist. For a more detailed discussion of Gilbert Hill, his relationship to his brother Aaron, and his role in the preservation and organization of SR's correspondence, see *Correspondence with Aaron Hill and the Hill Family*, pp. xlviii–xlix and 329; Christine Gerrard, *Aaron Hill: The Muses' Projector, 1685–1750* (Oxford University

li

GENERAL INTRODUCTION

and organization of Richardson's correspondence, since a significant number of endorsements on autographs as much as copies of letters are in his hand, too.[13] Richardson himself did extensive work in this vein across the entire correspondence and throughout the latter part of his life. In fact, emendations, additions, and endorsements appear in two distinctive hands: one a small but clearly legible rounded hand, the other the jittery and often difficult-to-read hand impacted by his later struggles with tremors and other symptoms of his neurological disease. Richardson's nephew William, son of his younger brother William, acted as copyist for one letter sent to Richardson and included in this volume,[14] and so did Jane Collier for a letter not originally intended for Richardson but clearly of interest to him and perhaps copied by her expressly for his collection.[15] Martha Richardson, finally, emerges as a copyist and editor with a far greater shaping influence on Richardson's correspondence than has previously been discussed.[16] Not only did we find two copies of letters to be in her hand – one sent to Richardson and one originally written by him – but we were also able to identify her as responsible for the numbering and, by implication, the ordering of considerable numbers of letters at some point in the history of Richardson's letter collection.[17] It seems unlikely, moreover, that this ordering worked in tandem with Richardson's own numbering of letters (which occurred later in his life and is often marked on the letters in his late, jittery hand) since their numbering systems overlap and conflict on three letters collected in this volume.[18] Instead, Martha Richardson's numbering probably represents an alternative arrangement of at least some of the letters, possibly instituted after Richardson's death when Martha and her sister Anne inherited the letters.

The presence of editorial interventions by one or more hands is another manuscript feature that reveals much about the letters' textual and material history.

Press, 2003), pp. 10–11 and 30; and Louise Curran, *Samuel Richardson and the Art of Letter-Writing* (Cambridge University Press, 2016), pp. 164–5.

[13] The endorsement, 'From Anonymous VI Ladies. Post Mark Reading. Directed to Mr. Richardson Bookseller in Salisbury Court, Fleet Street.', on his copy of Six Ladies to SR, <January or February> 1742, is a particularly lengthy example of this work.

[14] We have used SR to Carter, 12 June 1753, and Young to SR, 14 March 1754, as samples, which have both been identified as copies in William's hand by Betty Schellenberg; for further discussion of William's role as SR's amanuensis, see *Correspondence Primarily on* Sir Charles Grandison *(1750–1754)*, ed. Betty A. Schellenberg (Cambridge University Press, 2015), pp. xliii–xlv.

[15] We discuss Collier's copy of <Churchill to Collier?>, 30 June 1749, in more detail below.

[16] We identified her hand using two letters of hers to her sister Anne, of 7 and 20 July 1784, now in the Richardson Family Papers at Rice University, Fondren Library MS. 279.

[17] The copies in her hand are SR to Marsh, 21 December 1739; and Lowe to SR, 5 February 1749.

[18] These are Collier to SR, 9 July 1749, as well as Collier to SR, <Tuesday 19 September 1749>, and its enclosure, Collier to Cave, 19 September 1749. Letters captured by Martha's organizing system in this volume are numbered as follows: 3, 5 (x2), 6–14, 16–17, 19, 21–2, 24–5, 27 (x3), 28, 32–4, 36–8, 47–8, 59–62, 64–8, and 71.

lii

Most surviving manuscript letters in this collection carry a number of editorial emendations or notes in Richardson's hand – often the difficult-to-read hand of his later years – while several letters received sustained, sometimes repeated attention from Richardson as well as others and show extensive revision of wording as well as, occasionally, of content. Richardson's letter to his brother-in-law James Leake of August 1741, for example, shows heavy emendation by Richardson well after the letter had been copied for Richardson's records. Though neither this nor any other letter in the present volume received the level of editorial attention lavished on, say, the correspondence between Richardson and Lady Bradshaigh, it nevertheless illustrates the care with which Richardson continued to revise the texts of his letters and to annotate them as part of his autobiographical record.[19] In many cases, Richardson and other annotators sought to disguise the identities of correspondents or the people, places, and topics mentioned, so deletions and erasures occur in a significant number of letters. In most cases, the material so cancelled can be recovered quite easily, and we have noted where such deletions occurred. In at least one case, though – Richardson's letter to Edward Moore of 23 December 1748 – some of the text has been so thoroughly scratched out as to be almost unrecoverable. Several letters also carry emendations and notes in the hands of other readers of the letters: among these, Barbauld's edits, notes, and instructions to the printers of the *Correspondence* stand out, not only literally so because the ink in which she wrote them shows pale green against the grey and black of letter texts and other emendations but also because Barbauld's notes offer crucial insights into an otherwise opaque, largely undocumented editorial process.[20]

For the collection and reconstruction of Richardson's correspondence, Barbauld's edition is a double-edged sword. On the one hand, her six volumes record the only known text for the vast majority of letters that she included: of the 442 letters that make up the *Correspondence*, only 118 survive in manuscript.[21] In other words, were it not for Barbauld's collection, much of Richardson's correspondence – including some of the most interesting letters he and his correspondents exchanged – would now be lost to us. On the other hand, it may be precisely due to Barbauld's edition

---

[19] For other examples of heavy contextual annotation, often accompanied by considerable efforts to disguise living individuals mentioned in the same letters, see Lowe to SR, 18 May 1749; and Barber to SR, 26 August 1741.

[20] Channing to SR, <Early 1749>, offers a particularly interesting example of Barbauld's emendations and annotations. The standard discussion of her editorial work and its effects on the surviving correspondence is McCarthy, 'What Did Barbauld Do'; in addition, see William McCarthy, *Anna Letitia Barbauld: Voice of the Enlightenment* (Baltimore: Johns Hopkins University Press, 2008), pp. 412–16; and William McCarthy, 'Editing Richardson by Tug-of-War: Anna Letitia Barbauld and Richard Phillips in 1804', *Eighteenth-Century Fiction*, 29, no. 2 (2016–17), 263–76.

[21] See McCarthy, 'What Did Barbauld Do', 208; and Thomas Keymer and Peter Sabor, 'Samuel Richardson's Correspondence: Additions to Eaves and Kimpel', *N&Q*, 50 (2003), 215–18.

liii

GENERAL INTRODUCTION

and the working conditions that its publisher Richard Phillips imposed on her that so many manuscripts are now missing. It seems that, at least for some of the time that she worked on the *Correspondence* and in response to Phillips's pressure to provide more material faster, Barbauld edited and marked up the original letters and then sent them to the printers, who may have discarded manuscript copy after the texts had been printed. There is thus a good chance that Barbauld's selection of letters for inclusion in the printed *Correspondence* led more or less directly to the loss of those manuscripts, a process that becomes even more surprising when one considers that Phillips, who must have known that the manuscript letters were being used in this manner, was also their owner. The result of all of this is that, for 27 letters in this volume, only a printed version remains, most often in Barbauld's collection (see especially the Strahan correspondence, for which only the letters to Richardson are now known). A few others were printed in the periodical press, where the manuscripts may have met a similar fate as they did during the preparation of the *Correspondence*: much of Richardson's exchange with Elizabeth Carter surrounding his unauthorized use of her 'Ode to Music' in *Clarissa* survives only as published, again by Phillips, in the *Monthly Magazine* in 1812. Setting aside for a moment concerns for the preservation of manuscripts and the status of surviving texts, it is important to acknowledge that Phillips was the most important – almost the exclusive – publisher of Richardson's letters before the advent of the few scholarly editions of the twentieth century.[22]

In addition to his correspondence with friends, family, admirers of his writing, and business associates, this volume also contains an appendix featuring one order of payment to Richardson for printing jobs completed on behalf of the House of Commons as well as ten receipts for proceeds from annuities that Richardson appears to have collected for much of his life. While not part of the letters proper, these documents nevertheless tell an important part of the financial story that helps us better understand Richardson's business dealings, and in the receipt of 19 July 1715 we have the earliest record of Richardson's activities, private or public, as well as the earliest example of his signature.[23] The orders and receipts are also interesting media objects that merge a variety of financial and legal languages; and while the orders of payment are fully drawn up in manuscript, the receipts consist of printed forms that were then filled out and signed by government officials and by Richardson. The printing of such forms and other 'jobbing work' – handbills,

---

[22] These are *The Letters of Doctor George Cheyne to Samuel Richardson (1733–43)*, ed. Charles F. Mullett (Columbia: University of Missouri Studies, 1943); *The Richardson–Stinstra Correspondence, and Stinstra's Prefaces to Clarissa*, ed. William C. Slattery (Carbondale: Southern Illinois University Press, 1969); and *Selected Letters of Samuel Richardson*, ed. John Carroll (Oxford: Clarendon Press, 1964); as well as correspondence with SR in collections of letters by Henry and Sarah Fielding; David Garrick; Samuel Johnson; Charlotte Lennox; Edward Moore; and Edward Young.

[23] Eaves and Kimpel may still be correct in dating SR's acquisition of a 14 per cent government annuity to 'the late 1730s' (80), but the rediscovery of a receipt for a bankers' annuity from 1715 means that his financial activities began more than twenty years earlier.

liv

GENERAL INTRODUCTION

advertisements, financial and business documents, and other printed materials of less than one sheet – constituted the vast majority of printing firms' output throughout the eighteenth century.[24] Richardson's printing of bills for private business before the House of Commons from 1720 and of public bills, orders, and reports on behalf of the House of Commons from 1733 fell into this line of work, though we don't know whether he also printed forms and receipts of the kind included in the appendix to this volume.[25]

Besides this one outlier and another late receipt from 1751, the correspondence in this volume covers the period 1732–49, with the bulk of it concentrated in the 1740s; only ten letters date from the 1730s. By and large, Richardson and his correspondents were very careful to date their letters, and in most cases the writers and recipients are apparent or easily deduced, too. Where conjectural or unknown, we have followed Eaves and Kimpel in assigning dates or correspondents to most letters. In a few cases, however, internal and contextual evidence has required a redating, and in one important case it has led us to a wholesale reassignment of sender, addressee, and transmission history of the letter.

The first such reassignment within the chronology of Richardson's correspondence concerns a piece now only known from the *Correspondence*, a letter from William Strahan to Richardson that Barbauld dates to 16 September 1749; Eaves and Kimpel followed her lead. Presumably, the manuscript from which she was working did not carry a clear date, but with its gestures to travel, the knowledge or discovery of varieties in human nature, and mentions of business arrangements in Edinburgh, on first glance it appears to fit well with Strahan's other letters to Richardson sent during his travels through Scotland in 1749. However, Strahan's announcement of the birth of his son Samuel, so named in honour of Richardson, clearly dates the letter to 1745; Strahan was as meticulous in recording births, deaths, marriages, and other major life events of family members as he was in keeping business records, and he entered both into the same ledgers.[26] As a consequence, we should also treat it with caution when Barbauld locates Strahan in Edinburgh when writing this letter. While he is clearly at a distance from Richardson and feels the need to report news on a range of topics, any references to travel are metaphorical and all mentions of Edinburgh or 'the North' refer to business arrangements that do not necessitate Strahan's presence there or in fact

---

[24] See Maslen, pp. 35–6; James Raven, *Publishing Business in Eighteenth-Century England* (Woodbridge: The Boydell Press, 2014); Peter Stallybrass, '"Little Jobs": Broadsides and the Printing Revolution', in *Agent of Change: Print Culture Studies after Elizabeth L. Eisenstein*, ed. Sabrina Alcorn Baron, Eric N. Lindquist, and Eleanor F. Shevlin (Amherst: University of Massachusetts Press, 2007), pp. 315–41; and Peter Stallybrass, 'Printing and the Manuscript Revolution', in *Explorations in Communication and History*, ed. Barbie Zelizer (London and New York: Routledge, 2008), pp. 111–18.

[25] See Eaves and Kimpel, p. 56; Maslen, pp. 14–23.

[26] BL Add. MSS 48800–48918 and Add. Ch. 75421–75427; his family records are at Add. MSS 48802A, f. 88ff.

lv

GENERAL INTRODUCTION

often presume his absence. As far as we can tell from the available record, Samuel Strahan was born in London.

The other date change concerns two letters from Richardson to Thomas Birch, which survive in incompletely dated manuscripts: the first one to 19 April, the second one simply to 'Friday morn'. Eaves and Kimpel had cautiously assigned both letters to the '1740s' while noting that Richardson's mention of 'My Friend Grover' in the first letter meant that it had to have been written before the death of John Grover, assistant to the chief Clerk of the House of Commons, in September 1749. Two items of internal evidence, however, allow for a much more precise dating. In the first instance, both letters discuss the editing and printing of the second edition of Charles Yorke's *Some Considerations on the Law of Forfeiture, for High Treason* (1746); the two letters thus belong together. There are also indications that the second letter must have been written relatively close to the publication of the *Considerations'* second edition in mid-July because in this letter Richardson worries about last-minute changes Yorke is making while printing of the volume is already under way; the latest date for the two letters is thus established as before mid-July 1746. In connection with this second edition, Richardson also expresses concerns in the first letter regarding a bill under consideration in the House of Commons – itself merely a renewal of the Importation Act of 1738 – that received a late addition on 16 April 1746 according to which publishers of new editions of a book would also have to offer their customers any alterations or additions contained in such new editions for separate purchase. Richardson asks Birch to try to lobby members of the House against the bill, otherwise he foresees additional expenses for Yorke due to the alterations and additions to the *Considerations*. The first letter thus yields confirmation of the year for both letters and, since Richardson noted a day and month, establishes their sequence.

Our final and most extensive emendations to a letter in this volume concern an incomplete letter, dated 30 June 1749 but missing its opening and signature, that Eaves and Kimpel identify as having been sent to Richardson by an otherwise unidentified 'Miss Churchill'.[27] Our first change is to the addressee: internal evidence suggests that this letter was written *about* Richardson rather than *to* him, and that it was perhaps forwarded to him at a later date. This impression is further strengthened by our discovery that the letter is in the hand of Jane Collier, one of Richardson's protégées; the handwriting matches Collier's distinctive hand in a letter of hers to Richardson on 9 July 1749. However, internal evidence also shows that Collier was probably not the letter's original sender, who refers to 'my Fathers Business' in reviewing troops; to receiving wearisome social calls at Dalkeith House near Edinburgh (the seat in 1749 of Francis Scott, second Duke of Buccleuch); and to planning a tour through the Scottish Lowlands. Besides

---

[27] The discussion that follows draws from Sören Hammerschmidt, 'Mysterious Miss Churchill: Jane Collier's Copy of a Letter in the Richardson Correspondence', *N&Q*, 67, no. 3 (September 2020), 415–21, https://doi.org/10.1093/notesj/gjaa108.

lvi

GENERAL INTRODUCTION

not having any known direct connections to the family of the duke, Collier would not have been of sufficient social rank to worry about the frequency of visitors at Dalkeith; was to the best of our knowledge in London throughout 1749; and her father, a rector and theological controversialist, had died in 1732 and would in any event not have been of sufficient social or military standing to review troops.[28] It thus appears that Collier copied someone else's letter while disguising original recipient and sender, and that her copy somehow, through either her own agency or that of others, found its way into Richardson's collection of letters during his lifetime.[29] The letter does seem to be addressed to someone who moves within Richardson's circles with some regularity, since the sender gives cognizance to the recipient's pleasure in 'the Conversation of a Man who seems to understand human Nature so well'. Collier fits that description and might thus have been the letter's original recipient, but there is no direct evidence to confirm that possibility from the letter alone.

The letter's sender, on the other hand, can be identified with more certainty. It is not clear how Eaves and Kimpel arrived at her name – it appears nowhere in the letter, and they do not discuss the letter anywhere in the biography or in separate publications – but their 'Miss Churchill' is almost certainly Henrietta Arabella Churchill (1722?–56), daughter of Lieutenant-General George Churchill (c. 1690–1753), commander-in-chief of the land forces in Scotland. The most likely connection between Collier and Henrietta Churchill is to be found in the overlapping social circles of the Collier siblings and several branches of the Churchill family, with novelists Sarah Fielding and Henry Fielding acting as intermediaries. The Fieldings had familial and military connections to John Churchill, first Duke of Marlborough, and his family, and Henrietta Churchill's father was the illegitimate son and heir of the duke's brother, Admiral George Churchill (bap. 1654–1710). There is further potential for a military connection via Sarah and Henry's father Edmund Fielding (1680–1741), whose latter-day army career – promoted to brigadier in 1727 and to lieutenant-general in 1739 – exactly mirrors the years and promotions for Henrietta's uncle Charles Churchill (1679–1745), the illegitimate son of another of the Duke of Marlborough's brothers, General Charles Churchill (1656–1714). Collier may also have been in contact with another, more distantly related branch of the Churchill family

---

[28] For information on the still understudied Collier and her family, see esp. Eaves and Kimpel, pp. 202–4; entries for Collier in the *ODNB* and the *Orlando Project*; Jane Collier, *The Art of Ingeniously Tormenting*, ed. Audrey Bilger (Peterborough: Broadview Press, 2003), pp. 9–34; Jane Collier, *The Art of Ingeniously Tormenting*, ed. Katharine A. Craik (Oxford University Press, 2009), pp. xi–xxxviii; Sarah Fielding and Jane Collier, *The Cry: A New Dramatic Fable*, ed. Carolyn Woodward (Lexington: The University Press of Kentucky, 2018), pp. 2–20; and Thomas Keymer, 'Jane Collier, Reader of Richardson, and the Fire Scene in Clarissa', in *New Essays on Samuel Richardson*, ed. Albert J. Rivero (New York: St Martin's Press, 1996), pp. 141–61.

[29] SR took care to disguise the letter's sender even further by crossing out all references to Dalkeith, and he endorsed it by noting on the outside of the letter some of its contents.

lvii

GENERAL INTRODUCTION

via another family friend, the Salisbury-based scholar James Harris (1709–80), as well as through her social connections in Dorset more broadly. Harris's uncle, Anthony Ashley Cooper, third Earl of Shaftesbury (1671–1713), had encouraged and assisted the bookseller Awnsham Churchill (1658–1728) in his early bids for political office in Dorset, and Awnsham was not only 'distantly related to the Duke of Marlborough' but 'remained on friendly terms with his Tory kinsman George Churchill' – i.e. the duke's brother, Henrietta's grandfather – and 'was appointed an executor of George's will'.[30] Henrietta's father must therefore have had some form of contact with Awnsham and maybe others in the Dorset branch of the family during the administration of the will if not later. Members of that branch as well as of the duke's immediate family were patrons of Sarah and Henry Fielding from the 1730s to the 1750s. Given these consistent, repeated overlaps between Collier, Harris, the Fieldings, and the three branches of Churchills, it is very likely that George Churchill and his daughter Henrietta would at some point have come into contact with one or more members of the Collier–Harris–Fielding circle.

Richardson himself may not have known who the letter's sender was, or he may have confused letters and people when he created indexes while arranging his voluminous correspondence into volumes in the mid-1750s. The index for the volume of 'Letters, &c. Relating to Clarissa' lists two letters – 'Miss Carr to Miss Collier, on Clarissa' and 'Miss C. to Mr. R. congratulating him on his admirable Work' – that each fit some of the 'Churchill' letter's characteristics, but neither letter satisfies them all.[31] Following Eaves and Kimpel's identification, it was certainly written by a 'Miss C.' and, if we assume Richardson as recipient, could be read as 'congratulating him on his admirable Work' though we have seen that the letter does not in fact take Richardson as its intended recipient; this entry in the index, however, may well have led Eaves and Kimpel to identify Richardson as such. The first entry fits the letter's topic, and if Collier was indeed its intended recipient, then 'Miss Collier' would also correctly describe its addressee. It is, however, doubtful that Susan Carr (d. 1808), a friend of the Collier sisters, is the letter's original sender: though her father, Timothy Carr (d. 1771), rose to the rank of colonel, became first equerry to the king, and was present at Culloden in 1745, he never seems to have remained in Scotland sufficiently long or attained sufficient rank to count the review of troops in Scotland as one of his duties. Two possibilities then remain: first, that the entry in Richardson's index refers to a different letter once in Richardson's collection but now lost – one that was actually written by a 'Miss Carr' (possibly Susan) to a 'Miss Collier' (either to Jane or to

---

[30] Mark Knights, 'Churchill, Awnsham (1658–1728), of the Black Swan, Paternoster Row, London and Henbury, Dorset', *The History of Parliament: The House of Commons 1690–1715*, www.histparl.ac.uk/volume/1690-1715/member/churchill-awnsham-1658-1728 (accessed 19 May 2020).
[31] FM XV, f. 2.

lviii

GENERAL INTRODUCTION

her sister Margaret, who remained Susan Carr's close friend until her death in
1794); or second, that the entry does refer to the 'Churchill' letter in this volume
and Richardson misremembered the original sender, assigning it to 'Miss Carr'
because she was another 'Miss C.' associated in his mind with the Colliers. For
now, the letter in its surviving form remains above all an artefact of epistolary
practices common in Richardson's circles and across the eighteenth century: the
copying of (parts of) letters for circulation among social networks to which we
owe so much of Richardson's surviving correspondence.

CORRESPONDENCE PRIMARILY ON
PAMELA AND *CLARISSA*
(1732–1749)

Richardson to Thomas Verren Richardson[1]

<c. 1 August 1732>[2]

Printed source: The Imperial Review, 2 (August 1804), 609–16.

'An UNPUBLISHED Letter; from Mr Samuel Richardson,
to his Nephew, Thomas Richardson.'

Dear Tom;

As it is generally observed, that when relations come together
in the manner at present designed between your Father and me,
and which is also according to your own earnest desire, they
frequently disagree, by reason of greater expectations, on both
sides, of allowance and consideration to be had for each other, than
for mere strangers: As this, I say, is often the case, I think it is not
improper (that we may come to a thorough understanding before it
is too late), to let you know a few particulars of what I expect you
will make standard points of your observation; and you will be the
better able to judge how you can promise for yourself, or what you
are to expect from me: And, as I shall give here and there a reason,
as I go along, for what I say, and that some of them may have a
nearer relation to the time to come, than now, at your entrance,
it will not be amiss if you transcribe these lines, and keep them
by you for your better observation, that I may not be under the
necessity of repeating to you anything here set down: for, you must
know, I hate repetitions in such things as this, when a person of
your age is supposed to be duly apprized of his duty, &c.

Perhaps I shall be a little too serious for your present volatile
years: but, then, you must consider, that this you are entering
upon is a very serious and weighty affair; no less than what is to
be considered as the foundation of your future livelihood and
well-being in this world; and what (next to another point, that
you cannot be allowed to think of, for many years to come) of the
greatest importance to be well and maturely weighed: and therefore
I shall, without farther prefacing, tell you, in the first place, that I
expect,

---

[1] Thomas Verren Richardson (bap. 1717, d. 1732), eldest son of SR's brother William
Richardson, bound apprentice to SR on 1 August 1732 and died while in his employ, 8
November 1732; see Eaves and Kimpel, pp. 50–1.

[2] Written just as Thomas was beginning his apprenticeship in SR's print shop. The letter
subsequently provided the basis for 'Part II' of *The Apprentice's Vade Mecum* (1734).

RICHARDSON TO THOMAS VERREN RICHARDSON, <C. I AUGUST 1732>

1. That I shall be under less necessity of studying your temper, than you shall think yourself under of studying mine: and there is good reason for it; because I have lived so many years longer in the world than you have, and must not only have seen what is best for you to follow or avoid, but also must necessarily have so many other cares to pursue, that cannot easily or soon affect you, that my ease and quiet ought to be studied in every thing in your power; and that you may rather lighten me of my cares, than add to them.

2. That you behave to your fellow-apprentices with great condescension,[3] good manners, and evenness of temper, not expecting regards from them at one time, and playing antic[4] tricks with them at others; not desiring them to do for you, what you shall not be as willing to do for them: and you will be obliged to be more respectful to them, because they will be your elders, and know more of the business than you can do for some time, and are, besides, good men's sons.

3. That you treat the journeymen with complaisance and decency, as persons who are your elders and who, by due service and years, are become freemen of London,[5] or entitled to be so. You must, if you expect to be respected by them, shew a proper regard to them; do any civil, kind thing for them, that shall not hinder your own business, or injure me in loss of your time, &c.; and, if you expect any respect from them on my account, because of your relation to me, it will be exceedingly wrong, because I shall desire no such thing of them, but as you deserve it on your own: And let it be always remembered, that no man is to be ill used by you, if he happens to be poor or low in the world; for, how can you tell what your own fate may be? And even a man's being a very sorry man, a sot, a drunkard, (as, among so many, some may be,) does not entitle him to be ill used by you; for, pertness in youth is almost as great a fault as negligence, &c. in men: it will, therefore, become you to be serious, grave, even-tempered, and respectful to every body: and this you may be, and yet be cheerful and pleasant; for there is a proper medium between moroseness and melancholy, on one hand,

---

[3] 'Gracious, considerate, or submissive deference shown to another; complaisance', now obsolete (*OED*).

[4] I.e. grotesque or ludicrous.

[5] Earned with the completion of apprenticeship, 'the Freedom was the right to trade, enabling members of a Guild or Livery to carry out their trade or craft in the Square Mile' of the City of London, *The City of London*, www.cityoflondon.gov.uk/about-us/law-historic-governance/freedom-of-the-city (accessed 10 February 2021).

RICHARDSON TO THOMAS VERREN RICHARDSON, <C. I AUGUST 1732>

and flippancy and pertness, or sauciness, on the other. And this medium I must recommend you to aim at, not only to make you a good printer, but a good man.

IV.[6] If you see any bad example, learn to have a proper detestation of the action, without abusing the man that sets it: for, vice of all kinds is a misfortune when rendered habitual, as well as a fault, and deserves the pity of a person who has not a right to upbraid, and is not injured personally, – because it sinks the dignity of human nature, and makes the person suffer more by it than any body else. Endeavour, therefore, so to frame your conduct, as to shun in yourself what is odious in another: and be like the industrious bee, which collects its honey from the bitter as well as the sweet. Whatever you see in better men commendable, let it be your care to imitate it. Whatever you may be able to discern, even in myself, that may not be exactly right, make an useful inference of it for your own benefit, and endeavour to imitate what is better; for, we are none of us perfect.

V. Contract no intimacy with any young men in or out of the house, without apprizing me who they are, and knowing whether I approve of them for your companions: This may be, perhaps, a harder task for you to observe some time hence than at present: but as I should be fond to build you up in such a manner as may become my regards to you for the sake of your good Father and Mother, as well as for your own sake; and shall have a view to make you, if you are capable of so much good sense as to observe my instructions, an honour to your name, and credit to the Profession; I must absolutely insist upon it, and I caution you once for all, that if I see any affected disguise, or endeavour to conceal your acquaintance or any of your actions from my knowledge, I shall conclude you are in no good way: for, what must that young man be, who is studious to act under a mask, and can continue in the doing of those things which he thinks will not bear to be known? – I expect not from you absolute perfection; that cannot be found any-where: but this does not hinder but you should avoid these faults which you know to be so: for, he that knows his duty, and will not do it, shews nothing less than an abandoned mind.

VI. I cannot but observe to you, that there seems to be a kind of unpolished roughness in your behaviour, and a want of that sweetness and complaisance of temper which is absolutely necessary

---

[6] The numbering here switches to roman numerals.

5

to make a person respected and beloved. To avoid this, you should determine to study every one's temper, and carefully to avoid saying a thing, even in jest, that may discompose or shock any one: For, why should that be a pleasure to you, which would be a pain to another? – There is difference between an inoffensive jest, and making yourself merry at the expence of another person's quiet: but turn the tables; and see how you would like the same conduct from another: and 'twill make you avoid doing a disobliging thing to any one. 'Tis a barbarous temper, and a sign of a very ill nature, to take delight in shocking any one: and, on the contrary, it is the mark of an amiable and a beneficent temper, to say all the kind things one can, without flattery or playing the hypocrite, – and what never fails of procuring the love and esteem of everyone; which, next to doing good to a deserving object who wants it, is one of the greatest pleasures of this life. I must tell you also, that there seems at present in your temper a sort of faulty coveting after getting into your possession, books, &c. more for the sake of having them than reading them. You seem to me to aim more at satisfying your curiosity than informing your judgment: and this is a very great fault, which, as I am willing to believe it will wear off with your boyhood, so I hope it will be sufficient for your instruction that I have observed it to you. In a word, I would have you aim to be a good husband without being a niggard, and generous without being extravagant.

VII. I expect that you will never give me occasion to tell you twice of a proper or right thing; and that you will not lay me under the necessity of repeating any instruction that shall be of use to you, either with regard to your business, or conduct, or behaviour. This, common gratitude will oblige you to; because in all this I consider, and shall always consider, your good more than my own.

VIII. I hope you will not expect any distinctions from me, with regard to the relation between us, but as you deserve them. As I shall take a very great pleasure to encourage you in a manner proper to your years and to your merit; yet I do assure you, your merit must be the prime consideration with me: it is not sufficient with me, that you are the son of a Brother I love equal with myself. If you act not worthy of such a Father, and of the relation you bear, the disappointment will be so much the heavier, and so much the more to be resented: and I shall be always able to distinguish so properly as, I hope, to preserve my love to a good Brother, without favouring or affecting a naughty Kinsman: and, therefore, as it

will be best rather to deserve than expect distinctions; so it will
be always in your power to reap those advantages by your good
conduct, which your ill behaviour will never obtain from me: –
Remember this, that a mere stranger that obliges one, ought to be
far dearer to us than the nearest relation who, presuming upon the
ties of blood, does nothing that one would have him do: for, 'tis the
nature of a dog, and not of a man, that loves the better for being ill
used.

IX. Let it be your observation to avoid those faults in yourself,
which you see or hear me dislike in others. Is it not much better
that you mend by another's failings than by your own? But it
would be still more intolerable not to mend your own, when told of
them: And one thing I would very particularly inforce upon your
memory; which is, that you shew no impatience of being told of
your faults, but that you think every one your friend who tells you
any thing for your good. An enemy is usefuller to us by far than a
flatterer (who is indeed the worst enemy), because such an one may
be made a faithful monitor to us, by reproaching us of our failings,
which an ingenious nature wants only to know or be told of, in
order to mend or avoid.

X. Shun all loose words, or rash and inconsiderate expressions:
Your education hitherto, I know, has, or ought to have, made this
caution unnecessary to you: but, as you are coming among a set
of people of different manners and behaviour, you will observe
greater liberties than are decent, perhaps, taken in this respect by
some of the most profligate of them, (for, a printing-house is but an
indifferent school for good manners,) which, I hope, you will rather
dislike than give into: for, it would be a great affliction to me, that
you should so behave as to lose the fruits of the good education
your Father has been at a great expence to bestow upon you; and
that I should learn you a trade at so dear a rate as by the forfeiture
of your morals.

XI. With regard to your trade, I must desire you to avoid two
things, viz.,[7] idleness and eye-service: and, in your working-time,
by reading or any other amusement, do not waste your hours; for,
in this respect, you may become a very good or a very bad example
to the rest of the apprentices; who will soon take the same liberties
you give yourself; and so I shall have all the care and trouble of idle
and impertinent boys, without the profit that ought to accrue from

---

[7] 'that is to say, namely, to wit' (*OED*).

their diligence and good performance. Remember, there is a time for every thing, and you may employ your holidays or spare-time in reading: and this (as your business itself is a series of reading), I am persuaded, will be sufficient, except you should be so undeserving as to amuse yourself, through an idleness of disposition, with a book, when you should be at work.

XII. It need not be said that I shall expect from you (more than from another) a watchful eye for my interest, and to see nothing wasted or misapplied: but I would not have you quick to trifling and immaterial faults, so as to bring upon yourself the imputation of a spy or a tale-bearer: and this you must be very careful of; for, else, you will make all the house your enemies, and will lead a very uneasy life with them, especially in my absence: But your indenture will tell you that you must not see me wronged.

XIII. I am sometimes, when I think of some few things I have observed in you, afraid of an inattention and heedlessness that makes me apprehend I shall be obliged often to give you the same instructions, before you will observe them as I wish: If this should be so, and that you should shew an obstinate, stubborn temper, ready to commit faults, and impatient to hear of them then I should have no manner of comfort in taking you, and you had better never come to me; for I should surely, by a bad conduct, be quite estranged from you, and forgive it less in you than another. – I hope the few observations I hint at, are only the effects of your youth and inexperience; and so I am willing to think the best: but indeed I must tell you, that I take the pains to write this, because I may have occasion to say the less; because it may have the stronger impression upon you, and because I expect you shall alter any little thing in your temper and behaviour as you advance in age; – in short, that as you grow older, you grow wiser; and that you make such use of the hints I here give you, that the benefits accruing from them may rather appear the effects of your natural disposition, than that such hints were necessary. And, that you may be the better able to judge of me, I will tell you, it is my way very jocosely, when the world does not put me too much out of humour, to rally and banter for small faults; which, nevertheless, it is to be observed, I would have, seriously, mended: and if a pleasant behaviour has not a proper effect, then I become serious in my turn, and shall let you know it in a less agreeable manner: And this hint I leave you, to make a proper use of.

RICHARDSON TO THOMAS VERREN RICHARDSON, <C. I AUGUST 1732>

XV.[8] I expect, as to bed-time, working-time, spare-time, Sundays, &c. an entire conformity to the rules of the house, and those I shall from time to time give you; and that you take the directions of those I shall intrust with the management of things in my absence, with the same regard as if I gave you them myself: your readiness in this particular will be attended with this double benefit to yourself; – That, as he never knows how to command, that could not in his place obey; so it will shew me, that I may, so much the safer, in proper time, if it please God to continue my life, commit things to your management: and people will be the readier disposed, by the example of your submission to the rules of your elders, to pay regard to yours, when your good conduct shews you to be fit to be intrusted with a superior direction yourself.

XX.[9] Till you get a good insight into your business, if you are for talking with the men, or your fellow-apprentices, let it be about your business; and then you will not have occasion to talk impertinently or much; and every question you ask will bring with it some improvement. But it is very proper for you to remember that it is very unbecoming for young people to talk much, especially among their elders; they should rather hear than speak: and a close mouth, generally, is the sign of a wise head. What if your fellow-apprentices should happen to be pert, saucy, or talkative? Does not every one blame them for it, and call it by the name it deserves? And would you follow the worst examples? Nature has given two ears to one tongue: and what is this for, but to teach that *all* men, and much more *young* men, should hear twice as much as they should speak? And I earnestly desire that in your working-times I may see far more of the produce of your fingers, than hear of your tongue. Observe all those who speak much, how little is said that is fit to be remembered afterwards: and then think what a shame it must be in such who are always rattling and prating of what is not worthy to be remembered for an hour, or even fit to be repeated, as too generally is the case. It was once prescribed to a very talkative person, under a penalty which they consented to, to resolve to keep silence but one day, and instead of it, to write what they would otherwise have said: – What was the effect of

---

[8] The list here omits number XIV, possibly an indicator that the unknown editor for the *Imperial Magazine* cut material from the original letter.
[9] Another, larger jump.

RICHARDSON TO THOMAS VERREN RICHARDSON, <C. I AUGUST 1732>

this? They were quickly tired of writing, and what they did write was such stuff, that they were quite ashamed it should be seen: But this was a person of some modesty that could be ashamed; whereas the generality of the youth of this forward age are such confident creatures, that they know not how to talk, nor how to be ashamed. I do not expect you should never speak but in sentences, or that you should be a mute and a mope: There is a medium in all things: and that is what you are to aim to hit upon, as well in this as in all other cases.

There is one thing that is left behind, and more necessary than all the rest, and which, duly observed, will crown and secure all the rest; but which, I hope your good education and common sense will render it but just necessary for me to mention; that is, your duty to GOD, and inculcating the fear of Him in all your actions and views: This will make you just to every one, and will secure, like a strong wall, all your other virtues, and bring down a blessing upon all your honest endeavours: and if you hope to thrive and do well in the world, your due observations of this, whatever examples you, in this bad age, may see to the contrary, will make your hope reasonable and well grounded.

I told you I should be very serious with you: but I hope an article of this prime importance will not be thought by you too grave for any part of your life.

I have been longer than I intended; yet I could say more: but other things that time or particular occasions may make farther necessary, I shall, if God spare my life, inform you of as we go along, and as they shall be requisite. Meantime, copy out fair these articles, which may serve as preliminary ones to our coming together: and believe that they are the effects of that extraordinary care which I have for your welfare; and, by making a proper use of them, shew your gratitude to Your affectionate Uncle and Friend,

S. RICHARDSON

Richardson to Henry Lintot[1]

Sunday 10 October 1736

MS: Wisbech & Fenland Museum, 2003.35.277.1. Autograph letter sent (evidence of folding and seal).
Endorsement: 'To Henry Lintot, Esqr At Horsham, in Sussex' (in SR's hand).

Sir,

Mr. Coxeter[2] was with me on Saturday Afternoon, and I did not receive the Favour of yours till about Noon the same Day. As I thought of writing to you on the Subject, and attending your further Directions thereupon, I did not own, that I had received a Letter <from>[3] you, nor shall, till I have an Answer to this.

As I recommended Mr. Coxeter to you, (tho' upon no Experience of my own, but only on the Recommendation of another) and as I think he asked you much out of the way, and have told him so very plainly, for only once reading the Sheets which not a Printer (if you'll allow for me), you have employ'd in the Work, but must be as <cap>able of as he, as there is no collating by other Copies, &c. to be done;[4] I think it behoves me, to tell you, that I believe you may very well spare at least a good Part of the Money, as I imagine, from the Value of the Work, you'll not want a better Index than that you have, which appears to me, in so good a Light, that it will exceed most of the Kind. And your Man in the Shop can put the Pages, or Folio's, right to the New Edition, in which case you may spare the whole Expence – Had I known of this Index before, I should never have thought of commending any body to you for the Work. – I compos'd a Head-Page, a Half-Title, and a full Page, and sent it to every Gentleman concern'd, so that we

---

[1] Henry Lintot (bap. 1703, d. 1758), bookseller, and law printer to the king from 1749 (*ODNB*). Eaves and Kimpel mistakenly identified the addressee as Robert Dodsley.

[2] Thomas Coxeter (1689–1747), literary scholar and editor, who had also helped prepare the indexes for John Hudson's edition of the works of Josephus (1720). John Nichols associated Coxeter with Grub Street and wrote that he was 'without any settled pursuit' (Nichols, II, p. 512).

[3] Damage to the letter and smudging of ink has led to some loss of text in several places.

[4] 'collating' here probably carries the more general meaning, 'To compare critically (a copy of a text) with other copies or with the original, in order to correct and emend it', as well as the more specialized, 'To examine the sheets of a printed book by the signatures, so as to ascertain that they are perfect and in correct order' (*OED*).

RICHARDSON TO HENRY LINTOT, SUNDAY 10 OCTOBER 1736

shall be all in a Method, & such an one as I hope will please you, without any extra Expence.[5]

But whatever you may determine, as to the Index; which is all that will be, in any Case, left for him to do; I think you may, as if you had not wrote to me at all, <men>tion, that you, <*like*>*wise*, postpone any Thought of *that*, till your Return; for nothing can be done in it as yet, till the Press is forwarder. I will pay with all my Heart Six Guineas, & much more, if you have any Commands for it; and take it for a Favour that you'll be so free with me; but I think my self obliged to intimate, that by some general Hints from one or two Persons who have had Dealings with him, I think it as improper for you to make such an Advance, as it was for him, upon so *small an Acquaintance* to desire it. I submit the whole to you; but thought my self obliged, on the Score of my Recommendation, to say thus much. And so much for this Matter.

Every thing is very quiet about us; and I believe the Affair of the 'Spital-fields Rioters a little while ago,[6] and the unparalleled one of Capt. Porteus more lately at Edinburgh,[7] might give the Administration Grounds for apprehending some Disturbances, when the Gin Act took place,[8] and especially among the Dregs of the People. The Master of the Rolls, too, was threaten'd on this Occasion, and a Guard mounted at the Rolls Office for 3 or

[5] SR here probably refers to the second edition of Ephraim Chambers, *Cyclopaedia: or, An Universal Dictionary of Arts and Sciences* (1738). There is no direct evidence that the sheets for the *Cyclopaedia* were printed in SR's shop, but we do know that he printed the fifth edition (1752); that he owned a copyright share in the *Supplement to Mr. Chambers' Cyclopaedia* (1753) as well as maybe in the *Cyclopaedia* itself; and that Aaron Hill, earlier in the year, had asked SR to lend him a copy of 'your *Chamber's*' (see Hill to SR, 30 June 1736). The 'Gentlem[e]n concerned' in the composition and printing of the *Cyclopaedia*'s two volumes are thus the group of booksellers, among them Henry Lintot, who appeared on the title page.

[6] Not the silk weavers' riots against below-subsistence wages, now known as the Spitalfield riots (1769, with unrest brewing since 1765), but an earlier agitation against the import of Indian calicoes and printed linen (1719).

[7] John Porteous (*c.* 1695–1736), an army officer in Edinburgh whose lynching at the hands of a mob in 1736 became a fulcrum for parliamentary debates in London over how to govern Scotland and manage persistent anti-Union and Jacobean sentiments.

[8] The Spirit Duties Act (1735) sought to reduce the consumption of spirits, regarded as a primary cause of criminal behaviour, by licensing and levying increased fees on the sale of gin.

RICHARDSON TO HENRY LINTOT, SUNDAY 10 OCTOBER 1736

4 Days by way of Precaution;[9] but every thing, thank God, has passed very quietly only the Refuse of the Distillers here and there, being loth to give up so gainful an <Employ>, and <per>haps not knowing what else to turn to, are determin'd to die hard, & have substituted some other Liquors in the Room,[10] and a few have dar'd, in spight of the Act, to proceed in selling spirituous Liquors: but an Information from the Officers of Excise,[11] to each, will soon make these submit: – Complaints also are made of some of the lower Class of Apothecaries, who taking Advantage of a Clause in the Act in favour of their Fraternity, are turn'd Retailers in Gin, & against them the Distillers are the Complainants, & something will probably soon be done in this Affair, the Matter being brought before the Commissioners of Excise.

I have only to wish you Health and Pleasure, and that you may live long enough to mark out, if you shall think it proper, the *Successors* of the Timber you now design to fell, for some other good Purpose: How you call it, to pay your Debts; but then perhaps, it may be to build Towns or Hospitals to perpetuate your Name and your beneficent Disposition all over Sussex, & the adjacent Counties: I am, Sir, Your most Obedient Humble Servant

S. Richardson.

Chiswick 10 October, 1736?[12]

My Wife thanks you for your kind Remembrance, and desires her Respects to you; and the Captain[13] expressly charges me to thank you for being in your Thoughts, & to present his keenly[14] Service, and good Wishes.[15]

---

[9] The Master of the Rolls and Records of the Chancery of England, the second most senior judge in England and Wales after the Lord Chief Justice; Sir Joseph Jekyll (bap. 1662, d. 1738), lawyer and politician, held the position from 1717 to 1738.

[10] I.e. instead of gin.

[11] Officers charged with collecting excise duty, a tax on goods levied at the moment of manufacture rather than at sale.

[12] This date line appears to be in SR's contemporaneous hand, but given the question mark at the end it was probably added at a later date.

[13] Unidentified.

[14] 'bold, courageous' (*OED*).

[15] This postscript is written from top to bottom along the left margin of the letter.

ENCOURAGEMENT OF LEARNING, FRIDAY 18 MARCH 1737

Richardson to the Society for the Encouragement of Learning[1]

Friday 18 March 1737

MS: BL Add. MS 6190, ff. 32–3. Autograph letter sent (evidence of remainder of red wax seal, address, and folds).
Endorsement: 'To The Gentlemen of the Committee of the Honorable Society for the Encouragement of Learning' and 'These' (in SR's hand).[2]

Gentlemen,

I take the Liberty hereby to make an humble Tender to Your Honorable Society of the Original Papers and Letters of Sir Thomas Roe.[3] You will best judge how deserving they may be of your Approbation and Encouragement; and therefore to Your Determination I intirely Submit them; only taking Leave to mention,

That as the Work, if approv'd, must necessarily be expensive, and take up some time in Printing; and as Your Honorable Society may possibly in the Interim have other Works in View, which, tho' worthy of Your Encouragement, might be obstructed by so large an Undertaking, I am very willing to bear any Part of the Expence that shall be thought proper.

This, at the same time that it may ease the Society, will strengthen the Security so reasonably to be expected from every one whom You are pleased to encourage.

With very sincere Wishes for the Prosperity of all Your Generous Designs, I take the Liberty to subscribe my Self, Gentlemen, Your most Obedient and Faithful Servant

S. Richardson

---

[1] The Society for the Encouragement of Learning was founded in London in 1735 and dissolved in 1749; it was founded to encourage the publication of learned works and to secure the profits of such publications to their authors rather than the booksellers. See Clayton Atto, 'The Society for the Encouragement of Learning', *The Library*, 4th ser., 19, no. 3 (December 1938), 263–88.

[2] 'These' is a standard, formal manner of address, meaning 'these words I am sending you'.

[3] Sir Thomas Roe (1581–1644), a diplomat at the courts of James I and Charles I, first ambassador to Mughal India (1615–19), and ambassador at Constantinople (1621–9) as well as other European placements. He was also a literary figure who counted John Donne and Ben Jonson among his friends (*ODNB*). It is unclear when and from whom SR acquired the papers, which were finally published in 1740. SR wrote a dedication to the king, preface, and elaborate table of contents for this publication, which, despite its extensive advertising and promise of future volumes, failed to sell many copies. The table of contents foreshadows that prefixed to the second and subsequent editions of *Clarissa*.

RALPH ALLEN TO RICHARDSON, MONDAY 20 FEBRUARY 1738

Salisbury Court, Fleet Street,

Mar. 18. 1736–7.

Ralph Allen[1] to Richardson

Monday 20 February 1738

MS: Bath and North East Somerset Archives, Accession 386/1/38 p. 9. Copy in an undetermined hand.
Endorsement: 'A Copy of Mr Ralph Allen{'s} Letter to Mr Richardson the Printer Bath Feb: 20. 1737' (in an undetermined hand).[2]

Sir,
For the future pray let the letter dated from Bath the 14th of this month (when it <is> corrected by that which you will receive under this cover) be inserted in a large Character immediately after the foreign News, in the three publick Papers which Mr Nash have caused it to be printed in[3] – by the marks made to the inclos'd paper you'll see that 'tis our desire to have this letter divided in three distinct Paragraphs. I am your &c.

Ralph Allen

To Mr. Richardson

[1] Ralph Allen (bap. 1693, d. 1764), postal entrepreneur and philanthropist (*ODNB*); he was a patron of Henry Fielding and the model for Squire Allworthy in Fielding's *Tom Jones* (1749). SR became connected with Allen's printing proposals and advertisements for the Bath General Hospital, of which Allen was a founding member. Allen would later offer advice on revisions to the introductory materials in *Pamela* (which SR had already anticipated by dropping them entirely in the deluxe octavo edition) and on the treatment of Mrs Jewkes in *Pamela II* (which SR received too late to incorporate); the Allen and Richardson families – including SR's Bath in-laws, the Leakes – would remain socially close until after both men's deaths.
[2] The date in the endorsement is in Old Style, i.e. the new year begins on 25 March.
[3] Richard 'Beau' Nash (1674–1761), master of ceremonies and social celebrity in Bath (*ODNB*), and like Allen a founding member of the Bath General Hospital. Nash appears to have sent announcements of the Hospital's founding to three newspapers (one of these was the *London Evening Post*, where the announcement's revised version ran on 4, 18, and 25 March as well as on 1 and 8 April). Allen is sending SR textual corrections and printing instructions; SR is acting as Allen and Nash's London agent and may have been more deeply involved in the announcement's printing (he was printer for the *Daily Gazetteer* from 1735).

15

Richardson to Alexander Gordon[1]

Thursday 9 November 1738

MS: BL Add. MS 6211, ff. 62–3. Autograph letter sent (evidence of folding).
Address: 'To Mr. Gordon' and 'These' (in SR's hand).

Sir,

You desire to know the Price, from my Self, for the Treatise on
the Heaven;[2] and intimate that Mr. Bettenham has agreed for a
Guinea per Sheet. No. 1000, of a like Page and Character; I answer
therefore, that I have no manner of scruple to be determined by
Mr Bettenham's Price,[3] which is the common 3d[4] which a Printer
reckons[5] upon his Charges; but if my Work is accompanied with
Notes upon a smaller Character than the Text, or marginal
References or Lemma's[6] which Mr. Bettenham has <not>, and
which necessarily occasion an increased Expence to the Workman,
in this Case, your worthy Treasurer, Mr. Ward,[7] and your self, who
have been concerned in Printing, well know that a proportionable
(and I shall take care that it be no more than proportionable)
Expence will attend it. This I am glad you give me an Opportunity
to explain for the Sake of other Printers as well as my Self, who
may have the Honour of Serving the Society.[8] Your most humble
Servant

S. Richardson

9 Nov. 1738.

---

[1] Alexander Gordon (*c.* 1692–1754?), antiquarian, singer, and secretary of the Society for the Encouragement of Learning from 1736 to 1739 (*ODNB*).

[2] Possibly Archibald Campbell, *The Necessity of Revelation* (1739), printed 'At the Expence of the Society for the Encouragement of Learning' by William Bowyer. Campbell (1691–1756) was Church of Scotland minister, theologian, and Professor of Divinity and Ecclesiastical History at St Andrews University (*ODNB*).

[3] James Bettenham (1683? –1774), London printer employed by the Society in at least two instances; also 'ranked as a Nonjuror in Negus's list' (Nichols, I, pp. 65 and 302), a list that identified SR as a 'High-Flyer', a Tory or High Church adherent (Nichols, I, p. 312).

[4] 'Third': the printer's share after the total cost of printing.

[5] I.e. counts.

[6] Printer's heading, annotation or gloss.

[7] John Ward (1678/9–1758), antiquarian, Professor of Rhetoric at Gresham College, and a fellow of the Royal Society, chaired a committee to oversee the editing of Roe's manuscripts (*ODNB*).

[8] SR takes this opportunity to lay out (below his signature) the different costs that printers would charge depending on the variables of *composing* the text (i.e. typesetting), *press* work, and *reading* (i.e. proofreading). 'Thirds' represent the printer's share, and consist of half of the costs of composing, printing, and reading in SR's table. Thus the printer's 'thirds' are

Pica[9] without Notes (No. 1000) – –

Composing	– – – 0: 8: 0
Press	– – – 0: 4: 8
Reading	– – – 0: 1: 4

0: 14: 0 ⎫
— 1: 1: 0
Thirds – – – 0: 7: 0 ⎭

Pica with Notes – – – – –

*Composing if 10 shillings per Sheet	0: 10: 0
Press	– – – 0: 4: 8
Reading	– – – 0: 1: 8

16: 4 ⎫ — 1: 4: 6
8: 2 ⎭

*If 9 shillings Composing proportionally less
as per opposite. †

500 Pica without Notes – – – – – –

Composing	– – – 0: 8: 0
Press	– – – 0: 2: 4
Reading	– – – 0: 1: 4

0: 11: 8

Half which is 3ds of the whole — – – 0: 5: 10

750 Ditto   17: 6

750 Ditto – – – – – – – – –

Composing	– – – 8: 0
Press	– – – 3: 6
Reading	– – – 1: 4

0: 12: 10

Thirds   0: 6: 5

0: 19: 3

500   with Notes will be according to the Price paid
to the Composition, as the Work may deserve, from
9 to 12 shillings per Sheet and the Reading will be
proportionally, Two pence in the Shilling on the

added to the combined cost of composing, press, and reading to constitute the total cost,
here reckoned at 1: 1: 0. See Maslen, pp. 13–14, 21.

9   A unit of type size and line length roughly equivalent to a twelve-point font.

Price paid the Composition. – Pref. the
same, with or without Notes.

750 the same manner as 500; viz.

With notes, at 10 shillings to the Composition – – –	0: 10: 0
Press – – – – –	0: 3: 6
Reading – – –	0: 1: 8
	0: 15: 2
	7: 7
	1: 2: 9

†

1000	Composing, or, Case	– – –	0: 9: 0
	Press	– – –	0: 4: 8
	Reading	– – –	0: 1: 6
			15: 2
			7: 7
			1: 2: 9

Richardson to Thomas Birch[1]

Tuesday 5 December 1738

MS: BL Add. MS 4317, ff. 172–3. Autograph letter sent (evidence of remainder of black wax seal and folding).
Endorsement: 'To The Revd. Mr. Birch, These' and '5 Decemb. 1738.' (in SR's hand).

> Reverend Sir,
> I take the Liberty of a Line to you, to refer to your Consideration, whether something should not be done by way of Preface to Sir Thomas Roe's First Volume, and, if you think fit, to mention it at the Committee for their Opinion and Direction: And

---

[1] Thomas Birch (1705–66), historian and biographer (*ODNB*) who worked with SR on a variety of projects including the Society for the Encouragement of Learning and a number of historical compilations.

GOVERNORS OF THE BATH GENERAL HOSPITAL, TUESDAY 6 FEBRUARY 1739

in this Case, whether Dr Anderson[2] or Mr Carte,[3] or who else the
Society please, should be desired to draw one up to be laid before
them for their Approbation, those Gentlemen having read the
Papers, &c. – I should also be glad to know what Number of Sheets
the first Volume shall contain? Milton's Works lately publish'd Vol.
I. contains 182 Sheets and Half – Vol. II 161 & Half;[4] And this
makes me think, that 180 Sheets will make a sufficient Volume:
But for this, the Society may consult their Booksellers. Be so good
to excuse this Trouble, from, Reverend Sir, Your most Obedient
Humble Servant

S. Richardson.

Dec. 5. 1738

[2] Possibly James Anderson (bap. 1679, d. 1739), Presbyterian minister and historical writer
(*ODNB*); he corresponded with Alexander Gordon, the secretary of the Society for the
Encouragement of Learning from 1736 to 1739 (*ODNB*), who in turn was a correspondent
of SR (see, for example, SR to Gordon, 9 November 1738).
[3] Thomas Carte (bap. 1686, d. 1754), historian, notable Jacobite, and author of a *History of
England* (4 vols., 1747–55) (*ODNB*). He probably wrote the anonymous preface to Roe's
Negotiations and Embassies, 1620–1644 (1740), the first and only of the five intended volumes to be published.
[4] *A Complete Collection of the Historical, Political, and Miscellaneous Works of John Milton*, 2 vols.
(London: A. Millar, 1738) included a life of Milton by Birch.

Richardson to the President of the Governors of the Bath General Hospital[1]

Tuesday 6 February 1739

MS: Bath Record Office. Autograph letter sent (evidence of folding).

Sir,
I presume you have seen the Advertisement and Accounts
relating to your General Hospital, in the *Gazetteer* of last Saturday.
I put it there first, because of the Influence I have there,[2] to
induce it to be put in as small a Compass as possible, and at an

[1] The foundation stone for the Bath General Hospital was laid on 6 July 1738. The hospital
was first proposed as early as 1716, and the building opened to receive patients on 18 May
1742. Thomas Carew of Crowcombe (*c.* 1702–66), member of parliament (1739–47), was the
Board of Governors' first President (1739–41); SR's friend Dr William Oliver (see Lobb to
SR, 21 May 1743) was selected as the Board's first Deputy President.
[2] SR was printer of the pro-government *Daily Gazetteer* from its inception in 1735 to 1746.

19

easy Expence, for Example to others; and because that Paper is spread every where in the Country, to a very large Number. It will be in the *Daily Advertizer* to-morrow, for a Town Paper, and I have agreed for 2 Guineas. I would have put it into the London Evening Post; but they would not say when they would do it, and exorbitantly insisted on 5 Guineas; so that I would not be so bad a Husband[3] for the Charity to give it; and order'd it into the *General Evening Post*, a Paper next best receiv'd,[4] at a Guinea and half. This Saving will pay for its being repeated, if you chuse it in any of those I have named, or I will cause it to be further inserted as you shall direct in any other. I am, Sir, Your most Humble Servant

S. Richardson

London,

Febr. 6. 1738–9.

Already order'd.			
Daily Gazetteer	– Sat. Febr. 3.	as a Morning and Evening Paper
Daily Advertizer	– Wedn. Febr. 7.	for both Town and Country
General Evening Post	– Sat. Febr. 10.	

---

[3] 'With modifying word: a person who manages his or her household, resources, or affairs in the specified manner (e.g. well or ill, profitably or wastefully, etc.). Esp. in *good husband*: one who administers his or her affairs with skill and thrift; a frugal, economical, or provident person; a careful manager of (one's resources)' (*OED*).

[4] I.e. received by the next largest group of subscribers after that for the *London Evening Post*.

Richardson to Stephen Le Bas[1]

Friday 20 July 1739

MS: BL Add. 6190, f. 84. Copy in SR's hand.
Endorsement: 'Received of Stephen Le Bas. Esquire' (in SR's hand).

July 20. 1739.

Treasurer to the Society for Encouragement of Learning, the Original Letters and Papers of the Negotiations, &c. of Sir Thomas Roe belonging to me, and which were in the Society's

---

[1] Stephen Le Bas, treasurer of the Society for the Encouragement of Learning, 1738–41.

Custody.[2] And I promise to return them again at the Demand of the Committee, to be made such Use of in Printing and Publishing the same, as shall be judged fit by the said Society, with Consent of Saml. Burroughs, Esq,[3] or my self.

Saml. Richardson[4]

[2] The letters and papers of Sir Thomas Roe (1581–1644), diplomat, were in SR's possession. In April 1739 the Society had decided to produce an edition with SR as printer and editor. *The Negotiations of Sir Thomas Roe, in his Embassy to the Ottoman Porte*, edited by SR and the historian Thomas Carte, was published by subscription in 1740. Five volumes were planned, but the project was abandoned after this publication following lack of interest, according to Clayton Atto, 'The Society for the Encouragement of Learning': '105 unsold copies out of an edition of 750 were returned to Richardson in 1747' (268).

[3] Samuel Burroughs (d. 1761), from 1727 one of the Masters of the High Court of Chancery and author of *The History of the Chancery; Relating to the Judicial Power of That Court, and the Rights of the Masters* (1726) as well as other works concerning the judiciary and the law.

[4] Below this receipt, on the same sheet, is the following note: 'Received at the same time a small Parcel, presented the Society by Sir J. Evelyn which I promise to deliver with the above. W.m Mole'. Sir John Evelyn, 1st Baronet, of Wotton (1682–1763), Postmaster-general (1708–15), and politician, was the grandson of the diarist John Evelyn (1620–1706). William Mole remains unidentified.

Richardson to John Ward[1]

Friday 12 October 1739

MS: BL Add. MS 6211, ff. 64–5. Autograph letter sent (evidence of folding and address).
Address: 'To Mr. Professor Ward, At Gresham College' and 'These' (in SR's hand).

Good Sir,

I return you a thousand Thanks for the Favour of your most judicious and kind Corrections. I have transcribed *every one* of them into the Preface and Dedication; and, if a fair Copy be not necessary for the Perusal of the Committee, shall be glad, you will be so kind to lay them before the Gentlemen for their Perusal and Opinion, that it may go to Press, and the Volume be published with all convenient Speed. For this Purpose, I will send them

[1] John Ward (1678/9–1758), antiquary and biographer; appointed as professor of rhetoric in Gresham College, September 1720 (*ODNB*).

RICHARDSON TO CHARLES MARSH, FRIDAY 21 DECEMBER 1739

to the Society House, to Mr. Gordon, this Afternoon, against[2] your Meeting this Night, when your Opinion and Account of the Matter, will have proper Weight, &c. I am, Sir, (in haste) Your most Thankful and Obliged Servant

S. Richardson

12 Oct. 1739.

This relates to the volume of Sir Tho. Roe's Negotiations[3]

---

[2] 'In anticipation of, in preparation for, in time for' (*OED*, def. 10; now obsolete).
[3] This line is added in a different, undetermined hand.

Richardson to Charles Marsh[1]

Friday 21 December 1739
MS: FM XIII, 2, f. 26. Copy in Martha Richardson's hand.

Dec. 21st: 1739

Mr. Marsh

I am personally unknown to you; but think, in a Matter where Right is concern'd, I shall have your Attention. Proposals are published & handed about in your Name, for printing by Subscription Mr. Hill's[2] Ottoman Empire A Copy that is mine;[3] & which you can have no kind of Pretence to print: And which, if ever it be reprinted, will be done, with great Alterations & Additions. It will be your Interest therefore, and, I doubt not your

---

[1] Charles Marsh (fl. 1734–67), London bookseller who had circulated proposals for reprinting Aaron Hill's *Full and Just Account of the Present State of the Ottoman Empire in All Its Branches* (1709). Hill had asked SR to intervene on his behalf; see Hill to SR, 19 December 1739; and Hill to SR, 23 December 1739. In the event, Marsh did publish an edition of Hill's book in 1740.

[2] Aaron Hill (1685–1750), writer and entrepreneur (*ODNB*), patron of Alexander Pope and other writers. Hill, SR's earliest literary friend from the 1720s, championed *Pamela* and SR as a literary genius. See *Correspondence with Aaron Hill and the Hill Family*, ed. Gerrard; and Gerrard, *Aaron Hill: The Muses' Projector.*

[3] The Statute of Anne (1710) specified that previously published works would remain under copyright for twenty-one years. (Works published subsequently were protected for fourteen years and then, if the author were living, another fourteen years.) SR here asserts a traditional notion of 'perpetual copyright' respected by some in the Trade but not legally enforceable.

Inclination, to desist from this Undertaking, as soon as you are appriz'd of this. And I chuse to proceed in this courteous and civil Manner, rather than any other. And am Your humble Servant

S. Richardson

Salisbury Court
Fleetstreet,

Dec. 21. 1739.[4]

---

[4] 'To Mr. Charles Marsh; At Cicero's Head; in Round Court, in the Strand' (note in Martha Richardson's hand).

John Windus[1] to Richardson

September 1740

MS: FM XIII, 2, f. 29. Autograph letter sent.

September: – 1740.

Sir

I designed to have waited on you, but was taken suddenly ill on St. James' Guard,[2] from whence I thought it necessary to be relieved, before the time was out, to come home, bleed, and dilute, by which means the fever abated, and I think I am quite well again.

I return you thanks for the inclosed, your Friends[3] instructions are very full, and satisfactory: nevertheless it would be an addition to the Kindness, and shorten my labour, if He would be so good as to tell me, what is the proper proportion. – For Example – Suppose I have 500 Gallons of Must,[4] How many are to Ferment according to its natural Tendency, & How many to be Boiled into

---

[1] Possibly John Windus, the travel writer (fl. 1720–5), author of *A Journey to Mequinez, the Residence of the Present Emperor of Fez and Morocco* (1725) (*ODNB*).

[2] I.e. Horse Guard Parade facing St James's Park in Westminster.

[3] Probably Aaron Hill, who sent SR a long letter on his experiments in wine making at about the same time; see Hill to SR, 17 September 1740. George Cheyne had promoted the medical efficacy of wine in his *Essay on Regimen* (1740) and earlier that year had instructed SR to take wine for medicinal purposes; see Cheyne to SR, 20 April 1740; and Cheyne to SR, <May 1740>.

[4] 'Must' refers to a liquid undergoing fermentation.

Cute.[5] Then – Supposing 800 Gallons of the Must is to be boiled into Cute, to how many Gallons shall that be reduced. Lastly, how many days is it best to have the natural wine Ferment, before it is Fed with the Cute, and the proportion of Cute, in the whole, to the natural wine, and by what quan{ti}ties to feed it with at a time. I say Sir If it is not improper to trouble your Friend for instructions in the above particulars, it will be a great help to me, as also to know, whether It is to be fermented in an open vessell, while fed with the Cute, in a Close Cask, full, and so drawn off to admit every addition. I am Sir Your most humble Servant

John Windus

[5] 'Cute' is a type of sweet wine.

William Webster to Richard Hooker and Richardson [1]

Saturday 11 October 1740

Printed source: Weekly Miscellany, no. 407 (11 October 1740), [1].
First printing: The Weekly Miscellany.
Second printing: Pamela (1st edn, 1740); see *Pamela*, pp. 6-8.[2]

Mr. HOOKER,

AS the Design of your Paper is to promote *Virtue*, I beg leave, thro' your Hands, to convey a Letter to a very worthy Friend of mine, who is engag'd in the same noble Cause upon the same generous Principles. He has written an *English Novel*, with a truly *English Spirit* of unaffected good Sense, and yet with a great deal of Invention and Ingenuity. It is intitled, *Pamela*, or *Virtue Rewarded*. I chuse this publick Manner of giving the Author my Sentiments upon it, in hopes by this Means to quicken the Publication of it, and excite Peoples Attention to it when it does come out. *Yours,* &c.

[1] William Webster (1689–1758), clergyman and editor of *The Weekly Miscellany* (16 December 1732 – 27 June 1741) (*ODNB*). 'Richard Hooker' was Webster's editorial pseudonym. Attribution of this letter is inferred from conventions of 'puffing' (i.e. advertising) publications in the eighteenth century and from Webster's relationship with SR; see *Pamela*, pp. xlix–l. As published in the *Weekly Miscellany*, this letter was the first public hint of the novel's existence.
[2] The version printed in *Pamela* begins with 'To my worthy Friend', lacks the note to 'Hooker', and identifies SR only as 'the Editor of *Pamela*'.

WILLIAM WEBSTER TO RICHARD HOOKER, SATURDAY 11 OCTOBER 1740

To my worthy Friend, the Author of PAMELA, *&c.*

SIR,

I Return the Manuscript of *Pamela* by the Bearer, which I have read with a great deal of Pleasure. It is written with that Spirit of Truth and agreeable Simplicity, which, though much wanted, is seldom found in those Pieces which are calculated for the Entertainment and Instruction of the Publick. It carries Conviction in every Part of it, and the Incidents are so natural and interesting, that I have gone hand in hand, and sympathiz'd with the pretty Heroine in all her Sufferings, and been extremely anxious for her Safety, under the Apprehensions of the bad Consequences which I expected, every Page, would ensue from the laudable Resistance she made. I have interested my self in all her Schemes of Escape; been alternately pleas'd and angry with her in her Restraint; pleas'd with the little Machinations and Contrivances she set on foot for her Release, and angry for suffering her Fears to defeat them; always lamenting, with a most sensible Concern, the Miscarriages of her Hopes and Projects. In short, the whole is so affecting, that there is no reading it without uncommon Concern and Emotion. Thus far only as to the Entertainment it gives. As to Instruction and Morality, the Piece is full of them. It shews Virtue in the strongest Light, and renders the Practice of it amiable and lovely. The beautiful Sufferer keeps it ever in her View without the least Ostentation, or Pride; she has it so strongly implanted in her, that thro' the whole Course of her Sufferings, she does not so much as hesitate once, whether she shall sacrifice it to Liberty and Ambition, or not; but, as if there were no other way to free and save herself, carries on a determin'd Purpose to persevere in her Innocence, and wade with it throughout all Difficulties and Temptations, or perish under them. It is an astonishing Matter, and well worth our most serious Consideration, that a young beautiful Girl, in the low Scene of Life and Circumstance in which Fortune plac'd her, without the Advantage of a Friend capable to advise and protect her, or any other Education than what occur'd to her from her own Observation and little Reading, in the Course of her Attendance on her excellent Mistress and Benefactress, could, after having had a Taste of Ease and Plenty in a higher Sphere of Life than what she was born and first brought up in, resolve to return to her primitive Poverty rather than give up her Innocence. I say, it is surprizing, that a young Person, so

25

circumstanc'd, could, in Contempt of proffer'd Grandeur on the one side, and in Defiance of Penury on the other, so happily and prudently conduct herself through such a Series of Perplexities and Troubles, and withstand the alluring Baits, and almost irresistible Offers of a fine Gentleman, so universally admir'd and esteem'd, for the Agreeableness of his Person and good Qualities, among all his Acquaintance; defeat all his Measures with so much Address, and oblige him at last to give over his vain Pursuit, and sacrifice his Price and Ambition to Virtue, and become the Protector of that Innocence which he so long and so indefatigably labour'd to supplant: And all this without ever having entertain'd the least previous Design or Thought for that Purpose. No Art us'd to inflame him, no Coquetry practis'd to tempt or intice him, and no Prudery or Affectations to tamper with his Passions, but on the contrary, artless and unpractis'd in the Wiles of the World, all her Endeavours, and even all her Wishes, tended only to render herself as unamiable as she could in his Eyes: Though at the same time she is so far from having any Aversion to his Person, that she seems rather prepossess'd in his Favour, and admires his Excellencies whilst she condemns his Passion for her. A glorious Instance of Self-Denial! Thus her very Repulses become Attractions, and the very Means she used to guard, naturally conspir'd towards the Destruction, of her Virtue. The more she resisted, the more she charm'd; so that by a brave and resolute Defence the Besieg'd not only obtain'd a glorious Victory over the Besieger, but took him Prisoner too. I am charm'd with the beautiful Reflections she makes in the Course of her Distresses; her Soliloquies and little Reasonings with herself are exceedingly pretty and entertaining: She pours out all her Soul in them before her Parents without Disguise, so that one may judge of, nay, almost see, the inmost Recesses of her Mind. A pure clear Fountain of Truth and Innocence, a Magazine[3] of Virtue and unblemish'd Thoughts! I can't conceive why you should hesitate a Moment as to the Publication of this very natural and uncommon Piece. I could wish to see it out in its own native Simplicity, which will affect and please the Reader beyond all the Strokes of Oratory in the World, but those will but spoil it; and, should you permit such a murdering Hand to be laid upon it, to gloss and tinge it

---

[3] 'a storehouse for goods or merchandise' (*OED*).

WILLIAM WEBSTER TO RICHARD HOOKER, SATURDAY II OCTOBER 1740

over with superfluous and needless Decorations, which, like too
much Drapery in Sculpture and Statuary, will but incumber it; it
may disguise the Facts, marr the Reflections, and unnaturalize
the Incidents, so as to be lost in a multiplicity of fine idle Words
and Phrases, and reduce our sterling Substance into an empty
Shadow, or rather *frenchify* our *English* Solidity into Froth and
Whip-Syllabub.[4] No; let us have *Pamela* as *Pamela* wrote it; in her
own Words without Amputation, or Addition. Produce her to us in
her neat Country Apparel, such as she appear'd in on her intended
Departure to her Parents, for such best becomes her Innocence and
beautiful Simplicity. Such a Dress will best edify and entertain.
The flowing Robes of Oratory may indeed amuse and amaze,
but will never strike the Mind with solid Attention. In short, Sir,
a Piece of this Kind is much wanted in the World, which is but
too much, as well as too early debauched by pernicious *Novels*. I
know nothing Entertaining of that Kind that one might venture to
recommend to the Perusal (much less the Imitation) of the Youth of
either Sex, but what tends to corrupt their Principles, mislead their
Judgments, and initiate them into Gallantry and loose Pleasures.
Publish then, this good, this edifying and instructive little Piece for
their Sakes. The Honour of *Pamela*'s Sex demands *Pamela* at your
Hands, to shew the World an Heroine, almost beyond Example,
in an unusual Scene of Life, whom no Temptations, or Sufferings,
could subdue. It is a fine, and glorious Original, for the Fair to
copy out and imitate; our own Sex, too, require it of you, to free
us, in some measure, from the Imputation of being incapable of
the Impressions of Virtue and Honour, and to shew the Ladies
that we are not inflexible while they are so. In short, the Cause
of Virtue, in general, calls loudly for its Publication. Oblige then,
Sir, the concurrent Voices of both Sexes, and give us *Pamela* for
the benefit of the whole Race of Mankind; and as I believe its
Excellencies can't be long unknown to the World, there will not
be a Family without it, so I make no Doubt but every Family that
has it will be much improv'd and better'd by it. 'Twill form the
tender Minds of Youth for the Reception and Practice of Virtue
and Honour; confirm and establish those of maturer Age on good
and steady Principles; reclaim the Vicious, and mend the Age in
general; insomuch that as *Pamela* will become the bright Example

4 Whip-Syllabub: a sweetened drink made of milk or cream, beaten into a froth. In a figurative sense, an unsubstantial piece of writing; the *OED* cites this passage as illustration.

27

and Imitation of all the fashionable young Ladies of *Great Britain*, her truly generous Benefactor and Rewarder of her most exemplary Virtue, will also be no less admir'd and imitated among the *Beau Monde* of our own Sex. *I am, Your affectionate Friend*, &c.

Jean Baptiste de Freval[1] to Richardson

<Before 6 November> 1740[2]

MS: FM XVI, 1, f. 12. Copy in Gilbert Hill's hand.
First printing: Pamela (1st edn, 1740); see *Pamela*, pp. 4–5.
Endorsement: 'II.' (in SR's hand); 'To the Editor of the Piece intitled Pamela; or, Virtue Rewarded.' (in Hill's hand).

Dear Sir,

I have had inexpressible Pleasure in the Perusal of your Pamela. It intirely answers the Character you give of it in your Preface;[3] nor have you said one word too much in Commendation of a Piece that has Advantages & Excellencies peculiar to itself. For, besides the Beautiful simplicity of the Stile, and a happy Propriety and Clearness of Expression (the Letters being written under the immediate Impression of every Circumstance which occasioned them, and that to those who had a Right to know the fair Writer's most secret Thoughts) the several Passions of the Mind, must, of course, be more affectingly described, and Nature may be traced in her undisguised Inclinations with much more Propriety and Exactness than can possibly be found in a Detail of Actions long past; which are never recollected with the same Affections, Hopes, and Dreads, with which they were felt when they occurred.

This little Book will infallibly be looked upon as the hitherto much wanted Standard or Pattern for this kind of Writing. For it abounds with lively Images and Pictures; with Incidents Natural, Surprising, and perfectly adapted to the Story; with

---

[1] Jean Baptiste de Freval (fl. 1737–51), French translator living in London. SR printed de Freval's English translation of the Abbé Pluche's *History of the Heavens*, which was published in March 1740. For de Freval's interactions with SR, see the 'General Introduction' to *Pamela*, pp. xlix–l.

[2] Eaves and Kimpel's dating, based on the letter's inclusion in the prefatory material of *Pamela*'s first edition (1740).

[3] As 'the editor', SR prefixed an apologetic preface to the first volume of *Pamela* justifying its literary technique and morality.

Circumstances interesting to Persons in common Life; as well as those in exalted Stations. The greatest Regard is every where paid in it to Decency, and to every Duty of Life: There is a constant Fitness of the Style to the Persons and Characters described; Pleasures and Instruction here always go Hand in Hand: Vice and Virtue are set in constant Opposition; and Religion every-where inculcated in its native Beauty, and Chearful Amiableness; not dressed up in stiff melancholy, or gloomy Forms on one Hand; nor yet on the other, debased below its due Dignity, and noble Requisites, in compliment for a too fashionable, but depraved Taste. And this, I will boldly Say, that if its numerous Beauties are added to its excellent Tendency, it will be found worthy a Place, not only in all Families (especially such as have young Persons of either Sex in them) but in the Collections of the most curious and polite Readers. For, as it borrows none of its Excellencies from the romantick Flights of unnatural Fancy, its being founded in Truth and Nature, and built upon Experience, will be lasting Recommendation to the discerning and judicious, while the agreeable Variety of Occurrences and Characters in which it abounds, will not fail to Engage the Attention of the gay and more Sprightly Readers.

The moral Reflections and Uses to be drawn from the several parts of this admirable History, are so happily deduced from a Crowd of different Events and Characters, in the Conclusion of the Work, that I shall say the less on that Head. But I think, the Hints you have given me, should also prefatorily be given the Public, that it will appear from several Things mentioned in the Letters, that the Story must have happened within those thirty Years past:[4] that you have been Obliged to vary some of the Names of Persons, Places, &c. and to disguise a few of the Circumstances, in Order to avoid giving Offence to some Persons, who would not chuse to be pointed out too plainly in it, though they would be glad it may do the good so laudably intended by the Publication. And as you have in confidence submitted to my Opinion some of those Variations, I am much pleased that you have so managed the Matter as to make no Alteration in the Facts, and at the same Time have avoided the digressive Prolixity too frequently used on such Occasions.

---

[4] In SR to Stinstra, 2 June 1753, SR claimed that there was 'some slight Foundation in Truth' deriving from a story told by an innkeeper to a gentleman friend in the mid 1720s. On the origins of the story, see 'General Introduction' to *Pamela*, pp. xxxii–xxxv.

Little Book, charming *Pamela*! face the World, and never doubt of finding Friends and Admirers, not only in thy own Country, but far from Home, where thou may'st give an Example of Purity to the Writers of a Neighbouring Nation,[5] which now shall have an Opportunity to receive English Bullion in exchange for its own Dross, which has so long passed current among us in Pieces abounding with all the Levities of its volatile Inhabitants. The reigning Depravity of the Times has yet left Virtue many Votaries. Of their Protection you need not despair. May every headstrong Libertine, whose Hands you reach be reclaimed; & every tempted Virgin who reads you, imitate the Virtue and meet the reward of the high-meriting, though low-descended Pamela. I am, Sir, Your most obedient and faithful Servant,

J. B. D. F.

[5] France. Thomas Keymer has suggested that de Freval is pitching for the role of translator of *Pamela* into French here; see *Pamela: or, Virtue Rewarded*, ed. Keymer and Alice Wakely (Oxford University Press, 2008), p. xxiv. The anonymous author of *Pamela Censured* (London, 1741) agreed: '[Freval] insinuates a *French Translation*, and as I see one is since advertised to be published, it may not be amiss to congratulate the Gentleman, whoever he is, on his lucky Thought' (p. 14).

Anonymous to Charles Rivington[1]

Saturday 15 November 1740

MS: FM XVI, 1, ff. 33–4. Copy in Gilbert Hill's hand.
Endorsement: 'XVII' (in SR's hand); 'To Mr. Rivington, in S.ᵗ Paul's Church-yard' (in Hill's hand).

November 15th 1740

Sir,
When you have read these Lines, I think you will believe I am pleased with a Book publish'd under the Title of Pamela; and, as I dare say it will have a Second; perhaps many Editions, the Author may make such Alterations as he judges proper – I am persuaded he can Judge even of his own Work; for I am sure he judges well of those human Passions he paints in it.

[1] Charles Rivington (1688–1742), bookseller, founder of 'one of the most important book-trade dynasties in England' (*ODNB*).

ANONYMOUS TO CHARLES RIVINGTON, SATURDAY 15 NOVEMBER 1740

The Style methinks shou'd be a little raised, at least so soon
as she knows his Love is honourable, and when her Diffidence is
changed to Ease. From about the 4th Day after Marriage it shou'd
be Equal to the Rank she is changed to, and is to Fill, becomingly.
This the Author can do with a few Touches of which he is certainly
Master; because the Hero of his Fiction Speaks like a Gentleman;
and being Familiar Letters must not excuse her – She shou'd act
up to her Character in P.183 in Wit, Judgment and Education[2] –
In some parts the least Touch will give another Air – In several
places where her Husband is Styled My dear Sir, it is too near the
Vulgar. Call him Sir John, Sir James, Sir Charles or Sir any thing,
will do perfectly well – If he were Styl'd so from the first, it would
avoid the Idea apt to be join'd with the word Squire often used in
the Beginning – Or, if the Author choose, he may add an Episode
in his next Edition: to raise his Hero from Squire to Knight – or
Baronet; his Sister Davers being of Quality may bring him a Patent[3]
without his Knowledge, for his own Views to raise his Pride, in
hope to prevent effectually the Marriage she fears, and reconcile
their first Quarrel. – The Author of Cyrus's Travels added some
Episodes to his first Work, but not all with Judgment; his Sea-
Flight is too Romantic; but others were a great Improvement to
it.[4] The Word Curchee is to be sure affected wrongly; because her
Education with the Old Lady must have taught her it shou'd be
Curtsie, from the old way of Spelling Courtesie, or Curtsey from
the new. – p.184. Voluntierly shou'd be Voluntarily – One thing
more let me add; for 'tis one of the best Performances of the Kind,
and I wish it to be read as much as it deserves. – The Marriage on
Thursday has Superstition; Of which since he has so fully convinced
her, 'tis pity the Author shou'd countenance it, by making that the
Day; for 'tis easy to take one of the others – And if she repeated the
Sacred Name much seldomer, it wou'd have so much less the Style
of Robinson Crusoe,[5] as wou'd make it much more beneficial to the

[2] Throughout this letter, the anonymous writer refers to passages in the first edition of
Pamela. In the CEWSR edition, the relevant sections can be found on pp. 312, 318, 332,
and 402. For Rivero's editorial comments on this letter, the passages to which it refers, and
SR's textual responses, see *Pamela*, pp. 478 and 567.
[3] 'A document conferring some privilege, right, office, title, or property' (*OED*).
[4] Andrew Michael Ramsay, *Les voyages de Cyrus* (1727) was translated by Nathaniel Hooke as
The Travels of Cyrus, 2 vols. (London: Printed and sold by T. Woodward and J. Peele, 1727).
[5] For many contemporary readers, Daniel Defoe's *Robinson Crusoe* (1719) contained an egregious number of references to God and Providence.

ANONYMOUS TO CHARLES RIVINGTON, SATURDAY 15 NOVEMBER 1740

World – This Benefit to Mankind I am so convinced is the Author's Aim, and he is so capable of it, that I risk his neglecting all I have said by objecting to the Style, which seems strongly his Bent in her Character. I say I risk his Neglect of All, in order to induce him to peruse the whole Style again, with this last Objection in View. – I thank God I can solemnly Appeal to the Searches of Hearts, that 'tis not want of Veneration, but out of Veneration I object to these frequent Appeals. I am satisfied a Religious Sense of the Deity is the true foundation of Virtue; But Solomon's advice is, Be not Righteous overmuch – The Reflection P176 is Beautiful – But p177. 'I dropt down on my Knees in a Corner' – is better Struck out – In P.186. the Thing, Time, and Place, is rightly adapted.

I wou'd fain save Pamela some of the Penance she suffers from Lady D– tis rather too many Pages and may be shortened by One of the Author's Ability. She is too timorous after owning the Marriage to Lady D–; She should have a little more Spirit, and get away sooner out at Windows; or call her own Servants to protect and carry her to her Husband's Appointment.

Females are too apt to be Struck with Images of Beauty: If a little less Stress had been upon that Quality by so grave an Author, it wou'd be right. But one Part is easy to be helped. In Vol. II p216 she says 'Spanning my Waist with his Hands'; This Expression is enough to ruin a Nation of Women – I am certain when the Author considers, he will alter it.

As you will never know who I am, you can't tell my Wife (for I am a Married Man) that your Author exactly describes what Husbands call a good Wife – But he has performed in this Work so well, that if his Genius is not tired, I long to see what he can do upon a Plan of Equality in Rank. For Here he Sketches such Advantages on the Man's Side, that no Woman will dispute she owed most, if not all the Complacencies expected – I assert by Complacencies alone they are sure to govern all but Brutes: Yet they oftener chuse to be the Lady P.212; or some to be Lady Davers's. But as others, like Harriet in the *Funeral*,[6] will hear Reason when 'tis fairly Offer'd: I wou'd readily Subscribe for another Series of Familiar Letters on this Plan of Equality, if Possible to come up to the Performance of Pamela – But I dread

---

[6] Lady Harriot is a character in Richard Steele's comedy, *The Funeral, or Grief à-la-Mode* (produced 1701), who remarks at one point in the play: 'Why should I not obey Reason as soon as I see it?' (II.iii).

RICHARDSON TO ANONYMOUS, THURSDAY 20 NOVEMBER 1740

any thing like the 4.th Vol. of Gil Blas,[7] or the Sequel to the Beggar's Opera.[8]

Naughty I wish changed to some other Word: Bad, Faulty, Wicked, Vile, Abominable, or Scandalous. These wou'd in most places give an Emphasis for which we else must have recourse to the innocent Simplicity of the Writer, an Idea not Natural to the Moral of the Story, nor of Advantage to the Character of the Heroine.

My good Master p.197 *I hardly have got the Courage &c[9]* – Why not – *For I delight to call him by that Name* – P.305. *Dear lordly Master* – (O *my dear Parents* &c) – why not Dear lord and Master – And omit the whole Parenthesis – A few lines lower – *foolish thing that I am* – why not Foolish that I am.

Such are the Touches I speak of – But if I were able to be Author of a Piece so well wrote as Pamela, I doubt I shou'd despise the Advise of one Unknown.

Jokes are often more Severe, and do more Mischief, than more Solid Objections – To obviate some, why not omit P175 – *betwixt Fear and Delight* – and P181 – *I made shift to eat a bit of* &c. *but I had no Appetite to any thing else.*[10]

---

[7] Alain-René Lesage's *Gil Blas* was translated from French into English as *The History and Adventures of Gil Blas of Santillane* and published by Jacob Tonson, first in a two-volume edition in 1716 and then in a three-volume edition in 1725 and again in 1732. Volume IV appeared in 1735, printed for J. Nourse and F. Cogan.

[8] John Gay referred to his opera *Polly* as the 'second part of the *Beggar's Opera*' (*ODNB*). The play was suppressed and never performed during Gay's lifetime, though he published it in 1729.

[9] In *Pamela*, this passage reads 'My good Master, I hardly have yet the courage' (p. 332). Hill may have misread the 'yet' as 'got' in transcribing the original letter.

[10] At the end of this letter, SR has added: 'See Remarks on this good-natured Letter, p. 89' (see SR to Anonymous, 20 November 1740).

Richardson to Anonymous

Thursday 20 November 1740

Printed source: Daily Gazetteer, 20 November 1740, IV.
First printing: Daily Gazetteer (1740).

An Anonymous Letter relating to this Piece is come to the Editor's Hand,[1] who takes this Opportunity (having no better)

---

[1] SR himself.

RICHARDSON TO ALLINGTON WILDE, TUESDAY 23 DECEMBER 1740

most heartily to thank the Gentleman for his *Candid* and *Judicious* Observations; and to beg the Favour of a further Correspondence with him, under what Restrictions he pleases. INSTRUCTION, and not CURIOSITY, being *sincerely* the Motive for this Request.[2]

[2] This message appeared as part of an advertisement for *Pamela* and was probably a response to Anonymous to Rivington, 15 November 1740.

Richardson to Allington Wilde[1]

Tuesday 23 December 1740

MS: Bodleian, John Johnson Collection: Stationers' Company 1. Autograph note.[2]

YOU are desir'd by the Master, Wardens, and Stock-keepers, to come to *Stationers-Hall* on *Tuesday* the 23rd of this Instant *December*, 1740. at Eleven of the Clock in the Morning, to receive your Dividend.[3]

JOSEPH HAZARD, Beadle.[4]

N.B. The Dividend will not begin to be paid before Eleven o'Clock; and no Dividend will be paid after Two o'Clock, till *Monday* the 5th of *January*.[5]

Mr. Wilde,

If you please to receive for me my Dividend, you will much oblige Your most humble Servant

S. Richardson

23 Dec. 1740.

[1] Allington Wilde (1700–70), printer and bookseller in London, was the son of SR's master, the printer John Wilde (d. 1720) and brother to SR's first wife, Martha (m. 1721, d. 1731).
[2] SR's note is written at the bottom of a printed summons to a Stationers' Company meeting.
[3] SR had bought a yeomanry share of £80 in the Stationers' Company's stock in 1736, which allowed him to draw dividends on the Company's monopoly in printing almanacs, psalms, ABCs, and other religious and school books.
[4] Joseph Hazard (d. 1750), bookbinder and bookseller (1703–39) in partnership with SR's brother-in-law James Leake (1717–22); Beadle to the Stationers' Company (1738–50).
[5] Here ends the printed text and begins SR's note to Wilde.

Ralph Courteville[1] to Richardson

Tuesday 27 January 1741

MS: FM XVI, 1, f. 42v. Copy in Gilbert Hill's hand.
Endorsement: 'XXXI.' (in SR's hand).

Jan.y 27th 1740/1

Sir,

I shall take as a favour if you will Italick[2] the inclosed. I having been so hurried, have done it but slightly. The other Letter I could not Omit sending you, as it comes from a Gentleman well known among the Learned.[3] As I know the Author of *Pamela*, and have the highest regard for him, I rejoyce to be of Opinion with those who have such Sentiments of his Lucubrations as has his most Obliged and Obedient humble Servant

Ra. Courteville

---

[1] Raphael (Ralph) Courteville (fl. 1720–72), political journalist and propagandist on behalf of Walpole. He was reputed to be the author of the *Daily Gazetteer*, a pro-government paper printed and possibly edited by SR (*ODNB*, under 'Courteville, Raphael (fl. c. 1673–c. 1735), organist and composer', who may have been his father).

[2] To mark words for emphasis. Courteville has evidently sent SR a manuscript for publication. The *OED* does not record any use of 'italic' as a verb.

[3] See the following letter.

Knightley Chetwode[1] to Ralph Courteville

Saturday 24 January 1741

MS: FM XVI, 1, f. 42. Copy in Gilbert Hill's hand (originally sent to SR as enclosure with preceding letter).

Ryder-street, Jan.y 24th 1740/41[2]

Sir.

I thank you for Pamela, which I return you[3] per Bearer – I've read both Volumes, with great Attention & Delight; and my

---

[1] Knightley Chetwode (1679–1752), an Irish squire, friend of Jonathan Swift, and amateur poet; nephew to Knightly Chetwood (bap. 1650, d. 1720), Dean of Gloucester (*ODNB*), with whom he is often confused.

[2] 'Ryder-street' has been crossed through; the street lies near fashionable St. James's Square in Westminster.

[3] 'to' has been inserted, perhaps in SR's late hand, to read 'return to you'.

PHILO-PAIDEIAS TO RICHARDSON, MONDAY 30 JANUARY 1741

Opinion is, that if all the Books in England were to be \<xxxxx *1 word*\>,[4] this Book, next the Bible, ought to be preserved – I thank Mrs. Courteville[5] for it, and am hers and Your humble Servant,

Knightley Chetwoode[6]

[4] A word has been erased, and 'burnt' has been written in its place in SR's hand. The final letter of the erased word is d, suggesting that it may have been 'damned'.
[5] 'ourteville' has been crossed out.
[6] Much of the signature has been crossed out, and periods supplied, to read 'K. C.'.

Philo-Paideias[1] to Richardson

Monday 30 January 1741

MS: FM XVI, 1, ff. 43–4. Copy in Gilbert Hill's hand.
Endorsement: 'XXXII.' (in SR's hand); 'To the Author of Pamela.' (in Hill's hand).

January 30 1740/41

Sir

Accept this small poetic Essay on your excellent Book with Candour; and, if you think it will be of any Service to excite Attention, in the Minds of its Readers, you may print it in any future Edition;[2] and you'll oblige, Yours

Philo-Paideias.

On Pamela.

Too long have Tales obscene defil'd the Stage;
And Novels loose deprav'd the present Age,
With silly, long, Romantic Stories fill'd,
Where *mad knights*, woo, and the kind Princess yields;
Where, if the whining Lover says he dies,
The tender-hearted Lady soon complies.
From these Pert Miss catches the am'rous Fire,
And feels the Passions of unchaste Desire,
Scarce in her *Teens*, impure in Thought and Mind,
Great is her Inclination to be *Kind*:
Did Opportunity but serve, she'd run

[1] The pseudonym translates as 'friend of education'.
[2] The poem did not appear in any editions of *Pamela*.

36

PHILO-PAIDEIAS TO RICHARDSON, MONDAY 30 JANUARY 1741

To Ruin quick, and haste to be undone.
From those the *beardless Rake*, with lustful Eyes,
Views the Chaste Maid, till the Contagion flies
Swift through his Mind, and blots his sullied Soul;
While raging Passions Reason's Power controul.
In this small Treatise no loose words appear,
Such as may shock the chaste and modest Ear;
But honest Virtue, in its native Light,
With sweet attracting Graces, charms our Sight.
If to delight, instruct, and please us too, ⎫
Merits our Thanks, sure they are justly due; ⎬
From ev'ry truly grateful Heart, to you. – ⎭
From Vice you pluck the borrow'd Mask, and show
Its black Deformity before our View;
Improve our Minds, and teach us to beware
Of every tempting, fatal, flattering Snare;
To all make easy the Commands divine,
And Virtue with a brighter Lustre shine.
Ah! charming Book! for ever I cou'd read!
How sweetly there, does lovely Virtue plead!
How simple, unaffected, is the Style;
Yet beautiful and uniform the while!
Like *Pamela*, with Innocence it charms;
And ev'ry chaste, good, tender Passion warms.
Let ev'ry Fair one, Pamela in thee
The justest Pattern for example see;
In ev'ry Change, and ev'ry State of Life,
The humble Maid, good Mistress, and Chaste Wife
Let thy Merit plainly shew
Virtue's the chief, the only, Good below.
Tis that alone can ev'ry charm improve,
And make them truly worth Esteem and Love.
O may it have a right effect, and bless
Such good Endeavours with a Just Success!
Then shall our British Youth, with Virtue crown'd,
Through all the distant Nations be renown'd:
Succeeding Times shall bless this Author's care,
And strive to imitate the *Happy Pair*.

Stephen Duck[1] to Richardson

\<Monday 9 March 1741\>[2]

MS: FM XVI, 1, f. 75. Copy in Gilbert Hill's hand.
Endorsement: 'LXIV.' (in SR's hand).

Kew-Green. Monday Morn.

Dear Sir,

After your kind Present (Pamela) had visited almost every House in the Parish,[3] she returned home yesterday with the highest Compliments of all who had seen her. I had only before read her Misfortunes, and I thought it impossible to be more affected than I was with them. But you have a wonderful Art; for I was more mov'd with her Happiness than I was with her Troubles. Her discreet behavior to her Master, her Thanks and Piety to God, her Gratitude to her Friends, and Generosity to her Enemies, drew Tears from my Eyes, and made me see the amiable Face of Virtue in the noblest Light, and feel it's Force with the most sensible Pleasure.

I have neither Time nor Words to tell you the satisfaction I have had in reading this Book; but I will tell you this, that, were I able to compose so useful a Work in Prose, as well as I love Rhymes, I would willingly burn all I have made, and never attempt to make another.

I have inclosed in *this* the last Proof of my Epistle, with some little Alteration; and should take it as a Favor, if you would let Mr Roberts know that I would not have it published till to morrow Se'nnight.[4] I am, Dear Sir, Yours most gratefully,

S. Duck

---

[1] Stephen Duck (1705?–56), labouring-class poet and clergyman (*ODNB*). SR had printed Duck's popular *Poems on Several Occasions* in 1736.

[2] Eaves and Kimpel suggest that Duck refers to the heroine's change of fortune in *Pamela* rather than, as SR later claimed in his index to the manuscript volume of *Pamela* correspondence (FM XVI, 1, f. 7v), to *Pamela II* (Eaves and Kimpel, 627). This dating is further supported by Duck's reference to his forthcoming verse epistle, *Every Man in His Own Way: An Epistle to a Friend* (1741).

[3] Charlton, near Pewsey, in Wiltshire.

[4] Duck's verse epistle, *Every Man in His Own Way*, published by Robert Dodsley and the trade publisher James Roberts, was first advertised on 15 March 1741.

Richard Newton[1] to Richardson

Friday 15 May 1741

MS: FM XVI, 1, f. 48. Copy in Gilbert Hill's hand.
Endorsement: 'XLV' (in SR's hand); 'Extract from a Letter of D:ʳ Newton'[2] (in Hill's hand).

May 15th: 1741

Dear Sir,

I did not go to Oxford, as I intended, but to the Grange.[3] I have run over the first Part & made or rather suggested a very few Alterations; and say as I said before, that little Departures from Propriety out of the Sweet pretty Mouth of Pamela are so[4] natural, or more so, than Exactnesses, if what I have Suggested are Such.

---

[1] Richard Newton (1676–1753), educationalist and principal of Hart Hall, Oxford, which under his leadership became Hertford College (*ODNB*). SR had printed Newton's works and would, in a revision of Defoe's *Tour* (3rd edn, 1742), praise Newton's efforts to make Hart Hall a college.
[2] 'ewton' has been crossed out and the name disguised as 'N.—'.
[3] Newton's home in Lavendon, Buckinghamshire.
[4] 'so' has been inserted in SR's hand.

Ralph Courteville to Richardson

Monday 8 June 1741

MS: FM XVI, 1, f. 49. Copy in Gilbert Hill's hand.
Endorsement: 'XLVII.' (in SR's hand).

June 8 1741

Dear Sir,

It was with no small Concern, that I saw your Advertisement against those Poachers in Literature,[1] and from a true principle of

---

[1] In a note appended to his announcement of *Pamela*'s fourth edition in the *Gazetteer* for 7 May, SR wrote: 'Certain Booksellers having in the Press a spurious Continuation of these Two Volumes (in Letters from Pamela to Mrs Jervis her *Housekeeper*) the Author thinks it necessary to declare, that the same is carrying on *against* his Consent, and without any other Knowledge of the Story than what they are able to collect from the Two Volumes already printed: And that he is actually continuing the Work himself, from Materials, that, perhaps, but for such a notorious Invasion of his Plan, he should not have published'. The

Friendship cannot but think, as well as offer it as my Advice, that for the future you should to the Publick signify your intention of Presenting them with a Third Volume and am certain no One pretender could have hurt you – By what is now passed curiosity will Oblige many to see both – tho' I am convinced the same Hand as produced the other two cannot be out done, tho' a Pope[2] should attempt it. I am the worst Man living at Compliments: Therefore never presume farther than what is really my Sentiments; & hope you'll Excuse what is truly offer'd in the Sincere Intent of, your very Humble Servant.

R. Courteville

bookseller Richard Chandler (*c.* 1713–44) published the first volume of *Pamela's Conduct in High Life* on 28 May (the second followed on 12 September 1741). SR responded angrily to this publication in the *Gazetteer* of 30 May.

[2] The poet Alexander Pope, who meditated a satirical continuation of *Pamela* focusing on the main character's adventures in London; see Warburton to SR, 28 December 1742.

Philaretes[1] to Richardson

Monday 22 June 1741

MS: FM XVI, 1, ff. 50–1. Copy in SR's hand.
Endorsement: 'XLVIII.' and 'To the Author of PAMELA' (in SR's hand).

June 22. 1741.

Sir,

I believe few Persons, if any, sat down to read your Two Volumes of *Pamela* with more Prejudice than myself: I was frequently in Pain how you would come off in the nicest Scenes without offending the Modest, and the Virtuous; and often found fault with the *delaying* an *Attempt* to *escape* so *long*; and especially her *Return* when once got at Liberty: And I must own, that, if the *real Circumstances* of the Story did not forbid, a very agreeable Turn might have been given to it from her Retreat to her Parents. However, as I have now gone thro' the Whole, I can vindicate her in her Return to the 'Squire's; and am as much become prejudiced

[1] A 'Philaretes' (the same?) would write to SR again about seven years later to express disapproval with the rumoured ending of *Clarissa*; see Philaretes to SR, <Early 1748>.

40

PHILARETES TO RICHARDSON, MONDAY 22 JUNE 1741

in favour of the Performance, for the Entertainment of which you have my hearty Thanks. The strongest Colouring in it appears to me suited rather to damp the most outrageous Lust, and represent the *Rake* and the *Debaucher* as the most savage and monstrous creature in Nature. And I think 'tis plain, that Persons of this Character are afraid it will have this Effect on *young Sinners,* by the Attempt that has lately been made against it in that vile Pamphlet *Shamela.*[(a)2] As to the Complaint of *loose* and bad *Ideas* by the Author of *Pamela censured;* to me they appear only such as *he* has made by his own Turns and Inlargements; and therefore 'tis *he* that is accountable for them, and not *you:* And I am much mistaken, if Passages full as strong are not to be found in Milton, which, instead of being *blamed,* have been generally *applauded.* I might here, particularly, refer you to Book IV. Line 492. a *Description* of Eve *leaning* on *Adam* – Book VIII. Line 500, &c. Book IX. 1035, &c. And the *Reason* why *Eve* chose to hear the Story of the *Creation,* &c. from *Adam* rather than from the Angel himself; Book VIII. Line 50–54, 55, 56, 57–[3]

I shall only beg Leave to conclude this Letter to you with assuring you, that as no one has the Cause of Virtue and Piety more at Heart than myself, so I would be far from saying any-thing in favour of what I thought might in the least weaken the Guard of them, nor should I have troubled you with this Letter if I had not believed your Aim was to promote and cherish their noble Principles. And in this View I can read your Book; and, amidst all the wanton *Sneers* at it, apply the Words of an *inspired Writer* (which, by the way, I think would be a *good Motto* for the *Title-page*) –*[4] *To the Pure all things are pure; but unto them that are defiled and unbelieving nothing is pure; but even their Mind and Conscience is defiled.* I am, Sir, Your unknown, obliged Humble Servant,

Philaretes.

June 22. 1741.

P. S. I think that nothing can more evidently prove how much your Performance resembles *Nature,* than the Effect it produced on

---

[2] Footnote reads '(a) Written by Mr. H. Fielding'. Added in SR's late hand at an indeterminate date.

[3] References are to the twelve-book version of Milton's epic poem, *Paradise Lost* (1674).

[4] The footnote reads '* St. Paul to Titus, i.15'.

PHILARETES TO RICHARDSON, MONDAY 22 JUNE 1741

a young Miss not 12 Years old; who was so struck with the reading of it, that she broke out in these pretty unartful Lines.

I.
O Pamela! thy virtuous Mind
Riches and Honours has resign'd;
Riches were but Dross to thee,
Compared with thy Honesty.

II.
But since the Case is alter'd thus,
With Thankfulness thou mayst rehearse
The many Combats thou hast made;
And think with Joy, thou 'rt fully paid.

III.
Praise God for all his Mercies past:
Pray that his Favours still may last;
And in *Obedience* due express
Thy highest Love and Thankfulness.

P.S. I leave this Letter to your prudent Liberty.

The Passages in Milton, referred to in the foregoing Letter, are these that follow:

IV. 492.
So spake our gen'ral Mother; and with Eyes
Of conjugal Attraction, unreprov'd,
And meek Surrender, half embracing lean'd
On our first Father: Half her swelling Breast
Naked met his, under the flowing Gold
of her loose tresses hid. –

VIII. 500, &c.
She heard me thus; and tho' divinely brought,
Yet Innocence and Virgin modesty,
Her Virtue, and *the Conscience of her* Work,[5]
That would be woo'd, and not unsought be won,

---

5 Alongside this line, SR has supplied alternative text from Bentley's 1732 edition of Milton: 'her Consciousness of – Bentl.'. Richard Bentley (1662–1742), philologist and classical scholar (*ODNB*); his edition of *Paradise Lost* was roundly criticized for its many emendations of Milton's text.

PHILARETES TO RICHARDSON, MONDAY 22 JUNE 1741

Not obvious, nor obtrusive, *but retir'd*;[6]
The more desirable; *or*, to say all,[7]
Nature herself, tho' pure of sinful Thought,
Wrought in her so, that, seeing me, she turn'd;
I follow'd her, she what was Honour knew,[8]
And with obsequious Majesty approv'd
My pleaded Reason. To the nuptial Bow'r
I led her, blushing like the Morn: All Heav'n,
And happy Constellations on that Hour
Shed their selectest influence. The Earth
Gave sign of Gratulation; and each Hill:
Joyous the *Birds: Fresh Gales and gentle Airs*,[9]
Whisper'd it to the Woods; and from their Wings
Flung Rose, flung odours from the juicy Plant,
Disporting, till the am'rous Bird of Night
Sung spousal, and bid haste the Evening star.
On his Hill-top, to light the bridal Lamp.

IX. 1035, &c.
So said he; and forbore not Glance or Toy
Of amorous Intent, well understood
Of Eve, whose Eye darted contagious Fire.
Her hand he seized; and to a shady Bank,
Thick over-head with verdant Roof imbow'r'd,
He led her, nothing loth; Flow'rs were the Couch,
Pansies, and Violets, and Asphodel,
And Hyacinth, Earth's freshest, softest lap.
There they their Fill of Love and Love's Disport
Took largely; of their mutual Guilt the Seal,
The Solace of their Sin, till dewy Sleep
Oppress'd them, weary'd with their am'rous Play.

VIII. 50, &c.
——Such Pleasure she reserv'd,
Adam relating; she sole Auditress;
Her Husband the Relater she preferr'd

---

[6] 'bid retire – Bentl.' again supplied in the margin.
[7] Again, an alternative version from Bentley's edition is given: 'but – Bentl.'.
[8] 'I made Addresses. She what's – Bentl.' written alongside this line.
[9] Written alongside: 'Beasts and Birds: The gentle Gales. Bentl.'.

ANONYMOUS TO RICHARDSON, JULY 1741

Before the Angel, and of him to ask
Chose rather: He, she knew, would intermix
Grateful Digressions, and solve high Dispute
With conjugal Caresses: from his Lip
Not Words alone pleas'd her. –

Anonymous to Richardson

July 1741

MS: FM XVI, 1, f. 52. Copy in Gilbert Hill's hand.
Endorsement: 'L.' (in SR's hand); 'To the Author of Pamela.' (in Hill's hand).

July 1741

If a Man can act without Vanity, I would hope it from the
Author of Pamela, because he appears so great a Master of the
Passions; but he may rest assured, the Public so distinguish
between the original Pamela, and the attempted Imitation in
High Life,[1] as may well give Vanity. – I am pleased with Pamela
so much, as to be anxious for the Author's Reputation, and so
much a Friend as to offer Advice again,[2] though I shou'd be again
mistook, and have confuse{d}[3] instead of the contrary. The repeated
Advertisement about Pamela in High Life,[4] which does not deserve
so much Notice, makes me in pain for the Author of the Original
Pamela – He need not be in a Hurry; but may touch and polish his
Continuation at discretion; for though it is waited with Impatience,
yet if it is finished up to Expectation, no premature Imitation will
hurt the Profit of the Printer, nor the Credit of the Author; but
it will be a task so to finish it: For it is expected not merely equal
with, but to excell the first. – Higher Stations make Virtue and
Wisdom more conspicuous; Every Defect therein more obvious.

The Preface, which is properly the Postscript to the Work, may
say what the Writer pleases of the Imitator; but no Allusion, not
the most distant Hint relating to an Imitation, can be admitted in
Pamela's Story of herself, without being a Blemish. I don't mean,

[1] John Kelly's *Pamela's Conduct in High Life* and the anonymous *Pamela in High Life* – unauthorized continuations of SR's *Pamela* – were both published in 1741.
[2] This advice may have been offered in a previous letter, now lost.
[3] The manuscript reads 'confuse'. This is probably a copyist's error.
[4] *Pamela's Conduct in High Life* had been repeatedly advertised in May and June 1741, much
to SR's vexation.

ALEXANDER GORDON TO RICHARDSON, <BEFORE AUGUST 1741>

that no Incident shou'd have any resemblance; for though like Incidents sometimes cause a Charge of Poverty in Invention, yet the Different Event of, or a shining instead of a barely unblameable Behaviour in a like Incident, may show superior skill in the Author – But, I mean, nothing shou'd be in the Body of the Work like the Reflection, which Cervantes cou'd not forbear upon the Imitation of his Don Quixote.[5]

The long Episode of a Lady run away with in Italy, and rescued by an English Gentleman, exposes the Imitator's want of Skill to furnish proper Incidents for a Volume of his Heroine's Behaviour in High Life.[6] And the Punishments he has carved out for Mr Peters and Mrs Jewkes, with Pamela's Reflections thereon, give no advantageous Idea of her Improvements in High Life, no Mark of a Benign Temper, the true Spirit of Christian Charity, but rather of such an one as wou'd call down Fire from Heaven: a disposition reproved in these meek Words. Ye know not what manner of Spirit Ye are of.[7] I am Sir Your humble Servant

---

[5] In the author's preface to the continuation of *Don Quixote* (1615), Cervantes directly takes on writers of spurious continuations.
[6] In the first volume of *Pamela's Conduct in High Life*, pp. 58–71, 85–106.
[7] Luke 9:55.

Alexander Gordon[1] to Richardson

<Before August 1741>

MS: FM XVI, 1, f. 11. Copy in SR's hand.
Endorsement: 'I.' (in SR's hand).

> Dear Sir,
> If I shall not have the Pleasure of seeing you before my Departure for the Westerly World,[2] wishing you all Health and

---

[1] Alexander Gordon (*c.* 1692–1754?), antiquary and singer, and Secretary of the Society for the Encouragement of Learning (*ODNB*). SR had printed two works by Gordon: *Itinerarium Septentrionale: or, a Journey thro' most of the Counties of Scotland, and those in the North of England* (1726) and *The Lives of Pope Alexander VI and his Son Caesar Borgia* (1729). Gordon apparently still owed SR money for that work.
[2] In August 1741, Gordon 'sailed for Carolina as Secretary to the new Governor, James Glen' (*ODNB*).

ALEXANDER GORDON TO RICHARDSON, <BEFORE AUGUST 1741>

Happiness, and returning you, my dear Friend, cordial Thanks for your repeated Friendships and Goodness to me, I take Leave: And may God bless you and yours. What remains between us unpaid by me, shall, I hope, soon be done with Honour and Gratitude. According to Promise, I send inclosed your Letter sent me about Printing,[3] also a few scattered Thoughts about Operas: And I am, and ever shall remain, my dearest Friend, your affectionate, faithful, and humble Servant, while

Alexander Gordon.

My best Respects to Mrs Richardson, and the little Angel your Daughter.

Some Thoughts about Operas.[4]

In Italy, where their Language is best known and understood, Judges of Operas are so far from thinking the Drama a poetical Part of their Operas Nonsense, as we, unskilled in Italian, foolishly conclude in England, that if the *Libretto*, as they call it, [(a) be not][5] approved, the Opera, notwithstanding the Music is good, will [be] condemned. They in Italy very justly reckon, that the very Music of an Opera cannot be complete and pleasing, if the Drama is incongruous in its Composition; because, in order to please, it must have the necessary Contrast of the Grave and Light, that is, the Diverting, equally blended through the Whole. If there is too much of the first, let the Music express Love and the Tender never so much, it will turn out heavy and tiresome: If the latter prevails, it will surfeit with Jig and Minuit:[6] Wherefore 'tis the Poet's Happiness to adapt the Words for this agreeable Mixture; for the Music is but Secondary, and subservient to the Words; for if there is an artful Contrast in the Drama, there will be so in the Music, if the Composer be a skilful Master. Now, as in England the Practice has been to mutilate, curtail, and patch up a Drama in Italian, in order to throw in a Glut of minuitish Airs collected

---

[3] This letter is now lost.

[4] SR adapted Gordon's thoughts in Vol. IV, letter 16 of *Pamela II*, (see pp. 363–4). For information on Italian opera in the eighteenth century, see Margaret R. Butler's chapter in *The Cambridge History of Eighteenth-Century Music* (Cambridge University Press, 2011), pp. 203–71.

[5] SR's footnote reads: '(a) The Original being defaced, the Words between [ ] are supplied by Conjecture.'

[6] I.e. 'minuet'.

from all Authors, the Contrast thereby has always been broken; and the Opera damned, without knowing the Reason. And as arrogant beggarly Prompters, though Italians, have been employed in the Hotch-potch,[7] and in translating on Dramas from Italian into English, how could such Operas appear any otherwise but as incongruous Nonsense?

Recitativoes.[8]

To avoid the natural Dissonance and Irregularity in common Speech, Recitativoes in Musical and Dramatical Performances were invented; which, though the Time in pronouncing the Words in them is Scarce longer than in common Conversation; yet the Concatenation of Sounds is by this means so artfully contrived, as that the Cadences or Dialogue of Basses shall unite, and delight the Ear with their Opposites, the highest Tenors and Trebles. Therefore Recitativoes are a regular way of Speaking by Art, in order to avoid and correct the Irregularities of Speech often found in Nature, and to express the Passions without Offence to the Ear.

---

[7] 'A confused mixture of disparate things; a medley, a jumble' (*OED*).
[8] 'A style of musical declamation intermediate between singing and ordinary speech' (*OED*).

Richardson to James Leake[1]

August 1741

MS: FM XVI, 1, ff. 54–6. Copy in Gilbert Hill's hand.
Endorsement: 'LII.' (in SR's hand); 'To Mr Leake.'[2] (in Hill's hand).

August. 1741.

Dear Sir,
You desire to know when the 3rd Vol. of Pamela will come out; and you'll[3] have seen several base Advertisements and Papers against me in the Champion,[4] in Defence of the spurious

---

[1] James Leake (1686–1764), one of Bath's prominent booksellers and brother of SR's second wife, Elizabeth (m. 1733) (*ODNB*).
[2] 'Leake' is deleted and 'L of Bath' is inserted in its place in SR's late hand. This letter was highly edited and annotated by SR himself well after the date of original composition.
[3] 'you'll' is deleted and 'will' has been inserted in superscript in SR's hand.
[4] *The Champion* (1739–45), a periodical associated for a time with Henry Fielding.

RICHARDSON TO JAMES LEAKE, AUGUST 1741

High-Life, publish'd only to draw me into Controversy, to make that foolish Piece sell; and I will give you a Short Account of the Affair.[5]

Having heard that Chandler[6] had employed one Kelly[7] a Bookseller's Hackney, who never wrote any thing that was tolerably receiv'd, and had several of his Performances refused by the Stage,[8] I remonstrated against it, to a Friend of Kelly's. This brought Chandler to me, who when he found I resented the Baseness of the Proceeding; told me that he understood I had said, I had neither Leisure nor Inclination to pursue the Story. I told him it was true I had said so to several of my Friends who had pressed me on the Success to continue it; but that[9] was, upon a Supposition, that no one would offer to meddle with it;[10] in which case I had resolved to do it myself, rather than my Plan should be basely ravished out of my Hands, and, probably my Characters depreciated and debased, by those who knew nothing of the Story, nor the Delicacy required in the Continuation of the Piece. I told him that still I would decline continuing it, if he and others did not force me to it in my own Defence; but if they proceeded I must and would; and Advertise against them, as soon as they Published. He had the Impudence to propose to me, to join my Materials to their Author's, and to let it come out under my Name: A proposal I rejected with the Contempt it deserved. Next he offered to Cancel 4 Sheets he had Printed (though it was[11] no more than 4 ½ sheets, as I found afterwards) and to lose 9 Guineas they had advanced to their Author, if I would continue it, for him and his Partners. I told him, that if, contrary to my Inclination, I was obliged to continue it, I would suffer no one to be concern'd in it; having a young Family of my own that were intitled to All I could do for them. And insisted that if their Piece was so well Written as he pretended, (and much boasted to

---

[5] For a discussion of this letter and its importance in terms of the composition and publication of *Pamela II*, see *Pamela in the Marketplace*, pp. 55–9.

[6] Richard Chandler (*c.* 1713–44) (*ODNB*) commissioned *Pamela's Conduct in High Life* from journalist and playwright John Kelly (*c.* 1684–1751) (*ODNB*). Superscript insertions in SR's hand: 'Mr', prior to 'Chandler', and 'the Bookseller' after it.

[7] Superscript insertion in SR's hand: 'Mr', prior to 'Kelly', and 'of the Temple, as he stiles himself so' after it.

[8] Superscript insertion in SR's hand: 'to continue my Pamela'.

[9] 'I said it' is written in the margin in SR's hand.

[10] 'at least without consulting me: But that if such an Attempt were made, I was resolved' is written in SR's hand alongside this passage in the margin.

[11] Superscript insertion in SR's hand: 'they were'.

me, saying, they fell in nothing short of my two Volumes) he should have it publish'd under some other Title, and not infringe upon my Plan or Characters; which I represented to him in the Light it wou'd appear in to every Body; and I urged the Insignificance of his Plea of what Old Mr Osborn[12] had said, if he did say it when he might have consulted me, and had my Answer from my own Mouth and the Baseness as well as Hardships it was, that a Writer could not be permitted to end his own Work, when and how he pleased, without such scandalous Attempts of Ingrafting upon his Plan. He[13] went from me, as I thought, convinced of this Baseness, wishing he had not ingaged in it, and saying he would consult his Partners, and give me an Answer. I[14] never heard further from him only of his Boasts how well written their Piece was, and how determined they were to prosecute it, braving it out that if I did Advertise against them, they had Authors who could give me Advertisement for Advertisement let me say what I wou'd, and that I was like the Dog in the Manger wou'd neither eat myself nor let them eat.[15] Their[16] Author sent me the half Sheets[17] by means[18] of his Friend upon full Assurance that I would[19] be pleased with this Performance and by these I saw all my Characters were likely to be debased, and my whole Purpose inverted;[20] for otherwise, I believe, I shou'd not have prevailed upon myself to continue it; for Second Parts are generally received with Prejudice, and it was treating the Public too much like a Bookseller to pursue a Success till they tired out the buyers; and the Subject to be pursued as it *ought*, was more difficult and of Consequence, my Leisure, my Health and my Capacity to do it, were all Objections to the Attempt.

But on the other Hand, when it was represented to me, that *all* Readers were not Judges; and that their Volume, and another Volume after it, (which they design'd, and had intended to Publish with their 3rd had not my Menaces to Advertise against them,

---

[12] John Osborn senior (d. 1739), bookseller.
[13] SR has added a square bracket prior to this sentence.
[14] SR has added a square bracket prior to this sentence.
[15] See Fab. 64, 'A Dog in the Manger', in SR's edition of *Aesop's Fables* (1740) (*Early Works*, vol. I, p. 182).
[16] SR has added a square bracket prior to this sentence.
[17] The sheets of paper on which the text of a book is printed, here sent to SR prior to folding and binding into their final shape.
[18] In a later hand SR has crossed out 'by means' and substituted 'by the Hand of'.
[19] Superscript insertion in SR's hand: 'approve of'.
[20] SR has added 'and when I considered that their' prior to 'Second Parts'.

RICHARDSON TO JAMES LEAKE, AUGUST 1741

made them[21] try the Success of one first) (and still more and more[22] intended possibly by them, so long as the Town would receive them) would, by the Booksellers Interest and Arts, generally accompany the Two;[23] and moreover reflected upon the Baseness of their Proceeding; they likewise giving out that I was not the Writer of the two (which indeed, I wish, and did not intend should be known to more than 6 Friends and those in Confidence) but[24] they were written by one of[25] my Overseers, who was dead, and that I *could not* for that Reason, continue them – I set about the Work, but began not till I found their Volume in great Forwardness, and they in Earnest to proceed; and that was in the middle of last April. By which you may judge that its Appearance cannot be very sudden: For it is no easy Task to one that has so much Business upon his Hands, and so many Avocations of different Sorts, and whose old Complaints in the Nervous way require that he should sometimes run away from Business, and[26] himself, if he could. Then, Sir, to write up this Work, as it ought, it is impossible it should be done in the Compass of one Volume: For her Behaviour in Married Life, her Correspondencies with her new and more genteel Friends; her Conversations at Table and elsewhere; her pregnant Circumstance, her Devotional and Charitable Employments; her Defence of some parts of her former Conduct; which will be Objected to[27] by Lady Davers, in the Friendly Correspondence between them. Her Opinion of some of the genteeler Diversions when in London, as the Masquerade, Opera, Plays &c. – Her Notions of Education, her Friendships, her relative Duties, her Family Oeconomy –and 90[28] other Subjects as[29] Material, ought to be touched upon; and if it be done in a common Narrative Manner, without those Reflexions and Observations, which she intermingles in the New manner attempted in the two first Volumes, it will be consider'd only as a dry Collection of Morals, and Sermonising Instructions that will be[30] more benefitially to a Reader, found in other Authors;

[21] Superscript insertion in SR's hand: 'determined them to'.
[22] SR has added 'Volumes' here.
[23] Superscript insertion in SR's hand: 'I had written'.
[24] Superscript insertion in SR's hand: 'that'.
[25] Superscript insertion in SR's hand: 'who had been'.
[26] Superscript insertion in SR's hand: 'from'.
[27] Superscript insertion in SR's hand: 'her'.
[28] Superscript insertion in SR's hand: 'many'.
[29] Superscript insertion in SR's hand: 'equally'.
[30] Superscript insertion in SR's hand: 'with'.

PAUL BERTRAND TO RICHARDSON, TUESDAY 25 AUGUST 1741

and must neither Entertain or Divert, as the former have done beyond my Expectation.

Judge then, Sir, what a Scribbler such a one as I[31] and busied as I am otherwise, and oppressed by Tremors[32]

---

[31] SR has bracketed the phrase 'such a one as I'.
[32] The page ends here; the surviving letter is incomplete.

Paul Bertrand[1] to Richardson

Tuesday 25 August 1741

MS: FM XVI, 1, f. 58. Copy in Gilbert Hill's hand.
Endorsement: 'LIV' (in SR's hand).

Bath, August 25 1741

Sir,

The Honour of your Friendship, and the kind Reception you gave me at your House, call for thanks, especially from one that wou'd not be thought altogether undeserving: I therefore take this Opportunity of sending you mine together with my Regrets that I could no longer enjoy the Pleasure You, your pretty Family, the two agreeable Ladies[2] &c. gave me; but indispensible Business, and the Embarrass my Mind was in, occasioned by my Wife's Illness, were the Cause; which last, I hope, will be removed (as it is in a fair way of being) the next time I have the Pleasure of seeing you.

I was glad to read the two first sheets of Pamela,[3] I say of reading, divested of the Pathetic Accents of the Author: I will only say, for fear you should suspect me of Flattery, that I like them well; and that I am sure they will give you Honour and Reputation

---

[1] Paul Bertrand (fl. 1732–48), a merchant in Bath who handled monetary transactions for SR's friend and physician, George Cheyne (1672–1743); see also Cheyne to SR, 3 February 1739.
[2] Probably SR's second wife, Elizabeth Leake Richardson (1697–1773), and Elizabeth Midwinter (1724–1806), who lived with the Richardsons after the death of her father Edward Midwinter (d. 1736), a bookseller. Elizabeth Midwinter married the bookseller and prominent banker Francis Gosling (1719–68), a friend of SR's, on 12 November 1742.
[3] Bertrand received and read unbound pages of *Pamela II*; SR's continuation was published in duodecimo format, so the first two sheets would have contained the novel's first forty-eight pages.

PAUL BERTRAND TO RICHARDSON, TUESDAY 25 AUGUST 1741

superior to the first Parts; if I may be so bold to judge thus peremptorily without other Merit but strict Impartiality, and that of being your hearty well wisher.

The Doctor communicated me his Letter;[4] I was so free to tell him I thought it good, if you had asked him his Advice for some such future intended Work; but to a Man that had already completed his Design, and that only ask'd his Sentiments as to the Publishing, or for some few Remarks or Corrections, I thought it very needless because indeed your own Plan is very good. I will likewise take the Liberty to say (entre nous)[5] that I think the little amendments he has marked with his Pencil very trifling. I indeed like no Part of his Letter but that where he gives you Rules and Cautions for your Health, which I pray you to follow.

Let me tell you, that I retract the Advice I gave you of Transposing Lady Davers's Letters:[6] I now think your Introduction very natural and easy, and the Reader's Curiosity will be satisfied by soon meeting with the said Letters, and be agreeably led from Pamela's usual pious humble Style, to her more elevated one. As the Town already love Pamela, I hope their Fondness for the Lovely Creature, will even increase, and that this Second Part will be as warmly received as the First was: As I make no sort of doubt of it, take, Dear Sir, these my early Congratulations, together with my best Wishes for your Health, which I think the Public much Interested in. I am, Sir, Your most humble and most Obedient Servant

Paul Bertrand

---

[4] This is Cheyne to SR, 24 August 1741. SR drew up a lengthy response to Cheyne's criticism but may have refrained from sending it to Cheyne; see SR to Cheyne, 31 August 1741; and SR to Bertrand, 31 August 1741.

[5] I.e. between us.

[6] The letter in which Bertrand gave SR this piece of advice is now lost.

Mary Barber[1] to Richardson

Wednesday 26 August 1741

MS: FM XVI, 1, f. 53. Copy in Gilbert Hill's hand.
Endorsement: 'LI.' (In SR's hand); 'From a Lady in Dublin' (added in SR's late hand).

August 26 1741

When once a Man is out of the Way,
The farther he goes, the farther he goes astray.[2]

These lines have come into my Head a thousand times in relation to my worthy Friend Mr Richardson,[3] whom I have so shamefully neglected writing to, and whom I ought to have thank'd long ago for the Valuable Present he made my Daughter[4] of Pamela, which greatly delighted us all – The Truth is, she determined to thank him herself; but her Eyes were at that time, and long after, so weak, that she cou'd not Write; and when they grew better, she said she was asham'd to Write; Then it was so late, and my Head is so weakned with the Gout that I hardly ever Write at all, unless it be to my Son.[5] As this is the Truth I hope you will pardon us; for I do assure you, Sir, nobody can have a more sincere Respect, and Regard for you, than I and mine have, *or* was more rejoiced at the Universal Applause Pamela met with, which it so justly merited. It was indeed a long time before I knew who was the Author of it, so we had no prejudice in its favour and had read but a very Little way, before I sent to my Friend Faulkner,[6] and advised him to advertise, that he wou'd print it; but he happened to have got one at the same time, for though you were so kind to send the Book, we only imagined, that it was one you had printed, which you approved of, little thinking that you had time to write. I cannot say, that I have been so delighted with any thing that has been Publish'd for some Years past, as I was with it; and when I knew who wrote it, I was doubly delighted,

---

[1] Mary Barber (*c.* 1685–1755), poet living in Dublin (*ODNB*).
[2] A couplet presumably of Barber's own invention.
[3] 'ichardson' was crossed through at a later date.
[4] Mira (b. 1717).
[5] Rupert Barber (1719–72), artist known for his enamel miniatures and a pastel portrait he painted of Swift. In 1742, he married one of Patrick Delany's nieces, Bridget Wilson.
[6] George Faulkner (1703?–75), prominent Dublin printer and bookseller (*ODNB*). For his clandestine printing of *Pamela II*, see An English Printer in Dublin to SR, 12 November 1741; 'my Friend' was crossed through at a later date.

MARY BARBER TO RICHARDSON, WEDNESDAY 26 AUGUST 1741

by knowing that the generous, Virtuous, Noble, Sentiments with which it abounds, came directly from your Heart, every body in this Kingdom, whose Approbation was worth regarding, that I have met with or heard of, was highly delighted with it. the only objection I have heard made by the best judges, that is, by People of Taste and Virtue was, that the Scene where the Master and Mrs Jewkes had her in Bed between them, was a little too strongly Painted.

I think the Publishers of Pamela, in High Life as they Call it, have given you ample Satisfaction for the Envy and Ill-nature they shew'd you, by she{w}ing their great want of judgment in giving the World a second Part so infinitely below the first. I should be glad to know if Chandler is the Brother of the Milliner at Bath. I hope not; for I take him to be a Man of better sense than to shew so great a want of Judgment.[7] One great Beauty in Pamela is, that the Characters are so admirably kept up; which the other has no regard to: But they will bear no Comparison on any account.

I am sorry to tell you, that Dr Delany[8] one of the great Admirers of Pamela has been in long time past in great trouble on account of his Wife's ill State of Health.[9] The family are, and have been, all this Summer, going from place to place in the Country with her, Change of Air, being prescribed by the Physicians.

I know it will be a pleasure to you to hear, that my young Painter[10] has been blest with great Success here.[11] I have only room to intreat of you to Write to me, and give me a particular Account of all your Family; in whose welfare I shall for ever think myself interested. Do this, I beseech you, that I may know you have forgiven me: for till you do, I shall never forgive myself.

Mrs Newmans, Myra, & the Painter, desire you to accept their most humble leave[12]

---

[7] 'for I take him ... want of Judgment' has been crossed through.

[8] Patrick Delany (1685/6–1768), writer and cleric (*ODNB*). At a later date, 'elany' was crossed through.

[9] Delany's wife, Margaret, died in 1742 (*ODNB*). The widow of Richard Tenison, she had brought Delany an annual income of £1,600. Subsequently, Delany became involved in protracted litigation over her will.

[10] Her son Rupert.

[11] The passage from 'I am sorry ...' in the previous paragraph to '... great Success here' has been crossed through.

[12] In addition to her son Rupert and her daughter Mira, Barber here refers to two unidentified friends, the 'Mrs Newmans'. The sentence, in this copy, ends without punctuation mark, possibly mid-sentence. It was later crossed through, and at the bottom of the page SR has added in his late hand the note: 'See Answer No LVIII', i.e., SR to Barber, 3 September 1741.

JAMES LEAKE TO RICHARDSON, WEDNESDAY 26 AUGUST 1741

James Leake to Richardson

Wednesday 26 August 1741

MS: FM XVI, 1, f. 59. Copy in Gilbert Hill's hand.
Endorsement: 'LV.' (in SR's hand).

August 26. 1741

Dear Sir,

I am extremely obliged to you for your kind Letter, and the agreeable 2 sheets that accompany'd them:[1] I must assure you, they are, in my Opinion preferable to any Letters in the other Volumes and I have far a greater Desire to see the Conclusion, than I had last Week. Lady Davers mends apace, and I imagine soon her Good Sense will quite extinguish her former Severities; and that she will be as sincerely pleased with her Sister B, as she once detested her. The Suspicion of Mr B's new Amour I was glad to hear of. I doubt not but that part will be very serviceable to all Jealous Minds, and will either Cure or mend them. I expect their Children will be all brought from their Natural Stubbornness and Frailties, to be Great Comforts to their Parents[2] properly Lov'd and rever'd by them. The whole I imagine to be a Pattern for all Persons and Conditions not mentioned in the other Volumes; and will show Us all what we Should be. My Wife, Jemmy, and 3 Girls,[3] are all that have seen it, and have read or heard her twice with a great deal of Pleasure. I have not heard from Mr Allen since I sent the 2 sheets; so suppose he has return'd them himself. I am your most Affectionate Brother and Humble Servant

James Leake

---

[1] Leake, too, has received and read unbound pages of *Pamela II*; see Bertrand to SR, 25 August 1741.

[2] 'and in Return their Parents' is a superscript addition in SR's hand.

[3] These are James Leake's wife Hannah Hammond Leake (bap. 1699, d. 1751); his son James (1724–91), who succeeded him in the trade; and his three daughters Elizabeth, Ann, and Amelia.

Richardson to Paul Bertrand

Monday 31 August 1741

MS: FM XVI, 1, f. 64. Copy of a draft letter in Gilbert Hill's hand.
Endorsement: 'LVII.' (in SR's hand); 'Intended Letter to Mr Bertrand.' (in Hill's hand, 'Intended' added at a later point).

London, August 31 1741

Does not my good Mr Bertrand give up his Opinion merely because of the Pertinaciousness with which little Scribblers as well as great Authors, generally adhere to their own Plans? – Or from his kind Partiality, more in deference to his Friends' Judgment, than his own?

I must own to you, Sir, that your Opinion has so much Weight with me, that in my Thought I set about making it what you advised. But I found this Difficulty, and so forbear; viz. That I must have given up the Letters between the Parents and the Daughter, and only Narratively have given their Contents to Lady Davers, who desires an Account of what pass'd in the Fortnight in Kent.[1] And perhaps this would have been as well: – If you think so I would still do so; but if you don't, your Silence (for I wou'd not be too Troublesome to you) shall be taken by me, as if you'd have them stand as they are. For those five first Letters, as they now stand, wou'd have been too long and tedious to be brought in as Details, if I may call them so, of what pass'd on settling the Old Couple; though, as independent Letters, they make a direct Part of the Work.

I write to Dr Cheyne, and take the Liberty to mention something in my Letter in Defence of one or two Places to which he objects in the two Sheets. Methinks I would be glad, you would give yourself the Trouble of perusing that Letter; and I take the Liberty, unknown, to the Doctor, (for it is to *Mr Bertrand*) to send it upon to You, and beg you'll be pleased to Seal it up when read, and when Mr L— and Mrs L—[2] have read it, and give it him. The Reason why I give you this Trouble, is, that I may have the Pleasure of your Sentiments and theirs, if I *should* or should *not* (from what I have written) keep in the tender Parts, to which the Doctor objects,

---

[1] See *Pamela II*, pp. 35–9.
[2] James and Hannah Leake.

RICHARDSON TO MARY BARBER, THURSDAY 3 SEPTEMBER 1741

that is to say, if my Reasons are of any weight at all, the Nature of the Work considered?

Don't be afraid, dear Sir, that I am drawing You into a troublesome Course of Writing: Although I should be proud of Corresponding with Mr Bertrand; yet I intend your Trouble will end, if not *here*, with one more Letter, as to this Subject; I mean with regard to my Expectations upon you: And I return you many Thanks for the Contents of your last kind, very kind Letter.

Give me Leave to congratulate you, dear Sir, on the Hope you mention, of the Embarass you labour'd under in the nearest and tenderest Case that can affect a Mind like yours, being in a fair way of Being over. May it prove so! and all Happiness attend You and Yours, prays, Dear Sir, Your oblig'd and faithful Servant

S. Richardson

If you think the Letter to the Doctor, will be taken amiss, be pleas'd to keep it back, and I will send another and shorter.

Richardson to Mary Barber

Thursday 3 September 1741

MS: FM XVI, 1, ff. 65–6. Copy in Gilbert Hill's hand.
Endorsement: 'LVIII' (in SR's hand); 'To Mrs. Barber'[1] (in Hill's hand).

Sept. 3rd 1741

Dear Madam,

I receiv'd with great Pleasure your kind Letter of the 26th past, and thank you most heartily for its Contents. But am very sorry for the Occasion which so long depriv'd me of that Pleasure.

I congratulate you and your young Painter[2] upon his Success with all my Heart; but it is no more than I expected from the Opinion I had of his young Genius & his Application. May every Day add to his Fame & his Prosperity, till he rivals ancient and excels of Consequence modern Italy.

---

[1] 'arber' has been crossed out.
[2] Her son, Rupert.

57

RICHARDSON TO MARY BARBER, THURSDAY 3 SEPTEMBER 1741

As to my Wife and 4 Girls[3] they are all, God be Praised in tolerable Health. As to myself, I am sadly[4] afflicted with the Old Complaint, bad Nerves, and Startings and Tremors, and Dizziness, and worse for the hot Weather yet ever since that has come in, I cold-bath it, and Coach it about our rough Streets almost every Day, and find I must, as patiently as I can, bear what cannot be remedy'd.[5]

I am sorry Dr. Delany is hinder'd finishing his Work by so melancholy an Occasion.[6] The[7] First Volume is quite Stagnated, and People's Curiosity so much damp'd by the delay of the rest, that if I believe my Publisher, I cannot expect much from them now when they come. I have finished, long ago, the 2nd. But it would be wrong to publish that, without the whole, now it has been so long Delay'd. I Printed but 750 of the 2nd Edition of David, and the Publisher has brought me in an Account of 500 left. But this is so much like a Bookseller's gloomy and sometimes sordid Way, that I shall say no more of it.

I think it a particular Felicity that the poor Pamela has met with your Countenance and Approbation. The Scene you mention is undoubtedly very strongly drawn. But in the Continuation, Lady Davers will observe upon that and the other affecting one, in such a manner, as may perhaps excuse both a little. The unexpected success of the two first Volumes has made me still more diffident as to the Continuation. I have often wish'd, that I had the Happiness of your Advice and Conversation in some Particulars in which I doubt myself as well with respect to Capacity, as to Sex: I

---

3 The four daughters alive at this time are Mary (bap. 1735, d. 1783), Martha (bap. 1736, d. 1785), Anne (bap. 1737, d. 1803), and Sarah (bap. 1740, d. 1773).
4 'sadly' has been crossed out and 'greatly' has been substituted in SR's late hand.
5 These words have been edited (in SR's late hand). The late emendation reads: 'I also take cold-bath and take Coach Exercises about our rough Streets almost every Day.' A bracket marking this paragraph and the words '<sick> Exer<cising>' have also been written in the margin in SR's late hand.
6 The Irish clergyman, Dr Patrick Delany, whose writings SR had printed since 1732. Delany's writing had been delayed by the protracted illness of his first wife, Margaret (she died in May 1742); see Barber to SR, 26 August 1741. SR had printed the first volume of Delany's *Historical Account of the Life and Writings of King David* in 1740, with a second edition published the same year, both by John Osborn. Despite poor sales, SR had by this time printed a second volume and was waiting for Delany's manuscript for a third; the two additional volumes were eventually published by Osborn in 1742; see also Skelton to SR, 27 May 1749.
7 'Sale of the' has been inserted in SR's late hand.

58

having but a poor Notion of the requisite Delicacy of our own, in relation to some nicer points.

I did not design that any body should have known the Author; but those three or four Friends to whom I could not help owning it, would not let me have my own way: And I have suffer'd by it, as well in my own Mind, as in the Malice and Envy of others. But altho' I have been expostulated with, on one or two Hints in the Piece, that have not pleas'd some People, and altho' I am now known, I will not where the cause of Virtue is concern'd, trim one bit, in the future two Volumes, as some People expect I should and yet I have no Pleasure in giving Offence to any Body. Nor is it the Design of the Piece that I should. But yet 'tis impossible in general Conversation, now the Girl is lifted up into genteeler Life, to avoid some things, that may be a little touching, altho' I shall not Study for the Occasions, any more than to shirk them when they offer.[8]

I should rejoice, dear Madam, to hear of your better Health, and of every thing that gives you Pleasure. My humble Respects to the good Doctor, to Mrs. Newman, and your young Painter, as well as to the worthy Physician and I should have first said to your Spouse, tho' I am not personally known to him.[9] My Wife Joins in the same, most cordially. She often speaks of you and Miss with great Respect and Pleasure.[10] I am, Madam, Your most Faithful and Obedient Servant.[11]

[8] From 'Nor is it the Design' to the end of the paragraph is crossed out in SR's late hand.
[9] The 'worthy Physician' is Barber's oldest son, Constantine Barber (1714–83), who studied medicine and eventually became professor at Trinity College Dublin as well as president of the Royal College of Physicians of Ireland. Barber was married to Rupert Barber (d. 1777?), a Dublin woollen draper. It is not known who 'Mrs. Newman' was.
[10] 'Miss' is probably Barber's daughter, Mira.
[11] In his late hand, SR emends the final paragraph: 'My humble Respects to &c. &c. &c. My Wife Joins in the most cordial Respects to your Self, and the young Ladies, with, Madam, Your most Faithful and Obedient Servant'.

Richardson to Ralph Allen

Thursday 8 October 1741

MS: FM XVI, 1, f. 67. Copy in Gilbert Hill's hand.
Endorsement: 'To M^r. Allen of Bath' (in Hill's hand);[1] 'LX.' and 'Answer to N°.LIX.' (in SR's hand).

8th Oct. 1741

Good Sir,

I did indeed tarry near a Month before I wou'd put to Press the two Sheets I troubled you with, in Hopes of your kind Corrections. And then I proceeded supposing that your great Affairs would not allow me that desirable Favour.

You give me, Sir, no small encouragement in your Approbation of one or two Letters in the Sheets I sent you. And I wish I had in Time been favoured with your kind hint in relation to the genteel and generous Dismission of Mrs Jewkes. And yet, I hope, you will not be displeased, when you see upon what Terms she is continued in the Family, and the intire Reformation which her Lady's Example makes in her Morals and Behaviour.[2]

Pamela's Gratitude and Thankfulness to the Supreme Being, I have, on all such Occasions, as my Judgment wou'd enable me to think proper, kept up: And it was my Intention to avoid Affectation on this Head. And if Mr Allen,[3] when he comes to see the Piece, shall be of Opinion that I have, I shall think myself very happy: For I had rather have his Approbation, in any serious, pious or beneficient Turn, than that of Hundreds; since such wou'd be the Approbation of a Gentleman, the constant Tenor of whose Life distinguishes in him a Rectitude of Thinking, and a Benevolence of Mind, equal, at least, to all that the 4 Volumes of Pamela can pretend to inculcate.[4]

Your Objection to a Passage in one of the introductory Letters, is as just as it is kind; and I wish I had adverted to it before; But when I come to perfect the Design in the Publication of the New Volumes, I am advised to omit both the Introductory Preface in

---

[1] This has been subsequently crossed through.
[2] In a previous letter, now lost, Allen seems to have offered SR feedback on early print-offs of some of the sheets that would eventually constitute *Pamela II*, though they reached SR too late for inclusion in the first edition.
[3] The letters 'llen' have been subsequently crossed through.
[4] I.e. *Pamela* as well as *Pamela II*.

ANONYMOUS TO RICHARDSON, SUNDAY 11 OCTOBER 1741

the future Editions of the two first: And shall do it in an Octavo Edition I am Printing, which is to have Cuts to it, done by the Best Hands. And indeed the Praises in those Pieces are carried so high, that since I cou'd not pass as the Editor only, as I once hoped to do, I wish they had never been Inserted.[5]

I hope, Sir, to publish by the latter End of November: The Copy is all finish'd; But the Number Printed, being large, makes it tedious at the Press.[6]

If it wou'd be any Amusement at a Leisure Hour, for you, or your Lady, half a Line from Mr Leake[7] shall command for you the Sheets as done; and then, possibly the Octavo Edition will receive a Benefit by your kind Remarks, which this in Twelves cannot have. I am, Good Sir, with thankful Acknowledgements for the Favour of your kind Letter, Your most obliged and faithful humble Servant.

[5] In the same lost letter, Allen must have dispensed gentle criticism of one of the many letters of fulsome praise with which SR had stuffed the introduction to *Pamela* from the second edition onwards. SR had just published a fifth edition in duodecimo (on 22 September) and was preparing the lavishly illustrated sixth edition (to appear on 8 May 1742) in the larger octavo size, which contained engravings by Francis Hayman (1707/8–76) and Hubert-François Gravelot (1699–1773) (*ODNB*). In that later edition, SR would heed Allen's advice and cut the praise by replacing the commendatory letters with extensive synopses and contents lists.

[6] In the event, the two volumes of *Pamela II* did not appear until 7 December. The print run for this 'large' edition is not known; there are indications that the third edition of *Pamela*, in duodecimo like the first edition of *Pamela II*, ran to 3,000 copies (see *Pamela*, p. lxiv, n. 95) – itself a large edition for the period – and SR may have anticipated that his sequel would enjoy comparable popularity.

[7] The letters 'eake' have been subsequently crossed through.

Anonymous to Richardson

Sunday 11 October 1741

MS: FM XVI, 1, ff. 68–71. Copy in Gilbert Hill's hand.
Endorsement: 'LXI.' (in SR's hand).

October 11th 1741

Sir,

If the inclosed Letter from Lady Davers to Pamela will be of any Service to you in the Beginning of your 3rd Vol.[1] (where it

[1] I.e. the beginning of *Pamela II*.

ANONYMOUS TO RICHARDSON, SUNDAY II OCTOBER 1741

necessarily must come in, if at all) you have the Liberty of using it, with or without Alterations as it may best answer your Design, which (as a Friend to Virtue) I heartily wish to succeed, and am Yours, unknown, &c.[2]

We were within an Hour or two of setting out to wait upon our Dear Brother and Sister, when the unexpected Arrival of Lord and Lady Wickam made us defer our Journey a little longer. They design'd, it seems, to have been with us last night; but through a slight Accident which befel them on the Road, were forced to stop short at a neighboring Village, and so did not reach Davers-Hall till about Eight this morning.

Though they are both of them the best Natured and best behaved Persons in the World, and have a turn for Conversation the most easy and agreeable, and have besides been our intimate Friends for some Years, I can't help saying, that I could freely have dispensed with their visit at this juncture, and was resolved in my Mind (as soon as I heard they were come) no farther to press their stay than the common Rules of Civility and good Manners would necessarily oblige me.

Indeed, my dear Sister, (for I call you so with great Truth, as well as infinite Satisfaction) I was so full of my intended Journey, and had formed to myself such a Scene of Pleasure in our proposed happy Interview, that, had not Beck, who was looking toward the Window, and saw them drive into the Court, very artfully guarded against a Surprize; by imparting to me gradually the News of their arrival, I should have been too much Shock'd to have recover'd myself sufficiently to have receiv'd them without apparent Marks of disorder.

But, in they came; and with the best looks we could put on, we were all ready to bid them welcome.

After the usual Compliments were over upon our first Meeting, I pleasantly ask'd my Lord, Why he did not give me joy of my new Sister? I supposed, I told him, that he had heard of my Brother's Marriage, and I expected his congratulations. Why, Madam, said he, very gravely, I can't but say that I have heard that Mr. B. is

---

[2] George Psalmanazar (1679–1763), hack writer and impostor (*ODNB*), also sent SR proposals for a new scene involving Lady Davers (not included in this volume because not sent as a letter). As he did with the letter from Lady Davers offered here, SR rejected those proposals, though not without repeatedly noting his exasperation with Psalmanazar's 'Ridiculous & improbable' ideas in the margins (see *Pamela*, p. 551, and Eaves and Kimpel, pp. 144–5).

62

ANONYMOUS TO RICHARDSON, SUNDAY 11 OCTOBER 1741

Married. But I should not have taken Notice of it at the time, had
not You thought fit to begin the Discourse. Lady Davers is one of
the last Persons upon Earth, that I would willingly make uneasy.
And I can never imagine that such an unequal Match can be very
Pleasing to her. Indeed, my lord, said I, though I had once other
views for my Brother, (and then I smiled upon Lady Betty) there
is nobody in this Company, I assure you, but who thinks him very
happily Married, unless your Lordship and your good Lady should
be of a different Opinion; which however, I dare say, you will not
persevere in, when you know the Character of the lovely Creature,
whom I have the Honour and Happiness to call my Sister. Are you
really in Earnest, says he, still continuing his Gravity? I protest,
I don't know, what to make of this. Lord Davers, is my Lady in
Earnest in what she says? Certainly, my Lord, says he, we are both
highly delighted with my Brother's Match; and you will say that
we have ample Reason to be so, when you know all. Well, says
Lord Wickam, I will ask no more Questions, and immediately
coming up and saluting me, Madam, says he, I heartily give you
Joy. And then addressing himself to Lady Betty, May I give you joy
too, Lady Betty, says my Lord? If your Lordship pleases, says she
Smiling; for, upon my Word, I shall have great Joy, in so charming
an Acquaintance as Mrs B; and Lady Davers has been so good as
to promise me, that I shall very soon have the Happiness of being
perfectly acquainted with her. Nay to tell you the Truth, my Lord
(for Lady Betty you must know was a good deal Nettled at their
coming so critically and preventing us from setting out) had you
arrived two Hours later, we should all of us have been on the way
toward Mr B's House. I wish my Dear, says my Lord, turning
to Lady Wickam, that we had not come in this grave Dress; for
this good Company should not have staid an Hour here upon our
Account, for we wou'd have went with them. Lady Davers knows
that next to her own Lord who has been my intimate Friend from
my Childhood, there is no Man living whom I affect more, and
have a more sincere Esteem for, than her Brother Mr B. But,
indeed we dressed ourselves in this plain Manner out of Tenderness
to Lady Davers, whom we expected to find in a Condition very
different from what we have now the Pleasure to see her in. And,
my good Lady, added he taking me by the Hand, if you will put off
your Visit only for two Days, I will instantly dispatch a Servant for
other Cloaths for us, and my Wife and I shall take it as a Favour

63

ANONYMOUS TO RICHARDSON, SUNDAY II OCTOBER 1741

to bear you Company to Mr B's. I told my Lord that he was very obliging, and that I should be doubly Welcome, I know, to my Brother and Sister, when they saw, what Noble Guests I brought with me.

I had no sooner said this and rung the Bell, and order'd Breakfast to be served in, but Lady Wickam desired the Butler to bid her Woman come to her in the next room, and that he wou'd tell my Lord's Gentleman to attend his Master at the same time. Beck has since told me that they had Orders from their Lord and Lady to take the Coach and Servants home, and to be here again on Thursday Night without fail, with the New Coach, New Liveries, My Lord and Lady's Birth-day Suits,[3] Jewels &c.

When the Tea Things were removed, and the Servant had left the Room, Lady Wickam (who had all along been remarkably Silent and Attentive to what had been said) hoped, as she expressed herself, that I wou'd not think her Impertinent, if she begged a farther Account of this lovely Sister of mine; for truly, says she, Lady Davers, my Lord and I were told, that your Brother had thrown himself away, upon your Mother's Waiting-maid. And I should be glad, therefore, methinks, as you seem so vastly delighted with his Choice, that you would let us into more Particulars before we see the Bride. That shall be my Task, says Lady Betty; and I will give you a full History of the Bride in her own Words, this very Instant, if Lady Davers will permit me. Shall I fetch, Madam, says she to me, our charming Pamela's Journal, and entertain my Lord and Lady Wickam with the most Surprizing Story they ever heard. I'll send to Beck for it, my Dear, says I, presently. Indeed said she, you must let me fetch it; for I am quite unhappy till I begin. And away she ran, and was back again with it in a Trice.

And now, my Dear Sister, I wish for your own happy Memory, that I might recount what passed among us, while Lady Betty was Reading the charming Narrative. I can only tell you in short, that every Soul sighed for you, every Eye wept for you, every Heart aked for you, and every Tongue applauded you: When Dinner-time drew nigh, we agreed by joint Consent to postpone it, being determined one and all, that nothing should interrupt us till Lady Betty had read the Journal through. When the whole was finished, Lord and Lady Wickam, rising from their Seats came and wish'd us Joy

---

[3] 'A dress worn on the King's birthday' (*OED*).

64

ANONYMOUS TO RICHARDSON, SUNDAY 11 OCTOBER 1741

again of our happy Alliance in the most Affectionate and ingaging manner. They blessed your good Father and Mother, they Blessed your Sweet Self a thousand Times over, and they pronounced my Brother to be the happiest Man breathing. I'll be hanged, says Lord Wickam, looking earnestly upon Lord Davers, if this fortunate Brother of yours has not married Plato's Virtue. And, (as Tully has foretold us) we shall all certainly be in Love with her, when we see her.[4] Dear Lady Davers, says Lady Wickam, kissing me, secure me a Place in your amiable Sister's Breast, and let me be ranked in the Number of her most sincere Admirers and Friends. And pray, Madam, says Lady Betty, remember what you have promised me and don't let me be Jockied in the Wife, as I have been in the Husband; for a second Disappointment, I assure you, would be infinitely worse, than the first was; and I should be forced to wear Willow indeed.[5]

But my Paper admonishes me, that it is Time to put an end to this long Letter. And yet I cannot do it, without desiring you, my Dear Dear Sister, to forgive the cruel Part, which my passionate Pride incited me to act by you at B—n Hall. I am now as thorough a Convert to your transcendent Virtue, as my beloved Brother was, when, in the Rapture of his Soul, he took the well-judg'd Resolution to make you his Wife. I am in truth so like my Brother upon this Occasion, that I shall think every Minute a Day till I find myself in your Embraces, which I hope to do on Friday Night. In the mean Time, our best Love and most ardent Wishes attend you both. I am my dearest Brother's and Sister's most Affectionate Sister, and humble Servant

M. Davers

Tuesday Night

11' o Clock

P. S. I don't well understand, what Lord Wickam meant by Plato's Virtue, and what he said of Tully; but I take it for granted that my Brother can inform you, and that it was the highest

---

[4] Cf. Philip Sidney's rendering of Plato's concept of beauty, taken from the *Phaedrus*, in his *Defence*: 'if the saying of Plato and Tully [i.e. Cicero] be true, that who could see virtue would be wonderfully ravished with the love of her beauty' (*Defence of Poesie* [1595], F2r).

[5] 'Jockied' means to be cheated; to wear the willow is to mourn for a lost lover (see *OED*, def. 1.d.).

STEPHEN DUCK TO RICHARDSON, WEDNESDAY 14 OCTOBER 1741

Compliment, that Lord Wickam could pay you; for he is quite in Raptures, when he speaks of you.

My nephew who is greatly your Admirer, says, That, if you will forgive his Rudeness in the Parlour at B—n Hall, he will never draw his Sword again, but in Defence of Virtue and Pamela.[6]

[6] After an altercation between Lady Davers and Pamela, Lady Davers's nephew, Jackie, threatens to draw his sword on Pamela to prevent her leaving the room with Mrs Jewkes (*Pamela*, p. 364).

Stephen Duck to Richardson

Wednesday 14 October 1741

MS: FM XVI, 1, f. 72. Copy in Gilbert Hill's hand.
Endorsement: 'LXII.' (in SR's hand).

Kew, October 14th 1741

Dear Sir,

I hope you will receive your Papers[1] safe, which I have sent by the Waterman.[2] I have read them over and am mightily pleased with the diversity of Style and Manners so justly adapted to each particular Character. Homer's Achilles is not better distinguished by his Courage, Anger, and Impetuosity of Temper, than your Heroine Pamela, by her Virtue, Prudence, Gratitude, and dutyfull Behaviour.[3] But I know not how it is, I do not feel my Mind Affected and Interested so much for Pamela in this Third Volume, as I did in the two former. In this she is always Happy, in the others frequently Miserable, and had no sooner surmounted one Danger for which we rejoiced, than she encounter'd another, for which we equally grieved. In the first part of her Life, Plots, Intrigues, and Distress were continually moving Compassion for her, kept the Mind in a Happy Suspence, and made us concerned

[1] Part of the manuscript of *Pamela II*.
[2] A common method of transport of both persons and goods in this period.
[3] Duck alludes to a prominent critical debate in the early eighteenth century over the nature of the epic hero, epitomized by Achilles in Homer's *Iliad*. Richard Blackmore argued in the modern era a true hero could be proved through suffering (rather than action). John Dennis forcibly disagreed. See Blackmore's *Paraphrase on the Book of Job* (1700) and Dennis's letter in response to Blackmore in his *Original Letters Familiar, Moral, and Critical* (1721).

66

RICHARDSON TO STEPHEN DUCK, <OCTOBER OR NOVEMBER 1741>

for her besieged Virtue, 'till the Day of her Marriage; but I am
somewhat doubtful that these moving Incidents will be wanting in
this Second Part from the very Nature of the Subject which seems
too barren of Distress to excite our Pity. But, dear Sir, Pardon me,
I beg you; I wou'd not have said so much did I not love you, nor do
I say this to insinuate that the Book will not be a very useful one,
for I believe it will on several accounts, but my Affection and good
Wishes to you, make me afraid, lest it should not equal the former,
which wou'd make all your Friends be sorry especially Your most
Affectionate, humble Servant

S. Duck

Richardson to Stephen Duck

<October or November 1741>[1]

MS: FM XVI, 1, f. 73. Copy in Gilbert Hill's hand.
Endorsement: 'LXIII.' (in SR's hand).

My Answer to the preceding of Mr. Duck (Not sent)[2]

Dear Sir,

I am very thankful to you for your *general* Opinion so kindly
and like a true Friend given me:[3] But what I wanted was, that
you wou'd be so good as to point out *particular* Faults, which I
might correct before I put to Press our 8vo Edition, which is to
accompany an Octavo Size now Printing of the first Two Volumes.
An excellent Physician[4] was so good as to give me a Plan to break
Legs and Arms and to fire Mansion Houses to create Distresses;
But my Business and View was to aim at Instruction in a genteel
and usual Married Life. I expect not the Demand the two former
had: But I hate so much the French Marvellous[5] and all un-natural
Machinery, and have so often been disgusted with that sort of
Management of those Pieces,[6] that I am contented to give up my

[1] This letter is the draft of an answer to Duck to SR, 14 October 1741; SR would probably
have drafted his answer in the weeks following Duck's letter.
[2] 'of Mr. Duck (Not sent)' has been crossed through.
[3] See Duck to SR, 14 October 1741.
[4] See Cheyne to SR, 24 August 1741.
[5] SR and other English authors ridiculed implausible French prose fiction popular at the
time.
[6] 'of those Pieces' has been crossed through.

67

Profit, if I can but Instruct. I am very sensible that there cannot, *naturally*, be the room for Plots, Stratagem and Intrigue in the present Volumes as in the first. And *Nature* is my whole View, and such a Conduct in such a Life, as may generally happen, and be of Use. Hence you'll see in the succeeding Sheets, Plans for her Charity to the Poor, her Sunday Behaviour, Family Management, Table Conversations with her Polite Neighbours, the Pregnant circumstance to a mind so Apprehensive as Pamela's, a Debate about Mothers being Nurses to their own Children; an Intrigue of her Waiting-Maid with Lord Jackey, and her Behaviour in a Case so like[7] her own;[8] her Observations on a Tragedy, a Comedy, an Italian Opera, and a Masquerade; from the last of which will arise a Distress, that, possibly, will answer your kind Objection; in a Strong Jealous Scene. – Then her Opinion and Practice on the Subject of a first Education &c – And this is a general Sketch of my Design. (How it will be executed, is another thing). By all which you'll observe that *Instruction* is my main End, and if I can *Entertain* at the same time my View will be Complete; and when the four Volumes shall appear together, it will then be a piece of natural Life, with the *ups* and *downs*, the *Stormy* and the *Sedate*, that we generally find it, or (as to *Sedate*) hope to find it.

I only beg, my dear Friend, you'll take no notice to any one, that you have seen the Sheets. Because People will be asking for your Opinion, and I am so much convinced of your Friendship, that I should suspect your Partiality in my Favour, may wound your Judgment.[9]

I am, dear Sir, Your Faithful and Obliged Servant,

S. R.

---

[7] 'what' added as a superscription in SR's hand.
[8] 'was' added as a superscription in SR's hand.
[9] This entire paragraph has been crossed through.

An English Printer in Dublin[1] to Richardson

Thursday 12 November 1741

Printed source: Address to the Public, 9.
First printing: Address to the Public (1754).

I was yesterday in company with some Printers that I knew in London: Among other things in conversation, they familiarly commended Mr. Faulkner's *great diligence* in London;[2] and, after naming several pieces of which he had procured early copies, I understood he had been furnished with the Third and Fourth volumes of *Pamela*, sheet by sheet, as far as is done, from your Press; and is printing them off here with all speed – The truth of this information may be depended upon.

---

[1] Identified as such in the source for this letter, SR's *Address to the Public*. We have not discovered a more specific attribution.
[2] George Faulkner, the Dublin printer and bookseller (see Barber to SR, 26 August 1741). Faulkner had reprinted *Pamela* as well as Kelly's spurious continuation, *Pamela's Conduct in High Life*, in 1740. Now, SR is told, Faulkner has gone so far as to clandestinely print *Pamela II* from sheets smuggled out of SR's London print shop. Faulkner would be involved again in a similar ploy thirteen years later, when Dublin printers brought out an edition of *Grandison* reprinted from sheets stolen from SR's warehouses in London. *An Address to the Public* describes the controversy and SR's feeling of betrayal by a colleague with whom he had worked successfully in the Irish publication of *Clarissa* and with whom he had hoped to publish an authorized edition of *Grandison*.

Solomon Lowe[1] to Richardson

Monday 21 December 1741

MS: FM XVI, 1, f. 78. Copy in Gilbert Hill's hand.
Endorsement: 'LXX.' (in SR's hand).

Hammersmith, December 21 1741

Sir,
I writ to you sometime ago, about an Advertisement, which I sent you; and shou'd have been glad to have had it publisht if you had no Objection to it – Some greater Engagements, I presume, put it out of your Mind, because I heard nothing more – However,

---

[1] Solomon Lowe (d. 1750), grammarian and schoolmaster.

SOLOMON LOWE TO RICHARDSON, MONDAY 21 DECEMBER 1741

I design'd to have waited on you last Thursday, when I was in Town; but indeed was asham'd, fearing that my French Grammar[2] would never answer your Demands on me. But, be that as it may, I do assure you, Sir, if Providence should ever put it in my Power to pay you otherwise (as I am not without Hope that it will) you will find that I have a Heart full of Gratitude, though rather, because, in the little I have had to do with you, I have observ'd something so very amiable in your whole Manner, that I cannot forbear telling you, that I always think of you with Pleasure.

You will not wonder, therefore, if I trespass on you further to congratulate you on account of Pamela; which besides answering the great End you had in View, and that in the most engaging manner; has proved of so much Service to your very Brethren; witness the Labours of the press in Piracies, in Criticisms, in Cavils, in Panegyrics, in Supplements, in Imitations, in Transformations, in Translations, &c beyond anything I know of.[3]

But I check myself, for fear of offending you: On which Consideration (I flatter myself) you will pardon me; if (notwithstanding the Obligations I am under to you) I beg one favour more of you: and that is, that you be so good as to oblige my Wife and Daughters, as well as my Self, with a Sight of the two last Volumes of it,[4] which we will take care to return in very good Condition, and with many Thanks.

I wish you a good State of Health, and much Happiness; and if (in any thing) I should[5] be able to do you a Pleasure, you may most freely command, Sir Your most obedient Servant

Sol. Lowe[6]

---

[2] Solomon Lowe, *French Rudiments: Consisting of a Grammar of the Language* (London, 1740).

[3] See *'Pamela' in the Marketplace*, pp. 50–82, for discussions of the many unauthorized reprints, continuations, and spin-offs of *Pamela*.

[4] I.e. *Pamela II*.

[5] SR has added the word 'ever' here.

[6] SR has added a note: 'N.B. The Publication of the History of Pamela gave Birth to no less than 16 several Pieces under some of the above or the like Titles.' SR uses 'several' here in a now obsolete sense of separate.

David Mallet[1] to Richardson

<Between May and December 1741>

MS: FM XVI, 1, f. 15. Copy in Gilbert Hill's hand.
Endorsement: 'V.' (in SR's hand).

Dear Sir,

Do me the Favour to forward the enclosed to our Friend Mr. Hill.[2] I find there is a Second Part of Pamela Advertised:[3] If it is by the Author of the First I shall expect it with Impatience and with Pleasure.[4] If it is the Work of another Hand, I am resolved never to look into it. Believe me to be, Sir, Your most Obedient Servant

D. Mallet.
Strand on the Green[5]

---

[1] David Mallet (formerly Malloch) (1701/2?–65), poet and playwright (*ODNB*).
[2] Aaron Hill. Mallet's enclosed letter to Hill is now lost.
[3] I.e. *Pamela II*. SR first intimated to the public that he was working on his continuation at the end of an advertisement for the 4th edition of *Pamela* in the *Daily Gazetteer* of 7 May 1741 and in subsequent weeks; Mallet might here be referring to one of these early notices or to one of the advertisements announcing the publication of *Pamela II* on 8 December 1741. We have accordingly amended the date range suggested by Eaves and Kimpel.
[4] 'with' has been crossed out.
[5] An area in Chiswick, West London.

David Mallet to Richardson

<December 1741 or early 1742>[1]

MS: FM XVI, 1, f. 15. Copy in Gilbert Hill's hand.
Endorsement: 'VI.' (in SR's hand).

Dear Sir,

I thank you heartily for the Present of your Pamela. How very agreeable it was, you will fully Imagine, when I tell you, that the very Day I receiv'd them I read over both Volumes before I went to Sleep. I am with great esteem Sir Your Obliged and most humble Servant

D. Mallet

---

[1] Date range supplied by Eaves and Kimpel.

'Reverend Morley'[1] to Richardson

\<December 1741 or early January 1742\>[2]

MS: FM XVI, 1, f. 14. Copy in Gilbert Hill's hand.
Endorsement: 'IV.' (in SR's hand); 'Extract' (in SR's late hand, in red ink).

Sir

I return you many Thanks for your agreeable Present. I can
assure you, I receiv'd so much Pleasure from the former Part,
that I sent To-day as soon as it was light, for the two remaining
Volumes; and had read great Part of one of them through, when I
had the Favour of yours: But we are so great Admirers of them at
our House, and all our Acquaintance set so high and so just a Value
on them, that if I had twenty Sets, I could keep them all employ'd.
What I have said, or indeed what any one can say, in Praise of a
Performance writ in so elegant, and at the same time in so new a
Taste, falls so short of its real worth, that it must be look'd upon
rather as a Compliment to their own[3] Judgment, than a Tribute of
Praise to you; for every one that has any Taste, must admire it; and
it is the want of it only that can make any one dislike it. You will
excuse a Letter so coarsely writ, upon a Subject that requir'd so
much Care and Delicacy, because I have neither Light to see what I
write, nor time to digest my Thoughts in a proper Order, your Boy
waiting for an answer to what you sent me, which I suppose came
from Mr Wh——.[4] But I protest, I can hardly read the hand; and
therefore you will not wonder, when I tell you, I don't understand
the subject of the Letter; I only think in general, that as there is
a proper person appointed to do these kind of things, they ought
to go through his Hands, and every one ought to keep within
their own province, to prevent confusion, and Contradictions,
and sometimes what is much worse; I need not explain myself any
further to you. I have at last made shift to find out what is in Mr.

---

[1] The Reverend Morley remains unidentified. The first part of the letter indicates that he,
like others, has enjoyed *Pamela II*. The second half of this letter alludes to a situation about
which there is no further information.

[2] Date range supplied by Eaves and Kimpel based on Morley's discussion of *Pamela II*.

[3] 'own' is an insertion in SR's hand.

[4] Unidentified.

JOHN SWINTON TO RICHARDSON, TUESDAY 19 JANUARY 1742

W.'s letter; but I think there is something too personal, to make it safe to put it in against such a person as I know the Writer it alludes to, to be. I am, Sir, your most oblig'd Humble Servant

Reverend Morley.[5]

[5] The signature is in SR's hand.

John Swinton[1] to Richardson

Tuesday 19 January 1742

MS: FM XVI, 1, f. 79. Copy in Gilbert Hill's hand.
Endorsement: 'LXXV.' (in SR's hand); 'Extract from M[r]. Swinton's Letter, dated' (in Hill's hand).[2]

Jan.ry 19th 1741/42

The precise Number of the 3d & 4th Vols of *Pamela* Sold here, I cannot learn; but this I know, that all the Senior and more intelligent Part of the University[3] highly value and esteem them. Two or three Fellows of Colleges my Acquaintance, Men eminent for their Learning and Good Sense, are full of their Praises every time I see them; and my good Friend, the Dean of Christ's Church,[4] the last Evening I spent with him, assured me they were the finest Picture of Nature he ever yet saw. He said that the Passion of Jealousy was work'd up in so fine a manner, and the Part in which this was done had so many masterly touches in it, that the perusal of it gave him infinite Pleasure. He further added

[1] John Swinton (1703–7), Church of England clergyman and orientalist, was the humanities lecturer at Wadham College, Oxford, from 1735 to 1737. Following his involvement 'in a homosexual scandal', he resigned his Oxford fellowship in 1743 to become prebendary of St Asaph on 11 October (*ODNB*). He later moved to Christ Church to earn a Bachelor of Divinity in 1759 and became Keeper of the university's archives in 1767.
[2] 'Extract from M[r]. Swinton's' has been deleted and 'of a Letter from Oxford' added in SR's hand.
[3] The University of Oxford.
[4] 'ean', 'st's', and 'urch' have been crossed through. John Conybeare (1692–1755), bishop of Bristol (1750–5), was dean of Christ Church from 1733 until his death (*ODNB*) and an outspoken opponent of Richard Newton's politics and educational reforms at Hart Hall/Hertford College; see Newton to SR, 15 May 1741. SR printed many controversial pamphlets by Newton, including an attack on Conybeare as well as Conybeare's response (1735).

73

ANONYMOUS TO RICHARDSON, SUNDAY 24 JANUARY 1742

that he had read the 3rd and 4th Vols. with great Eagerness twice, and was determin'd to give the whole a *3rd* reading immediately. I doubt not but all Persons of Good Sense & ellegant Taste, and admirers of Nature, entertain the same Sentiments of that inimitable Performance. I am Good Sir, Your most Faithful and most Obedient humble Servant

J.S.[5]

---

[5] Swinton's initials have been crossed through.

Anonymous to Richardson

Sunday 24 January 1742

MS: FM XVI, 1, ff. 80–1. Copy in Gilbert Hill's hand.
Endorsement: 'LXXVI.' (in SR's hand); 'Anonymous. Deliver'd at North-End' (in Hill's hand).

Jan.ry 24th 1741/2

Sir,

Being One among the many Thousand Admirers of your excellent Pamela, I was glad to hear you had determined to oblige the World with a Sequel to the two first Vols. but at the same time was in Pain for your Success; it being the Fate of almost all Second Parts to be treated with Indifferency, be their Merit what it will: Accordingly even yours I heard greatly censured, before I had read them; but, this not checking my Curiosity, I sent for them, and must own, have perused them with inexpressible Delight. – But first let me thank God for giving me Grace, to feel the Conviction, that none but those unhappy Wretches, who want the Blessed Influence from above, can disrelish so divine a Performance.

– And now what shall I say of it? or rather what *can* I say of it equal to its deserts? The sparkling Beauties of this bright Galaxy stand so thick they strike Confusion on the dazzled Sight, nor will permit me to single out any Star of different Magnitude. – In general, then, I think your Style very just and accurate as applied in its several Branches; in the Narrative and Historical, simple and familiar, but not mean or low; in the Descriptive somewhat more lively and florid, but not unnatural or fantastical; and in the Devotional, truly pious & Sublime without the least Tincture of

ANONYMOUS TO RICHARDSON, SUNDAY 24 JANUARY 1742

Superstition or Enthusiasm. The Characters so livelily Imaged, that 'tis[1] Nature's Self: The Manners diligently observed, and the Passions so nicely distinguished, and so deeply traced even to their own[2] very Source, That surely none but he that form'd them cou'd inspire thee with[3] more than Philosophical Penetration. How benignly is every Foible reprimanded! how invitingly is every Virtue recommended! For so well read art Thou in human Nature, that like a Skilful Physician, Thou not only shew'st the Cause of any Malady, but at the same time prescribest a proper Remedy. – And then how noble, how Christian how Godlike is the End! *To Cultivate the Principles of Virtue & Religion in the Minds of Youth!*[4] This, Sir, may be all that is intended, but what more blessed Consequences must follow from the Perusal of this Piece, be it read but with a tolerable Turn of Mind? Will it not be of Service through every Stage of Life, and to every Individual? Will the Coquet any longer delight in her vain Triumph? or the Prude in Sullenness and ill-nature? Will not the profuse and Vain force themselves from the Enchanting Circle? and the worn-out Debauchee, instead of re-enjoying his past Follies in Idea, contemn them with the utmost Abhorrence, and with a truly penitent Heart turn to God e'er it be too late to hope for Mercy?

– And what can be more serviceable to these noble Purposes, than those admirable Reflexions that are scatter'd throughout the Whole, Reflexions made in so nice a Taste, and upon such Sound Principles that I cou'd not help culling them out, and Transcribing them, in order to consider them in a closer View; and indeed the more I consider them, the more I admire them, as we do the Works of Nature, and doubt not but they were both form'd under the direction of the same God.

Sir, I am only speaking of the 3 first Volumes, for I want Words to express the inimitable Excellency of the last. Be it enough, that in my humble Opinion, I think it one of the most Entertaining, most Instructive Books, that have as yet appear'd in the *English* Language.

– This in general, perhaps I may touch upon the Particulars hereafter; but I must not Subscribe my Name, least, lying under

---

[1] 'our' inserted in SR's hand.
[2] 'own' crossed out in SR's hand.
[3] 'such' inserted in SR's hand.
[4] A phrase taken from *Pamela*'s title page.

ANTHONY FULFORD TO RICHARDSON, MONDAY 25 JANUARY 1742

great very great[5] Obligations to you, the Dictates of a sincere
and grateful Heart should be mistaken for Sycophancy and mere
Compliment, which meanesses not to despise after reading *Pamela*,
wou'd be as impossible as not to admire and revere the great[6]
Genius, that shines so conspicuous in the composure of it. I am,
Sir, Your most obliged and humble Servant.

[5] 'very great' has been crossed through.
[6] 'great' has been crossed through.

Anthony Fulford[1] to Richardson

Monday 25 January 1742

MS: FM XVI, 1, f. 82. Copy in Gilbert Hill's hand.
Endorsement: 'LXXVII.' (in SR's hand).

Jan.ry 25 1741–2

Sir,
After the Approbation of my learned Friend,[2] I have sent
you those Lines I read to you with a few Amendments; by way
of Prologue, they may be of no disservice to your new Edition
of Pamela. I take it to be of a quite different nature than those
Commendatory Letters you design to Omit. Friendly prefatory
Verses we have most of the Antients as Examples of it; and many
of the most Considerable Moderns, in that respect, Copying
them: however, I will Submit it to your own determination. I don't
desire you verbally to conceal the Author of them; and was I not
at present about taking a Dignified Degree in Oxford,[3] shou'd not
scruple publickly Subscribing to them; but indeed the Author of
any Verses wou'd appear inconsistent with that Character. I heartily
wish you good Success in your Undertaking; and am, Sir, Much
your Humble Servant

A. F.[4]

[1] Anthony Fulford (*c.* 1714–54), Vicar at Toller Porcorum in Dorset (1747–54).
[2] Unidentified.
[3] Fulford was awarded the MA in 1741. 'Dignified Degree' was not a technical term. However, 'dignified' referred to ecclesiastical matters (*OED*).
[4] 'ulford.' inserted in SR's hand to complete the last name.

76

Anonymous to Richardson

\<Before Tuesday 26 January 1742>

MS: FM XVI, 1, ff. 83–4. Copy in Gilbert Hill's hand.
Endorsement: 'LXXVIII' (in SR's hand); 'To the Author of Pamela; or, Virtue Rewarded' and 'Received Jan.ʸ 26ᵗʰ 1741/42' (in Hill's hand).

Sir,
Among the many Addresses and Expressions of Admiration or rather Affection your Excellent Piece called Pamela must have given you the Trouble of, none has probably come from a Meaner Hand than the Present. Nor can any thing New be said by this Time of that Master-piece of Human Wit, in which tho' Art is every where diffused, it can be traced no-where; in which tho' all is elaborate & Exact, yet all is easy and flowing; whose irresistible Influence over the Heart, eludes and turns into Ridicule the rigid Rules of Criticism; and whose Morality (which is severe enough for a System for Angels) has the unaccountable Power of gaining our Love, whilst it makes us hate even our dear selves. And tho' I know not how to make my Presumption in this address appear pardonable, yet being convinced from the Feeling you every where discover in your Writings that you are as much Master of the Practice as the Theory of Virtue; and that the animated, the glorious, the striking Representations you have drawn of Seraphic Excellence and Perfection are copied from your Heart, not your Fancy; having conceived so high an Opinion of your Worth, I could not be at rest without giving vent to the Overflowings of a rude, though Sincere Admiration and Gratitude. And if you should send me any Answer, as I know not how good-natured you may be, I really think, tho' I am not Superstitious I should regard a bit of Paper from your Hands, in the same manner as Bigots[1] do Amulets and Relics of Saints.

I hope and wish for the good of the Public that you will again and again employ your exquisite Hand and well-disposed Heart to awaken a harden'd and lethargic Age. This is a bad Character, though more hopeful than that of a Profligate and abandon'd one (which I don't think applicable to the present bad as it is). If you should oblige your Country with any more of your Productions, I beg leave to recommend to you (for where shall such another

---

[1] 'a superstitious adherent of religion. *Obs.*' (*OED*); here especially aimed at Catholics.

ANONYMOUS TO RICHARDSON, <BEFORE TUESDAY 26 JANUARY 1742>

Hand be found) that you would give us the Representation of Virtue in the lowest Stations of Life, as you have already in the higher. Perhaps my Thought is Chimerical,[2] but I would fain persuade myself that some Way might be found by which People of moderate or even of small Fortunes, might enjoy a Share of the transporting Pleasure of Benevolence, which it is commonly thought, none but the Rich can taste of. I am myself but about 26 years of Age, and consequently have a reasonable Prospect of many Years, in which I might do an infinite deal of Good, if I had the Advantage of Fortune, or of such a Capacity as yours. You have procured yourself the Blessing of Thousands: The Consciences of the Guilty you have awaken'd; you have confirmed the staggering Virtue of the Weak, and better'd the Hearts of the most perfect: The Man of Fortune too can command the Prayers of Numbers every Day and every Hour: And must I like your poor Esau have no Blessing because I want what it was not in my Power to procure myself?[3] If I had Reason to think my Heart ill-disposed for doing worthy Actions, I shou'd not be so concern'd at my want of the Opportunities; but as I have the Pleasure to reflect, that 5 or 6 People in a rising Way owe their All to me, besides many[4] pieces of kindness I have done to others, I think it something of a Pity but I, as well as some other People I know had[5] more in our Power to do good by some other Means, since the above mention'd two are out of our reach. To make but one or two People happy in a whole Year, or perhaps not so much as one or two in a Year, is mere trifling. If one could have the Prayers of some Hundreds whom one had relieved from Poverty, Diseases, or Vice, &c. one might imagine such a Number might have some Influence at the Throne of Heaven.

If you could find Time to throw together a few Thoughts on this Subject (for certainly your Thoughts on any Subject relating to Virtue must be ripe and well digested) I should think myself infinitely obliged to you for communicating them by Letter. I once was so happy as to be Instrumental in reclaiming a Rake by means of an Anonymous Letter I sent him; I have been thinking, that I

---

[2] Here in the sense of 'vainly or fantastically conceived, imaginary, fanciful' (*OED*).
[3] Elder son of Isaac, cheated out of his inheritance and his father's blessing by his brother, Jacob (Genesis 27:1–46).
[4] 'particular' inserted in SR's hand.
[5] 'it' inserted in SR's hand.

78

ANONYMOUS TO RICHARDSON, <BEFORE TUESDAY 26 JANUARY 1742>

might lay out Time to very good Purpose by giving useful Hints to inconsiderate People of both Sexes, in the same Manner; and if you approve of it I shall never let slip an useless Hour after this Time. To Conclude this enormous Letter; if you will oblige me with a few Lines, directed to Mr. Willis at the South-sea House Coffee-House, Bishopsgate Street,[6] the Favour shall never be forgotten by, Sir, Your Sincere Friend & Admirer.

P. S. On looking back upon the above, I begin to fear you may be apt to mistake my Warmth for Flattery, as the Style of Sincerity is often usurped by those who are Strangers to that Virtue. To shew you therefore that I don't praise your Admirable Piece at the Expence of my Sincerity, I will venture to hint an Imperfection in it, viz. That it might, perhaps, have shewed more Effectually Mr. B's Address in assaulting the Virtue of a Lady of Pamela's excessive Delicacy, and likewise shewed more effectually her Prudence and Strictness of Chastity, had Mr. B. instead of treating Pamela as his Servant, given her voluntarily a Settlement of £100 per Annum as[7] allowance proportion'd to the Education she Receiv'd from his Mother, and afterwards begun his Attack, and carried on his Designs, till Pamela had found herself Obliged to give up the above Settlement, and loose his kindness entirely.[8] The Articles he offers must Startle a Virgin; whereas to yield her Chastity to one she loved, and owed so much to, might appear more disinterested. I hope you will forgive this and am as above &c.

---

[6] Coffee houses were popular sites for exchanging semi-anonymous letters. Correspondents would use real names, initials, or pseudonyms in providing ways for others to contact them. There were two South Sea Houses: one, the Old South Sea House, in Broad Street and the other, the New South Sea House (built 1720–27), at the junction of Bishopsgate Street and Threadneedle Street. Both had coffee houses associated with them. Evidence exists for the Bishopsgate coffee house being active in the 1740s, but little else is known; see Bryant Lillywhite, *London Coffee Houses: A Reference Book of Coffee Houses of the Seventeenth, Eighteenth, and Nineteenth Centuries* (London: Allen & Unwin, 1963), p. 541. It is impossible to determine whether 'Willis' is an actual name or a pseudonym.

[7] 'an' inserted in SR's hand.

[8] Lady Davers's nephew, Jackey, promises to settle £100 per year on Pamela's maid Polly in return for sexual favours, and Polly happily complies, in *Pamela II*, pp. 245–57. SR had published the sequel only a month before this letter, so it is not clear whether his correspondent had read the passage and did not remember it as the source for his idea, or whether he serendipitously hit on the same plot element. SR does not refer to *Pamela II* in his response to and refutation of the idea, either; see SR to Anonymous, 27 January 1742.

Richardson to Anonymous

Wednesday 27 January 1742

MS: FM XVI, 1, ff. 85–6. Copy in Gilbert Hill's hand.
Endorsement: 'LXXIX.' (in SR's hand); 'Answer to the foregoing Letter' (in Hill's hand).

Jan. 27 1741/2

Sir,

Altho' I am an absolute Stranger to You, yet the Favour of your Letter, and more particularly the Benevolence that appears every where in it to your Fellow-Creatures, intitles you to my Acknowledgements, and the Answer you desire from me.

But what shall I say as to the principal part of the Subject, to a Gentleman who must know, That the Will[1] to do good according to our Power, is all that is required of us. It must needs be a very great Pleasure to such a Mind as yours seems to be, that at so early an Age you have been the means of doing great good to several Persons; and still more of being an Instrument of reclaiming a wicked Man; And whatever your own[2] Heart can suggest to you to do in the same Way, will no doubt if prudently performed yield you great Pleasure upon Reflexion. As to the Power you so earnestly wish for; If I may be excused for quoting the little Work you mention with so much Favour, it will be observed that the *poor Pamela* took as much Delight in dispensing her Lady's Bounty to worthy Objects, as the *rich Mr. B.* could: And her Benevolence was no less distinguishable in the one Station, than in the other; altho' in the one it was but a passive Virtue as I may say, while in the other it was an active one. And why? Because in the one she *wanted* the *Power*; which in the other she *had*: And hence you will observe, Sir, that the same Piece gives the Example you wish for of Benevolence in Low Life; and she frequently Observes, that if her Will to do good should not be proportionably inlarged with her Power, she must be a very ingrateful Creature, and unworthy of her Elevation.

I am much obliged to you, Sir, for the Instance you give in Postscript of your Sincerity in the Favour you express for this Piece. But I believe when you reconsider the Matter with all its

---

[1] 'Will' underlined for emphasis in SR's hand.
[2] 'worthy' inserted in SR's hand.

RICHARDSON TO ANONYMOUS, WEDNESDAY 27 JANUARY 1742

Circumstances; and how much the Settlement of the 100 £ per Annum must have subjected her to the World's Censure; who would have thought she must have paid the highest Consideration for it: which[3] must have destroy'd or weaken'd the Influences of her Example.[4] How likely, had it been in her own Power, her Duty to her poor Parents, wou'd have made her share that Allowance with them: How apprehensive they would have been of her taking it, who were so scrupulous about her accepting a few Guineas, and some of her Lady's Apparel. How little Mr. B. doubted obtaining all his Ends, by taking Advantage of the low Fortune of her Parents and distressful Circumstances; How much his Love was increased by her unexpected resistance; How obstinately she refused taking any Money from him either for herself or Parents, till she knew what the one or the other was to do for it; I say, Sir, If you weigh the Matter with these Circumstances, I believe you will think that[5] would not have been an Alteration for the better: Especially as she every where expresses in her low State (what you Suggest)[6] a great contempt of Money, and that this is one of her Virtues, and accounts the more naturally for her despising and rejecting the most alluring Temptations. However, Sir, I can see in this very Objection a virtuous and a generous Motive in the Objector; and I thank you for it, as I shall do any Gentleman who will be so kind as to suggest any thing that would make the Piece more Perfect, as I am very sensible it might be made.[7] I am, Sir, Your humble Servant.

[3] 'however unjust' inserted in SR's hand.
[4] See Anonymous to SR, <Before 26 January 1742>.
[5] 'what you suggest' inserted in SR's hand.
[6] The content of this bracket has been crossed out in SR's hand.
[7] 'made' crossed out in SR's hand.

SIX LADIES TO RICHARDSON, <JANUARY OR FEBRUARY> 1742

Six Ladies to Richardson

<January or February> 1742[1]

MS: FM XVI, 1, ff. 16–17. Copy in Gilbert Hill's hand.
Endorsement: 'VII.' (in SR's hand); 'From Anonymous VI Ladies. Post Mark Reading. Directed to Mr. Richardson Bookseller in Salisbury Court, Fleet Street.' (in Hill's hand).

To the Editor of Pamela, or Virtue Rewarded

Sir,

I beg pardon for adding to the Number of Impertinents that have sollicited you about the above-mention'd Books; but I and a few Female Friends that often meet, have read your two First Volumes with great Pleasure, your Continuation with no less, and think it quite worthy of the First:[2] You seem to speak at the beginning of your First and Third Volumes, as if the Story was Fact: You say it is founded in Truth & Nature: The Characters I own are Natural; but as you mention it to have Happen'd in so late a Date of Years, and intimate in your Advertisement at the End of your 4th Vol. that Pamela is not Dead, we can't think that People of the Distinction, that Mr. and Mrs. B[3] seem to be of, wou'd care to be pointed at as they must be, by People then Conversant in the Polite World, notwithstanding your altering some of the Incidents, Names, & Places. If you have, as you say, had regard to Truth, a Couple so much talk'd of in three Counties, the Admiration of a large Acquaintance, the Masquerade Affair so Public in London, cannot but be known by somebody, and would Mr. H,[4] and several others, that do not appear in the best Light, consent to have their Characters made Public? What we desire of You then, Sir, is, that you would favour this with an Answer, and say upon your Honour, which we take you to be too much of a Gentleman to violate, whether the Story is real or feigned? The Question, I own, is bold, after you have told us you have said all you think necessary, or yourself at Liberty to say: Yet we are not satisfied, but desire you to tell us, whether its Fact, or spurious; and do assure you upon

---

[1] Date range supplied by Eaves and Kimpel since the 'Ladies' have recently read *Pamela II*.
[2] 'your two First Volumes' is *Pamela*; 'your Continuation' is *Pamela II*, which SR had published on 7 December 1741.
[3] I.e. Pamela and her erstwhile-tormentor-turned-husband, Mr B.
[4] The name by which Jackey, Lady Davers's rakish nephew, goes in *Pamela II*.

82

SIX LADIES TO RICHARDSON, <JANUARY OR FEBRUARY> 1742

Honour you may freely Speak, for it shall go no farther than the above Company.

If you answer, it is true, pray send me Word, what Mrs. B did with her Wedding-ring the Night she Sup'd with Sir Jacob Swynford, as Lady Jenny; for she says in her Letter to Mr. B, it was never off of her Finger, and sure he could see a plain Gold Ring.[5]

If you answer, it is Fiction, who was the Author? We are prepared to hear either way.

Perhaps you will say you have given your Word to Answer no Questions: But that will be no Excuse; for you may give a few hints and say upon Honour, whether the Story is real or feign'd. Your Silence shall not serve your Turn; for we are so desirous to have an Answer to our Question, that we cannot, nor will not, cease Writing, till you favour us with it.

If there is such a Person as Mrs. B, I dare say, she will not be against your[6] Satisfying our Request, it redounding so much to hers, and Mr. B's Honour. If there is not, tell us ingenuously, that our Admiration may be turn'd upon the Author that could Paint the Heinousness of Vice, and the Reward of Virtue, in such true Lights and Natural Colours.

Lady Gainsborough[7] and Lady Hazlerigg,[8] we know, are exemplary Ladies, but can't find their Story in your Account. We shall esteem Ourselves, Sir, Your Obliged Humble Servants.

P.S. Don't let it be long before we hear from You. I cannot but repeat the Confidence you may repose in us; and assure you, if there is a Mrs. B, and you acquainted us with the real Names and Places, it should go no further than the Company I have

---

[5] This scene occurs in *Pamela II*, pp. 206–17, but the letter is addressed to Miss Darnford and not to Mr B. In the octavo third edition (1742), SR seems to address this point by specifying that Sir Jacob stares so much at Pamela's face that he does not notice her ring.

[6] 'your' is inserted in SR's hand.

[7] 'ainsborough' has been crossed out by Barbauld. Baptist Noel, the fourth Earl of Gainsborough (1708–51), had married his gamekeeper's daughter, Elizabeth Chapman, in 1728. She accordingly became the Countess of Gainsborough. In 1786, an essay in the *Universal Magazine* suggested that the Countess had been the real-life inspiration for SR's Pamela (see B: I, lxviii; and *'Pamela' in the Marketplace*, p. 102).

[8] 'azlerigg' has been crossed out, and 'Lady' has been inserted by Barbauld. Reference here is to Lady Hesilrige, *née* Hannah Sturges, a coachman's daughter who married Sir Arthur Hesilrige, Baronet, after being pursued and harassed by him while in service to his mother. An account of her life, *Memoirs of the Life of Lady H—, the Celebrated Pamela*, was published in 1741, in which Lady Hesilrige was being proposed as a possible original for SR's Pamela (see also B: I, lxviii; and *'Pamela' in the Marketplace*, pp. 100–4).

SAMUEL VANDERPLANK TO RICHARDSON, ‹JANUARY OR FEBRUARY› 1742

mention'd. We are Six in Number, and have sworn ourselves to Secrecy in this Affair.

Pray Direct your Answer, For Mrs. Lancelet, to be left till call'd for, with Mrs. King the Letter Carrier in Reading Berks.[9]

[9] Berkshire. 'Mrs. Lancelet', probably a pseudonym for the 'Six Ladies', may refer to the character of the surgeon Mr. Lancelet in *The Fortunate Country Maid* (1741), discussed in *'Pamela' in the Marketplace*, pp. 94, 111. Letter carriers distributed letters from the post office to local businesses and residences. 'Mrs. King' has not been identified. The entire paragraph has been crossed through in the pale greenish-grey ink that marks Anna Barbauld's editing of SR's correspondence for publication (1804). The letters exchanged between SR and the 'Reading Ladies' were not included in the *Correspondence*, but Barbauld discusses them in her 'Life of Mr. Richardson' and incorporates several phrases almost verbatim (B: I, lxvii–lxviii).

Samuel Vanderplank[1] to Richardson

‹January or February› 1742[2]

MS: FM XVI, 1, f. 20. Copy in Gilbert Hill's hand.[3]
Endorsement: 'X.' (in SR's hand).

Sir,

I will venture to add to the Number of Impertinents, by telling you that in my Opinion this pretended (Nameless) Lady is no Friend, there's such an Envious sort of Criticism runs through the Whole, as puts me in Mind of what your Ingenious Friend said, viz. 'I never says he, could endure a Lukewarm Approbation, because I always found it Neighbour'd by too fierce and Hot an Envy[4] – But if this is a Lady, she's a Bold Pullet.[5] I thank you for

[1] Samuel Vanderplank (d. 1750), SR's landlord at North End.
[2] In their list of SR's correspondence, Eaves and Kimpel suggest a date of 'c. March' for this letter, but in their narration of SR's exchanges with the 'Six Ladies' from Reading, they propose (correctly, we think) that SR and Vanderplank discussed the Ladies' identities in response to their first letter: in calling himself an 'Impertinent', Vanderplank explicitly quotes Six Ladies to SR, ‹January or February› 1742, whereas he makes no clear references to their second letter, Six Ladies to SR, ‹March› 1742.
[3] The entire letter has been crossed through in red ink.
[4] The friend is Aaron Hill, who had insisted that SR accept his enthusiastic praise of *Pamela*; see Hill to SR, 22 October 1741.
[5] A pullet is a young domestic hen, and so figuratively 'A young or inexperienced person (in early use *spec.* a young woman)' (*OED*, def. 2).

84

SIX LADIES TO RICHARDSON, <MARCH> 1742

the Pleasure you have given my Girls To-day,[6] and am always Yours very Sincerely

S Vanderplank

Friday Night.

---

[6] Vanderplank had two daughters, Hannah (d. 1803) and Ann; the families were on visiting terms. Hannah married Sir Edward Hulse on 23 February 1742. Ann was 'an intimate friend' of Sarah Wescomb by 1746 (see Eaves and Kimpel, p. 198).

Six Ladies to Richardson

<March>[1] 1742

MS: FM XVI, 1, f. 17v. Copy in Gilbert Hill's hand.
Endorsement: 'VIII.' (in SR's hand); 'From Reading Ladies. Nº 2' (in Hill's hand).

Sir,

We wou'd not have imagin'd you would have paid so little regard to the Number Six, that so justly admir'd your Pamela's and gave them their due praise (when they declared Secresy which we again repeat) as not to Answer the Question we desired.[2] This therefore comes, Sir, to beg you would do it next Week, or give us good Reasons why you cannot, and say, as we before desired you, upon Honor whether the Story is real or feign'd, which you may do without any Breach of Trust. Your obliging us soon will prevent our giving you more Charge, for we told you we would not cease Writing till we were Satisfied; and you may expect us to be as good as our Word. Don't fail answering us next Week, that we may Stile ourselves Your Obliged Humble Servants.

N. B. Remember you're to direct to Mrs. Lancelet to be left till call'd for with Mrs. King the Letter-Carrier in Reading, Berks.[3]

---

[1] Date proposed by Eaves and Kimpel.
[2] See Six Ladies to SR, <January or February> 1742.
[3] Berkshire. This paragraph has been crossed through in the pale greenish-grey ink that marks Barbauld's editing of SR's correspondence for publication (1804); see Six Ladies to SR, <January or February> 1742.

85

Richardson to Six Ladies

\<March\>[1] 1742

MS: FM XVI, 1, ff. 18–19. Copy in Gilbert Hill's hand.
Endorsement: 'IX.' (in SR's hand); 'Intended Answer to Reading Ladies. To the Lady who writes in the Name of N°. 6.' (in Hill's hand).[2]

Madam,

I must confess that I chose to wait for your Second Favour, before I answer'd the first. For surely, thought I, it is impossible but these fair Inquisitors against[3] they wrote again[4] will not want being reminded that it must appear a little unwarrantable to a Stranger, that desirous to know the Secrets of other Ladies, who are so Industrious to conceal their own Names.[5]

You will excuse me, Madam, therefore, from entring into the Subject you write upon, till I am made acquainted with the following Particulars, at least:[6]

I. To whom is it[7] I am to reveal a Secret, that[8] upon the Face of the Matter, appears to be intrusted to me as such? – Whether really Six Ladies? – If so, the Name of each. –[9] Nor can this[10] be thought impertinent,[11] because no one surely, should intrust his Secret to an absolute Stranger, no, nor even to every one who Styles himself a Friend. And when I know each Lady's Name, I must take some Time to inquire into the Character of each; so far I mean, as to be well assured, that there is no one among the Six, that one ought to scruple trusting with a Secret. – For let me tell you, Ladies, it was never since the Beginning of the World, known, that a Secret was

---

[1] Date proposed by Eaves and Kimpel.
[2] 'Intended' and 'Reading Ladies. To' has been crossed through in the pale greenish-grey ink that marks Barbauld's editing of SR's correspondence for publication (1804); see Six Ladies to SR, \<January or February\> 1742.
[3] I.e. coming to the time that.
[4] 'against they wrote again' has been crossed out by SR as well as by Barbauld.
[5] SR emended this, with deletions and insertions in his late hand, to read: 'reminded when they write again that it must appear a little unwarrantable to a Stranger, that Ladies who are desirous to know the Secrets of others should be so Industrious to conceal their Names'.
[6] ', at least:' has been crossed out by SR as well as by Barbauld.
[7] SR has emended to 'it is'.
[8] 'that' has been crossed out and replaced with 'which' by SR.
[9] The three dashes preceding these argumentative questions have been deleted in an undetermined hand with looped cross-outs.
[10] 'Expectation' inserted by SR.
[11] Insertions in SR's hand change this to 'an Impertinent one'.

RICHARDSON TO SIX LADIES, <MARCH> 1742

communicated to, and kept by a Society of Six Ladies. And pardon me, Madam, but I have ever had some Doubt, whether those who are the most desirous to obtrude themselves into a Trust are the fittest Persons in the World to keep it.[12]

II. You must next acquaint me, Madam, with the Nature[13] of the Oath by which each Lady has bound herself to Secrecy in this Affair. – [14] You'll be so good also as to favour me with the Words of this Oath,[15] and in what manner[16] it was administer'd and taken. Nor can this Expectation be[17] out of the way; because if the matter be[18] important in the Ladies Opinion as to require an Oath of Secrecy, surely it behoves the Person who is to communicate the Secret so earnestly desired to be revealed, to be satisfied in every minute[19] Particular relating to this Solemn Point; especially as he has not the Honour to know any of the Ladies, or, indeed (but by the curious Notice of the Demand upon him)[20] whether it be made by Ladies or not. –[21] And not rather by some Gentleman, who having, *as he thinks*, found out some Inconsistencies between different Parts of the Story, and the Editor's Preface;[22] has got his sister, or Lady, perhaps, to write in the Name of No. VI. and this may be rather suspected, perhaps, because Gentlemen are more accustom'd to take Oaths, especially *voluntary* ones, than[23] Ladies.[24]

You see, Madam, what a Curiosity you have raised by *your*[25] Curiosity; and I hope the fair Assembly will have the Justice to think mine *at least*[26] to be satisfied as theirs.

---

[12] 'inviolate' inserted in SR's hand.
[13] 'Nature' underlined by SR.
[14] The dash has been deleted by an undetermined hand with a looped cross-out.
[15] Barbauld has crossed out the sentence to 'Oath'. 'Words' has been underlined by SR.
[16] 'manner' has been underlined in an undetermined hand.
[17] 'thought' inserted by SR.
[18] 'so' inserted by SR.
[19] 'minute' crossed out by Barbauld.
[20] 'curious Notice' has been crossed out and replaced with 'Curiosity' by SR, while Barbauld has crossed out 'curious Notice … him)' and inserted 'expressed' after SR's 'Curiosity'.
[21] Dash deleted by an undetermined hand with a deletion mark.
[22] 'having, … Editor's Preface' crossed out by Barbauld.
[23] 'take Oaths … <ones,>' has been crossed out by SR and replaced with 'swear', while 'to take … than' has been crossed out by Barbauld.
[24] 'Swear' has been added in SR's hand.
[25] 'own' has been inserted in an undetermined hand and then crossed out in SR's hand.
[26] 'as proper' has been inserted by SR.

RICHARDSON TO SIX LADIES, <MARCH> 1742

For let any one of the fair Assembly make the Case her own; and suppose she had intrusted some favourite Gentleman with a Secret she was very desirous should not pass his Breast; what would she think of him, if he should break his Trust, and reveal the Matter to half a Dozen curious Ladies at once, even tho' he perfectly knew them all, and had a high Opinion of their Taciturnity?[27] But what still wou'd she say were the Indiscretion heighten'd, by his not knowing[28] one of the Ladies, and that he broke his Trust upon an inquiry made by[29] an Anonymous Letter, written in the Name[30] of Six Ladies, an[31] Answer requir'd to be directed to a strange Name, and to be left at a Letter-carrier's, till call'd for? –

But if there really be such Six Ladies, I am convinced that they have chosen to divert themselves with the Editor of Pamela, because they know how to Direct to him, and he makes me no doubt but he shall have made their Jest complete, by writing[32] so largely on the Subject. But he has really so much Honour for the whole Sex, that he can never think that[33] Time ill-bestowed that[34] can contribute to the Amusement or Diversions of Six Ladies at once.

Mean time, being willing to draw some Benefit to the Work,[35] he thinks it proper to observe[36] that he is commission'd in any future Editions, to make such Corrections and Amendments, as any kind Correspondent shall suggest a Necessity[37] for; the Piece being really calculated to Instruct as well as Divert; and to answer that End, shou'd be as little Objectionable,[38] as possible.[39]

---

[27] SR has emended the passage in his late hand to read: 'even were they all perfectly knewn to him and he had a high Opinion'.
[28] 'any' inserted in SR's hand.
[29] 'by' has been crossed out and replaced with 'in' in SR's hand.
[30] 'in the Name' has been crossed out and replaced with 'at the Request' in SR's hand.
[31] 'an' has been crossed out and replaced with 'his' in SR's hand.
[32] 'as now' inserted in SR's hand.
[33] 'that' amended to 'the' in SR's hand.
[34] 'that' has been crossed out and replaced with 'which' in SR's hand.
[35] 'from his very Curiosity' inserted in SR's hand.
[36] 'observe' has been crossed out and replaced with 'declare' in SR's hand.
[37] 'Necessity' has been crossed out and replaced with 'Reason' in SR's hand.
[38] 'Objectionable' has been crossed out and replaced with 'liable to Objection' in SR's hand.
[39] Barbauld has crossed through the entire final paragraph with an X.

Philopamela to Richardson

Tuesday 21 March or Wednesday 22 March 1742

MS: FM XVI, 1, ff. 87–8. Copy in Gilbert Hill's hand.
Endorsement: 'LXXXI.' (in SR's hand); 'March 21 or 22nd 1741/2' (in Hill's hand).

Dear Sir

It is as impossible for me to express to you the Pleasure and Satisfaction I have receiv'd by the Perusal of Pamela as it is for Pamela herself to say or do any thing but what is perfectly just and beautiful, or for me not to approve of all *her meditations, and Actions*, so inexpressibly agreeable are the former, and so noble and Generous the latter. There is not a part in the whole Performance that I do not sincerely admire, & which has not an effect, more or less, on my Passions; I entirely agree with her in every thing, sympathize in all her Distresses and Misfortunes, & feel Pleasure or Pain only where Pamela does. One while I am overcome with anger against her Wicked Master; then melted with Pity for the distressed Virgin; This Hour my Soul is carried away by the Tempest she raises in me; the next I am brought to a Calm by her fine Reflections. In short, she absolutely governs me, and can, when she pleases, excite such Tumult in my Soul, which it is in her power alone to appease; and I can truly say of her, what Mr. B. says of the whole Sex, that I am but a mere weathercock to be turn'd this way or that, just as Pamela Pleases.[1] I am, I assure you, Sir, so delighted & affected, by this Book that my Friends tell me I talk in no other Language than Pamela's; and I have often us'd all my Endeavours to forget the dear Girl; but I find it impossible, for the sweet Idea still[2] recurs to my Mind, and does not permit my Thoughts to attend any thing else; I have often made my addresses to the soft God of sleep, and us'd all means to be favour'd by him; but Pamela always gets the Victory over this dull Deity, and charms, and haunts me sleeping or waking, & if ever Sleep locks up my Senses, I am sure to be delighted by Pamela in sweet

---

[1] In *Pamela II*, it is actually Mr H./Jackey who is compared to a weathercock when Pamela begins to uncover his attempts to bribe her maid, Polly, for sex: 'He looked like a Man Thunder-struck. His Face was distorted, and his Head seemed to turn about upon his Neck, like a Weathercock in a Hurricane, to all Points of the Compass. His Hands clenched as in a Passion, and yet Shame and Confusion struggling in every Limb and Feature' (*Pamela II*, p. 254).

[2] Here used in the now obsolete sense of 'always' (*OED*).

PHILOPAMELA TO RICHARDSON, WEDNESDAY 22 MARCH 1742

pleasing Dreams; and thus she is never absent from my Thoughts. Even when I have thought myself most gay and chearful, Pamela has turn'd me into Pity and Compassion, and made me as it were, quit this Soul of mine, and acquire a far different one. One Day I remember, I took up Pamela, to read the celebrated jealousy piece, and thought my temper of mind was such, that all the long Winded whining Descendants of Andrew Cant cou'd not move me;[3] but had not read two Pages, before my Eyes discover'd by the pearly Fugitives, that flow'd from Those Fountains in two little Streams, the Temper of my Soul, which was not a little eas'd by these relieffull tears, to use Pamela's own beautiful Epithet.[4] Her Reflections on going to throw herself into the Pond are extremely natural, and contain in my opinion the best Arguments against self-Murder, and I am sure set in the most beautiful Light.[5] Mr. B's Observations on Marriage, and the conduct of married People towards each other, are inexpressibly just; and the Curtain-lecture, as Pamela phrases it, is necessary to be read by all married People;[6] as indeed the whole Book contains Instructions for all Parts of Life; for the Ladies, the three great characters of a Virgin, Bride and Wife are excellently drawn, and kept up to, thro' the whole, and I confess I almost thought it impossible that the Author of Pamela, who cou'd draw such amiable Characters as Pamela and Mr. B. when married (the Masquerade excepted) shou'd with the same Justice have represented the odious Mrs. Jewkes and rustic Sir Jacob Swynford. But what can one imagine too great for the Author of this celebrated Piece? Nothing is impossible to him.[7]

---

3 Andrew Cant (1584/90–1663), Church of Scotland Minister, Royalist, and Covenanter who was 'well known' for his 'courage and eloquence' (*ODNB*). He is mocked in William Meston's Hudibrastic poem, *The Knight* (1723) (the third edition's longer title was *The Knight of the Kirk: Or, The Ecclesiastical Adventures of Sir John Presbyter* (1728)): '[He] neither wanted Zeal nor Cunning, / And was profoundly skill'd in punning, / And in the Pulpit many Times, / Instead of Reason vented *Rhimes*'. Cant's son, Andrew Cant (d. 1685), became principal of the University of Edinburgh from 1675 until his death (*ODNB*).

4 In *Pamela II*, when Pamela believes that Mr B. is unfaithful to her, she writes to Lady Davers: 'I weep in the Night, when he is asleep; and in the Day, when he is absent: And I am happy when I can, unobserv'd, steal this poor Relief. I believe already I have shed as many Tears as would drown my poor Baby' (*Pamela II*, p. 404); the specific term 'relieffull tears' is nowhere to be found.

5 In *Pamela*, pp. 158–60.

6 Mr B. gives his 'lecture' in *Pamela*, II, pp. 408–11; Pamela calls it a 'Curtain-lecture' in *Pamela II*, pp. 52–3.

7 'Nothing is impossible to him' has been crossed through in an undetermined hand.

PHILOPAMELA TO RICHARDSON, WEDNESDAY 22 MARCH 1742

Were I to enumerate to you[8] all the Beauties of Pamela, I am
sensible I shou'd have nothing to do but transcribe the Whole; I
shall therefore only mention to you (and thro' your Kindness to
the World) one Passage, which has exceedingly struck me. It is
in the Second Volume, where having spoke a little before of the
Wickedness of her Master, she adds, 'I need not rail against men
so much; for my Master, bad as I have thought him, is not half so
bad as this Woman! – To be sure she must be an Atheist! – Do you
think she is not.'[9] I the rather mention this, because I know few
have seen the Beauty of it, or remarked the fine Sentiment. For my
part, I think it *even* exceeds that passage of Tully in his Book de
Natura Deorum where he says,

—'Tubulus Si Lucius umquam,

  Si Lupus, aut Carbo, aut Neptuni filius,

ut ait Lucilius, putasset esse deos, tam perjurus aut tam impurus
fuisset?'[10] (i.e. If, as Lucilius says, Lucius Tubulus, Lupus,[11] Carbo,
or the Son of Neptune, had believed the Existence of the Gods,
would any of them have been so perjured or so Wicked?) I say
not this, Sir, to blame the Author of Pamela for it, as a borrowed
Sentiment; for had Pamela read Tully, which, when she wrote
this, could not be, tho' it might afterwards, Mr. B. having taught
her Latin, yet tho' the Thought is much the same, Pamela has
much more beautifully express'd it; and the Thoughts throughout this Book are quite new and uncommon; few, very few borrowed; and those that are taken from others, are put into much
better Language, and so prettily brought in, and connected with
such a variety of entertaining Incidents, that the *Utile dulci*[12] is
more found in this Book than any I know of. Our Ancestors,
I need not acquaint you, Sir, have always made their Boasts of
Homer's, Plato's, Cicero's, Vergil's, Milton's, but it is the distinguishing Character and Credit of this Age, a perfect Pamela, an

[8] 'to you' has been crossed through in an undetermined hand.
[9] In *Pamela*, p. 227.
[10] With minor misspellings, this is from Cicero, *De Natura Deorum*, Book 1.23, in which he
refutes arguments proving the existence of the gods from general consent or agreement
(Loeb 268, pp. 24–7).
[11] 'Lupus' is an interlinear addition, possibly but not definitely in the copyist's hand.
[12] Horace, *Ars Poetica*, l. 343: 'the useful with the agreeable' (Loeb 194, pp. 478–9).

91

PHILOPAMELA TO RICHARDSON, WEDNESDAY 22 MARCH 1742

Original indeed, quite Natural, and I will venture to add abounding with Instances of the true Sublime, and I could point to finer Sentiments in the four Volumes of Pamela, than in Homer or Virgil. And of Longinus's five Fountains of the Sublime, Pamela abounds in Three, Greatness of Thought, moving the Passions, and proper Diction; and of the two other I cou'd produce Instances.[13] And as to the Sublime's always leaving an agreeable Idea (a)[14] after we have read it, every one that has seen Pamela can Testify.

I have only to add, that as you have thought fit to Publish the Objections, stupid and Absurd as they are, that have been made against Pamela, in your Two First Volumes, and have taken notice tho' undeserving of it, of the T{r}oilus's (so must I call all Cavillers against Pamela)[15] you will not neglect the Aristotle's and Longinus's, among whom I presume to rank myself; and shall consider this as a Favour confer'd on, Sir Your humble Servant

Philopamela

(a) See this Observation confirmed, and beautifully expatiated upon, by A. H. Esq p. 107 of this Collection.[16]

[13] Cf. Longinus, *On the Sublime*. The other two sources of the sublime according to the translation by William Smith are 'a skilful Application of Figures' and 'the Structure or Composition of the Periods in all possible Dignity and Grandeur' (*Dionysius Longinus on the Sublime: Translated from the Greek, With Notes and Observations, and Some Account of the Life, Writings and Character of the Author* (London, 1739), p. 16).

[14] The footnote is written and subsequently crossed out in SR's hand.

[15] In the introduction to the second edition of *Pamela* (1741), SR had included excerpts of letters from Aaron Hill in which the latter responded to objections against the novel; see *Pamela*, pp. 463–77. A 'caviller' is 'a captious or frivolous objector, a quibbling disputant' (*OED*). In the tradition from Chaucer to William Shakespeare's play *Troilus and Cressida*, Troilus became synonymous with foolishness and inconsistency.

[16] SR's note refers to Hill to SR, 15 January 1741.

Richardson to William Warburton[1]

Wednesday 17 November 1742

MS: FM XVI, 1, f. 89. Copy in Gilbert Hill's hand.
Endorsement: 'LXXXII.' (in SR's hand); 'To the Rev.ᵈ M.ʳ Warburton' (in Hill's hand).

17th Nov. 1742

Reverend Sir,

My Friend Mr. Woodward[2] acquainted me some Days ago, that if I had had the Honour of being known to you, before I had enter'd upon the 3rd and 4th Volumes of Pamela,[3] I might have received great Benefit from the Hints you could have favoured me with.

This, Sir, and the Approbation the first Genius of the Age has honoured the First and Second Vols. with,[4] makes me bold to court your Corrections, if in your *unbending Hours*,[5] such a low Performance may obtain the Favour of your Perusal. For I am Collecting together the Observations and Castigations[6] of several of my kind Friends in order, if the Piece should happen to come to a future Edition, besides the new one of the 3rd and 4th which is near Publishing, that it might be benefitted by their Remarks and that I might have a corrected Copy for the Press.

I beg, Sir, that the Octavo Edition which has received a good many Alterations from the former, may be permitted a Place in one Corner of your Portmanteau.[7] And that you will excuse me

---

[1] William Warburton (1698–1779), bishop of Gloucester, religious controversialist, literary critic, and editor of Shakespeare (1747) and Pope (1751) (*ODNB*).

[2] Thomas Woodward (fl. 1726–43), bookseller, was like SR involved in the publication of pro-government periodicals and published the French translation of *Pamela* (1741) in collaboration with bookseller John Osborne, Sr (d. 1745), one of the original publishers of *Pamela*.

[3] I.e. the two volumes of *Pamela II*.

[4] SR's friend and physician George Cheyne had reported Alexander Pope's 'great Approbation and Pleasure' in reading *Pamela*; see Cheyne to SR, 12 February 1741. According to Barbauld, SR's brother-in-law James Leake had reported the same of Pope and Ralph Allen; see B: I, lviii–lix.

[5] Johnson's *Dictionary* defines 'unbending' as 'devoted to relaxation', citing the phrase 'unbending hours' from Nicholas Rowe's preface to his tragedy, *The Ambitious Step-Mother* (1700).

[6] 'Castigations' has been underlined and 'Corrections' written above it in SR's hand.

[7] 'A case or bag for carrying clothing and other belongings when travelling' (*OED*). SR was sending a copy of the significantly altered and richly illustrated octavo edition of *Pamela* and *Pamela II* as a present.

for thus presuming on a slight Hint my Friend, as above, gave me. But of which however, I shou'd not have had the Courage to take Advantage, had not the Piece been designed to promote the Cause of Virtue, among the *many* who cannot relish higher Performances; and had it not been receiv'd with an Approbation, as much beyond its Merit, as its Writer's Expectation.

A good Journey,[8] and Health and Happiness, attend you, Sir, is the Wish of Your faithful and Obedient Servant

S. R.

---

[8] Warburton was probably returning to Brant Broughton in Lincolnshire, the rich living that he held until 1746.

William Warburton to Richardson

Tuesday 28 December 1742

Printed source: B: I, 133–5.
First printing: Barbauld, *Correspondence* (1804).

To Mr. Richardson.

Dec. 28, 1742

Good Sir,

This very day, on receiving my things from London, I had the pleasure to find in the box an obliging letter from you, of the 17th past, with a very kind and valuable present of a fine edition of your excellent work, which no one can set a higher rate upon. I find they have both lain all this time at Mr. Bowyer's.[1]

I have so true an esteem for you, that you may depend on any thing in my power, that you think may be of any service to you.

Mr. Pope and I, talking over your work when the two last volumes came out,[2] agreed, that one excellent subject of Pamela's letters in high life, would have been to have passed her judgment, on first stepping into it, on every thing she saw there, just as simple nature (and no one ever touched nature to the quick, as it were, more certainly and surely than you) dictated. The effect would have

---

[1] William Bowyer the younger (1699–1777), printer in Whitefriars (*ODNB*).
[2] *Pamela II* had been published on 8 December 1741.

<JAMES LEAKE, JR> TO RICHARDSON, THURSDAY 21 APRIL 1743

been this, that it would have produced, by good management, a most excellent and useful satire on all the follies and extravagancies of high life; which to one of Pamela's low station and good sense would have appeared as absurd and unaccountable as European polite vices and customs to an Indian.[3] You easily conceive the effect this must have added to the entertainment of the book; and for the use, that is incontestable. And what could be more natural than this in Pamela, going into a new world, where every thing sensibly strikes a stranger?[4] But, when I have the pleasure of seeing you in town, we will talk over this matter at large; and, I fancy, you will make something extremely good of our hints. I have a great deal to say upon this subject, that, when we are together, you will not only understand more perfectly, but I shall be able to conceive more clearly by the use of your true judgment.[5]

At least, I shall be always zealous of shewing how much I am, Good Sir, Your very obliged and most affectionate, humble servant,

W. Warburton

[3] In making this suggestion, Pope (and Warburton) were responding to the popularity of 'innocent eye' fiction in the early to mid eighteenth century. Works like Montesquieu's *Persian Letters* (1721) presented an outsider's view of cosmopolitan life, including satiric depictions of the follies and foibles of the present day.

[4] Pamela had excused herself from this task repeatedly in the third and fourth volumes of the novel, suggesting that such commentary would be 'impertinent' to those like Lady Davers, 'who are no stranger to what is worthy of notice in London' (*Pamela II*, p. 305), and apologizing repeatedly when she does critique social mores (e.g. pp. 307–8).

[5] If this meeting ever came to pass, SR did not pick up Warburton's and Pope's ideas.

<James Leake, Jr>[1] to Richardson

Thursday 21 April 1743

MS: Laing III, 356, 264–5. Copy in SR's hand.

Bath. April 21. 1743

Dear and honoured Sir,

I should have given you a Letter sooner on a Subject you must naturally want to be informed of, if the ill Health of our Family had not prevented. Indeed I should have wrote to you long before,

[1] On the strength of references to 'my father', scholars since Eaves and Kimpel have suggested that this anonymous letter was written by James Leake, Jr (1724–91), the son of SR's

if it had been thought necessary to acquaint the Friends of the late good Doctor of his Indisposition: But his Friends of this Place were not less surprized than his absent ones, at the News of his Death.[2]

It was about ten Days before his Decease, that a Vomiting & Purging confined him at home, together with the Symptoms of the Disorder that has lately spread itself so universally.[3] On Thursday, about five Days after that Seizure, my Father visited the Doctor. Mr. Bertrand did the same the Day following. But my Father's Illness coming on the Same Evening, prevented me paying the Duty I owed to a great and good Friend. We continued daily our Enquiries; but never received an Answer that alarm'd us with the Apprehension of his Danger: But, alas! this whole time he wasted prodigiously. His Looseness and Sweatings grew more violent till the last three Days; when the former stopt, and from that time hardly any thing passed him; nor did any thing stay in his Stomach, but Bristol Water,[4] of which he drank very largely, and with it sweated very much.

Tho' the Doctor's Friends were not apprehensive of his imminent Danger, he himself was. He talked to his Family of his Death, as of a natural Consequence; tho' he did not imagine it so near: And it was not till the Day before it happened, that he consulted a Physician. Dr. Hartley was then sent for;[5] but he was at Mr. Allen's;[6] and when he came down in the Evening, Dr. Middleton, Mrs. Cheyne's Brother,[7] was come over from Bristol, and had been with the Doctor. He went into the Bed-chamber; but the Doctor was dozing. The next Morning, he visited him about Eight. He was then very easy; but his Pulse was gone. He did not know Dr. Hartley, as he had not seen him in his Illness; but he

---

brother-in-law by his second marriage, James Leake (1686–1764). The Leake family ran printing and bookselling businesses, first in London (which SR initially managed and then took over in 1720) and then in Bath (*ODNB*).

[2] SR's friend and physician, George Cheyne, had died on Wednesday 13 April 1743.

[3] An influenza epidemic spread throughout Europe in 1742, reached London in March 1743, and resulted in significant illness and death in the British Isles in April and May 1743.

[4] 'the water of warm springs at Clifton near Bristol, used medicinally' (*OED*).

[5] David Hartley (bap. 1705, d. 1757), philosopher and physician; his philosophical and proto-psychological treatise, *Observations on Man* (1749), would later be printed by SR and sold in Bath by James Leake, Sr, and his associate, William Frederick.

[6] Presumably Ralph Allen, philanthropist and friend of Cheyne and SR; see Cheyne to SR, 5 September 1742.

[7] John Middleton (1710?–60), physician and man-midwife with a successful practice in Bristol, was one of Cheyne's brothers-in-law.

RICHARDSON TO SAMUEL LOBB, TUESDAY 11 MAY 1743

was still sensible. It was not above Ten Minutes after he left him, that the Doctor left the World. His Death was easy, and his Senses remained to the last.

To consider the Circumstances of your Health, and that there is taken from you by the Divine Wisdom, one, in whose Mind the Direction of it was a good deal lodged, it is impossible but we must look to the Almighty Disposer; and then see the same Power capable of making up that Loss to you a thousand different ways. Reflexions of this Sort are natural; and we must know that these and much greater, are as natural to you. Even the wisest Sentiments on this Head would be but a Repetition of your Thoughts: The World has lost a great and able Physician: You, my dear Sir, a truly valuable Friend; and I, one greater than my Merits............[8]

Extract from a Letter.

As long as Health shall be reckoned a Blessing, and the Preservation of Life a Duty, both Rich and Poor must condole the Death of their common Benefactor: And those Honourable Families which have so frequently and successfully resorted hither for his Advice, must now be daily more sensible of the Power of Diseases, and apprehensive of their approaching Fate.

[8] SR's copy ends here with a line of dots that indicate he did not copy the remainder of this letter; the following 'Extract from a Letter' may be more material from the same letter or, more likely, a short piece from another letter, possibly also from James Leake, Jr, with further thoughts on Cheyne's death.

Richardson to Samuel Lobb[1]

Tuesday 11 May 1743
MS: Yale (Osborn). Copy in SR's hand.

Dear and Reverend Sir;
I cannot express the Pleasure your most agreeable Request has given me; and that, as well from the Nature of it, as from the much-respected Person with whom you do me the Honour to join me. Indeed, my dear, good Mr. Lobb, you are very kind to me on

[1] Samuel Lobb (1690–1761), Rector of Farleigh Hungerford, near Bath, from 1736. For information on the Lobb family, see Eland.

97

SAMUEL LOBB TO RICHARDSON, SATURDAY 21 MAY 1743

this Occasion: And only in *one* thing unkind, that you could seem to think any Preface to so agreeable a Signification needful. You have, in short, Sir, by this Instance of your Favour laid me under such an Obligation, that nothing but the Urgency of Business, and the Shortness of Time, could hinder me from personally thanking you for it, on the 19th of this Month; as it is my Hope once more to see Bath.

God preserve to You both, and give Ye Joy of my dear little Joseph![2] I call him mine, already, because I will date my Relationship to him, from the Date of your kind, your very kind, Letter.[3]

My humblest Respects to good Mr. Allen,[4] and his excellent Lady, and to the Gentleman with whom you do me the Honour to join me, on this Occasion.[5] My Wife and Miss Leake desire the Return of their Compliments to You both:[6] And Mrs. Lobb has my best Thanks for her concurring with You, as I presume to hope, in the Favour you have done, to, Dear Sir, Your-much-obliged and affectionate Friend and Servant,

S. Richardson

London, May 11. 1743.

[2] Joseph (1743–1811), a future dealer in textiles, was Samuel Lobb's younger son; his elder son, William (1736–65), corresponded with SR from 1750 at the latest.
[3] Lobb had asked SR to be godfather to his son, Joseph, in a letter now missing.
[4] Ralph Allen (see Allen to SR, 20 February 1738) lived at Prior Park near Bath from 1742.
[5] This 'Gentleman', who seems to have been involved in Joseph Lobb's baptism and elicited such respect from SR, remains unidentified, although Eaves and Kimpel report a Lobb family tradition to the effect that the 'Gentleman' was Henry Fielding (see Eland, p. 49).
[6] Elizabeth Leake Richardson and an unidentified female relation.

Samuel Lobb to Richardson

Saturday 21 May 1743

Printed source: B: I, 173–6.
First printing: Barbauld, *Correspondence* (1804).

Dear Sir,
I should have thought a compliance with my request,[1] without any marks to distinguish it from those that are usual on such

[1] To stand godfather to his child (Barbauld's note); see SR to Lobb, 11 May 1743.

SAMUEL LOBB TO RICHARDSON, SATURDAY 21 MAY 1743

occasions, a very great obligation upon me; but a compliance so big with generosity as your's, in terms that express just what I was wishing, but, really, was far from having the presumption or vanity to expect, shews not a bare esteem, but the affection of a sincere friend; and this accompanied with such a respect for one, indeed, of the best of wives and mothers; and with such tenderness for the dear little stranger you so kindly consider already as your own. So unexpectedly engaging a compliance as this, affected me on my first perusing your most obliging letter; and every time I think of it, still affects me in a manner I can no other way give you the idea of, than by referring you to what you must have felt yourself, if at any time, with such warm wishes for an interest in the friendship of a person you most highly valued, you have had your expectations so agreeably disappointed and exceeded, as by a goodness that admits of but few examples, mine have now been.

I do not pretend, by thus referring you to your own sentiments of gratitude, that mine are equally grateful. The true sterling generosity is uniform and of a piece on all occasions, if exerting itself; and, therefore, shews itself as much in acknowledging, and, where there is the opportunity, in returning obligations, as in seeking and embracing opportunities of conferring them.

On the 19th of May, through the goodness of God, we had all the friends with us we had invited, but Mrs. Leake, and Mrs. Oliver, who were not horsewomen enough to accompany our other friends.[2] What an additional pleasure would it have been, could your affairs, and the time, have permitted you to have indulged your kind disposition of making one of the company.

Our much esteemed friends, Mr. and Mrs. Allen,[3] desired me to send you their best compliments, and to Mrs. Richardson, of whom Mrs. Allen speaks with great respect and good-liking.

The god-father and god-mother of our dear little fellow surprised us with their liberality on the occasion. The evening

[2] 'Mrs. Leake' is probably Hannah Hammond Leake, wife of SR's brother-in-law, the bookseller James Leake, and sister-in-law of SR's second wife, Elizabeth Leake Richardson (the 'Mrs. Richardson' mentioned later in this letter). 'Mrs. Oliver' is probably the wife of Dr William Oliver (1695–1764), eminent physician and philanthropist at Bath, and the inventor of the Bath Oliver, a now traditional savoury biscuit or cracker given to his patients (*ODNB*).

[3] Ralph Allen (see Allen to SR, 20 February 1738) had married his second wife, Elizabeth Holder (d. 1766), on 24 March 1737 after his first wife, Elizabeth Buckeridge, died in February or March 1736 (*ODNB*).

99

ALEXANDER POPE TO RICHARDSON, TUESDAY <LATE 1743?>

my friends were going, I gave the nurse, who is a widow with seven children, three guineas, without any intimation that any thing more was likely to come to her share; for this she was very thankful; but when, the next day, I added the other three guineas,[4] she was almost beside herself, and, in the surprise of her joy, she fell down on her knees, stammering out a million, ten millions, of thanks, with a most beautiful and natural remark on the goodness of God, in the care of the fatherless and widow. It was very affecting to see the natural workings of a grateful mind.

I am, Dear Sir, Your most obliged and affectionate friend and servant,

S. Lobb

[4] Presumably from SR.

Alexander Pope[1] to Richardson

Tuesday <Late 1743?>[2]

MS: William A. Clark Memorial Library, Misc Mss. Autograph letter sent (evidence of red wax seal, address and folds).

Address: 'To Mr Richardson' (in Pope's hand).
Endorsement: 'Note from Alexander Pope to Richardson author of Sir Charles Grandison – sent me by Rich in 1732. Robert Gilmore' (in an undetermined hand).[3]

Dear Sir
You are the first Man I shall see when I am able to get to Town. I am in a very ticklish State, dreading any Cold, from the Asthmatic Complaint; which follows me close, or I had been

[1] Alexander Pope (1688–1744), the foremost poet of his time.
[2] George Sherburn, in his *Correspondence of Alexander Pope*, 4 vols. (Oxford: Clarendon Press, 1956), assigns the note to the end of 1743 based on Pope's health that year. Sherburn identifies the recipient as the painter and friend of Pope, Jonathan Richardson the elder (1667–1745), dismissing the endorsement explicitly identifying SR as the recipient because 'Pope did not correspond with the novelist Richardson, who would not have welcomed a visit from Pope' (Sherburn, *Correspondence*, IV, p. 487). We now know, however, that SR and Pope were on friendly terms shortly after the publication of *Pamela* (see, for example, SR to Warburton, 17 November 1742; and Warburton to SR, 28 December 1742).
[3] The date 1732 is doubtful for this letter, since there is no evidence that SR and Pope had yet come into contact. The endorsement itself, by an unidentified Robert Gilmore, cannot have been written before the end of 1753, after *Grandison* had first been published. 'Rich'

RICHARDSON TO THOMAS BIRCH, FRIDAY 21 DECEMBER 1744

sooner there. No Thanks are equal to your noble, & (what yet Ennobles it more) friendly Present.[4] Believe I am indebted to you, not in part, but Whole, & All Yours.

A. Pope.

Twit'nam.[5] Tuesday.

probably refers to John Rich (1692–1761), pantomimist and theatre manager at Lincoln's Inn Fields and Covent Garden (*ODNB*).

[4] SR liked to present friends and correspondents with copies of his novels, so perhaps Pope received a copy of the recently published illustrated sixth edition of *Pamela* and *Pamela II*.

[5] I.e. Twickenham, where Pope had built his famous villa and gardens beginning in 1719.

Richardson to Thomas Birch

Friday 21 December 1744

MS: BL Add. MS 4317, f. 174. Autograph letter sent (evidence of remainder of red wax seal and folds).

Address: 'For The Revd Mr Birch' (in SR's hand).

Reverend Sir,

The widening the Lines will occasion the intire over-running of the Half-Sheet you have seen, and another, compos'd, which you have not seen; and the Distances between the Lines will be then too short. I think you had better have the whole done without Distances, and a wider Page. It will then make a handsomer Appearance, and be Bulky enough for a Shilling Price.[1] I shall attend your Pleasure, before I proceed. I am, Sir, Your most humble Servant

S. Richardson

Friday Noon.
Decemb. 21. 1744.

[1] Birch must have seen proofs for a pamphlet he intended to publish and asked SR to alter the spacing between words within each line of type, which for SR creates an aesthetic problem – the increased spacing throws off the composition of the page and reduces its visual appeal – as well as one of increased labour and associated costs because his compositor will have to revise ('over-run') the type that has already been set for a number of the pamphlet's pages; see also SR to Birch, 28 December 1744; and SR to Birch, 12 February 1745. None of the ESTC entries that identify Birch as author in this period could even remotely be described as pamphlets, so either this publication was scrapped at the last moment (unlikely, considering how far SR's work on it had progressed by the following February) or Birch had decided to publish anonymously. The only anonymously authored pamphlet identified by Maslen as definitely printed by SR in 1745 is *A Method to Prevent, Without a Register, the Running of Wool from Ireland to France* (Maslen, no. 471).

101

RICHARDSON TO THOMAS BIRCH, TUESDAY 12 FEBRUARY 1745

Richardson to Thomas Birch

Friday 28 December 1744

MS: BL Add. MS 4317, f. 176. Autograph letter sent (evidence of remainder of red wax seal and folds).

Endorsement: 'Mr. Richardson. 28 Dec. 1744' (in Gilbert Hill's hand).

> Reverend Sir,
> Tis Pity the Page and the Manner of Capitaling[1] were not ascertained at first; for this Half Sheet has now been twice over-run, line by Line, in the Composing-Stick, which is very little less Trouble than new Composing. And what is worse, the first time a Half-Sheet beyond what you saw a Proof of; and now the Second above Two Half Sheets, beyond this, composed, and about to be put into Frame, to be sent you:[2] All which must be as expensive as troublesome. I forget the Number (so long in hand) that you order'd to be printed, if it were not 750. Be pleased to write that on the Proof, on Return. The Compositers are employ'd in Over-running the Pages they had out: But for the Holidays, you would have seen them. I am, Sir, wishing you the Felicities of the Season. Your most humble Servant
>
> S. Richardson
>
> Friday Night.
> Decemb. 28. 1744

[1] 'The provision or supply of a word with a capital letter. Now *rare*' (*OED*).
[2] I.e. SR's compositor has had to revise the typesetting for Birch's pamphlet twice – almost as much work and cost as setting type anew – because of changes to page layout and capitalization after the type setting had already been completed, which has also expanded the number of pages to be printed to complete the pamphlet; see also SR to Birch, 21 December 1744; and SR to Birch, 12 February 1745.

Richardson to Thomas Birch

Tuesday 12 February 1745

MS: BL Add. MS 4317, f. 177. Autograph letter sent (evidence of folding).
Endorsement: '12 Febr. 1744/5' (in SR's hand, on the outside of the letter).

> Reverend Sir,
> You have once or twice mention'd the fine Paper of the Pamphlet; I ought to have acquainted you that you gave no Orders

102

for finer Paper till one or two Half Sheets were wrought off. But the Whole is printed on a finer Paper than common for Pamphlets; the same as the Journals of the House of Commons. And what Destination may be desired, will be most visible in the Binders Way: by the Cover, Gilding, &c.[1] – You'll please to order what Number you'd have, and send for them; which, I presume you had rather do, than to have them sent to your House. You'll direct the Binder as I suppose, having had no Commands from you on that Head.[2] I am, Sir, Your most humble Servant

S. Richardson

Tuesday Morn.
Febr. 12. 1744/5

---

[1] SR is telling Birch that the quality of paper is less important than the particulars of the binding. In the eighteenth century, sheets were sold unbound, and purchasers selected binding and gilding to suit their taste, wealth, and status.

[2] SR's printing jobs for Birch and his friends seem to have involved more last-minute changes and created more additional work than most; see SR to Birch, 21 December 1744; and SR to Birch, 28 December 1744 for this pamphlet, as well as SR to Birch, <1746>; and SR to Birch, 19 April <1746>, for Charles Yorke's *Considerations on the Law of Forfeiture, for High Treason*.

William Strahan[1] to Richardson

Saturday 16 September <1745>[2]

Printed source: B: I, 147–51.
First printing: Barbauld, *Correspondence* (1804).

Edinburgh, Sept. 16, 1749.[3]

Dear Sir,
When I sit down to write to you, I present you before my eyes, with a smile of complacency overspreading your intelligent countenance, as if telling me, before I put pen to paper, that you

---

[1] William Strahan (1715–85), printer (*ODNB*). Born and apprenticed to the trade in Edinburgh, Strahan moved to London in 1736 and had established his own printing business there by November 1738.

[2] Barbauld dates this letter to 1749, and Eaves and Kimpel follow her lead, but Strahan's mention of his son Samuel, whose birth date he meticulously recorded in one of his business ledgers (now at the British Library) as 15 September 1745, indicates the need for a revision of this letter's date. Barbauld may have inserted the letter into the sequence of Strahan's reports from his travels to Scotland in 1749 because it seemed to fit thematically.

[3] The place and date are probably Barbauld's insertions.

WILLIAM STRAHAN TO RICHARDSON, SATURDAY 16 SEPTEMBER <1745>

expected to hear nothing new from me; but that's your fault, not
mine. Had you been less assiduous in storing your mind with
every sort of useful knowledge, you would yet have had something
to learn. *I* have the pleasure of daily making new discoveries,
which *you*, who have long ago travelled over the whole territories
of human nature, are already intimately acquainted with. In this
respect, I am happier than you. – 'I am glad of it, Mr. Strahan; I
envy not your superior ignorance, I assure you.'

This moment I was going to say several bright things, which, as
I am afraid I shall not be able to recollect again, I am sorry to tell
you, you will probably lose for ever; but was interrupted by several
people, who insist on my company, whether I will or no. I must
therefore hasten to tell you, that I have had the pleasure and honour
of your kind epistle;[4] that my face, sleek as it is, I am very sensible
will, in time, if it lasts, undergo a change, which I now neither
hope for nor fear – that I hope I shall be able to tell you this, to *your
face*, twenty years hence: – that my wife says she loves you, as does
also her old infirm mother;[5] poor conquests you would say, if you
were not Mr. Richardson: – that I have not yet seen Mrs. A——,[6]
but intend it soon: – that Mr. —— is in Ireland,[7] from whom you
need never expect any thing: – that —— is in the North just now, but
having got a good post, you will surely recover his money;[8] please,
therefore, send me down another copy of the bill, with a letter
annexed, (directed to Mr. George Balfour, writer to the Signet in
Edinburgh,)[9] impowering him to receive it for you; this you will
be so good as to do directly. I have spoke to him, and he will take
particular care of it. Mr. Hamilton has franks to forward to town.[10]
That I am very greatly pleased Mr. Hamilton has your good opinion
and approbation; he is full of your kindness in all his letters.

---

[4] That response is now lost.
[5] Strahan had married Margaret Penelope Elphinston (1719–85), daughter of an episcopal
clergyman in Edinburgh, on 20 July 1738. Her mother was Rachel Honeyman (d. 1750),
niece of the bishop of Orkney (*ODNB*).
[6] Unidentified.
[7] Unidentified.
[8] Unidentified, though clearly someone who owed SR money.
[9] George Balfour (1711–51), Scottish lawyer.
[10] Probably Gavin Hamilton (1704–67), bookseller and paper maker in Edinburgh (*ODNB*),
who from 1739 had been in business with his brother-in-law John Balfour (1715–95), a
brother of George Balfour's. A frank was 'The superscribed signature of a person, e.g. a
member of Parliament, entitled to send letters post free' or, metonymically, 'A letter or
envelope bearing such a superscription' (*OED*).

WILLIAM STRAHAN TO RICHARDSON, SATURDAY 16 SEPTEMBER <1745>

Allow me also, Sir, to acknowledge, (and I do it with the utmost sense of gratitude) the great honour you have done me, in admitting me to such a share of your conversation and friendship, which I have reason to value and be proud of on many accounts. You have indeed laid me under so many repeated obligations, and oblige too in so obliging a way, that I am afraid I must remain your poor insolvent debtor as long as I live: yet I will beg leave to say, that, if I do not deceive myself, I think I shall ever endeavour to pay all I can towards the interest of them, since the principal I am afraid I shall never be able to discharge. I know you may justly reproach me with neglecting one affair in particular you recommended to me;[11] but I can with great truth say, it proceeds not from indolence, or any worse cause, but purely from an almost irresistible dislike to that sort of employment, which I really did not perceive in myself before, but which I am determined nevertheless to conquer.

I take this opportunity also to acquaint you, that my spouse was yesterday, between six and seven in the morning, safely delivered of a boy.[12] She and I had long ago determined, if this child should be a male, to name it Samuel, after you; to make him, as it were, a living monument of your friendship; but without intention of putting you to expence, as I never make any formal christening. This, I hope, you will do me the honour to accept of.

I shall ever retain that just value and esteem for your singular humanity and goodness, which such a variety of amiable qualities never fail to command; and it shall always be my sincere wish, that you may enjoy a good state of health, to enable you to do all the good that is in your heart to do; that your young and promising family may exceed all your expectations of them; and that they, with Mrs. Richardson, (whose invincible honesty of heart, and unaffected love and veneration for you, must daily gain ground in the affections of a heart like your's) may all concur to make life serenely agreeable to you. I am, &c.

William Strahan.

[11] This 'affair', probably a business venture, remains unidentified.
[12] Samuel Strahan (1745–7), one of three children not to survive to adulthood, the other two being Anne (1748–9) and David (1754–5). For Strahan's announcement of the death of Anne, see Strahan to SR, 21 September 1749.

Richardson to Charles Ackers[1]

Thursday 30 January 1746

MS: location unknown (owned by Dr. Charles Turner in 1968). Autograph letter sent.
Printed source: Transcript by D. F. McKenzie in *N&Q*, n.s. 11 (1964), 299–300.
Endorsement: 'For M[r]. Acres' (in an undetermined hand).

Mr. Acres:
The Gazr. of Monday last.[2] having given Offence to several Persons of Quality; I think it but a Piece of Benevolence, to give you a Caution that you take nothing from it for your Magazine, relating to Mr. W. and Lady T. —[3] It was inserted in the Gazr. without my Knowledge; and I have had a good deal of Trouble about it, and perhaps shall have more. I have no other Motive but Such as one Printer ought to be govern'd by another. I am Your humble Servant

S. Richardson

[1] Charles Ackers (also spelled Acres) (1702/3–82), printer, had been responsible for printing the *London Magazine* since its foundation in 1732.
[2] SR printed and edited the *Daily Gazetteer*, possibly from 1735 but definitely from 1738, until he severed all connections in mid 1746; like the *London Magazine*, the *Daily Gazetteer* was a pro-government political paper that tended to draw significant political scrutiny from the opposition on those involved in its production.
[3] Identified by McKenzie as probably Etheldreda, Viscountess Townshend (*c.* 1708–88), whose politics leaned towards anti-government opposition views, and her lover Thomas Winnington (1696–1746), a politician whose star was on the rise within the government (*ODNB*). The item in the *Daily Gazetteer* that gave SR so much trouble may have reported on a break in their relationship.

Richardson to Thomas Birch

Wednesday 19 April <1746>[1]

MS: BL Add. MS 4317, f. 171. Copy in Gilbert Hill's hand.

Salisbury Court April 19th

Reverend Sir

My Friend Grover[2] informs me, that a Bill is now depending in the House of Commons and likely to pass,[3] which will oblige Authors, when they publish a second Edition of their Works, to print any Additions there may be seperate, for the Benefit <of the>[4] Purchasers of the First. I must use your Canal[5] to acquaint the Author of the *Considerations &c.*[6] with this Affair which I am sorry for, as well upon his Account as my own, as it will create a further Charge in a work, between Ourselves, already expensive and Troublesome enough. I can think of no way to prevent it, unless you and the Author, who I am satisfied from many circumstances is a person of Consequence, will make interest with such Members as attend to learned matters to throw out the Bill. I need not point out to you Misters West, Lyttelton and Hoblyn[7] as proper Persons

---

[1] This date is most immediately indicated by SR's news of 'a Bill now depending in the House' and corroborated by his concerns for the bill's consequences for the second edition of Yorke's *Some Considerations on the Law of Forfeiture* (see relevant notes below); Eaves and Kimpel tentatively assigned this letter to the '1740s'.

[2] John Grover, who died in September 1749, was assistant to Nicholas Hardinge (1699–1758), chief Clerk of the House of Commons, politician, and poet (*ODNB*). SR worked with them as a printer of bills and other official documents, including the House's *Journals*.

[3] The bill itself, ordered to be brought in on 24 March 1746, had merely been a continuation of the Importation Act of 1738 (12 Geo. II, c., 36), which forbade the importation of reprints of books that had originally been composed or published in Britain. On 16 April, however, the House had instructed the committee charged with bringing in the bill to insert a clause 'to provide, that upon the Publishing of a new Edition of any Book, with Alterations or Additions, there be printed and published also a proper Number of such Alterations or Additions, by themselves, of the same Size with the former Editions' (*Journals of the House of Commons*, XXV, 127). The amended bill passed in the Commons on 22 May 1747 and received the Royal Assent on 17 June to become part of the Continuance of Laws Act (22 Geo. II, c., 46) in 1748.

[4] Manuscript has been torn and repaired.

[5] 'A medium of communication, means, agency. *Obs.*; now CHANNEL' (*OED*, def. 7).

[6] *Some Considerations on the Law of Forfeiture, for High Treason* (J. Roberts, 1745; 2nd edn, 1746; 3rd edn, 1748). The 'Author' was Charles Yorke (1722–70), lawyer and politician (*ODNB*); see also SR to Birch, <Before mid-July 1746>.

[7] SR may refer to James West (1703–72), politician and antiquary (*ODNB*); George Lyttelton (1709–73), first Baron Lyttelton (from 1756), politician and writer (*ODNB*); and Robert Hoblyn (bap. 1710, d. 1756), politician and book-collector (*ODNB*).

RICHARDSON TO THOMAS BIRCH, FRIDAY <BEFORE MID-JULY 1746>

to apply to on the Occasion. I am, Reverend Sir, Your Obedient humble Servant

J. Richardson[8]

[8] The signature is clearly 'J'. Perhaps this is a mistake by the copyist.

Richardson to Thomas Birch

Friday <Before mid-July 1746>[1]

MS: BL Add. MS 4317, f. 181. Autograph letter sent.

Revd. Sir

I send you the last Cancelling[2] we have receiv'd. I should have sent it before. But, really, it was uneasy to my Folks to set about it;[3] and they delay'd it as long as they could; and I had some Concern to oblige them to it,[4] loving chearful Service, and loth to give them the Trouble (tho' I paid them for it) of breaking what they call their <pleasures>, and setting up, and taking down their Cases,[5] and going off and on the other Work they had under their Hands. Nevertheless, This only to yourself: for, whoever the Gentleman be; as his Aim is Exactness, and our trouble proceeds from his Diffidence, in a Subject very important, tho' it may not engage, as the Act is passed into a Law, many Buyers, I would not wish him to be made uneasy about our little Inconveniencies.[6] The worst is

[1] Eaves and Kimpel date this letter to the '1740s'. Like SR to Birch, 19 April <1746>, this letter seems to be about the second edition of Yorke's *Considerations*, which was advertised as 'This Day ... publish'd' in the *General Advertiser* on July 18 and in the *London Evening Post* on July 19; see also relevant note below.

[2] A cancel is 'usually executed after the completion of the original press run and sometimes after the distribution of the first copies ... cancels as they were known in the trade went from a tiny piece of paper containing a single punctuation mark pasted over the error to recomposing one or more sheets of an edition' (*Oxford Companion to the Book*, 2 vols., ed. Michael F. Suarez and H. R. Woudhuysen (Oxford University Press, 2010), I, p. 583).

[3] 'Folks' is a very late usage of a now obsolete term for 'retainers, followers; servants, work-people' (*OED*).

[4] 'to oblige them to it' is a superscript insertion.

[5] 'Cases' are compartments holding printing type.

[6] SR probably refers to *Some Considerations on the Law of Forfeiture, for High Treason* (J. Roberts, 1745; 2nd edn, 1746; 3rd edn, 1748), whose anonymous 'Gentleman' author was Charles Yorke (1722–70), a lawyer and politician known, among other things, for 'over-thinking everything' (*ODNB*). Bibliographical evidence for the second edition indicates

108

RICHARDSON TO SAMUEL LOBB, FRIDAY 16 MAY 1746

still to come, to avoid the Confusion of so much Cancelling. But in this I will be as careful[7] <as possible> I am, Sir, Your most humble Servant

S. Richardson

Friday Morn.

that Yorke made a number of last-minute changes while printing was already under way, especially to the contents pages and the introductory section containing extracts from the Acts of Parliament. Yorke's pamphlet supported his father, the Lord Chancellor Hardwicke (1690–1764), in a debate over whether the forfeiture of estates should extend to the children of rebels or be confined to the rebels themselves; Parliament passed a large number of laws to seize lands and disarm the Highland Clans in the years following the Jacobite Rising of 1745.

[7] There is a tear in the manuscript at this point.

Richardson to Samuel Lobb

Friday 16 May 1746

MS: Yale (Osborn). Autograph letter sent (evidence of folding).
Endorsement: 'M.[r] Richardson' (in an undetermined hand).

Reverend Sir,
　　Your Corrections and Additions came too late: Yet were of so much Importance, that I thought proper to cancel 12 Pages for them. – I will make the Charge as gentle to you as possible. But, indeed, my Dear Friend, Nothing should be imperfect in your Copy, after it is given into the Printer's Hands. Into the Hands of a Printer too, who thought he did you pleasure in dispatching.[1] I would not cancel for the Words *they were,* in p. 6. which were in your Copy; but have made an Erratum of them. – They are now completed, and wait your Order. I printed 500 of them. I hope the Manner and Paper will please you.[2] That I did not write to acquaint you, that I was willing to be your Printer; was, That I

[1] Here used in the sense of 'making haste' (*OED*).
[2] Lobb must have been late in sending changes for *The Benevolence Incumbent on Us, as Men and Christians, Considered. In a Sermon Preached at the Assizes Held at Taunton, April 1. 1746. Before the Honourable Sir Thomas Dennison, and Sir Michael Foster, Knights, Justices of His Majesty's Court of King's Bench* (1746), which SR was printing (though not recorded in Maslen), so that SR opted completely to reprint twelve pages of the thirty-two-page sermon. In the end he did not charge Lobb at all; see also SR to Lobb, 4 July 1746; and SR to Lobb, 12 January 1748.

RICHARDSON TO SAMUEL LOBB, FRIDAY 16 MAY 1746

thought you ought not to doubt of it: *In* my Way, or *out* of my Way, in *whatever* Service, I shall always take great Pleasure to Serve Mr. Lobb. In the next place, I was exceedingly taken up, and still am, in the writing Way;[3] so that I forbore writing on all the Occasions, where I could trespass; and never was more in Arrear, than at the Time.

I have searched my *assimilating* Drawer: But if you had not repeated the Contents of your kind Letter and your Soul, I protest to you, I should have been at a Loss to know what they were: – It was a wrong thing of me, not to take more Care of the Originals. I promise you, that my Error shall not be repeated.[4] As I had not so much as read them (Fie upon me!) I was at a Loss to know how you got down, with your better Half, and your, perhaps, more than Third: – (Excuse the Ternian Style!);[5] Unused to Fatigue and Journeyings, as I observed on the Effect the Weather had on you when you favour'd us with your Company's at N. End. It was well for You, Sir, perhaps, that it was my own Fault; Since had you *not* written to me on your Getting down, I should have asked you, If you thought, I had no Concern for my Friends after they were out of my Sight? — How long you liv'd at Bath, before at Farley?[6] And Twenty other as free Questions; which, being so much in fault, I will say no more of.

But as to the *perverse Revenge* you mention, I do assure you, I had it not in my Head or my Heart.[7] And yet I hope, I stand so well in your good Opinion, as that I might safely have referr'd You to *Your* Cabinet, as You did *Yourself* to *mine*. –

But to be serious, I had not complain'd, as You call it, to Mr. Leake,[8] if I had had mere Forms in my Head. I have long, intentionally, discarded that from my Friendships. Whenever I seem'd to shew any Regard to it, it was from Diffidence more than Judgment, or Choice, lest I should appear disrespectful in the

---

[3] SR had been busy in revising *Clarissa*, which he had outlined before 20 June 1744 and was ready to send parts in manuscript out to friends by November 1744.

[4] 'wrong' crossed out.

[5] SR is joking about calling a spouse a 'better half' and seems to refer to Lobb's younger but growing son, Joseph, as, 'perhaps, more than a third'; SR was Joseph's godfather (see SR to Lobb, 11 May 1743). 'Ternian' may be a mistake for 'tertian', which refers to thirds or sets of three; while 'getting down' means 'coming to London'.

[6] I.e. Farleigh Hungerford, about six miles from Bath, where Lobb was Rector from 1736.

[7] Lobb's 'perverse Revenge' is unknown.

[8] SR's brother-in-law, James Leake, who was a common friend.

RICHARDSON TO SAMUEL LOBB, FRIDAY 16 MAY 1746

Want of it; where my Reverence was an Obstacle to my Freedom: But when I presumed to think my Heart was known, I troubled not my self about it. What, for a month together, after I had last seen you, I wished to hear from you, or master for,[9] was purely to know how you got down: How Mrs. Lobb bore her Journey:[10] How you found *our* other Son:[11] And then I could have sat down, and hoped a Continuance of all I wish'd for you, afterwards; without tiezing you with Impertinencies, or mere Ceremonies. – Then, Sir, I had a Wish to see something from the young Gentleman, *before* he commenc'd Author, which I doubted not would have justify'd the Opinion I had conceived of him; and what I still expect and hope from him. – But as to what he mentions and his Papa, too, of Receptions, at London and North-End, and such-like undue Acknowledgements, believe me, dear Sir, they were as little expected or *deserved*. –

My Wife, and her Girls, desire their affectionate Respects, to You, and Yours. We join to thank you for your good Wishes, express'd in so amiable a manner, in yours – tho' only the Substance of what was mislaid.

I beg my Compliments to your Patron: He is a Gentleman whom I greatly *R*espect, for the Regard he most kindly express'd for you.[12] You should not make it so difficult, as I am apprehensive you do, for the Worthy to know you. To be forc'd to undergo a Probation to your self: To be under a Necessity to preach at Bridgwater, to know if you *could* at Taunton, before the Judges! – Let me tell you, my Friend, I should have had a poor Opinion of their *Judgments*, and other Qualifications, had they not given your Discourse the Approbation every good judge (I humbly presume, for my own Part, to say) must give it.[13]

---

9 Meaning unclear.
10 Susanna Lobb, *née* Shipley (1700–77).
11 Presumably Samuel Lobb's older son, William (the 'young Gentleman' a few sentences later), who would start a correspondence of his own with SR later that year. See SR to William Lobb, <July 1746–March 1750>; and SR to Lobb, 4 July 1746.
12 Lobb's patron was SR's friend Ralph Allen, postal reformer and philanthropist in Bath.
13 Lobb must have exerted some effort to be allowed to give his sermon before the judges at the court sessions ('assizes') in Taunton, apparently with the condition that he first give a sermon at Bridgwater, another parish about forty miles from Bath. For the rest of the letter, an entire section of the sheet has torn off along two folds in the paper, rendering the letter all but incomprehensible. Significant parts of the text are lost, which we indicate with <xxxxx>.

RICHARDSON TO SAMUEL LOBB, FRIDAY 4 JULY 1746

As to the Tenaciousness you mention (if I may call it so, led to
call it <xxxxx> have as little an Opinion of your own Judgment,
as you might justly have had <xxxxx> you been influenc'd by any
Remarks of mine in Disfavour, were it practical <xxxxx>

Let me beg your Allowance for the Contradiction, or
Impropriety, if any <xxxxx> or any other. Altho' my whole Heart
is at your Service; yet is my Head up<xxxxx> now, and in half as
many different Places: – You'll hardly believe it, wh<en><xxxxx>
before you. But I was resolved, when I begun, (in this *Half-Sheet*
Length) <xxxxx> however little it may be to the Purpose – But had
I been a Woman, I sho<uld><xxxxx> Adieu, Dear and Reverend
Sir! – May God bless You, and Yours, and all *you love* <xxxxx>
mine, here included) – Prays, Your affectionat<e> <xxxxx>

London 16 May, 1746.

Richardson to Samuel Lobb

Friday 4 July 1746

**MS: Yale (Osborn). Autograph letter sent (evidence of folding and
endorsement).**
Endorsement: 'The Author of Sir Charles Grandison to my relation. JL' (in an
undetermined hand).[1]

Reverend Sir,
I have been pretty much hurry'd since my last, or yours of May
27. (so long ago, I am asham'd to say it is dated!) should not have
been so long unanswer'd. As to the Price of Paper and Printing,
let That alone, till we see what the Discourse will do towards
reimbursing itself.[2] In this I consider you as a Bookseller, as I
generally do every Author, who is at his own Expense in putting
his Works to the Press: – For which the Booksellers thank me not.
You would not, I dare say, have me use my Friend worse than I
would use a London Bookseller.

[1] This endorsement is probably by Samuel Lobb's younger son, and SR's godson, Joseph
Lobb ('JL').
[2] SR has printed *The Benevolence Incumbent on Us, as Men and Christians, Considered* for Lobb
and is now offering to wait to be paid until Lobb can pay him from proceeds; he would go on
to waive the cost entirely. See also SR to Lobb, 16 May 1746; and SR to Lobb, 12 January 1748.

112

RICHARDSON TO SAMUEL LOBB, FRIDAY 4 JULY 1746

I think, my dear Worthy and Reverend Friend, you do not judge quite right, when you wish me to write first to Master Billy:[3] I have a very great Opinion of him; You need not tell him so, lest it be a Balk[4] to him, & set his Modesty at Variance with his Genius, in which Case, I question not, but the former would keep down, the latter, if it once gets it down. He should, therefore, be only told, to write free, easy, and familiar, as if to his most intimate Friend, of like Age, if he pleases: – Without Doubt; And chuse his Subject himself: I would not leave so little Room for future Excellence, as to suppose him qualify'd for Every Subject *I* could give him. – I forgot that – Nevertheless, as he is to write to a Friend, and a Lover of him, and not to a Critick, or Carper, I think, he should begin first – Yet Difference of Years, I stand not upon; I would not have *him* suppose I do. – I have always made the several young Ladies, who oblige me with their Correspondence, begin first. I would not, that they should put me in Mind of Sex,[5] when I don't intend to think of it: And they may be sure, by my Earnestness in putting them upon Writing to me, that I am very desirous of their Favour: And I am not so sure that they pursue their own voluntary Option, unless they begin first: – Many a pretty Correspondence have I lost, on Account of this Presuming Nicety: But when I want Nature and Ease, not Art and Study, I persist, and put up with the Loss; taking the Difficulty as a Test of the Delight or Reluctance to the Correspondence, as they will or will not get over it.

If Master Billy is permitted to read the above, he'll see, that he can have no possible Difficulty in writing to me. When I was young, I was very sheepish; (so I am indeed now I am old: I have not had Confidence enough to try to overcome a Defect so natural to me, tho' I have been a great Loser by it) but this was my Rule to get Courage, when I was obliged to go into Company I had been taught to have an Opinion of. – I let them all speak round[6] before I open'd my Lips after the first Introductions: Then I weigh'd, whether had I been to speak on the same Occasion, that

---

3 Samuel Lobb and his older son, William, had visited SR and a correspondence been proposed by mid May; see SR to Lobb, 16 May 1746; and SR to William Lobb, <July 1746–March 1750>.
4 'a stumbling-block, obstacle. *Obs.*' (*OED*).
5 I.e. 'remind me of their sex': SR insists that he does not want the accidents of age or sex to affect how friends correspond with him.
6 In the sense of taking a turn in speaking.

113

RICHARDSON TO SAMUEL LOBB, FRIDAY 4 JULY 1746

each Person spoke upon, I should have been able to deliver my self as well as they had done; And if I found I should have rather chosen to be silent, than to say something they said, I pre<ser>v'd my Silence and was pleased. And if I could have spoken as well as others, I was the less formulaic: While those who were above my Match, I admir'd, endeavour'd to cultivate their Acquaintance, by making my self agreeable to them by my Modesty, if I could not by my Merit; and to imitate them, as nearly as my Abilities and Situation would permit: Situation, I say, For Business, which was not to be neglected, in order, if possible, to secure my Independence, was not to be neglected; and that generally hurry'd me to my Garret, and my narrow Circle (Printers you know must be in the uppermost Floors, for the Light Sake)[7] and so I kept my Sheepishness, when it had given me very little Reason to be so civil to it. – Now Master Billy (He will see how easily one may turn from Father to Son, where Father and Son so well understand each other) you will by this Time observe, that you cannot have an easier Task set you, than to begin to one, who can scribble such a Quantity without a Subject; Who can be so easily transcended; and who loves the Castigation of a Friend; and should be willing to have you improv'd by my Errors and Inaccuracies: Since a diligent Mind may be as much benefitted by observing what another does that he should not do; or that would not look pretty in himself; as by the most set and laborious Lessons, that could be attempted to be drove into his Head. The rest, my dear Master Billy, I leave to your Self: Only, since I have slid from your Papa's into your Way; I will just detain you from Your Pen and Your Book, while You can make my sincere Compliments, and present my best Wishes, of Health and Prosperity to Every One whom you love and honour; This is now done; – And I am with great Truth, dear Mr. Lobb, Your most faithful and affectionate Friend and Servant

S. Richardson

London, July 4. 1746.

---

[7] Printers required unobstructed daylight for their work, so printing presses were often located on the top floors of printing houses.

Richardson to William Lobb[1]

<July 1746-March 1750>[2]

MS: Yale (Osborn). Autograph letter (incomplete).[3]

what Intelligence, could I but prevail upon you to enter into a <Co>rrespondence with me. You are capable of being *Flint* and *Steel* yourself. You want but *Tinder* to receive your Sparks. Such you <m>ust think me, susceptible of your Fire, tho' almost burnt out, and <on>ly fit to catch your Sparks as they fall. *Proceed, my dear Billy Lobb.* You yourself will find Improvement from frequent and familiar <wr>iting: Familiar Writing no one obtains a Mastery in, who begins not <yo>ung. To[4] My early Years Fortune was not propitious. What would I <ha>ve given for your Opportunities? – Such a Father – Such an Encourager – I <ha>d a very good Father; But he could not be such an Encourager – such <a> Promoter – such an Improver – go on, *my dear Billy Lobb!* – Your <Fr>iends expect great Things from you! The Almighty has blessed your <s>unrise! Take Care that you set not unhappily, from Faults, from <N>egligences of Your own. Nor yet be too sure, from Encouragement, <of> your Ground. *Doubt* my Dear Youth,[5] And Doubt will make You *assured.* And never <d>epart from your Modesty. If you excel thousands, think there are <hun>dreds who may excel you. You would not, I am sure, triumph over <th>e Lowest, when you may emulate the Highest. The famous Wotton <at> Ten Years of Age was sent to the University.[6] His Fame at 12 <w>as so great that the Learned and Pious Bishop Lloyd sent for him, to <m>anage and order his

---

[1] William Lobb (*c.* 1736–65), elder son of SR's friend Samuel Lobb; became Fellow of Peterhouse, University of Cambridge in 1758.

[2] Date range suggested by Eaves and Kimpel based on SR to Lobb, 4 July 1746, in which SR discusses conditions for a correspondence with William; and on SR to William Lobb, 10 April 1750, by which point the correspondence is well established. The tone of this letter, with its many exhortations to William, seems to place it close to the start of their correspondence; it especially echoes comments about William in SR to Lobb, 16 May 1746.

[3] Only this final page of an originally multi-page letter survives. The page is heavily damaged or cropped on the left edge, which has resulted in some loss of text.

[4] 'To' is an insertion in SR's hand.

[5] 'my Dear Youth,' is an insertion in SR's hand.

[6] William Wotton (1666–1727), linguist and theologian; 'a prodigious natural linguist who could read Latin, Greek, and Hebrew verses when aged five', Wotton acquired a BA in 1680, an MA in 1683, and a BD in 1691 (*ODNB*).

RICHARDSON TO JOHN SHARPE, <SUMMER 1746>

Library, and assist him in some of his learned <Di>squisitions.⁷ At 17 he was thought to excel the most Learned of his <A>ge. Shew, my dear Billy Lobb, that you can bear Praise. People <t>hat deserve it, best bear it. Good Reason why!⁸ They are most used to it. Praise is <f>amiliar to them – To be proud of it, is to deserve to forfeit it. Yet <it> is honest to love it, and desire it. But before that the *Desire* and *Deserts* <go> together. I know they will in you,⁹ They must. Adieu, for the present, *my <de>ar Billy Lobb.* Remember, once more, that the Eyes of all your <Fri>ends and Favorers are upon you. More particularly the Eyes of him <w>ho is with great and affectionate Regard, my dear Youth, Your true Friend, and obliged Correspondent

S. Richardson

<B>est Respects, to all whom you <d>eservedly Love and Honour.

⁷ William Lloyd (1627–1717), bishop of Worcester, was Wotton's early patron in his previous position as bishop of St. Asaph (*ODNB*). Ironically, William Lobb's grandfather, Stephen Lobb (d. 1699), a dissenting minister, had been instrumental in advising James II to incarcerate the bishops – including Lloyd – in the Tower for resisting the king's declaration of religious toleration; see Eland, p. 23.
⁸ 'Good Reason why!' is an insertion in SR's hand.
⁹ 'in you,' is an insertion in SR's hand.

Richardson to John Sharpe¹

<Summer 1746>

MS: PRO TS 20/45 f. 4. Autograph letter sent.
Address: 'To John Sharpe, Esq' (in SR's hand).
Endorsement: 'From Mr. Richardson, the Printer' (in an undetermined hand).

Sir
I have enquir'd about Short-hand Writers: Have heard of one Mr. Ewen Schoolmaster in Meeting-house Yard, Poor Jewry-Lane, near Aldgate. He takes down the Tryals at the Old Bailey.²

¹ John Sharpe (1700?–56), lawyer and Solicitor to the Treasury (from 1742), was tasked with managing the logistics of the prosecution and trials (held in autumn 1746) following the Jacobite Rebellion (1745). In the course of securing documents, testimony, and witnesses as well as coordinating the detention, transport, and trial of prisoners, he seems to have asked SR for recommendations for shorthand writers to record the proceedings.
² Ewen remains unidentified. The Old Bailey was the site of criminal trials from its rebuilding in 1673 after the Great Fire of London. Accounts of the trials began to be published immediately and by the eighteenth century had become a commercial success.

RICHARDSON TO JOHN SHARPE, <SUMMER 1746>

Mr. Burnham is another; To be heard of at Mr. Clark's
Bookseller at the Royal Exchange.[3]

Mr. Weston, over-against Water-Lane, Fleetstreet, has so often
advertised himself, that I suppose I need not mention him.[4]

Give me Leave to add, that Mr. Basketts Pretension of his
Patents is without Foundation.[5] Dr. Sacheverell's Tryal was printed
by Mr. Tonson: Lord Macclesfield's by Mr. Buckley;[6] And all
his Father[7] pretended to was to have Copies at a Price from the
Printers, to serve the House of Lords with them. I am, Sir, Your
most faithful and obliged Servant

S. Richardson

Your own Office, Wednesday Morn.

---

[3] Burnham remains unidentified. There were two John Clarkes who sold and published
books from a shop at the Old or Royal Exchange; the younger Clarke became Master of the
Company of Stationers in 1760 while the older Clarke, a well-known publisher of divinity,
may have been the target of *A Letter to Mr. John Clark, Bookseller; Upon His Printing on Both
Sides in the Present Debates Among the Dissenting Ministers* (1719).

[4] James Weston (1688?–1748?), stenographer notorious for aggressively advertising his ser-
vices and his book, *Stenography Completed, or, The Art of Short-hand Brought to Perfection*
(1727) (*ODNB*).

[5] SR is probably weighing in on a case in the Court of Chancery, *Baskett v. University of
Cambridge*, in which the King's Printer, Thomas Baskett (d. 1761), and his brother Robert
(d. 1767?), who had inherited the printing business and patents from their father John
(d. 1742), were seeking an injunction against the university for infringing on their exclusive
right to print acts of Parliament; the case was not settled until 1758 (establishing that the
university had a concurrent authority to print) but had already been argued in front of a
judge once in the autumn of 1745.

[6] Jacob Tonson I (1655/6–1736) and Samuel Buckley (1674?–1741), both well-known booksellers of the previous generation, had published the trials of Sacheverell and Lord Macclesfield
'by order of the House of Peers' in 1710 and 1725, respectively. Henry Sacheverell (bap.
1674, d. 1724), Church of England clergyman and religious controversialist, was impeached
for seditious preaching and publications in 1709–10 (*ODNB*). Thomas Parker, first Earl of
Macclesfield (1667–1732), lord chief justice and lord chancellor, was centrally involved in
the prosecution of Sacheverell, and was himself impeached for embezzlement, corruption,
and financial abuse in 1725 (*ODNB*).

[7] 'he' corrected to 'his' and 'Father' inserted, all in SR's hand.

Richardson to Arthur Onslow[1]

Wednesday 29 October 1746

MS: FM XIII, 3, f. 57. Copy in SR's hand.[2]

Sir,

Your <Honour>[3] will be pleased to excuse a Trouble that has Gratitude and Veneration for its Foundation; both inhanc'd by the distinguishing Favour of your Letter,[4] in which you give me Hope, that at some happy Hour of your Leisure, I may be admitted to your chearful and chearing Presence.

I could not, Sir, deny to my self the Pleasure of having it in my Power, by so great an Instance of your Goodness to me, to give Pleasure to a Mind, one of the worthiest that I know in Man. I accordingly inclosed it in a Letter to Mr. Hill: And the opposite Leaf is a[5] Copy of the Return I had to it.[6] As I presume to be but the Vehicle of a worthy Man's Grateful and Just Sentiments, I will only add, that I am, with equal Truth and Obligation Sir, your Humble &[7] Most Faithful & Obedient Servant

S.R.[8]

S. Court, Fleetstreet. Oct 29. 1746.

---

[1] Arthur Onslow (1691–1768), speaker of the House of Commons from 1728 to 1761 (*ODNB*).
[2] SR has copied this letter at the top of Hill to SR, 25 October 1746.
[3] SR has emended 'Your Honour to' 'You'.
[4] Now lost.
[5] SR has crossed out 'the' and written 'a' after it.
[6] See Hill to SR, 29 October 1746.
[7] 'Humble &' has been crossed out by SR.
[8] Signature has been crossed out by SR.

Mr. Bennet[1] to Richardson

<1746 or 1747>[2]

MS: FM XV, 3, ff. 10-11. Copy in Gilbert Hill's hand.
Endorsement: 'Letter 3' (in Martha Richardson's hand); 'Mr. Bennett justifying the Harlowes' (in Gilbert Hill's hand); 'Mr. Bennet Justifying the Harlowes' (in SR's hand, on the outside of the letter); 'Clarissa Papers' (in SR's late hand, on the outside of the letter).

Sir,

I have read over very attentively Mr. Cibber's Letters, as likewise Yours to him:[3] and I think with Sir R. d'Coverley much may be said on both sides;[4] but I cannot help inclining to his Opinion with regard to the Character of Lovelace, as entertain'd of him by the Harlowe Family.[5]

Wou'd not You think Yourself Justify'd in endeavouring to *force* Your Daughter to marry Solmes, rather than risque her being snap'd up by a Lovelace, knowing the latter to be an avow'd Libertine?

No, You will say, I suppose: because She promises not to marry at all, if You will be silent about Solmes; will give up her Fortune to You, and put an End to her Correspondence with Lovelace.

What reason have You to depend on all this? did she not correspond with Lovelace before Solmes made any offers? was not Lovelace permitted to address her before the Rencounter between the Brother and Him? did She not at that time countenance his Addresses? and can it be *depend<ed> on* that She cou'd guard against the insinuations of suc<h> an Intriguer who had doubtless

---

[1] 'Mr. Bennet' remains unidentified; for SR's own speculation as to his possible identity, see SR to Hildesley, 13 July 1754, n. 2. A 'George Bennet, A.B. Late of St. John's College, Oxford' published the serialized *Pamela Versified: or, Virtue Rewarded. An Heroic Poem* in July 1741, but the venture seems to have collapsed after the second instalment in August; see *'Pamela' in the Marketplace*, pp. 44–6.

[2] Date range proposed by Eaves and Kimpel.

[3] These letters are now lost.

[4] A reference to a character from *The Spectator*, Roger de Coverley. Said to have been created by Joseph Addison, the character was a country gentleman and member of the Spectator Club. The phrase, 'Much might be said on both sides', however, is actually used by Mr Spectator when trying to avoid giving offence to Sir Roger in *Spectator* 122.

[5] The letter from actor Colley Cibber to which Bennet refers seems now lost, but we know that Cibber felt some sympathy and admiration for the character of Lovelace (see Cibber to SR, 30 March 1748).

JAMES HERVEY TO RICHARDSON, SATURDAY 24 JANUARY 1747

made some impression on her, or She wou'd not have enter'd into a Literary Cor<respondence> <xxxxx *1+ words*><?>[6]

Before the Rencounter I will suppose the Father had no Objection to his *Libertinism*, but Solmes's offer suiting his Avaricious disposition, he now makes *that* a pretence to hide his true Reason – but this is begging the Question; for who can pretend to say the *Rencounter* was not his inducement for breaking off the Match, let Who will, have been the Aggressor? – I believe such an Affair in any Family wou'd put an end to all intended Alliances.

Supposing I have stated the Matter right, I really think the Father is *almost*, if not quite, justify'd: And that Cla: will be absolutely condemn'd for throwing herself into the Arms of so Libertine and impetuous a Man as Lovelace.

If Lovelace appear'd to all the Family a Sober well bred Man (whatever his true Character might be) then the Family wou'd be condemn'd, and Cla: almost applauded.

I have read *Miss C.'<s>* Letter with infinite pleasure,[7] and if I may judge of the Lady's Mind by an Elegant Remark she has made, You will neve<r> Draw Clarissa's picture, unless *She* sets for it. I am Sir Your most Obedient Humble Servant

---

[6] The sheet on which this first page of the letter is written has been heavily cropped along the right and bottom edges sometime after the letter was copied into SR's letter book, which resulted in some loss of text along both edges. After the publication of *Pamela*, SR compiled autograph letters and copies into dedicated volumes.

[7] Possibly Elizabeth Carter. See Carter to SR, 16 December 1748. Carter was referred to as 'Miss C.' not only by SR but by others in the period.

James Hervey[1] to Richardson

Saturday 24 January 1747

MS: Morgan MA 1024.11. Autograph letter sent (evidence of folding and sealing wax).
Endorsement: 'Jan. 24 1747 Rev. Hervey at Weston, near Northampton' (in SR's hand, on the outside of the letter); 'Jan. 24. 1747' (in SR's late hand, on the letter's first page).

---

[1] James Hervey (1714–58), Church of England clergyman and writer (*ODNB*). Hervey was negotiating for SR to print second editions of his *Meditations Among the Tombs* and *Reflections on a Flower-Garden* (both 1746); see also Hervey to SR, 3 November 1747.

JAMES HERVEY TO RICHARDSON, SATURDAY 24 JANUARY 1747

Dear Sir,

I thank You for the Answer which your Letter brought to my Queries. – I wish, You woud inform me, What might be the Expence of two neat Frontispieces. – As also, How the Print of a Duodecimo Edition can be dearer than that of an Octavo.[2] When there is the same Number of Letters in both, consequently the Trouble of setting the Press must be equal for both. And I suppose, a larger Type can hardly be dearer than a small one.[3] – I own, I am very much inclined to prefer the Duodecimo Size. All my Acquaintance chuse to have the Book in the Pocket Size. – The Price, I fancy, may be pretty near the same. Especially, if we allow a little better Character & Paper. Which I would gladly have done. – The Quantity, & of Course the Bulk, of the second Edition will be somewhat larger than those of the first. This will be occasioned by the Corrections & various Additions which I shall make. Which, I imagine, will augment the whole to another Sheet. – I shall interleave a printed Copy,[4] & proceed upon the Corrections out of hand. In the mean Time let me desire You to favour me with an Answer; or, if You acquiesce in my Proposal, to make choice of an elegant Type, & beautifull Paper, & send me a Specimen in Duodecimo. Perhaps, the second Edition may make its Appearance with the returning Flowers, Let Us try to have like the Season & the Subject.[5] Which will recommend the Piece, & oblige, Dear Sir, your most humble Servant

J. Hervey

Weston. Jan. 24. 1746

[2] 'Octavo' and 'duodecimo' are measures of how often a printed sheet has been folded (here: three and four times, respectively) to make up the pages of a book. Generally, though not necessarily, the more often a sheet has been folded, the smaller the book's individual pages will be. In the end, Hervey settled for octavo until the fourth edition, when he switched to duodecimo.

[3] The word 'larger' has a 2 written above it, the word 'small' has a 1, both in what looks like Hervey's hand.

[4] 'Interleaving' a book means to insert blank pages on which corrections or additions can be written.

[5] It would take until 1748 for the second edition to appear, significantly enlarged, under the title *Meditations and Contemplations*; see SR to Hervey, 28 January 1747.

Richardson to James Hervey

Wednesday 28 January 1747

MS: Morgan MA 1024.1. Autograph letter sent (evidence of folding).
Address: 'To the Revd. Mr Hervey Jan. 28. 1747' (in SR's hand on the outside of the letter).
Endorsement: 'What I have heard of his Work:' (added to the address in SR's late hand on the outside of the letter); 'Jan. 28. 1747' (in SR's hand at the top of the letter's first page).

Reverend Sir,

It would save a good Deal of Trouble to yourself, if, as you seem so very desirous to have your Piece printed after a particular manner, you would point out the Book, the Page, the Type, you would have it printed after; and then you'd *have*, as well as *give*, a Specimen, without sending you down a Twelves Page[1] or two at random.

Methinks I should be very loth, that my Opinion should be asked, only to make me appear tenacious afterwards, when it is a Rule with me, and I believe with most Printers, when his Author knows his Mind, and the Printer knows it to be his Mind, to acquiesce with it.

I was obliged to answer your Queries at random; and must, unless you let me know what you absolutely determine upon. The Print and Paper of the First Edition I thought, not bad. But no Print I believe can come up to your own Delicacy.

As to the Frontispieces; those, like the Print, must be prescribed by yourself: There are Books; There are Designs; There are Frontispieces; which you might choose out of, as to the Manner, at least; and then I could ask an Engraver proper Questions, and be able to satisfy your Queries as to his Part. As they may be done, they may come to *Two* Guineas, or *Ten*. Have you, Sir, thought of Designs for them? – That would help towards an Answer to your Question.[2]

---

[1] I.e. a page in duodecimo format, for which each printed sheet has been folded four times to create twelve pages; see Hervey to SR, 24 January 1747. Hervey was deliberating in what format and design to reprint his *Meditations Among the Tombs* and *Reflections on a Flower-Garden* (both 1746); see Hervey to SR, 24 January 1747; and again Hervey to SR, 3 November 1747.

[2] Hervey apparently decided on one frontispiece facing the title page of each volume of what would finally become the *Meditations and Contemplations* (1748) plus another illustration, of a tomb, in volume one.

RICHARDSON TO JAMES HERVEY, WEDNESDAY 28 JANUARY 1747

Small Print is dearer than large: Your Book wants Bulk, and it would be thinner, I think, in a smaller Type: The Sheet you would add – But I am answering without knowing to what: When I see the Copy, and am told the Manner by another Book, I shall be able to write with Certainty; if Writing, rather than Printing, be necessary.

You asked me by your former, If I had heard any Objections – A Gentleman, who is an admirable Judge (to whom I presented one), this Day told me, that he thought the Subject was too much ornamented: And, tho' a fine Scholar, found fault with the Learning display'd in the Notes. A Flower-Garden, and a Tomb, he would have it, required only plain and good English, for English Readers, and for Youth for whom, by the Style, he said, the Piece was principally calculated; since he thought it too fanciful for the Solid and Learned.[3] I am not of his Opinion; for I think every Person, whether in Years, or in Youth, may be delighted and instructed by it; tho' I think the Learning may be spared, if you please: And I mention it the rather, for you to think of, as possibly your Additions may be of that Sort. – His Daughter, he says, is highly pleased with the Piece; wants to see you; and calls you, Her *Dainty*[4] *Favourite*.

I am sure, by your inquiring after Objections, you will not be displeased with my Communicativeness. I am, Sir, Your faithful and obedient Servant,

S. Richardson.

London, Jan. 28. 1746–7.

---

[3] This 'Gentleman' remains unidentified but may have been identical with the 'judicious friend' whose opinion on Hervey's *Meditations* – 'too flowery for prose, too affected … *prose run mad*' – SR mentioned to Lady Bradshaigh three years later; see SR to Lady Bradshaigh, 31 March 1750.

[4] 'Valuable, fine, handsome; choice, excellent; pleasant, delightful. *Obs.*' (*OED*).

Joseph Highmore[1] to Richardson

<Autumn 1747>[2]

MS: FM XV, 2, f. 86. Copy in Gilbert Hill's hand.
Endorsement: 'Mrs Brand' (in Hill's hand, crossed out); 'Letter 47' (in Martha Richardson's hand); 'Clarissa' and 'Mr Highmore' (in SR's late hand, 'ighmore' has been crossed out).

Mr. Lovelace is so determin'd a Villain, so resolutely wicked, and perseveres in his hellish Purposes with such unshaken Constancy, that to suppose him at the same time to have any Thought of Religion and especially any Veneration for it, is not only utterly inconsistent with his Character, but, instead of being any Recommendation, is, on the contrary, the greatest Reproach to Religion: And I think it wou'd be doing greater Honour to it, to suppose him an Infidel, or even an Atheist. What Sort of an Idea must a Man have of God, who shall act in the cursed Manner he is represented to do; and yet flatter himself that he shall be pardon'd and accepted by that Being, whom he is confessedly and resolvedly affronting in so egregious a manner, on the weak pretence, that, after gratifying every wicked Inclination, and committing the worst and basest Crimes that human Nature is capable of (if human Nature is capable of them), he designs some time or other to repent and reform? I say, what Notion must such a Man have of God and Religion? And can any reasonable Man, and one who is religious himself, think he does Honour to both, by pretending that this Conduct, and these Sentiments, are consistent? I own I cannot conceive any thing more derogatory to the Honour of God and his moral Perfections, or less serviceable to the Cause of true Religion, than such Suppositions. No! Let the Dog be an Atheist, or worse, if worse can be; or, at least, say nothing about his religious Sentiments; unless he is represented as an abominable[3] Hypocrite.

---

[1] Joseph Highmore (1692–1780), painter, who painted scenes and characters from *Pamela*, *Clarissa*, and *Grandison* as well as two portraits of SR and one (destroyed during World War II) of his second wife, Elizabeth Leake Richardson (*ODNB*).

[2] Date suggested by Eaves and Kimpel; Highmore's questioning of the necessity of a preface indicates that this letter was originally written prior to publication of volumes I and II of *Clarissa* in December 1747. This copy consists of selections and abstracts rather than representing a complete transcription of the original letter.

[3] Originally 'admirable' but amended by the copyist.

JOSEPH HIGHMORE TO RICHARDSON, <AUTUMN 1747>

May it not be said, if the Editor has the highest Opinion of that Gentleman's Knowlege, Judgment, Experience & Candour, that it seems inconsistent with this Testimony to his Abilities to pay no Regard to his Advice, but rather to follow that of others, whose Talents he says nothing of? – And also may not that Gentleman be somewhat offended at the Intimation which follows, That the Period of Life, to which he is now arrived, may be the Cause why he contents himself with Amusement, rather than Instruction, altho' he is here complimented with being happy in having got over those dangerous Situations, which require Advice and Cautions, and has filled up his Measures of Knowlege to the Top?[4]

Two first Vols. by way of Specimen, and to be determin'd with regard to the rest, &c.

Meantime, &c. deleted[5]

A young Lady of an excellent Understanding & Disposition, of the sweetest Manners, and greatest Delicacy, with the strictest Notions of Religion, Virtue, and filial Duty.

I believe it wou'd not be difficult to find more than Two of the Editor's Friends, that wou'd agree in leaving out many Parts; particularly of Lovelace's Stratagems –

If these Observations are not of Weight enough to alter any Part of the Preface, if there be one – & whether a Preface be at all necessary?

---

[4] Highmore here refers to and quotes from the preface to *Clarissa*, in which SR rejects the advice of an unidentified 'Gentleman' to focus the novel's narrative on the main character, transpose much of it from first-person epistles into third-person narration, and cut everything else (see *Clarissa*, I, pp. v–vii). SR's correspondent R. Smith believed that Highmore was referring to himself as that 'Gentleman', but that seems to be a misreading (see Smith to SR, <Autumn 1747>); SR's friend Aaron Hill was probably right that the 'Gentleman' was Colley Cibber instead (see Hill to SR, 3 December 1747).

[5] The copyist here indicates passages left out from the original letter; the first is actually an abstract of a passage in the preface to *Clarissa* (*Clarissa*, I, p. vii).

R. Smith[1] to Richardson

<Autumn 1747>[2]

MS: FM XV, 2, ff. 87–8. Copy in Gilbert Hill's hand.
Endorsement: 'Letter 48' (in Martha Richardson's hand); 'Mr. R. Smith' (in SR's late hand).

> Sir,
> The Arguments contained in the foregoing seeming to be much built upon by the Writer, and the Decision of great Importance, I shall venture to be equally plain in the following Remarks, that no Doubt may remain, if possible, to the Objector himself.
> To suppose Mr. Lovelace, Villain as he is, has some Veneration for Religion, as the Best upon the Whole, is no more than what all Men, virtuous or not, must necessarily have: And, since this Gentleman has *filled up his Measures of Knowlege to the Top*, as he repeats of himself from the Preface,[3] he cannot but know, that Theoretical and Practical Religion are two different things; that Nominal Christianity may be where Real is not; and that the Actions of Him who calls himself Most Christian may not always be even al-most Christian; in other Words, that the Passions will drive harder, and to a different Goal, than the Understanding. This being the Case, Where is the Inconsistency to suppose, that Lovelace, a Man of great natural and acquired Talents, has yet the Sense to own a God, without which he cannot account for himself? and, altho' he ought to dread his Vengeance for the Violation of the eternal Laws of Rectitude, yet that his Passions, always importuning, should mislead his Judgment, seldom or never exercised on those Topics which are above the World? In short, is any Man *quite* so good, as his Profession demands? And are not some much worse, than they wou'd like to acknowledge? which shews, that their Reason disallows the Course of their Actions: So that they may justly say of themselves, with Medea
> — Video meliora, proboque;

---

[1] 'R. Smith' remains unidentified even though he offered some of the most incisive commentary on *Clarissa* as well as responses to several suggestions for alterations from SR's correspondents; see also Smith to SR, 3 February 1749; and Smith to SR, 20 May 1749.

[2] Date suggested by Eaves and Kimpel; it comments on Joseph Highmore to SR, <Autumn 1747>.

[3] This passage quotes Highmore to SR, <Autumn 1747>.

R. SMITH TO RICHARDSON, ‹AUTUMN 1747›

Deteriora sequor —[4]

This also accounts for Lovelace's putting of{f} his Repentance to a long Day: Which all the World knows is not a singular Case.

But, if, on the contrary, the Editor makes use of this Gentleman's Scheme of making Lovelace an Infidel or Atheist, What will the Adviser do to secure the admirable Clarissa's Character, in entering upon Terms with such an open Profligate, when, before, she had rejected Wyerly on this very account?[5] From bad Principles what but similar Practices must flow? since as the Fountain, such is the Stream: And bad Principles avow'd, must always be a Criterion to judge of the Heart; for out of the Abundance of the Heart the Mouth speaketh:[6] Whereas, when loose Principles are not avow'd by the Tongue, and a Veil of Bravery is thrown over the Actions; there, if a Person is deceiv'd, it must be analogous to the simplicity of the Dove being over-reach'd by the subtlety of the Serpent.[7]

How inconsistent is the Gentleman in advising Lovelace to be made an Infidel or Atheist in the same Paragraph, which concludes with proposing him to be *represented as an Hypocrite*! An Hypocrite may be supposed to conceal real Infidelity under a sanctimonious Appearance; for, if he believes in God, he cannot hope to delude him: An Atheist discovers his Enmity to Mankind by wishing the Bonds of Society to be dissolved, and disputing the Being and Authority of the Governor of the World.

Why shou'd the Gentleman be angry with the Editor's Friends, unknown, and supposed without Talents? when he is at the same time, so conscious of his own Abilities, that he ought rather to despise his Competitors in the Field of Cavil? – But what if, on the contrary, the Editor might think, that to expatiate on the Characters of his other Friends was intirely superfluous, being Gentlemen already long known to the learned & ingenious World? I profess I am not acquainted with his Sentiments on this Subject: But, if my Conjecture be right, what must be the Consequence, with regard to this Gentleman; who has offer'd nothing like an Argument; tho' he has endeavour'd to depreciate the Editor's other Friends, and the Editor

---

[4] Ovid, *Metamorphoses*, Book 7, lines 20–1: 'I see the better and approve it, but I follow the worse' (Loeb 42, pp. 342–3); spoken by Medea in trying to resist her infatuation with Jason.
[5] Cf. *Clarissa*, VII, pp. 72–3.
[6] This phrase appears in both Luke 6:45 and Matthew 12:34.
[7] Proverbial, a characterization and contrast found throughout the Bible, e.g. Genesis 3:1, Corinthians 11:3, and esp. Matthew 10:16.

JAMES HERVEY TO RICHARDSON, TUESDAY 3 NOVEMBER 1747

himself, who is, in Tully's Words *omni laude & vituperio longe major?*[8] as his divine Clarissa will be the Wonder of this Age, and probably the great Exemplar of the following; and to whom may be applied that of Horace in a far nobler Sense than to the Witch Canidia;

– Tu pudica, tu proba,

Perambulabis astra, sidus aureum.[9]

As the Work itself, for the copious Variety, and general Usefulness of the Matter, and the short Time in which it was completed, is most like Virgil's

– Nec longum tempus; & ingens

Exiit ad coelum ramis felicibus arbos.[10]

I am the Editor's, and the Friend's of the Editor's Most humble Servant

Elisha Brand.[11]

---

[8] Marcus Tullius Cicero. The online Loeb edition of Cicero does not include this phrase, but it translates as 'greater by far than all praise and blame'. Smith may be trying to convey a general sentiment attributed to Cicero in the eighteenth century.

[9] Horace, Epode 17, lines 40–1: 'O chaste and respectable lady, you will walk among the constellations as a golden star' (Loeb 33, pp. 314–15). In Epodes 5 and 17, Canidia is an antagonistic figure who threatens Horace's poetic prowess; in these two lines, he seeks to placate her.

[10] Virgil, *Georgics*, Book 2, lines 80–1: 'then fruitful slips are let in, and in a little while, lo! a mighty tree shoots up skyward with joyous boughs'. The passage refers to the grafting of fruit trees; it actually continues, 'and marvels at its strange leafage and fruits not its own' (Loeb 63, pp. 140–3).

[11] Smith here takes as pseudonym the name of a character, Elias Brand, whom he probably helped create but who only gained his questionable prominence in the third edition (1751) of *Clarissa*; see T. C. Duncan Eaves and Ben D. Kimpel, 'Richardson's Helper in Creating the Character of Elias Brand', *N&Q*, n.s. 14 (1967), 414–15.

James Hervey to Richardson

Tuesday 3 November 1747

Printed source: B: II, 180–2.
First printing: Barbauld, *Correspondence* (1804).

Weston, Nov. 3, 1747.

Dear Sir,

I can hardly forbear saying, that I almost envy the generosity which breathes in your letter. I hope it will always tend to fill my heart with conscious shame; and to enlarge it with some inferior degrees of emulating benevolence. Before this incident, I could not so much as guess at the solid worth of Mr. Richardson: but now I beg leave to regard him, not as a printer whom I employ, but as a choice friend, whom I highly honour, cordially love, and for whom I shall frequently pray.

And now, my dear friend, let me ask, whether you know any virtuous and valuable person in distressed circumstances, to whom a few guineas might be a seasonable and acceptable present. If you do, be so kind as to inform me at your leisure; and withal permit me to put such a little gift into your hand, to be transmitted to the worthy object.[1]

I agreed with Mr. Rivington for the impression now printing off, at the rate of twenty-five guineas, and two dozen of copies, bound and lettered for my share. I was willing to transfer my right to him; because I imagined it would be natural for him, in such a case, to push the sale, and be more concerned for the reputation of the book.[2]

I assure you, Sir, if any of my thoughts are so happy as to please you, I shall entertain the more chearful hope with relation to the work that is going to appear; and shall be the more easily induced to form some other attempt of a public nature.[3] O! that my capacities were equal to the arduous, but delightful task, which your pen has assigned! Nothing could be more pleasing to my own taste, than to explain the meaning, point out the beauties, and enforce the evangelical truths, with which the admirable prophecy of Isaiah is most copiously enriched, most illustriously adorned.[4]

---

[1] The specific 'incident' mentioned above remains unidentified, but SR and Hervey were deeply invested in acts of charity to relieve poor families and individuals (see also the exchange between Hervey and SR in January 1747; and Hervey to SR, 29 February 1748).

[2] SR was in the process of printing Hervey's *Meditations and Contemplations* (2 vols., 1748), sold in London by John Rivington (1720–92) and his brother James (1724–1802), and in Bath by SR's brother-in-law, James Leake. The book was very popular, reaching three editions within the first year and twenty-six editions by 1800. SR printed editions 2, 4–5, and 7–10 (1748–53), as well as two of the meditations it contained as separate pamphlets (both 1746). These seem to have been counted as the first edition (see also Hervey to SR, 29 February 1748, and their letters of January 1747). Despite selling his copyright to Rivington, Hervey earned about £700 from the *Meditations and Contemplations*, all of which he gave to charity.

[3] Hervey would in fact go on to write another very successful book, the three-volume *Theron and Aspasio* (1755), which went into three editions within the first year.

[4] SR seems to have suggested that Hervey undertake an extended explication of the Book of Isaiah, considered one of the more complicated of the books of prophecy.

JOHN HEYLYN TO RICHARDSON, THURSDAY 12 NOVEMBER 1747

I almost despair. – Nevertheless, I should be very glad, if, in some future vacant half-hour, you would suggest such a form and method of executing this design, as might be most acceptable and useful. I am, dear Sir, with very great respect and affection, Your sincere and cordial Friend,

J. Harvey.

John Heylyn[1] to Richardson

Thursday 12 November 1747

MS: FM XV, 2, f. 3v. Copy in Gilbert Hill's hand.
Endorsement: 'D^r. Heylin' (in Hill's hand).

Hampstead, Novr. 12. 1747.

Dear Sir,
I write this only to assure you, that I have perused the Title and Preface with the Application you desired; and find nothing I would choose to alter or omit, except in the Title – *With a View to both Worlds*; especially as that is included in the *most important* preceding.[2]

[Then, after enumerating the Errata in the Sheet, the Dr. adds] I have nothing more but to repeat my Thanks for the Pleasure I have had, and still expect from your inimitable Pen. I am, Dear Sir, Your faithful Servant,

John Heylin.

[1] John Heylyn (1684/5–1759), theologian and mystic, Rector of St Mary-le-Strand from 1724, prebendary of Westminster Abbey from 1743, and a chaplain in ordinary to George II (1733–48) (*ODNB*).

[2] Heylyn suggests amending the title page of *Clarissa* and SR adopted his suggestion: in the title page of the first edition, the subtitle is '*Comprehending* THE MOST IMPORTANT CONCERNS OF PRIVATE LIFE'.

130

Mary Heylin[1] to Richardson

Tuesday 24 November 1747

MS: FM XV, 2, f. 3r. Copy in Gilbert Hill's hand.
Endorsement: 'Mrs Heylin'[2] and 'On Clarissa' (in Hill's hand); 'Letter 5' (in Martha Richardson's hand); 'Clarissa' (in SR's late hand).

Nov. 24. 1747.

Good Sir,

I could not answer it to myself, was I not personally, or by a Line, to return you Thanks for the Pleasure you have given us in reading Clarissa: But must beg Pardon for my Impertinence, when I accuse you of Cruelty in raising our Expectations to the highest Pitch of Woman's Curiosity and Impatience and then unkindly leaving us in Suspense, till the Opinion of the World shall determine you when you shall give us the Sequel. As none can pretend to censure so charming a Story, unless it fall into the Hands of the Ignorant and Envious; and as the one ought to be pitied, as much as the other despised; I really think, Sir, (excuse my Freedom) you should by no Means delay obliging your Friends, as well as the thinking Part of Mankind, with the proceeding Volumes of so useful and entertaining a History.[3] The just Esteem I have of your unparalleled Good Sense makes me consider you as singled out by Providence for the Improvement of this degenerate Age. And, Oh Sir! who would wish for Riches, or any of the gaudy Pomp this Life affords, could they, in Lieu of it, be blest with such a happy Understanding as you are Master of! But I will say no more (as I am

---

[1] It is not known who 'Mary Heylin' was. The letter is copied on the reverse of John Heylyn to SR, 12 November 1747, and endorsed as from 'Mrs Heylin', but John Heylyn's second wife, Elizabeth (*née* Ebbutt) had just died on 9 June 1747; his surviving daughter (d. 1759) remained unmarried and was called Elizabeth; the wife of his brother, Edward (1695–1765), one of the founders of the Bow porcelain factory, was called Jane; and his surviving son, John (1712–68?), a merchant in Bristol, would not marry Elizabeth Staunton (1732–?) until 1761. It is of course always possible that the copyist made a mistake in transcribing the letter, or that 'Mary' was a nickname; in that case, given the letter's content and placement, John Heylyn's daughter Elizabeth Heylyn is the most likely candidate.

[2] 'eylin' has been crossed through, perhaps when SR later edited this letter.

[3] The first two volumes of *Clarissa* were published on 1 December 1747, with a note in the Preface that 'it was resolved to present to the World, the Two First Volumes, by way of Specimen; and to be determined with regard to the rest by the Reception those should meet with' (*Clarissa*, I, p. vii). Heylyn was reading the first two volumes in proof.

ELIZABETH CARTER TO RICHARDSON, SUNDAY 13 DECEMBER 1747

sensible my Pen is not equal to paint your true Merit,) than that I am, Your constant admirer, obliged Friend, and Humble Servant

Mary Heylin[4]

[4] Again the letters 'eylin' have been crossed through to obscure the name.

Elizabeth Carter[1] to Richardson

Sunday 13 December 1747

Printed source: MM, no. 228 (1 July 1812), 533–4.
First printing: MM (1812).

Canterbury, Dec. 13, 1747

Sir,

I was, very lately, extremely surprized on receiving an account that you have thought proper to print an Ode, which, I apprehend, no one had a right to publish, if I did not choose to do it myself.[2] To print any thing without the consent of the person who wrote it, is a proceeding so very ungenerous and unworthy of a man of reputation, that, from the character I have heard of you, I am utterly at a loss how to account for it, unless you were misled by some false representation, from the person of whom you received these verses, that the printing them would not be disagreeable to me. If this be the case, you will, I am persuaded, make no difficulty of letting me know who that person is, who has acted in a manner so very unfair. If you should think fit to satisfy me in this point, you will be pleased to direct a letter for me at Mrs. Hall's, in the Palace, Canterbury.[3] I am, sir, Your humble servant,

Eliz. Carter.

[1] Elizabeth Carter (1717–1806), poet, translator, and writer (*ODNB*).
[2] SR had inserted Carter's 'Ode to Wisdom' in the second volume of *Clarissa* without her knowledge (*Clarissa*, II, pp. 48–50); see also SR to Carter, 18 December 1747. In a letter of 20 January 1748, Carter told Catherine Talbot that she 'immediately wrote a twinkation to Mr. Richardson about it' (*A Series of Letters Between Mrs. Elizabeth Carter and Miss Catherine Talbot, from the Year 1741 to 1770*, ed. Montagu Pennington (1809), p. 249).
[3] Elizabeth Hall (m. 1760, d. 1774?) was the 'Miss Hall' of many of Carter's letters and poems; Carter often resided with the family when visiting Canterbury. The Palace, formerly the residence of the Archbishop of Canterbury, had been deserted since the Long Parliament took it over in 1647, with some sections serving as private homes.

Richardson to Elizabeth Carter

Friday 18 December 1747

MS: Houghton Library, MS Eng 759.6.[1] Autograph letter sent.
First Printing: Memoirs of the Life of Mrs. Elizabeth Carter, ed. Montagu
Pennington (1807), 69–70.

Be pleased, Madam, to receive a faithful Relation of the
Occasion of the Trespass I have made, for which you call me to
severe, however just, Account, in your Favour of the 13th.[2]

I have a worthy Kinswoman, Miss Elizabeth Long her Name,
who shew'd me the Ode to Wisdom, as a Piece she knew I should
admire. She had obtained the Promise of a Copy of it, when in
Wiltshire, a few Weeks before (at Mr. Long's, I think).[3] And one
was accordingly sent her.

I wanted not Matter for the Piece I had then ready for the
Press. I had a Redundance of it; and after it was written, parted
with several beautiful Transcripts from our best Poets, which I
had inserted, in order to inliven a Work (my Characters being
all *Readers*) which perhaps is too solemn. But the Ode being
shewn me, as written by a Lady; and the Intention of my Work
being to do Honour to the Sex, to the best of my poor Ability, I
was so pleased with it, that I desired my Kinswoman to give me
what Light she could, as to the Author, and to write down into
Wiltshire, to be informed, whether any Exceptions would be likely
to be taken if I should insert it.

She said, She had her self when in Wiltshire, been desirous
of knowing who the Author was: But had no other Intimation
given her, than that the Ode was really written by a Lady; and
by one whom she had had the Honour once to see. Whence she
conjectured the Lady to be a Descendant of the famous Mr. Norris
of Bemerton.[4]

---

[1] The manuscript, which is difficult to read in several places, has been checked against the
earliest printed versions: Montagu Pennington's *Memoirs of the Life of Mrs. Elizabeth Carter*
and *MM*, no. 228 (1 July 1812), 534.
[2] See Carter to SR, 13 December 1747; as well as her reply to the present letter in Carter to
SR, 31 December 1747.
[3] Eaves and Kimpel have speculated that this Elizabeth Long may be the Mrs. Long mentioned in Elizabeth Leake Richardson's will and perhaps also the Mrs. Long who died
impoverished in 1784 and who told Anne Richardson of SR's 'burning the letters of his
wild young friend' ('Samuel Richardson and His Family Circle', *N&Q*, n.s. 11 (1964), 469).
[4] John Norris (1657–1712), Church of England clergyman and philosopher (*ODNB*).

RICHARDSON TO ELIZABETH CARTER, FRIDAY 18 DECEMBER 1747

She wrote, however; but could get no further Light: But said, that as these were sure Copies of it: As it had been given to her without Restriction: As I thought the Piece excellent in itself; and that the inserting it with the Distinction I talked of, could bring no Disreputation to the Author; – No Name to be mentioned – she was of Opinion, that no Offence could be given or taken.

By this time my little Work was so far advanced at Press, that I was obliged to resolve one way or other; and I ventured to insert it. – I presumed not to make my Character, tho' the principal one, claim it; only doing intentional Honour to it, by setting it to Musick; which is done in a masterly Manner. I caused it to be engraved, and wrought highly, the more to distinguish it.[5] And all this Trouble I might have spared, and the Expense with it; as, tho' the Ode would have been an Ornament to any Work, and an Honour to any Character, it was not expected –

Upon the Whole, give me Leave to say, that I was not, in this re-acknowledg'd Trespass, govern'd by any low or selfish Views. I should have been the last to have forgiven my self for *such*, if I had. – And the rather, as This is the first Charge of the kind, that ever was made against me.

You will give me Leave, Madam, to desire your Acceptance of the Two little Volumes (in Half-binding as an unfinish'd Work)[6] – Not by way of Satisfaction or Atonement; but to see how the Ode is introduced. — That Satisfaction or Atonement shall be whatever you will be pleased to require. For I think I would sooner be thought *unjust*, or *ungenerous* by any Lady in the World, than by the Author of the Ode upon Wisdom.

I send them by the Canterbury Coach. And am, Madam, Your sincere Admirer,

S. Richardson

Salisbury Court

Fleet Street – Dec. 18th 1747[7]

---

5 SR included not only the text of Carter's poem but an oversized fold-out engraving of a musical score supposedly composed by Clarissa (*Clarissa*, II, pp. 48–50). The composer he employed remains unidentified.

6 Vols. I and II of *Clarissa*.

7 At some point, this letter was cut up. An undetermined hand had added 'I send them by the Canterbury Coach', words that have been pasted back into this copy in the original hand. The signature and the dateline likewise have been cut away and supplied by the undetermined later hand.

Anonymous to Richardson

Monday 21 December 1747

MS: FM XV, 2, f. 4. Copy in Gilbert Hill's hand.
Endorsement: 'Letter 5' (in Martha Richardson's hand); 'Clarissa' (in SR's hand); 'Anonymous' and 'Advice to publish' (in Hill's hand).

Decr. 21. 1747.

Mr. Richardson,
I write in the Name of several of the Readers of Clarissa to advise you to[1] publish the rest of the Book, not only as we are impatient to read it, but as it is certainly your Interest: For now People who have read the two first Volumes are desirous to finish it; and if it comes out some Months, hence, they will have forgot it, and not care whether they ever read the others.[2] I am Your Friend.

[1] 'advise you to' is an insertion in the copyist's hand.
[2] Vols. III and IV were published on 28 April 1748, vols. V–VII on 6 December 1748.

Elizabeth Carter to Richardson

Thursday 31 December 1747

Printed source: MM, no. 228 (1 July 1812), 534–5.
First printing: MM (1812).

Canterbury, Dec. 31, 1747

Sir,
I have been almost constantly engaged ever since I received the favour of your letter,[1] or I should have acknowledged it sooner. I am much obliged to you for giving me so particular an account of how you came by the Ode; and, by your naming Wiltshire, I can nearly guess who first gave away the copy, contrary to an express promise.[2] Mr. Cave, to whom I at first denied it, though I would

[1] Referring to SR to Carter, 18 December 1747.
[2] In a letter (20 January 1748) to Catherine Talbot, however, Carter wrote of 'resent[ing] the very unfair dealing in the person, whoever it was, who gave away copies without my leave, or any restriction' (*A Series of Letters Between Mrs. Elizabeth Carter and Miss Catherine Talbot, from the Year 1741 to 1770*, ed. Montagu Pennington (London: Printed for F. C. and J. Rivington, 1809), p. 249).

PHILARETES TO RICHARDSON, <EARLY 1748>

have been glad to oblige him, has now my leave to print it. But I have taken care the manner in which it is introduced shall cast no reflection upon you;[3] though I think there should be great caution used in publishing any thing where there is not the highest reason to believe it would not be disagreeable to the author.

I ought not to conclude my letter without acknowledging you have introduced the Ode in a way that does it honour, and in a work with which I am greatly pleased. I am much obliged to you for the agreeable entertainment it has given me, and am, sir, Your very humble servant,

E. Carter.

---

[3] The 'Ode' appeared, with minor variations, in the December issue of the *Gentleman's Magazine*, not without a small jab at SR and the unidentified inhabitant of Wiltshire who passed on the copy: 'We have had the following beautiful Ode above a year, under an injunction, which was general on all the copies given out, not to print it; but as it has appeared in *Clarissa* with several faults, we think ourselves at liberty to give our readers so agreeable an entertainment, from a correcter copy' (*The Gentleman's Magazine, and Historical Chronicle*, 17 (December 1747), 585). Edward Cave (1691–1754), printer, was proprietor of the *Gentleman's Magazine* from its inception in January 1731 until his death (*ODNB*).

Philaretes[1] to Richardson

<Early 1748>[2]

MS: FM XV, 2, f. 32. Copy in William Richardson's hand.
Endorsement: 'Without Date' (in William Richardson's hand); 'Letter 27' (in Martha Richardson's hand).

Sir,

I have read the two first Volumes of your Clarissa, in which there are a great many Letters that charm me; though I must own (since you desire the Judgment of the Public in that particular) I think several of them might be shortened very much to their Advantage.[3] Your Clarissa is an Angel; and I could not have

---

[1] A 'Philaretes' (the same?) had written to SR about seven years earlier and approved of the ending of *Pamela*; see Philaretes to SR, 22 June 1741.
[2] Date suggested by Eaves and Kimpel based on the letter's comments on the first two volumes of *Clarissa*, which had been published on 1 December 1747.
[3] See *Clarissa*, I, pp. vii–viii for SR's invitation to the public.

136

RICHARDSON TO SAMUEL LOBB, TUESDAY 12 JANUARY 1748

borne her Family's barbarous Treatment of her with Patience, if
I had not been calmed with the Hope, that she would have met
with the Reward of her Piety and Virtue, and been happy with
Lovelace at last. But since I have heard that you design the End
shall be unhappy, I am determined to read no more: The Idea of
Clarissa's Misery or Death would haunt and torment me through
the Whole; every Instance of her Merit would increase my Pain,
when I considered, that she must be miserable notwithstanding;
and I should read the Account of her Death with as much Anguish
of Mind, as I should feel at the Loss of my dearest Friend. I know
a great many Gentlemen that are of my Mind, and I believe your
Book will sell very indifferently, unless you alter it in that Respect.
I am, Sir, Your humble Servant

Philaretes.

Richardson to Samuel Lobb

Tuesday 12 January 1748

MS: Yale (Osborn). Autograph letter sent (evidence of folding and seal).
Address: 'To The Reverend Mr Lob<b> SR' (in SR's hand).

Reverend Sir,
I am so great a Lover of voluntary and chearful Correspondence,
that I cannot but take the Favour of your Letter now before me,
extremely kind. Mr. Lobb and I want not Monthly, nor even Yearly
Communications with each other to keep up a Value for each. And
I am sure he thinks so, by his long Silence.

But I am surprized at what seems to be at this time the principal
Motive of your writing. Lord, Sir, have you no Memory? – My
Demand is long ago satisfy'd. – Don't you know, that my Godson
paid it? – How can you <be so>[1] forgetful? –[2]

<But it> is my fault, I must own. I did not give the young
Gentle<man> a receipt: And you not being able to find it among

---

[1] The letter is heavily damaged along one of the folds, so significant portions of the address
and text are lost. Some text has been supplied from an incomplete transcription in Eland,
pp. 52–3. Eland seems to have had access to the letter when it was less damaged.

[2] In a previous letter, now lost, Lobb must have asked SR how much he still owed him for
printing *The Benevolence Incumbent on Us, as Men and Christians, Considered* (1746); SR had
apparently decided to waive the charges entirely. See SR to Lobb, 16 May 1746; and SR to
Lobb, 4 July 1746.

137

JOSEPH SPENCE TO RICHARDSON, THURSDAY 21 JANUARY 1748

your Dis<char>ges, supposed you had not paid it. Dear, dear Sir, for the future <alwa>ys take Receipts. You see, if you had not an honest Man for your Printer, how it might have been. But you Gentlemen of Learning, and of a better World, are such Strangers to this! – Be pleased now to take a Receipt –

I do acknowlege to have received full Satisfaction, by the Hands of my Godson, for the Printing Part and Paper of and for an Excellent Sermon preached, and directed to be printed, by his worthy Papa; and for all Demands upon him, Friendship excepted; As Witness my Hand this 12th Day of January, 1747/8.

Saml. Richardson.

My sincere Respects to your good Spouse; And my Love to your <xxxxx *1 word*> Sons! –Many, many happ<y> <Y>ears to you All, are the hearty <Wish>es of, dear Sir, Your affectionate Friend and humble Servant

S. Richardson

Joseph Spence[1] to Richardson

Thursday 21 January 1748[2]

Printed source: B: II, 319-27
First printing: Barbauld, *Correspondence* (1804).

Allegory of Art and Nature.

Stratton-street, January 21, 1748.

Dear Sir,

I have read over your contents, and return them to you, with many thanks.[3] Even the reading of them (which contents, I think, never did before) gave me, several times, those fine emotions which you know I am so fond of;

---

[1] Joseph Spence (1699–1768), literary scholar, anecdotist, as well as (from 1728) Professor of Poetry and (from 1742) Regius Professor of Modern History at Oxford (*ODNB*).

[2] Only draft notes survive for this letter in manuscript, written on the back of a letter from Philip Alston to Joseph Spence of 6 January 1748; the draft follows the printed version below.

[3] SR seems to have given Spence a preview of the table of contents eventually prefixed to the second edition of *Clarissa* (1749).

JOSEPH SPENCE TO RICHARDSON, THURSDAY 21 JANUARY 1748

> Those feelings of the soul! – that charming pain,
> That swells and agitates the heaving breast,
> And bursts in tears of pleasure at the eye.[4]

I have a moral feeling for you, of another sort; on seeing how much you suffer from the contrariety of advices that have been given you. Such a multitude of opinions can only serve to confuse your own judgment, which I verily believe would direct you better, without any help, than with so much.[5]

I wish you would take up a resolution (which perhaps may be new to you) of neither trusting others, nor distrusting yourself, too much. If you bundle up the opinions of bad judges in your head, they will only be so much lumber in your way; and even the opinions of good judges, in general, when they come to decide about particulars in your Clarissa, are much to be suspected.

Have they sufficiently considered your design and manner of writing in that piece? Do they know the connections and dependencies of one part upon another? Are they acquainted with your various ends in writing it; your unravellings of the story; and your winding up of the whole? Without these lights,[6] a very good judge may give a very wrong opinion about the parts that compose it. Another defect in those that are called the best judges is, that they generally go by rules of art; whereas your's is absolutely a work of nature. One might, for instance, as well judge of the beauties of a prospect[7] by the rules of architecture, as of your Clarissa by the laws of novels and romances.

A piece quite of a new kind must have new rules, if any; but the best of all is, following nature and common sense.

Nature, I think, you have followed more variously,[8] and at the same time more closely, than any one I know. For Heaven's sake, let not those sworn enemies of all good works (the critics) destroy the

---

[4] These lines seem to be of Spence's own composition.

[5] Not only had SR invited, and continued to copiously receive, advice from friends on revising and shortening *Clarissa*, but in a Preface to volume I he had also announced that the further publication of the novel's volumes would depend on how readers received it.

[6] 'Pieces of information or instruction; facts, discoveries, or suggestions which explain a subject' (*OED*).

[7] 'The view (of a landscape, etc.) afforded by a particular location or position; a vista; an extensive or commanding range of sight' (*OED*).

[8] 'with variation or variety; differently, diversely' (*OED*).

139

JOSEPH SPENCE TO RICHARDSON, THURSDAY 21 JANUARY 1748

beauties you have created. If you indulge them all in their wicked will, they will cut every tree in your garden into a bird or a beast.[9]

What I have just said will hold stronger against lopping. You love the Scriptures. There, you know, a good man is said to be like a tree by the rivers of water.[10] You are, as yet, flourishing in all your verdure; for God's sake, don't let them make a pollard[11] of you! Upon reading the contents of the whole, I am more and more convinced that much ought not to be parted with. Pruning is always proper. If you see a dead branch, or a straggling bough, that offends your eye, cut it away; but do not labour to find out faults where they do not meet you.

For fear I should fall into too grave and critical a way myself, if you please, I'll tell you a story. I wish it was shorter; but you will be so good as to take it as you find it. – But, hold! shall I call it a dream or a story? A dream, you know, may be as long as one pleases, and so I'll e'en call it a dream!

As we had a tolerable afternoon yesterday, I went, as usual, into the Park;[12] and, after a turn or two in the Mall, stept to the pretty coffee-house at the end of it, just without Buckingham-gate.[13] I had the second part of your Clarissa in my pocket,[14] and was so eager to go on with the story, that I could not help pursuing it even in the coffee-room. I seated myself there by the fire, and after reading about ten leaves, my eyes (which are still very bad with my cold) would not suffer me to go any farther. I laid my book down upon the table, and in a few minutes sunk insensibly into a gentle slumber, to the hum of three or four critics, who were gravely debating over their coffee, on the other side of the room.

---

[9] Spence's reference is to topiary, here in the shape of animals, a gardening practice that had been fashionable in English gardens in the late seventeenth century but had become outmoded by the early eighteenth century.

[10] Psalm 1:3: 'And he shall be like a tree planted by the rivers of water, that bringeth forth his fruit in his season; his leaf also shall not wither; and whatsoever he doeth shall prosper' (also echoed in Jeremiah 17:8).

[11] 'A tree which has had its upper trunk and branches cut back, so as to produce new growth and a uniform shape' (*OED*).

[12] St James's Park in the City of Westminster, in the early eighteenth century a fashionable space where the *beau monde* walked up and down one of the main thoroughfares, The Mall, to see and be seen.

[13] The entire area around St James's Square, Pall Mall, and St James's Street was a hotbed of fashionable coffee houses in the early eighteenth century.

[14] Spence was reading the second volume of the first instalment of *Clarissa*, which had been published in an eminently portable duodecimo format one month earlier.

JOSEPH SPENCE TO RICHARDSON, THURSDAY 21 JANUARY 1748

Our thoughts in sleep are often only a continuation of the dreams we have while we are awake. At least, it was so with me now; for I was no sooner asleep, than I found myself again walking by the side of the Mall, with several of the same persons in it that I had left there so lately. But there was one lady, whom I had never seen there, I think, before, and who soon engaged all my attention. She was tall; of an easy air, and noble deportment; with a face more charming than one of Guido's angels.[15] There was grace in all her looks and motions; her dress was rather negligent than set; she had very little head-dress, and her hair fell in easy ringlets down to her shoulders; her bosom was shaded with lawn,[16] but not imprisoned in stays,[17] as one could discern through her long robe of white satin, which was collected there, though it flowed all loose, and at its full liberty, behind her.[18] As I and several others were admiring her (for no man could look steadily on her without admiring her) a little, pert, busy woman, with much of the air of a French milliner, came tripping to her, and cried (half out of breath) 'O! Ma'am, I'm most extremely glad of having the pleasure of meeting your la'ship here! but, for God's sake, who dressed you to-day? Never did Heaven give so many beauties to any one person to be so hideously neglected as your la'ship's are. Those beautiful auburn ringlets to be suffered to run to all that wildness! why, they wander at least three fingers-breadth lower than they ought to do! Then these wide unmanaged sleeves! and that intolerable length of your robe, that hides the prettiest feet in the universe! That length of robe is what I can't nor won't bear with!' As every thing she said was accompanied with much action, these last words were followed by a very violent one; for just as she had finished them, she applied a pair of scissars (which she had till then concealed) to the robe, which had so much offended her, and running them along with the greatest impetuosity, in a moment as it were, divided all the

---

[15] Guido Reni (1575–1642), early Italian Baroque painter known in particular for his mythological and religious subjects.

[16] 'A kind of fine linen, resembling cambric' (*OED*).

[17] 'A laced underbodice, stiffened by the insertion of strips of whale-bone (sometimes of metal or wood) worn by women (sometimes by men) to give shape and support to the figure'; a corset (*OED*).

[18] At a time when hoop petticoats were at their widest and most flamboyant during the century, and corsets and close-to-the-head hairstyles were *de rigueur* in fashionable women's dress, Spence's dream lady notably stands out for her more natural, toned-down but also loose or 'unmanaged' aesthetic.

JOSEPH SPENCE TO RICHARDSON, THURSDAY 21 JANUARY 1748

lower half of it from the upper. A gentleman, who stood just by me, and had observed the whole affair with a particular attention, seemed more than ordinarily moved at it. 'What! (says he) shall it be allowed to so mean a creature to insult so noble an one, thus in the sight of day, and in my sight, who am so well acquainted with the dignity of the one and the vileness of the other?' 'Do you know them? (said I.) For Heaven's sake! who are they?' 'These are not real ladies (replied he) but allegorical ones.' 'Allegorical ladies! (cried I) I am extremely glad of it; for I don't know that I ever saw an allegorical lady before, in my life; but, pray, what are their names?' 'That fine lady (says he) with so free and graceful an air, is NATURE; and that little busy French milliner, who has cut off the most flowing part of her robe (perhaps only to make pincushions and patchwork of it at home) is ART. Now you know who they are, you will, I doubt not, be the more ready to join me to catch that wretch, and conduct the noble sufferer out of this crowd. Let us fly, then! (cried he, taking me by the hand) let us fly! –' And at that instant I started out of my sleep, awakened by a sudden quarrel that had arisen between the critics in the coffee-room. It seems they had taken up your book, which I had dropped heedlessly on the table. Three of them maintained, with great clamour, that it ought to be reduced to half its bulk; that a story ought to be short and quick, and the events crowding in upon one another; that a giant-novel was a monster in nature; and several other things that put me in mind of the restraining character of the milliner in my dream. I could not help smiling a little to myself. I put your book into my pocket, which they had flung down again upon the table, in the impetuosity of their arguments; and left them to debate over a point, which they seemed very little to understand.

I am now safe again in my room, where I should be glad to see you on Saturday, if it suits your convenience. I will have a vegetable[19] dinner that day, of which you may take a part or not, as you please. If it should be inconvenient to you to stay, it may, however, be of service to me; for, with such temperate diet, I shall be the less subject, perhaps, to these hurrying dreams.[20] I am, in the mean time, very sincerely and affectionately, Your's,

J. Spence.

[19] I.e. 'vegetarian'. SR himself had repeatedly been urged by his physician and friend, George Cheyne, to abandon or at least considerably reduce his meat intake in favour of a vegetarian diet; after Cheyne's death in 1743, SR had been backsliding a little on that account.
[20] 'that hastens under pressure or excitement; moving with excited haste' (*OED*).

142

JOSEPH SPENCE TO RICHARDSON, THURSDAY 21 JANUARY 1748

MS: Yale (Osborn), OSB MSS 4. Autograph draft.[21]

[22]confused with so many different advices
why not so much to be minded, in<serted>
　　In part<s> his No Novel; & they
go by the Novel Rules. – don't know
the whole.
　　As to the manner of writing
warbles his native wood notes wi<ld>.[23]
against my self.
　　[24]A Piece quite of a new kind
must have new rules, if any: but　　penultimate　　*Dream*, ultimate
the best rule, following Nature
& common sense.
　　So connected that 'tis difficult　　<xxxxx *1 word*>[25]
to detach parts, without hurting
many others.
　　The Moral Emotions upon
only reading the Contents.
　　Observe the writer's end.
　　Not to seek how much
he can leave out; & to omit
only where something appears　　The difference of his ways
to be wrong.
　　&. If Sale to be consulted, or
the conduct of the Novel to be
observ'd,　　　　　　　　　The effect of the Contents.
　　(The Sunshine-Evening of a　　did not enable me to do
stormy day).[26]　　　　　　what I talked of.
　　[27]Who would judge of a Prospect　　Why I go on as they did
by the Rules of Architecture?　　not

21　The draft begins with paragraph three in Barbauld's printed version.
22　This and the following paragraph have been crossed out.
23　A reference to John Milton's *L'Allegro*, in which Shakespeare, 'Fancy's child, / Warble[s] his native wood-notes wild' (ll. 133–4).
24　This and the following four paragraphs have been crossed out.
25　Illegible because heavily smudged or scraped.
26　Untraced.
27　This and the remaining paragraphs have been crossed out.

143

'JOHN CHEALE' TO RICHARDSON, TUESDAY 9 FEBRUARY 1748

If[28] you bundle up the
opinions of bad judges in your
head, they will only be so   Trees into birds a<nd> beasts
much lumber in your way.
     & as to your Opinions
of good Judges of writing;
     Even those to be rejected, if
they don't know your design, manner of writing, & the ends you
propose by it
         <pleasing> charming pain
     The painful pleasure that   Those feelings of the Soul; that
<sw>ells the heaving[29] breast,   painful bliss[30] That swells &c
& bursts in tears of pleasure
at your Eye.

---

[28] 'I hope' has been overwritten with 'If'.
[29] 'moral' has been crossed out and replaced with 'heaving'.
[30] 'charming p<angs>' has been crossed out and replaced with 'painful bliss'.

'John Cheale'[1] to Richardson

Tuesday 9 February 1748

MS: FM XVI, 1, f. 90. Copy in Gilbert Hill's hand.
Endorsement: 'John Cheale, Esq.' (in Hill's hand); 'Letter 60' (in Martha Richardson's hand).

Fendon, near Arundell.[2] Feb 9. 1747/8

Mr. Richardson,
     As a great Admirer of your last Performance, The History of Miss Clarissa Harlowe, I take the Liberty of troubling you with a Short Criticism, which, considering my Employment, I think I have a Right to lay before you.

---

[1] John Cheale (bap. 1699, d. 1751) was Norroy King of Arms, an office at the College of Heralds with jurisdiction over heraldic matters in England north of the Trent. The letter, however, was actually written as a prank by Charles Lennox, second Duke of Richmond (1701–50), politician and cricket enthusiast (*ODNB*).
[2] Findon, in West Sussex.

JAMES HERVEY TO RICHARDSON, MONDAY 29 FEBRUARY 1748

In P. 176. of the First Volume is this egregious Blunder in Heraldry: *Little did the old Viscount think when he married his Darling, his only Daughter, to,* &c.[3] How can you then know so little of the English Peerage, as to call this old Viscount's Daughter *Lady Charlotte* Harlowe? A Viscount's Daughter is only Miss before Marriage, and then only Mrs. Harlowe; which I wonder your Brother Booksellers of the genteel Side of Temple-Bar did not inform you of.[4] I thought it my Duty to let you know this, and am Your obedient humble Servant,

John Cheale, Norroy King at Arms.

There are other Absurdities in your Book; but depend upon it, that by this I have mentioned, you have highly affronted all the Dukes, Marquisses, and Earls Daughters, in England, Scotland, and Ireland.[5]

---

[3] *Clarissa*, I, p. 176.
[4] Temple Bar divided the mercantile City of London, where SR lived and worked, from the more genteel City of Westminster.
[5] 'Cheale' claims that SR's mistake in calling a viscount's daughter 'Lady Charlotte' will insult daughters of dukes, marquises, and earls who would properly be called ladies.

James Hervey to Richardson

Monday 29 February 1748

MS: Morgan MA 1024.11. Autograph letter sent (envelope only).

Printed source: B: VI (facsimile page).
First printing: Barbauld, *Correspondence* (1804).
Address: 'To Mr. Richardson in Salisbury Court' (in Hervey's hand, on the outside of the letter).
Endorsement: 'Rev. Hervey Weston. Febru. 29. 1747 5 G. Present'd To Rev. Spence's poor Woman.' (in SR's hand, on the outside of the letter).[1]

Dear Sir,
I am sorry, it was not consistent with your Conveniency, to transmit my Meditations from your Press, a third Time into the World It is like to prove their Loss & Detriment. The Paper

---

[1] 'Rev. Spence' is SR's friend and correspondent, Joseph Spence. The 'poor Woman' remains unidentified, a subject of Hervey's, Spence's, and SR's charity.

145

is not so fair nor the Types so elegant Which gives me some Dissatisfaction.[2]

I heartily thank You for your kind Congratulation, on the Acceptance with which the Public has condescended to honour the Performance. Your entertaining & improving Piece[3] I hope will meet with much greater Encouragement, & (which I dare say is the one Scope of your Desires) be productive of more abundant Good May the great Author of Holiness & Happiness bless them both, how far so ever they spread how long so ever they Live!

I have desired Mr. R— to advance five Guineas, & deliver to You, for the Releif of that distressed & worthy Person, whom You are so kind as to recommend to my Charity With Pleasure I bestow it, to releive the pressing Necessities of a valuable Woman; & with double Pleasure because it will be a Compliance with your Inclination[4]

Wishing You & your Family every desirable Blessing, I remain, Dear Sir your affectionate Friend & humble Servant

J Hervey

Weston. Feb. 29. 1747

---

[2] See Hervey to SR, 3 November 1747; SR had printed the 'second' edition (actually the first collected edition) and would print again the 'fourth' edition.
[3] I.e. *Clarissa*.
[4] See Hervey to SR, 3 November 1747. 'Mr. R—' is John Rivington, who with his brother and business partner James was publishing Hervey's *Meditations and Contemplations*.

Samuel Lobb to Richardson

Tuesday 1 March 1748

Printed source: B: I, 177–81.
First printing: Barbauld, *Correspondence* (1804).

Dear Sir,

A certain friend, that at present shall be nameless, has laid me under a very great and unreturnable obligation, by a very singular and quite unexpected favour.[1] Now, though it be ever so much

---

[1] This friend is SR himself, who had waived charges for printing Lobb's *The Benevolence Incumbent on Us, as Men and Christians, Considered* (1746); see SR to Lobb, 12 January 1748.

SAMUEL LOBB TO RICHARDSON, TUESDAY 1 MARCH 1748

against me, I will do him the justice to give you his true character; or else, you know, how will you be able to form a judgment? If any good quality may be said to be born with a person, generosity and he were certainly born together. I do not mean that they were twins; it is part of his very self. Now you must be sensible that such a person (which is another consideration that makes terribly against me) can never confer a favour, but he makes it as big again as it would be (were it conferred by another of less generosity), by the very manner of his conferring it. The case therefore, in short, is this. This friend has obliged me, as above, so long as the 12th day of January last; and now it is the first day of March, and, in all this time, that is, in the space of near six-and-forty days, has not had from me so much as a bare acknowledgment. And now, in spite of your own generosity, tell me the truth: do not you feel your breast rise with some degree of indignation; and have you not already passed sentence upon me, as chargeable with the crime I pretend to such an abhorrence of? Why, really, while I have the case, as I have stated it, in view, without my defence, I am apt to take your part, and feel some of that very indignation myself; but still I will not plead guilty, till, after your having fairly weighed what I have to allege in my behalf; you declare, that in spite of your prejudice in my favour you must be against me. That, indeed, will sink me at once! That will bring me on my knees: – but I hope better things. Thus, then, stands my defence. – I received the favour, with all the sentiments the nature of it, and the manner of conferring it, could inspire. I admired the benefaction. I loved my friend for his generosity. I felt myself warmed with all the gratitude an ingenuous mind would wish to feel. I was full of it. I must also confess, that, being then a visitor at the house of a gentleman of the very same stamp for generosity and goodness, one Ralph Allen, Esq.[2] in the impatience of my gratitude, or, perhaps, rather of my pride to shew him what a footing I had in the friendship of one, whose character I knew he was no stranger to, I shewed him my friend's letter, without so much as once thinking, till afterward, of the construction[3] it was capable of – that of an invitation to go and do likewise. I own, even that after-thought gave me no real pain; for as he needs no intimations of that sort, so, from his knowledge both of my circumstances and my character, I was satisfied he

[2] Allen, widely known as an exceptionally benevolent philanthropist, was a mutual friend.
[3] Used here in the sense of 'interpretation' (*OED*).

147

RICHARDSON TO SAMUEL LOBB, MONDAY 7 MARCH 1748

could not suspect me of being guilty of such a meanness. But to return to my other friend; with the same grateful sentiments, and, I will not deny it, with the same pleasing vanity, I betrayed his generosity to more than he is acquainted with: but he knows the above-mentioned gentleman's lady; he has some knowledge of Dr. Oliver, of Bath; and a greater of Mr. and Mrs. Leake, of the same city, who were of the number of those to whom, in the fulness of my heart, I shewed the letter I was so proud of.[4] So that, I flatter myself, you will allow that I have nothing further to account for, but my deferring so long my acknowledgements to himself. Why, what if I hesitated a little whether I ought to accept of the favour? But, indeed, no: my friend's generosity furnished him with an expedient by which, I know, he designed to remove that difficulty. For he throws in my way a pretty little godson of his, whom he knows I love as well as himself, in such a manner, that my refusing his kindness might be construed a faulty disregard to that little fellow.[5] I am, &c.

S. Lobb.

[4] Elizabeth Allen; William Oliver, a physician; and James and Hannah Leake, SR's in-laws; see Lobb to SR, 21 May 1743.
[5] Lobb's second son, Joseph, for whom SR had stood godfather; see SR to Lobb, 11 May 1743; and Lobb to SR, 21 May 1743.

Richardson to Samuel Lobb

Monday 7 March 1748

MS: Yale (Osborn). Autograph letter sent (evidence of folding).
First printing: Barbauld, *Correspondence* (1804), I, 181–3.

Reverend and dear Sir,
Your kind Acceptance overpays the Present.[1] And your equally-kind Letter, by its agreeable Length, and the Heart that it incloses, more than makes Amends for the Delay you blame your self for. – I must have overvalued the Trifle almost as much as you do, had I presumed to harbour the least hard Thought of a Friend I esteem so much, (and that for his unquestionable Goodness of Heart,)

[1] See Lobb to SR, 1 March 1748.

148

RICHARDSON TO SAMUEL LOBB, MONDAY 7 MARCH 1748

because he observed not a Punctilio. I am even sorry, that you should seem to think your self under the Necessity of apologizing on this Score. Had you been as many Weeks as Days in answering, well as I love to hear from you, I should only have doubted your Health; and been sollicitous to have put a private Inquiry after it, into my next Letter to Bath: And injoined it to be kept private; lest it should have been a Reflexion on my own Expectations for a Thing so much in the Way of my Business, and so very a Nothing in itself.

I was a little concern'd at first reading your Letter, <where you mention>[2] the shewing of mine to several of my worthy and valued Friends. But was easy, when I consider'd, that you, undesignedly, gave greater Reputation to your own amiably-grateful Disposition, in the over-rate,[3] than could be due to me, had the Matter been of much higher Value.

My sincere Respects to Your other Self, and kindest Love as well as Blessing to my Godson; not forgetting the other young Gentleman; from whom not only I, but all who have seen or heard of him, expect great Things; and who will never forget (from such a Monitor, as he has the Happiness to have) that *Great* means, at least includes, as of necessary Consequence, *Good.*[4] I am, my good and reverend Friend, Your truly obliged and faithful Servant,

S. Richardson

London, March 7, 1747/8.

---

[2] Wording obscured by tear along a fold in the letter, confirmed by Barbauld's transcription.
[3] 'An excessive rate or charge', now obsolete (*OED*).
[4] SR is sending his respects to Lobb's wife and two sons; the 'Monitor' is Lobb himself. See also SR to William Lobb, <July 1746–March 1750>.

Colley Cibber[1] to Richardson

Wednesday 30 March 1748

Printed source: B: II, 167–70.
First printing: Barbauld, *Correspondence* (1804).

Wednesday Morn.
March 30, 1748

Sir,

Is it possible? How could an author, so snubbed, and disappointed of approbation as you have been from me, ever recover into such spirit? Lovelace's sixth letter, p. 52,[2] has thrown out such lively strokes of his uncommon, and yet natural character, such almost justifiable sentiments of his intended treatment of Clarissa, that scarce a libertine reader will forbear to triumph with him, over the too charming, and provoking delicacy of his Clarissa. I am in the same rapture with Miss Howe's reply to her narrative, p. 60.[3] I have not patience to dwell on its particular parts, that have seized upon my approbation. I am afraid of talking nonsense upon it. Would you were here, while I am reading! I could not help saying thus much, before I come to something, which I confess I am in apprehension of meeting with to displease me. The Lord grant I may be disappointed![4]

I have got through 210 pages,[5] with a continual resolution to give every occasional beauty its laudable remark; but they grow too thick and strong upon me, to give me that agreeable leisure. I read a course of full five hours and a half, without drawing bit (as the jockeys call it);[6] in which time my attention has got the better of my approbation, which all the while longed to tell you how I liked it. But hold, said I, be quiet, and (as Congreve says) while the lady is singing,

Let all saucy praise be dumb![7]

---

[1] Colley Cibber (1671–1757), actor, writer, and theatre manager (*ODNB*). Cibber is reading the manuscript of *Clarissa*, copies of which SR was circulating among friends to receive feedback ahead of publication – his page numbers refer to that manuscript copy.
[2] Vol. III (Barbauld's note). In *Clarissa*, III, p. 52.
[3] Vol. III (Barbauld's note). In *Clarissa*, III, p. 60.
[4] Cibber may indicate that he is worried Lovelace's plans might come to fruition; see also his reference to 'the life [Clarissa] is to lead at London' below.
[5] Vol. III (Barbauld's note).
[6] 'to draw bit: to pull the reins in order to stop or check the horse' (*OED*).
[7] Cibber quotes William Congreve, 'On Mrs. Arabella Hunt, Singing' (1710), line 33.

ANONYMOUS ('CLARISSA') TO RICHARDSON, WEDNESDAY 6 APRIL 1748

And yet it is impossible any longer to contain. Miss Howe's expostulatory letter (p. 213) wherein she sets her own, and her friend's differently amiable temper, in the most lively light, must charm every sensible heart that reads them. O Lord! Lord! can there be any thing yet to come that will trouble this smooth stream of pleasure I am bathing in. But the book again lies open for me. — I have just finished this letter of Miss Howe's; with that charming chicken's neck at the end of it.[8] What a mixture of lively humour, good sense, and wanton wilfulness, does she conclude it with! How will you be able to support this spirit? In Clarissa's following letter you have, with admirable art, removed the objection of Clarissa's not having followed Miss Howe's advice not to delay any moment in her power to marry Lovelace, as the only means to redeem her from misery.[9] And yet I tremble for the life she is to lead at London. But to read and write, at the same time, grow troublesome. Shall I call upon you this afternoon? Your's,

C. Cibber.

[8] In *Clarissa*, III, p. 218, Anna Howe recounts how she once wrung a chicken's neck because it would peck at another chicken; this is also the letter in which she compares her own and Clarissa's tempers (III, p. 214).
[9] *Clarissa*, III, pp. 218–26.

Anonymous ('Clarissa') to Richardson

Wednesday 6 April 1748

MS: FM XV, 2, ff. 4–5r. Copy in Gilbert Hill's hand.
Endorsement: 'Letter 6' (in Martha Richardson's hand); 'The Author supposing herself Clarissa'[1] (on first page) and 'Anonymous' (as running header, both in Hill's hand).

April 6. 1748

Sir,

I wou'd only beg the Favour of you to let Mr. L......[2] know, that when I went some time ago out of Friendship to see his Mother

[1] 'The Author' has been crossed out and the whole phrase been amended to read 'A Lady supposing herself to be meant by Clarissa' in SR's hand in red ink.
[2] Lovelace.

151

ANONYMOUS ('CLARISSA') TO RICHARDSON, WEDNESDAY 6 APRIL 1748

before she died,[3] I little thought, that he had a Design to insult me with a Sort of History of those Misfortunes which he himself has been the original Cause of: For, whatever Abuses may have been thrown upon him, I can never believe, that any Person related to my Family had a Hand in them; for I dare say, that they are intirely Ignorant of the Abuses on both Sides. And, as to myself, I never mentioned his Name to any Creature breathing; neither did I ever do myself the Honour or 'Credit of pretending to have refused a Man whom I thought unworthy my Acceptance, and who, it seems, so sincerely despised me.[4] For, give me Leave to say, I was too much ashamed (for my own Sake) of the Usage that I met with from him, and which was too publicly known for me to inlarge upon, or say anything of the Matter: Therefore you are either imposed upon yourself, or else you endeavour to impose upon the World. But let that be as it may, it is equally indifferent to me; for it is not the Opinion of the World, that will either acquit or condemn us hereafter: And that Philosophy of Temper, with which you reproach me, will teach me to bear all things. I write not this, Sir, with any Design of putting an End to your History; for if Mr. L... finds himself the easier by abusing of me, I am satisfied; for I have suffer'd too much already to be greatly concerned at such usage; and the less, as I am not conscious of deserving it from him; neither has he any great Reason to be concern'd himself about what I may farther suffer from my Relations, upon his Account: For, in the first Place, I do not think, that I shall live many Years longer; and, in the next, he will be the last Person that I shall apply to for Relief.

P.S. You begin your Story, That neither Mr. L....'s Honour, &c.[5]

Item[6] Whether it is honourable to endeavour to engage the Daughter's Affections in a secret Manner, and never speak a Syllable of it to her Friends?

3   This does not occur in *Clarissa*.
4   Not actually a direct quote, but a paraphrase of Anna Howe's reflections on the conduct of Clarissa's sister, Arabella: 'Her *outward eye*, as *you* have own'd, was from *the first* struck with the figure and address of the man [i.e. Lovelace] whom she pretends to despise, and who 'tis certain thoroughly despises her' (*Clarissa*, I, p. 87).
5   Using 'begin the story' somewhat loosely, this probably refers to a moment in the novel when Lovelace aligns his honour with that of Clarissa in an attempt to isolate her from her family and gain her trust and affection: 'he declares, "That neither his own honour, nor his family's ..., permit him to bear these confirmed indignities"' (*Clarissa*, I, p. 114).
6   The word was used to introduce individual entries within a list; now archaic. Within this letter, the word is represented by a capital 'I' in secretary hand, followed by a truncation mark.

152

RICHARDSON TO WILLIAM WARBURTON, THURSDAY 14 APRIL 1748

Whether, if a Man had no such Design, but would have shunned it, it was honourable to desire her to go to Public Places with him, in order to be remarked, and have her Character afterwards reflected upon? And,

Lastly, Whether it is not extremely honourable and generous to deny it; and endeavour to justify himself at her Expense?

Believe me, Sir, that I have a pretty good Memory still, tho' I have lived a few Years longer than you seem to imagine, or rather, than you wou'd have the World imagine I have done.

Item. Whether a Man can propose any solid Satisfaction to himself in artfully endeavouring to impose upon others?

Observe, that even a Worm will turn, when trod upon.[7]

You have been pleased, Sir, to quote some Texts of Scripture yourself; or I should not take the Liberty of referring you to the 1st Verse of the xvii Chapter of St. Luke[8] as an Answer to the History of Clarissa[9]

---

[7] Proverbial. First recorded in print in John Heywood, *Dialogue of Proverbs* (1546), it also appears in Shakespeare's *Henry VI, Part 3*, act 2, scene 2.

[8] 'Then said he unto the disciples, It is impossible but that offences will come: but woe *unto him*, through whom they come!' (Luke 17:1).

[9] SR follows this letter with a note: 'every word of this extraordinary Letter proves that the Lady, whoever she was, most egregiously flattered herself in supposing that the Character of History of Clarissa *cou'd* <be> meant for her!!!'.

Richardson to William Warburton

Thursday 14 April 1748

MS: Lilly Library, University of Indiana, English literature mss., 1630–1800. Autograph letter sent (evidence of folding).
Endorsement: 'Mine to Mr Warburton on Pref to Vol. III, IV', 'Apr 14. 1748', and 'Clarissa' (in SR's hand, on the outside of the letter); 'To Mr Warburton.' (in Gilbert Hill's hand, on the letter's first page); 'Letter 9' (in Martha Richardson's hand, on the letter's first page).

London, April 14. 1748.

RICHARDSON TO WILLIAM WARBURTON, THURSDAY 14 APRIL 1748

Reverend Sir,

Most heartily do I condole with you the heavy Loss you so affectingly deplore.[1] I have made my poor Clarissa say that the finer Sensibilities make not happy.[2] Who can wonder that Mr. Warburton should most sensibly feel so severe a stroke as this;[3] however apprehensive he might be of it, not only from the good Lady<'s> Illness, but from her advanced Life. Since to *apprehend* and to *know*, must have very different *Effects* on the Mind; as the one admits of Hope; the other not.[4] But it would be highly impertinent in me to offer any thing more[5] on this awful[6] Subject to You. —

I am infinitely obliged to you, Sir, for your charming Paper.[7] But how shall I take it upon myself? – I must, if put to me, by Particulars, suppose it to be suggested to me, at least, by some learned Friend, so disguising, as You may not be supposed to be the Person. And I have transcribed it, that not even my Compositor may[8] guess at the Author. – But it is really so much above my Learning and my Ability, that it will not be supposed mine by anybody.[9]

Will you, good Sir, allow me to mention, that I could wish, that the '*Air* of Genuineness' had been kept up,[10] tho' I want not the Letters to be *thought* genuine; only so far kept up, I mean, as that they should not prefatically be owned *not* to be genuine; and this for fear of weakening their Influence where any of them are aimed to be exemplary: as well as to avoid hurting that kind of Historical Faith, which Fiction itself is generally read with, tho' we know it to be Fiction.

---

[1] Probably the death of his mother, Elizabeth Warburton, *née* Hobman. Most sources, from the nineteenth century onward, list her death as occurring in late 1748 or 1749. We cannot verify the date of death and speculate that she had died before Richardson wrote this letter.

[2] 'Oh! my dear! The finer Sensibilities, if I may suppose mine to be such, make not happy!' (*Clarissa*, III, p. 116).

[3] 'as this' crossed out.

[4] 'the other not' crossed out.

[5] 'more' crossed out.

[6] Here used in the sense of 'Worthy of, or commanding, profound respect or reverential fear' (*OED*).

[7] 'charming' crossed out. Warburton had sent SR a copy of a proposed preface for volumes III and IV of *Clarissa*, which SR included in the first two editions but dropped afterwards.

[8] 'not' crossed out after may.

[9] In the left margin SR writes, with a mark comprehending this paragraph, some words impossible to make out: 'That "<xxxxx *1 word*>" in <xxxxx *1 word*><y or g>'.

[10] Warburton's preface discusses *Clarissa* within the context of a history of fiction.

RICHARDSON TO WILLIAM WARBURTON, THURSDAY 14 APRIL 1748

Then as to what you are pleased to hint, that I pursued in my former Piece[11] the excellent Plan fallen upon lately by the French Writers, I would only observe, that all that know me, know, that I am not acquainted in the least either with the French Language or Writers. And that it was Chance and not Skill or Learning, that made me fall into this way of Scribbling.

But these Points I absolutely submit to Your Determination. If they could be easily alter'd, and you were of Opinion that they *should* be alter'd, I then will hope for that Favour. But if you are not of that Opinion, it shall go just as you have favoured me with it. And in either Case, I repeat my most hearty Thanks to you for the Favour, and Condescension as I shall always think it, in bestowing your Thoughts on so light a Subject.

I forbore my acknowledgments of this Favour till one could be composed; which I inclose, lest you should have no Copy. – But, on second Thoughts, it will, perhaps, be more to your own Satisfaction, that I inclose your own MS.[12]

I hope, that all the good Family of Prior Park, are in good Health.[13] God preserve yours to you, together with Freedom of Spirits,[14] the greatest Blessing in this Life, is the Prayer of Reverend Sir, Your most obliged and faithful Servant

S. Richardson

[11] I.e. *Pamela*.

[12] This paragraph crossed out in original. SR seems to intend sending Warburton a copy of the printed preface at first, but then reconsiders and returns him his original manuscript.

[13] 'good' crossed out. Having married Ralph Allen's favourite niece, Gertrude Tucker (d. 1796) on 5 September 1745, Warburton by this point enjoyed great intimacy with Allen and his family.

[14] For this phrase, see, for example, George Cheyne, *Dr. Cheyne's Account of Himself and of His Writings: Faithfully Extracted from His Various Works* (3rd edn, 1744).

William Warburton to Richardson

Monday 25 April 17<48>[1]

MS: Yale (Osborn). Autograph letter sent (evidence of folding).[2]
First printing: Barbauld, *Correspondence* (1804), VI (facsimile page).

Dear Sir

I heartily thank you for the 2nd and 3rd Vols. of Clarissa.
I suppose 2 more will finish the work and to those another
advertisement of the same length which you have affixed to
these may not be improper.[3] This *was* but a ge<neral> criticism
on the *spirits of the Fable*. That will aff<ord> a more particular
examination of the conduct of <this> work in which we find that
too great a sensib<ility> & impatience under the force put on her
selfe satisf<action> necessarily & fatally drew after it that long &
terrible attack & combat on her Virtue which near so entangl<ed>
her in the miseries of life that nothing could free her from or
make her tryumphant over them, but divine <grace> which now
comes, like the God in the catastrophe <of> the Ancient fable,
to clear up all difficulties. The r<apid> & necessary connexion of
all these parts on one anot<her> will afford occasion – of remarks
advantageous to <the> conduct of your work – explain the fineness
of <the> moral – and remove that silly objection against the *to<o>*
tragical catastrophe. Tis not so! tis happy, if a<n> overflow of divine
grace upon the human mind <can> make the close of life (from
whence happiness accor<ding> to the ancient sage is to take its
denomination) happy.[4] But the objection arose both from want of
sense & of religion. I give you this hint that you may work up the
concluding scene of her life as seraphicly as you can, cast over it
that sunshine that may be able to dispell all the impressions that

---

[1] Year supplied by Barbauld.
[2] The letter is now heavily damaged, especially along its right edge, so Barbauld's facsimile has been used to supply lost or illegible words.
[3] Warburton had supplied SR with a preface to volumes III and IV, in which he advertised the verisimilitude and didactic value of SR's narrative and situated it within a short history of fiction; see also SR to Warburton, 14 April 1748. He may have mistaken the volumes SR had sent him for perusal.
[4] The 'ancient sage' may be Athenian statesman, lawmaker, and poet Solon (*c.* 630–560 BCE), who supposedly told Croesus, the last king of Lydia (r. *c.* 560–546 BCE), that the vagaries of life and fate made it impossible to tell whether someone's life had been a happy one until the day they died.

ANONYMOUS TO RICHARDSON, FRIDAY 20 MAY 1748

the foregoing had made upon minds really & not pret<endly>
tend<er> for as these last only pride themselves in what they have
not they will never be brou<ght> to own that an author's address
can ravish from them what they think it an honour to pretend
to — So good a work as yours deserves a sensible defense rather
than a childish revery of a cake-house vision. Dear Sir ever most
affectionately yours.

W. Warburton

P.P. Apr. 25 17<48>

Anonymous to Richardson

Friday 20 May 1748

MS: FM XV, 2, ff. 5v–6. Copy in Gilbert Hill's hand.
Endorsement: 'Anonymous' (running head) and 'Finding fault with Length,
Lovelace's Character, &c. Dated May 20. but not receiv'd till July 20 following'
(both in Hill's hand); 'Letter 7' (in Martha Richardson's hand).

May 20.

Sir,
As a former Work of yours was universally read, and by many
esteemed, among which I was one, give me Leave to mention
some Particulars relating to Miss Clarissa. All its Readers I have
met with are offended at the tedious Repetitions; and, when they
hoped to come to something of Moment, they were hardly anything advanced in the History. Others wished the Author had
recollected Mr. Prior's Advice, not to *tire his Friend to grace his
Story*.[1] Another (and that a Man of Learning) decided, 'Twas Much
ado about Nothing, & many Things of the like Nature. For my
Part, who always consider'd Conciseness, as well as Perspicuity,
Essentials in a well-written Book, was the more concerned, as there
are many excellent Observations, which will not be attended to,
for want of the Patience necessary to separate them from the Heap

---

[1] Not traced in any of Matthew Prior's writings, but a version of the line – 'tire my Friend
to grace my Song' – appears first in the anonymous, 'In Answer to a Lampoon on Several
Ladies of Quality' (in *Tunbrigialia: or, Tunbridge Miscellanies, for the Year 1730*, p. 27) and
then in the Reverend James Barber, *The Law-Suit: or, The Farmer and Fisherman* (1738),
p. 34.

157

SOLOMON LOWE TO RICHARDSON, MONDAY 23 MAY 1748

of Matter by which they are surrounded; and what would have
been incomparable in two Volumes, make four that will hardly
meet with a second Perusal. 'Tis further wondered, a Gentleman
of a universal good Reputation can support such a Character as
Lovelace thro' such a Multitude of Convictions as must have
convinced any Man higher in Intellectuals than a mere Brute,
which still adds to its capital Fault the Length, and is the only Part
I think unnatural: For, to do you, Sir, but Justice, you have the
Talent in Perfection of knowing Human Nature, and keeping close
to it, except in the Instance above: And the Passions are so raised
by the Perfections and Distresses you paint, as by no Means to be
satisfied, till the Catastrophe shews whether Vice or Virtue is to
prevail. And now, if the rest of your Friends, (for I am one in the
true Sense of the Word) are of the same Opinion, another Edition
may let me have only that Part of your Mind which is admired by
all the Good Part of the World, as well as by, Sir, Your humble
Servant &c.

Solomon Lowe to Richardson

Monday 23 May 1748

MS: FM XV, 2, ff. 101–2; XVI, 1, f. 90v. Copy in Gilbert Hill's hand.
Endorsement: 'Mr. Solomon Lowe' (running head, in Hill's hand); 'Letter 59' (in
Martha Richardson's hand).

May 23, 1748.

Sir,
I thank you for the Loan of the 3rd Volume of Clarissa; which
I have read with great Satisfaction.[1] As you did me the Honour
(when you left the Book for me) to desire my Animadversions on
it; I cannot but say something; at least to shew you that I am not
insensible of the Obligation.

But, to confess the Truth, I find the Characters so well pointed,
the Sentiments so shrewd, and the Language so sinewy; that I
know not where to fix on a Fault worth the mentioning. Yet I
cannot but say I am amazed (as I have, long, played the Critic) that

---

[1] Given the coincidence of Lowe's page numbers with the published volume, this must have
been a printed pre-publication copy.

SOLOMON LOWE TO RICHARDSON, MONDAY 23 MAY 1748

I should not be able to catch you Napping, in so long a Work, and so difficult to carry on with Spirit: When I durst engage to expose Mr. Pope, not only in every Page of his Homer, but in almost every Line of his famed Universal Prayer.[2]

You will perhaps smile at my Fancy of making an Index to a Novel; which you will see (by the inclosed) it came into my Head to begin (amidst a Croud of other Attendances) at P.[3] But so it is: Among my Acquaintance, I declare it to be as worthy of one, as the Tatlers or Spectators;[4] tho' there is nothing in the Whole that is handled in a Common-place Manner; but everything delicately interwoven into the several Pieces, suitably to the several Characters of the Writers. – The Numbers prefix'd to each Article are for the easier throwing the Particulars into Alphabetical Order. – If you approve of what I have done, and will be pleased to correct it; I will proceed in the same Manner (or rather Alphabetize directly) what shall occur of the like Nature, in the next Volume you shall favour me with[5] – In the mean time I must beg Leave to keep this Volume a little longer, that our Folks may have Time to go thro' it; having been hinder'd by their Preparations for the Holidays.[6] – When you come to N. End, and shall find yourself most at Liberty; I will do myself the Pleasure to wait on you:[7] Against[8] which time you may possibly steal half an Hour from your better Employments, to run over the inclosed on Mr. Pope; and will be so good as to mark with your Pencil what you disapprove, or have any Scruple about, for one Subject of our Conversation, when

---

[2] What Lowe had to say about Alexander Pope's translations of the *Iliad* (1715–20) and *Odyssey* (1725–6) or about his *Universal Prayer* (1738) remains unknown, though it probably focused on grammatical concerns, in which Lowe was a specialist. He never seems to have published any of his criticism of Pope, at least not under his own name.

[3] Location untraced. Enclosures and index now missing.

[4] *The Tatler* (1709–11) and *The Spectator* (1711–12) were periodical essays conceived and largely written by Joseph Addison (1672–1719) and Richard Steele (1672–1729), writers and politicians (*ODNB*). Extremely influential throughout the eighteenth century and beyond, the *Tatler* (published three times per week) and the *Spectator* (published six times per week) were focused on short essays on political, cultural, and social topics.

[5] SR never included an index with *Clarissa* but did so from the start with *Grandison*.

[6] Lowe is asking SR to keep the loaned volume longer so that those in his circle, including family members, may have time to read it. The holiday to which he refers is presumably Easter.

[7] The school at which Lowe was Master, Blyth House Boarding School in Hammersmith, was close to SR's retreat at North End.

[8] 'In anticipation of, in preparation for, in time for. *Obs.*' (*OED*).

159

SOLOMON LOWE TO RICHARDSON, MONDAY 23 MAY 1748

I have an Opportunity of paying my Respects. I am, Sir, Your most obedient Servant

Sol. Lowe.

The Scruples that occurred to me on reading the 3rd Volume of CLARISSA.[9]

P.82. Rather than give the Reader the Trouble of turning back to P.75. better, perhaps, to address this Letter 'Mr. Lovelace, To John Belford, Esq.r in Continuation' – And so P.84. 88. 99. 103[10] – according to your own Practice, Letter 20 and 21. P.119 and 128.

90. Rather than Santa Katharina's, &. better perhaps (according to the common Appelation) St. Catherine's, &c.[11]

102. Do not the two partly's coincide?[12] — No.

152. Afternoon, as here, methinks I wou'd always use, instead of P.M. which tho' common among Astronomers, are not so familiar to the Populace.[13]

206. 'Your Mamma is answerable to any-body rather than to her Child, for whatever was wrong in her Conduct toward Mr. Howe.' – Is not the Child wronged more than any-body? Vide p. 196. 2.[14]

352. *Phil*-tits[15]

Of all the *New Words and Phrases*, with which you have enrich'd our Language, more than any Writer I ever read, I can't say I dislike any but

---

[9] At some point in the document's history, the list of 'Scruples' was separated from the rest of the letter by SR or later collectors and eventually wound up in a different volume of the Forster Collection. SR adopted most of Lowe's suggestions.

[10] Addresses letter 11 as well as letters 12–13 and 16–17, titled 'Mr. Lovelace; in Continuation' in the published version.

[11] In letter 13.

[12] Refers to the phrase 'partly for her sake, and partly because I will never marry' in letter 16.

[13] SR has changed the date line of letter 27 to read 'Sat. Afternoon'.

[14] In the published version, the sentence in letter 39 reads: 'Your mamma is answerable to *any-body*, rather than to her *child*, for whatever was wrong in her conduct, if any thing *was* wrong, towards Mr. Howe.'

[15] In letter 76, Lovelace lists 'wrens, *phil*-tits, and wagtails' as prey he disdains as a rake with an eye for 'the noblest quarries'. All three are actual birds, but the latter two also have salacious connotations. See 'tit' and 'wagtail' in Francis Grose, *A Classical Dictionary of the Vulgar Tongue* (1785).

349. *Podagra-men.*[16]
91.   Excurse, I hestitate about.[17]

---

[16] Lovelace's neologism in letter 75 for Lord M., who apparently suffers from gout in his big toe, a condition called podagra.
[17] SR has retained the phrase 'But how I *excurse!*' in letter 13.

H. Morgan[1] to Richardson

Tuesday 9 August 1748

MS: FM XV, 2, ff. 15–16. Copy in Gilbert Hill's hand.
Endorsement: 'Letter 10' (in Martha Richardson's hand); 'Mr. H. Morgan' (in SR's hand).

August 9.th 1748

Dear Sir

Your agreeable Letter found me on my second Death Bed in a Relapse, occasion'd by my natural impatience after Liberty & Action, for having left the Country Air, & resuming Business (accursed Business) too soon, I pick'd out a delicate Scotch misty day for my first flight; which bearing a little too heavy on my Pinions, Opprest me down to the Ground. But the goodness of my unabus'd constitution, Surmounted this difficulty also, and set me once more on the Wing.

You pay Sir too great a compliment to my taste and Judgment, to think them worth consulting, tho' I shall begin now to entertain a little better Opinion of both than I have, as they are extremely charm'd with Clarissa. Those truly ingenious Letters have catch'd me by the Soul, and will not let go. A pox upon you! – I was going to say – you know not the mischief you have done yourself and me by sending me this Syren Daughter of your prolific Brain; for it has taken off not a little of that attention, which I ought to have applied, now on the close of Business, towards getting in my almost £1200. and you know who will suffer by that as well as myself.

---

[1] Possibly SR's solicitor in at least one suit launched in 1731 in the Court of Chancery to recover money owed for printing. Morgan is otherwise untraced.

H. MORGAN TO RICHARDSON, TUESDAY 9 AUGUST 1748

You have Sir entertained me with a delicate Nosegay[2] indeed! compos'd of such a beautiful variety of Flowers that I am puzzl'd which to admire most! The Scrupulous piety and struggling Reluctances of your Heroine are nobly adapted to a well-inform'd mind that judiciously resists imposition. The raillery of that notable Baggage (as Sir Roger de Coverly Says) her Friend and confidante,[3] is happily struck without the vain Flights of Levity; for her notions are not only just, but pleasantly convey'd. Her reasonings too are close and cogent when she becomes Serious. In short she rivals the Capital Figure so powerfully, that I can't give Clarissa the Palm, without a kind of Check of Conscience, and a fervent look towards Miss Howe. Belford's is an Amiable Character, a conscientious Rake he! who looks with an awful decency upon a Devotée to virtue. Old Harlowe is drawn with all the Dogmatic haughtyness of a parental Tyrant, And the young one full of the Pragmatical Coxcomb up to the very brim. A piece of ambitious inflexibility this. Bell has a<ll>[4] the arrogance of an assuming[5] Sister, and the Malignancy of disappointment: Methinks I see her bite her lips.[6] B<ut> as for your Hang-Dog Lovelace, I know not well what to make of him. He is a compound of good & bad Quality<,> an Amphibious[7] creature, an Original[8] Character, not unlike the Devil in the Serpent, and bent like him on the destruction of Innocence. I think it incumbent upon you to impanel a Jury of Ladies upon him in the close of your next Volume, And let Miss Howe stand Foreman — Forewoman I would

---

[2] Literally 'a bunch of flowers or herbs' (*OED*), often worn to ward off bad smells and thought to protect against airborne disease, the term had also come to designate collections of wholesome literature.

[3] While attending a performance of Ambrose Philips's tragedy, *The Distrest Mother* (1712; based on Racine's *Andromaque*), Sir Roger approvingly calls Hermione 'a notable young Baggage' for her bravado (*Spectator* 335); Morgan here applies the epithet to Clarissa's confidante, Anna Howe.

[4] The letter is heavily cropped along its right edge, which results in a loss of text in several places.

[5] SR has inserted 'elder' at this point.

[6] Morgan refers to characters in *Clarissa*: 'Miss Howe', Clarissa's best friend; 'Belford', Lovelace's best friend; 'Old Harlowe', Clarissa's father; 'the young one', Clarissa's brother James Jr; 'Bell', Clarissa's older sister Arabella.

[7] Combining qualities or categories, often used negatively; mixing elements that do not belong together.

[8] Several meanings overlap here: (1) 'Created, composed, or done by a person directly ...; not imitated or copied from another'; (2) 'Of a person: given to independent exercise of the mind or imagination'; but also (3) 'a singular, odd, or eccentric person' (*OED*), thus negative because without precedent and therefore impossible to classify.

162

ANONYMOUS TO RICHARDSON, FRIDAY 2 SEPTEMBER 1748

have said; or at least Counsel[9] against him<.> In short, my good
Friend, I must have him hang'd at all Events; and yet – there are
some Lady's of my acquaintan<ce> who are only for giving him the
discipline of the Blanke<t.>[10] I argued vehemently for a punishment
more condign,[11] and at last, proposing to commute for[12] Castration,
I found it high time to withdraw to avoid being Sentenc'd into my
own Brazen Bull;[13] and consequently to alter my Opinion as to
the Jury, which, for the sake of Justice, ought I think to consist of
Parents – But as I could talk all day upon this entertaining Piece, I
will restrain myself here at the present, and conclude this Letter, as
I shall my life, with being Dear Sir Your most affectionate humble
Servant ever oblig'd &c

H. M.

[9] 'a counsellor-at-law, advocate, or barrister' (*OED*).
[10] 'to toss in a blanket': 'to throw (a person) upward repeatedly from a blanket held slackly at
each corner' (*OED*); now a game, it used to be a form of punishment.
[11] 'Since the end of 17th c. commonly used only of appropriate punishment' (*OED*).
[12] 'To change (a punishment, or a sentence) for ... another of less severity' (*OED*).
[13] The ancient Greek historian Diodorus of Sicily recounts that the brazen ('bronze') bull was
a torture device invented by Perillos of Athens for Phalaris, tyrant of Akragas, in which
prisoners were roasted alive; according to Diodorus, Perillos became his own invention's
first victim.

Anonymous to Richardson

Friday 2 September 1748

MS: FM XV, 2, f. 6. Copy in Gilbert Hill's hand.
Endorsement: 'Letter 8' (in Martha Richardson's hand); 'Pressing for Publication'
(in Hill's hand).

Wedn. Morn. Sept. 2. 1748.

Sir,
   As I am a well-wisher to you, and your Writings, I take this
Opportunity of informing you, that you'll greatly oblige Multitudes
of both Sexes, if you'll expeditiously publish the Residue of
Clarissa.[1] From Your unknown Friend & Servant

It will be taken extremely kind, if you'll give us a public
Advertisement when you intend it.

[1] By the time this letter was written, volumes III and IV had been published, and volumes V
through VII would appear three months later.

163

John Channing[1] to Richardson

Monday 5 September 1748

Printed source: B: II, 337–40.
First printing: Barbauld, *Correspondence* (1804).

Sept. 5, 1748

Dear Sir,

I called on you the day before I left London,[2] when you exacted a kind of promise of a line or two from me.

I set out from London with as much glee as ever prisoner left his dungeon; and most cordially wish that my affairs were so circumstanced as never to see that foul beast again. Every stage gave me fresh spirits, and the country appeared even more charming, than ever it had appeared before even to me. The smoke, the gloom, the hurry of the town, seemed more than ever my aversion, and I was ready to envy the meanest cottager I past by. Our journey was safe and agreeable: only the humanity of my friend and companion, Mr. P—,[3] frequently hurt him. The poor post horses were the objects of his compassion, and every lash they received, gave him very sensible displeasure. For my own part, I never was much inclined to the Cartesian doctrine;[4] and yet, I don't know how it was, my spirits were so high, and the pursuit of my journey so much at heart, that I was almost ready to think with that whimsical philosopher, that those animals felt little more than machines; at least I was willing to excuse the brutality of the drivers, who treated them as such. We arrived here on Saturday, after having been overturned[5] only once; a singular happiness, as we were both quite unhurt.

---

[1] John Channing (*c.* 1703–75), apothecary and Arabist (*ODNB*). Barbauld thought that Channing helped SR create the character of Elias Brand in *Clarissa* (see B: II, 332–3n) but Eaves and Kimpel have identified R. Smith as the more likely candidate; see Smith to SR, <Autumn 1747>.
[2] Despite the dislike Channing expresses for London in this letter, he maintained an apothecary shop on fashionable Essex Street, off the Strand, from 1745 until his death.
[3] Unidentified.
[4] Channing here refers to the mechanistic physiology of René Descartes (1596–1650), first forwarded in the *Discourse on the Method* (1637), according to which the functioning of human and non-human animal bodies can be explained entirely without reference to a soul, which he considered exclusive to humans.
[5] 'To tip or topple over. *Obs.*' (*OED*).

JOHN CHANNING TO RICHARDSON, MONDAY 5 SEPTEMBER 1748

Sunday was devoted to the public worship. All the family went to the parish church; and here I was most agreeably surprised with a rural concert: – artless, indeed, and unadorned; but whose natural, pathetic, unaffected harmony charmed me as much, or more, than the best choir I had ever heard, accompanied by even a Green or a Handel.[6] The forty-third, and the hundred and thirty-seventh Psalms, were performed by no mean voices, in four parts. Both these have been ever reckoned fine pieces of ancient poetry; the last, particularly, has ever been justly admired as an inimitably fine composition; and Brady's paraphrase of it, which they sung, one of his best.[7] I have prevailed on them to give me a copy of that music in score, and am much mistaken if it do not please our connoisseurs in music as much as it did me. The chief composers, as I learn from the parson of the parish, are the clerk's son, and another day-labourer. There are several good voices, one in particular, a girl, whose pipe,[8] for strength and sweetness, equals any I have ever heard: she has the misfortune to have lost one eye, and is likewise a day-labourer. This epistle should have been sent you from the top of a neighbouring hill, whither your humble servant sallied forth, a morning or two after his arrival, furnished with pen, ink, and paper, and trusting to his nearer approach to the clouds for inspiration.[9] I had even fixed on a little hillock for my desk, and found my spirits and imagination in a tolerable way for writing something or other, to a friend whose candour might be trusted to;[10] but a young companion missed me at home,[11] and soon traced me out, so as to render my design impossible; and hereby you are spared a week longer. I wish you were with me,

---

[6] Georg Friedrich Händel (1685–1759), German expatriate composer active in London from 1711 (*ODNB*); and either John (bap. 1677) or, more likely, James Green (bap. 1692), brothers who collaborated on a series of compilations of *Psalm Tunes* (2nd edn, 1713) that also incorporated music used in provincial churches; James's name appears alone on title pages from 1718 (*ODNB*).

[7] Nicholas Brady (1659–1726), poet and Church of England clergyman, collaborated with playwright and poet laureate Nahum Tate (*c.* 1652–1715) on a metrical translation of the psalms, *New Version of the Psalms of David* (1696), which became the standard version in Anglican churches until the mid nineteenth century (*ODNB*).

[8] 'The voice or vocal cords, esp. as used in singing' (*OED*).

[9] In the sense of being closer to heavenly influences. Ironically, both the divine inspiration of God and the source of poetic inspiration in classical mythology, Apollo, are conventionally represented as the sun.

[10] I.e. to SR.

[11] Both companion and home remain unidentified.

165

EDWARD MOORE TO RICHARDSON, SATURDAY 1 OCTOBER 1748

at the top of that hill, whose lofty summit commands one of the most beautiful vales in the country, with a little river winding through it. Methinks I feel more strongly than ever the force of that divine poetry, which displays the beauty of the rural scene, at this season; the little hills rejoicing on every side, the pastures clothed with flocks, the vallies covered over with corn,[12] and the whole scene sounding the praises of the great Parent and Preserver of universal nature. But whither am I going? – I must leave room enough to tell you, that wherever I am, I shall ever remember the many obligations I am under to you, and embrace with the greatest pleasure, every occasion of assuring you, that I am, dear Sir, your most obliged, and affectionate humble Servant,

J. Channing.

[12] In British usage, wheat.

Edward Moore[1] to Richardson

Saturday 1 October 1748

MS: FM XV, 2, ff. 17–18. Copy in Gilbert Hill's hand.
Endorsement: 'L11' (in Martha Richardson's hand); 'Mr Edw. Moore' (in SR's hand, subsequently crossed out).

Oct. 1. 1748

Dear Sir

I find myself more obliged to you for the 5th Volume of Clarissa than I imagin'd — But you are not to expect from this friendly Beginning that I intend to write you a civil Letter. On the contrary I am commanded by three fair Ladies to handle you a little roughly. You are accused of having acted very rudely by these Ladies, in sending me down with the afforsaid Volume in my Pocket; by means of which they are grown so out of Conceit with themselves as to think better of another; And this, I need not tell you, is a Circumstance that no Woman can either be easy under, or forgive him who occasions it. They were early of Opinion that the Character of Clarissa was meant as an Affront to the Sex, but they

[1] Edward Moore (1712–57), playwright and writer (*ODNB*).

166

EDWARD MOORE TO RICHARDSON, SATURDAY 1 OCTOBER 1748

never imagin'd You would have carried Matters so far as in this Book. Their only hope is that her History will gain no Credit in the World; if it should, they say, they are to thank Mr. Richardson for the Contempt that must be put upon them, Since he has been pleas'd maliciously to instruct the Men in what a Woman ought to be, instead of advising them to bear with what she really is. The Lady's unaccountable Behaviour upon the last Outrage, however, is matter of some Comfort to them: for they are of Opinion, there, that the Author either knows nothing of the Sex, or has thought proper to drop the Character by making her guilty of the most unpardonable absurdity: For would the prudent Clarissa, they ask, forego the only means upon Earth of recovering her Honour from the Stain of Violation? Would not she with Tears, and upon her Knees, have solicited this common and only Reparation? And does not every Father and every Brother, under the Penalty of Death, demand this Justice of the Ravisher? The Wounds of a Lady's Honour admit of no Cure but Marriage; and to be made an honest Woman of, upon such an Occasion, is the virtuous Clamour of the Whole Sex. If Clarissa, therefore, had acted like a Woman, She would have adhered to a known Maxim, and that is, when Young Ladies are no longer Maids, it is high time for them to be made Wives. But this, we are affraid is only an Absurdity by Design; and I am ordered to ask the Author if he has not intended by it to revive the Custom of ravishing? For it is the Opinion of some People, that shall be nameless, that most Men would be Lovelace's in this Point, if every Woman was as easily to be got rid of afterwards as a Clarissa. They have, besides this, a Grand Objection to the whole Work – And here indeed I am at a loss how to defend you – For they have taken it into their Heads that the plain Tendency of these five Volumes is to put People out of Conceit with all other Reading. If you know your own Innocence, you are called upon to defend it; but if you have nothing to say in Extenuation of your Offences, I would advise you for the future to keep within Doors: For if either of these Girls should happen to lay Hold of you, perhaps your Turn of Ravishment might be next. It is for this Reason, I suppose, that they are so desirous of seeing you – I would give a Hundred Pound for an Hour with Mr. Richardson, is the Cry of all of them – Nay, they have carried their Wickedness so far as to tempt me with Bribes to steal them into your Company – But I trust that I have more Grace than to be accessary to a Rape. You

EDWARD MOORE TO RICHARDSON, SATURDAY 1 OCTOBER 1748

may be assured that every mitigating circumstance has been urged in your Defence; but all that I could say has gone for nothing: For it seems I am so partial to the Man that I shut my Eyes to the Book – I deny the Fact – I speak only of the Book – I like the Book as well as the Man – But, to trouble you no longer with this disagreeable Dispute, I have brought them to own one Thing; and that is, if the Man has any one Virtue in the World he must be the best Creature living: For to have a Heart to conceive the Mischiefs of a Lovelace, and to have the smallest spark of Goodness in that Heart, is of more Merit than the whole Catalogue of Virtues in Another. For I am affraid it is a sad Truth, that the best Security against Vice is the Want of Ability to sin with Safety. If this detestable Remark of mine is right, and you should happen to have a single Virtue (which I have almost ventured to assert), I hope you will allow that I have gained a Point; and that this will prove with how much Regard and Esteem I am Dear Sir Your Oblig'd & Affectionate Humble Servant

Edw.d Moore[2]

Oct.r 1.st 1748

If You do me the Favour of a Letter, it must be in a Post or two[3] directed at Ashley Palmer's Esqr.[4] at Eaton, near St. Neots Huntingtonshire.[5] We have a Strange Curiosity here to see in what sort of a Hand Mr. Lovelace's Letters were written.

---

[2] Signature has been crossed out.
[3] The directions from here to the end of the sentence were crossed out at an unknown date.
[4] Ashley Palmer (d. 1792) was the nephew of the wife of Edward Moore's eldest brother, the Reverend John Moore (1708–74). Palmer's sister, Sarah Palmer (1721? –1801) – about whom Edward Moore wrote a poem, 'The Trial of Sarah ****, Alias Slim Sal, For Privately Stealing', at about the time of this letter – and his wife, Susanna Palmer (1736? –1829), may have been two of Moore's 'three fair Ladies'.
[5] Now in Cambridgeshire.

Richardson to Edward Moore

Monday 3 October 1748

MS: FM XV, 2, ff. 19–20. Copy in Gilbert Hill's hand.[1]
Endorsement: 'Letter 12' (in Martha Richardson's hand); 'Mine to Mr. E. Moore' (in SR's hand).

A Question to you, dear Sir, if you please — Are they the three Ladies at St. Neots,[2] or is it the ingenious Author of certain Fables calculated for the *Castigation* as well as Improvement of Ladies in general,[3] who imagine that the Character of Clarissa is meant as an Affront to the Sex?

Let me declare my Opinion of the three, altho' I have not the Honour to know them – It is, that they must undoubtedly be Ladies of the highest Merit, by the generous Preference they are able to give to another against themselves – Since none but the highest[4] minded can emulate Minds exalted.

But, Lord, Sir, how do these Ladies Mistake the Tendency of the five Volumes you have seen, as well as that of the two others to come, when they suppose, that it is to put People out of Conceit with all other Reading! – All, I do assure you, that is Meant, and can be presumed on this head, is, that the poor Clarissa may be admitted to fill a Gap in the Reading World; while Mr. Moore and Mr. Fielding[5] are (as a certain Duke lately said of a certain Genius in his Retirement) reposing their Understandings.[6]

You are pleas'd to say of your humble Servant, 'That to have a Heart to conceive the Mischiefs of a Lovelace, and to have the *smallest Spark* of Goodness in that Heart, is of more Merit than the whole Catalogue of Virtues.' – How, Sir! – But to say nothing of *myself* – Let me ask – Have you read Lovelace's Bad, and not his

---

[1] Julian Browning Rare Books & Manuscripts in 1997 listed the ALS (autograph letter sent) and reported that it was addressed to Moore 'At Ashley Palmer's, Esq. at Eaton'. See *The Scriblerian and the Kit-Kats*, 32, no. 2 (2000), 390.

[2] 'St. Neots' has been crossed out. See Moore to SR, 1 October 1748.

[3] A reference to Moore's *Fables for the Female Sex* (1744), which was about to go into a third edition.

[4] 'est' has been crossed out.

[5] 'oore' and 'ielding' have been crossed out.

[6] Allusion untraced. Fielding was working on *Tom Jones*, published in February 1749. Moore had produced *The Foundling* (in February 1748) as well as the anonymously published *Trial of Selim the Persian* (reviewed by Fielding in the *Jacobite's Journal* of 16 July), but his next play, *Gil Blas*, would not be produced until 1751.

RICHARDSON TO EDWARD MOORE, MONDAY 3 OCTOBER 1748

Good? – Or, does the Abhorrence which you have for that Bad, make you forget, that he has any Good? – Is he not generous! Is he not, with Respect to *Meum* and *Tuum* Matters,[7] just? Is he not ingenuous?[8] Does he not on all Occasions exalt the Lady at his own Expence? – Has he not therefore many Sparks of Goodness in his Heart; tho', with regard to the Sex and to carry a favourite Point against them he sticks at nothing? – And are there not many Lovelaces in this Particular? – Men, who, if they do not so much Mischief as Lovelace did, do, nevertheless, all that is in their Power to do? Ah! My dear Mr. Moore![9] – But I will only Repeat, that there are more Lovelaces in the World, than the World imagines there are.

You are pleas'd to say, 'that there is a strange Curiosity with you, to see in what sort of a Hand Mr. Lovelace's Letters are written!' – Let me observe, that *Clarissa* is said in several Places of her History to write a fair Hand. Methinks I should have been glad to have had *hers* enquired after, rather than that of Mr. *Lovelace*. — And so, I dare say, it would, had Ladies been the Inquiristers.[10]

Adieu, my dear Mr. Moore![11] (I am unluckily pressed in time) – May you be as happy as I think you deserve to be! You will then be *very* happy: my Compliments to the Ladies unknown, I wish I could not say *unknown*. You know how much I love the whole Sex – And that my Love extends to all those of ours whom they esteem. *You*, therefore, will allow me to say, that I am, very particularly, your Affectionate & Oblig'd Humble Servant

S. Richardson

London Octr. 3. 1748.

---

[7] The copyist has left a gap, or there was an erasure at some point, and the phrase '*Meum* and *Tuum* Matters' is written in SR's hand. 'Meum' and 'tuum' are Latin for 'my' and 'your', i.e. Lovelace is scrupulous about property matters.

[8] 'Noble in nature, character, or disposition; generous, high-minded' *(OED)*.

[9] 'oore' has been crossed out.

[10] 'sters' has been crossed out.

[11] 'oore' has been crossed out.

Jane Collier[1] to Richardson

Tuesday 4 October 1748

Printed source: B: II, 61–5.
First printing: Barbauld, *Correspondence* (1804).

Oct. 4, 1748.

Dear Sir,

I have been farther considering of that part in Mrs. Fielding's proof, which relates to Mrs. Teachum's method of punishing her scholars;[2] and give me leave to tell you my reasons for thinking it rather better to remain as she has left it, than to have it altered even as *you* proposed.

As this book is not so much designed as a direction to governesses for their management of their scholars (though many a sly hint for that is to be found, if attended to) as for girls how to behave to each other, and to their teachers, it is, I think, rather better that the girls (her readers) should not know what this punishment was that Mrs. Teachum inflicts; but they should each, on reading it, think it to be the same that they themselves had suffered when they deserved it; for though Miss[3] Fielding (as well as yourself) is an enemy to corporeal severities, yet there is no occasion that she should teach the children so punished that their punishment is wrong; for it is the governors only that should be taught that lesson, and this may be done in her Book upon Education;[4] and this is my reason for leaving it as it is with regard to her little readers.

And now, as to her elder readers, I have this reason, which chiefly indeed regards this future Book upon Education.

You know that people are very much divided in their opinions concerning the punishment of children, and in this, as in most other things, they are pretty positive; so that, as soon as it is seen,

---

[1] Jane Collier (bap. 1715, d. 1755), novelist and essayist (*ODNB*).
[2] SR was printing Sarah Fielding's *The Governess; or, Little Female Academy* (1749), an educational book aimed at child readers, and had sent her proofs with suggestions for emendations, which Fielding had shared with Collier. Collier and Fielding had been friends since their childhood in Salisbury in the 1720s. Collier here refers to a section titled 'An Account of a Fray', in which Mrs Teachum metes out unspecified punishment to her nine charges for fighting over an apple.
[3] I.e. Sarah Fielding. Collier moves between 'Mrs.' and 'Miss' throughout this letter.
[4] This tantalizing project never seems to have come to fruition.

JANE COLLIER TO RICHARDSON, TUESDAY 4 OCTOBER 1748

by this small hint, that Miss Fielding is against corporeal severities, all the party of the Thwackums' (as Mr. Fielding calls them)[5] will say at once, that they are sure her notions of education cannot be worth reading, as she has already shewn herself an enemy to what they call proper discipline; and so she will lose the very chance of a fair reading from one half of those that read; whereas if she leaves this place as it is, all these aforesaid Thwackums' will say, upon seeing the words, *severe punishments*, *&c.* 'Aye, this Book upon Education will be worth reading, for I find the lady has a just notion of severities;' which they, of course, will suppose to be bodily; and, when they come to find the contrary set forth in this future Book on Education, as the reasons for it will be there set forth, they may happen to be convinced.

And now, as to the other party, they will easily infer, that as no whipping is mentioned, no whipping is implied, and therefore they also are engaged in favour of this other book.

You see how I have run on as usual upon this thing; but I trust that you will do just what you like best; for Mrs. Fielding desired you would determine upon it; and if you would still have it altered, then be so kind as to put in what you would have, and Miss Fielding will be perfectly satisfied with it, and I am sure I can answer for myself, that I shall *know* that you must be in the right.

Your dear little Patty's story (for dear I must call her) is extremely pretty,[6] and I should send it to you, but I want to read it to my sister;[7] but will bring it or send it before it is long. Pray send me word how you do to-day – I want to know not only how you do, but what you do, to-day; but a verbal answer to this will satisfy Your very sincere Friend, and humble Servant,

J. Collier.

---

[5] The character of the hypocritical, unjust educator in Henry Fielding's novel *Tom Jones* (1749).

[6] Martha ('Patty') Richardson (bap. 1736, d. 1785); the story she had written is not recorded.

[7] Margaret Collier (1719–94), herself a correspondent of SR (*ODNB*). See *Correspondence of Richardson's Final Years (1755–1761)*, ed. Shelley King and John B. Pierce (Cambridge University Press, 2019).

HENRY FIELDING TO RICHARDSON, SATURDAY 15 OCTOBER 1748

Henry Fielding[1] to Richardson

Saturday 15 October 1748

MS: Yale (Osborn) (copy in SR's hand); Amsterdam (copy in SR's hand, first half only, in SR to Johannes Stinstra, 2 June 1753).
Endorsement: 'Copy of Mr. H. Fielding's Letter follows this, Oct. 15, 1748. Taken out to lend Mr. A. Millar, at his Request. A very exact one' (in SR's late hand, on the back of Mary Delany to SR, 18 June 1748); 'Mr. Fielding on the 5th Volume' (in SR's hand, in the index to his correspondence relating to *Clarissa*, FM XV, 3, f. 2r).

Oct. 15. (1748)

Dear Sir,

I have read over your 5th Vol.[2] In all the Accounts which Loveless[3] Gives of the Transactions at Hampstead,[4] you preserve the same vein of Humour which hath run through the preceding Volumes. The new Characters you Introduce are natural and entertaining, and there is much of the true Comic Force in the Widow Bevis.[5] I have seen her often, and I Promise you, you have drawn her with great exactness. The Character of Loveless is heightened with great Judgment. His former Admirers must lose all Regard for him on his Perseverance, and as this Regard Ceases, Compassion for Clarissa rises in the same Proportion. Hence we are admirably prepared for what is to follow. – Shall I tell you? Can I tell you what I think of the latter part of your Volume? Let the Overflowings of a Heart which you have filled brimfull speak for me.

When Clarissa returns to her Lodgings at St. Clairs the Alarm begins,[6] and here my Heart begins its Narrative. I am Shocked; my Terrors are raised, and I have the utmost Apprehensions for the poor betrayed Creature. – But when I see her enter with the Letter in her Hand, and after some natural Effects of Despair,

---

[1] Henry Fielding (1707–54), author and magistrate (*ODNB*).
[2] Fielding had evidently been reading parts of *Clarissa* prior to publication. He warmly recommended the novel to readers in the 2 January and 5 March 1748 issues of *The Jacobite's Journal*, a periodical written and edited by Fielding.
[3] Fielding's misspelling of 'Lovelace' may correspond to contemporary readers' pronunciation.
[4] Much of volume V is set in Hampstead, where Clarissa flees and hides from Lovelace before he finds her and returns her to London.
[5] One of Clarissa's fellow lodgers at the house in Hampstead. Lovelace flirts with the widow and tricks her into assisting him in his plots against Clarissa.
[6] The house in London to which Lovelace takes Clarissa, a brothel run by Mrs Sinclair.

173

Fig. 1 Henry Fielding to Samuel Richardson, 15 October 1748

clasping her Arms about the Knees of the Villain, call him her Dear Lovelace, desirous and yet unable to implore his Protection or rather his Mercy;[7] I then melt into Compassion, and find what is called an Effeminate Relief for my Terror. So I continue to the End

[7] *Clarissa*, V, pp. 217–18.

HENRY FIELDING TO RICHARDSON, SATURDAY 15 OCTOBER 1748

Fig. 1 (Continued)

of the Scene. When I read the next Letter I am Thunderstruck; nor can many Lines explain what I feel from Two.[8]

---

[8] Lovelace's announcement to Belford that he has raped Clarissa, in the two lines that make up the entirety of letter 26: 'And now, Belford, I can go no farther. The affair is over. Clarissa lives' (*Clarissa*, V, p. 222).

HENRY FIELDING TO RICHARDSON, SATURDAY 15 OCTOBER 1748

What I shall say of holding up the Licence?[9] I will say a finer Picture was never imagined. He must be a Glorious Painter who can do it Justice on Canvas, and a most wretched one indeed who could not do much on such a Subject. The Circumstance of the Fragments is Great and Terrible; but her Letter to Lovelace is beyond any thing I have ever read.[10] God forbid that the Man who reads this with dry Eyes should be alone with my Daughter when she hath no Assistance within Call.[11] Here my Terror ends and my Grief begins which the Cause of all my Tumultuous Passions soon changes into Raptures of Admiration and Astonishment by a Behaviour the most Elevated I can possibly conceive, and what is at the same time most Gentle and most Natural. This Scene I have heard hath been often objected to.[12] It is well for the Critick that My Heart is now writing and not my Head. During the Continuance of this Vol. my Compassion is often moved; but I think my Admiration more. If I had received no Hint or Information of what is to succeed I should perceive you paving the way to lead our Admiration of your Heroine to the Highest Pitch, as you have before with wonderfull Art prepared us for both Terror and Compassion on her Account. This last seems to come from the Head. Here then I will end: for I assure you nothing but my Heart can force me to say Half of what I think of *the* Book. And yet what hinders me? I cannot be suspected of Flattery. I know the Value of that too much to throw it away, where I have no Obligation, and where I expect no Reward. And sure the World will not suppose me inclined to flatter one whom they will suppose me to hate if the{y} will be pleased to recollect that we are Rivals for that Coy Mistress Fame. Believe me however if your Clarissa had not engaged my Affections more than this Mistress all your Art and all your Nature had not been able to extract a single Tear: for as to this Mistress I have ravished her long ago, and live in a settled cohabitation with her in defiance of that Publick Voice which is supposed to be her Guardian, and to have alone the Power of giving her away. To explain this Riddle. It is not that I am less but

---

[9] The marriage license that is part of Lovelace's plot to trick Clarissa into returning to Mrs Sinclair's (*Clarissa*, V, pp. 201–5).

[10] *Clarissa*, V, pp. 231–44.

[11] Harriet Fielding (1743–66), by this time Henry's only surviving daughter.

[12] Probably a reference to the scene in which Clarissa threatens to kill herself with a penknife (*Clarissa*, V, pp. 342–5).

JOHN CHANNING TO RICHARDSON, WEDNESDAY 26 OCTOBER 1748

more addicted to Vanity than others; so much that I can wrap my self up as warmly in my own vanity, as the Ancient could involve himself in his Virtue.[13] If I have any Merit I certainly know it and if the World will not allow it me, I will allow it my self. I would not have you think (I might say know) me *to be* so dishonest as to assert that I despise Fame; but this I solemnly aver that I love her as coldly, as most of us do Heaven, so that I will sacrifice nothing to the Pursuit of her. Much less would I bind my self, as all her Passionate Admirers do, to harbour in my Bosom that Monster Envy which of all Beings either real or imaginary I most heartily and sincerely abhor. You will begin to think I believe, that I want not much external Commendation. I will conclude then with assuring you. That I heartily wish you Success. That I sincerely think you in the highest manner deserve it. And that if you have it not, it would be in me unpardonable Presumption to hope for Success, and at the same time almost contemptible Humility to desire it. I am Dear Sir Yours most Affectionately

Hen. Fielding

I beg you to send me immediately the two remaining Vols:

---

[13] The 'Antient' is Horace, in his 'Ode to Maecenas' (*Odes*, Book 3, 29, lines 54–5): 'mea / virtute me involvo' (Loeb 33, pp. 214–15).

John Channing to Richardson

Wednesday 26 October 1748

MS: FM XV, 2, f. 24. Copy in Gilbert Hill's hand.
Endorsement: 'Mr. Channing' (in SR's hand); 'Letter 16' (in Martha Richardson's hand).

October 26.th 1748.

Dear Sir,
I sat up with your Heroine till near one o'clock this morning;[1] but there's no parting from *such* company, especially in distress. Pray favour me with a little more, if 'tis not too much to ask of you;

---

[1] Channing has been reading part of the final volumes of *Clarissa* in manuscript, which SR was circulating among friends to receive feedback ahead of publication.

JOHN CHANNING TO RICHARDSON, SATURDAY 29 OCTOBER 1748

for 'till I have gone through the whole, or at least as far as I can, I shall think on no other subject. I have visited all your characters by turns all night long; and shall continue with them to day, much more than with any body else. I want words to express what I wou'd say – but! your bookselling curtailers I can never forgive.[2] Excuse the impatience of, Dear Sir, ever yours &c.

J. C. . .

[2] Several of SR's advance readers, among whom were apparently members of the book trade, had suggested SR shorten *Clarissa*; see, e.g., Highmore to SR, <Autumn 1747>, and Hill to SR, 3 December 1747.

John Channing to Richardson

Saturday 29 October 1748

MS: FM XV, 2, f. 24. Copy in Gilbert Hill's hand.
Endorsement: 'Mr. Channing' (in SR's hand); 'Letter 17' (in Martha Richardson's hand).

October 29.th 1748

Dear Sir,
With sincere thanks I return you the Sheets you so kindly entrusted me with Yesterday,[1] (as well as those I had forgot belonging to the sixth Volume) every letter of which I have read, except Mowbrays last.[2] This I began, but cou'd not read three lines of it; wholly engross'd by our departed friend.[3] May you and I have the same infinite support in that moment, 'when flesh and heart shall fail.[4] I am Dear Sir Yours &c. &c.
J. C. . .

[1] Channing is reading part of the final volumes of *Clarissa* in manuscript ahead of publication; see also Channing to SR, 26 October 1748; and Channing to SR, 31 October 1748.
[2] Mowbray's account to Belford of Lovelace's immediate response to Clarissa's death appears in *Clarissa*, VII, pp. 249–51. Channing expands on his reasons for refusing to move immediately from Clarissa's death to Mowbray's account in Channing to SR, 31 October 1748.
[3] I.e. Clarissa.
[4] 'My flesh and my heart may fail, but God is the strength of my heart and my portion forever' (Psalms 73:26).

178

John Channing to Richardson

Monday 31 October 1748

Printed source: B: II, 333–6.
First printing: Barbauld, *Correspondence* (1804).

October 31, 1748

Dear Sir,

I returned your papers on Saturday, with sincere thanks, myself very truly affected with them.[1] I had attended the last moments of your heroine with such emotions of soul, as every unsteeled reader must experience. But who, without a much longer pause, could leave the company of a departing saint, and enter that of a brutal Mowbray?[2] *His* character, no doubt, is as well preserved, as all the rest have been; but till I have paused and reflected some time, I can no more be entertained with any thing such a character can say, than I should have been with a buffoon or a harlequin, playing tricks over the fresh dug grave of my father.

It may be accounted a partiality to my own opinion; but to me, the desire of having your piece end happily (as 'tis called) will ever be the test of a wrong head, and a vain mind.[3] Let Belton *feel* all that wickedness can feel;[4] and Clarissa *enjoy* all the serenity which piety, and piety only, can bestow. How much more instructively will these scenes be formed to touch the hearts both of good and bad, than any which can be drawn upon the contrary plan! Two deaths pictured in the strongest contrast: one filled with the gloomy remorse created by a life spent in wanton impiety; the other, glorious in that peace which is the promised conclusion of a life devoted to Heaven and virtue. – The one, like the tempestuous sea, which cannot rest, whose waters cast forth mire and dirt;[5] the other, all humble resignation, and unclouded hope!

---

[1] Channing has been reading part of the final volumes of *Clarissa* in manuscript ahead of publication; see also Channing to SR, 26 October 1748; Channing to SR, 29 October 1748; and Channing to SR, 28 November 1748.

[2] Mowbray's account to Belford of Lovelace's immediate response to Clarissa's death appears in *Clarissa*, VII, pp. 249–51; see also Channing to SR, 29 October 1748.

[3] A number of SR's readers, among them Lady Bradshaigh and the pseudonymous 'Philaretes', had asked SR to let Clarissa live at the novel's end; see Lady Bradshaigh to SR, 10 October 1748; and Philaretes to SR, <Early 1748>.

[4] The cruel, drawn-out end of Lovelace's rakish friend, Thomas Belton, is reported by Belford in *Clarissa*, VII, pp. 27–34.

[5] Isaiah 57:20: 'But the wicked are like the troubled sea, when it cannot rest, whose waters cast up mire and dirt'.

JOHN CHANNING TO RICHARDSON, MONDAY 31 OCTOBER 1748

Your reader will be shocked, forsooth, at poor Belton's horrid end – be it so: perhaps too at Clarissa's coffin, and her familiarity with an object naturally undesirable; and yet I can assure you, my dear friend, some scenes I have myself been present at, very much resembling those you represent, the memory of which I could wish never to lose. And give me leave to say, the reader who would be most shocked by them, has perhaps the most need of them.

My own father was removed from this world, by a painful, lingering, tedious illness.[6] The morning of the day on which he died, his pains and oppression of breathing were so excessive, that by the consent of his physicians he was blooded,[7] with an expectation of alleviating them; it had its effect. My brother[8] and self, were in the afternoon sitting by him, when, bidding me feel his pulse, he charged me on my duty, to tell him truly how long I imagined he might be yet continued? Being answered, scarce an hour. I bless God for it, said he – Be sure, children, that you cultivate true religion and virtue – never think hardly[9] of God, or his providence, from what you have seen me suffer. God has been kind and merciful to me, in all this dispensation; and, I bless him for it, I can look forward with comfort and pleasure. I am now easy, and believe I shall go off[10] without pain. Then, asking for a little wine – I drink to all your welfares; I take my last solemn farewel of you, said he; God bless you all, and be for ever with you. I will now try to sleep, and let me not be disturbed – He seemed to dose, and in a few minutes expired, without any external appearances of the least uneasiness.

Can I remember this; can I have this parting, awful[11] (and let me say too pleasing) lesson, repeated, and not take time solemnly to reflect upon it? 'Tis too solemn, too pleasing, too interesting,[12] to admit at present any other. Will God himself visit the good man upon his bed of languishing? Will he make all his bed in his sickness?[13] Will he put underneath him his everlasting

---

[6] John Channing Sr (d. 1725), apothecary.

[7] Bloodletting, part of a humoral understanding of the body in which bodily fluids had to be kept in balance, was standard medical practice in the eighteenth century.

[8] Wingate Channing, otherwise unidentified.

[9] 'With severity or rigour; harshly, cruelly, sorely' (*OED*).

[10] 'To die, pass away' (*OED*).

[11] 'Worthy of, or commanding, profound respect or reverential fear' (*OED*).

[12] 'That concerns, touches, affects, or is of importance; important. *Obs.*' (*OED*).

[13] Psalm 41:3: 'The Lord will strengthen him upon the bed of languishing: thou wilt make all his bed in his sickness.'

JOHN CHANNING TO RICHARDSON, FRIDAY 28 NOVEMBER 1748

arms,[14] and support him under the tottering ruins of mortality? Have I seen this in picture,[15] and in reality? I am, your's, &c.

J. Channing.

[14] Deuteronomy 33:27: 'The eternal God is thy refuge, and underneath are the everlasting arms.'
[15] 'A vivid or graphic description, written or spoken; *esp.* a description emblematic or illustrative of a particular concept, quality, or character' (*OED*).

John Channing to Richardson

Friday 28 November 1748

MS: FM XV, 2, ff. 25–6. Copy in Gilbert Hill's hand.
Endorsement: 'Letter 19' (in Martha Richardson's hand); 'Mr. Channing' (in SR's hand); '<d> for Lady B.' (in SR's late hand).[1]

Nov.r 28.th 1748.

Dear Sir,

I have just finished your Clarissa: & I can't help telling you before I go to bed how much the whole has pleas'd me, and most heartily to thank you for it.[2] Whoever accuses you of want of strict poetical justice, must have quite different notions from mine, & I think will never be able to make me alter my opinion. To tell you, or indeed endeavour to tell you, how great an esteem I have for the whole, wou'd look so much like flattery, that I shall be silent upon that head; only give me leave to say, that when I had read the whole, *I wish'd to have that pleasure to go over again*; or a new work of yours of the same length, or double if you please, to begin upon. For tho' I doubt not many new beauties will appear upon a reperusal which have hitherto escap'd me, and will therefore afford a pleasure of a different sort; yet the pleasure arising from a work *quite new*, can never be repeated on a second reading. I'm sorry

[1] '<d> for Lady B.' has been crossed through. The 'd', in secretary hand, represents 'deletion'. Lady Bradshaigh, among many other correspondents, had tried to sway SR from the tragic end he envisioned for Clarissa, an end he had defended in a postscript at the end of volume VII. Since Channing rejects the idea that the novel should have ended any other way (see also Channing to SR, 31 October 1748), SR may have intended to keep this letter from Lady Bradshaigh when they set out to reread and edit his correspondence.
[2] Channing has been reading *Clarissa* in manuscript ahead of publication; see Channing to SR, 26 October 1748; Channing to SR, 29 October 1748; and Channing to SR, 31 October 1748.

181

JOHN CHANNING TO RICHARDSON, FRIDAY 28 NOVEMBER 1748

Brand's other Letter was omitted;[3] as I am likewise that *Sinclair's End*, was not *as circumstantially describ'd*, as that part of the horrid Scene you have inserted.[4] Will it look like vanity in me? I must say it notwithstanding; I think your post-script unnecessary, and too great a Deference paid to the opinions of many of your friends; who, I'm confident, most of them, will retract every thing they have said; and agree that Clarissa's apotheosis is every way as strict poetical justice, and a much more glorious one, (due indeed to her exalted Character) as the happiness or unhappiness bestow'd upon the other Characters.

To tell you that there are no blemishes or inequalities in the whole, wou'd be saying what cou'd never yet be said of any humane composition. Through the whole however, I can truly tell you, that no one has offer'd itself to me worth mentioning, or which I can recollect. On a second reading perhaps there may: but I have been too much pleas'd, and too earnestly engag'd, to stop to look out for trifles, or pick little faults, as subjects for dull criticism – I ever read to be pleas'd, and instructed. Pleasure I'm sure I have received, & I hope instruction likewise. My Wife and her Companion went out this Evening a visiting, and gave an opportunity of sitting down alone to read that part of your work which follows the Copy of the Will to the conclusion.[5] The deserv'd distress of the Family, the solemn scene of the funeral, the description of every circumstance by Col: Morden, the Posthumous Letter to Lovelace; his wild rage, his in vain attempted mastery over his own torturing reflections, his affected outside Levity – are pictures *so* drawn, as I never yet have seen; nor ever expect to see again: But must have done, or shall be suspected of the Flatterer, while I mean the Friend.

In spite of knowing the whole a fiction, in *spite ev'n of your Postscript,*[6] every different human passion is excited; Love admiration, esteem; of the highest & most exalted kind: pity,

---

[3] In the third edition of *Clarissa* (1751), SR in fact restored not one but two letters by the pedantic Elias Brand; the first edition only included one: *Clarissa*, VII, pp. 109–13.

[4] Channing wishes that SR had provided as much detail describing Mrs Sinclair's death scene (*Clarissa*, VII, p. 268) as he did describing Belton's death (see Channing to SR, 31 October 1748), though the novel spends considerable time and imaginative energy depicting Mrs Sinclair's agonies prior to death (*Clarissa*, VII, pp. 258–68).

[5] Referring to *Clarissa*, VII, pp. 310ff.

[6] 'Postscript', in addition to being underlined, is written at least twice as large as the rest of the letter.

JOHN CHANNING TO RICHARDSON, FRIDAY 28 NOVEMBER 1748

resentment, indignation; ev'n to execration: in short, you carry me with you wherever you please; & enrage, calm, or transport me; and make all your Characters living and real.

You'l{l} excuse a late visit: let me only tell you that the other day I happen'd into the company of a Mowbray and Beau Fribble,[7] each of whom had a Volume of your work in his hands; Skipping like monkeys[8] from Letter to Letter. Your's Gentlemen: what so busily employ'd about? – this d–d Clarissa. L–ds what a rout is here about a woman! don't you like her Character? – I can only tell you she's such a woman as I never met with yet, and hope never to have to do with. What say you Sir. Laud such a multitude of reading without coming at the Story. 'Tis quite tiresome, a man can never get through with any tolerable patience by my Sawl.[9] I hope you will {be} sufficiently[10] mortified by the opinions of these two admirable Connoisseurs.[11]

I carried my Boy to Mrs. R. .[12] & drank a dish of Tea with her this morning.[13] I have the pleasure to tell you she and all your family are well, and[14] of subscribing myself Dear Sir, with great esteem Your much oblig'd &c &c &c.

J. C. . . . . .[15]

---

[7] Mowbray is one of Lovelace's libertine friends in *Clarissa*, whereas Fribble is a foppish character in David Garrick's *Miss in Her Teens* (1747).
[8] Johnson's *Dictionary* glosses 'monkey' as 'An ape; a baboon; a jackanapes' as well as 'A word of contempt, or slight kindness'.
[9] 'Laud' and 'Sawl' are, respectively, alternate phonetic spellings of 'Lord' and 'Soul' (*OED*).
[10] 'sufficiently' is written in SR's hand to supply text that has been erased. He apparently forgot the preceding 'be'.
[11] 'Connoisseurs' is written in SR's hand to supply text that has been erased. This whole paragraph has been crossed through.
[12] Elizabeth Leake Richardson, SR's second wife, may have been at North End while SR remained in London to supervise the printing of *Clarissa*. Channing presumably visited her there with his son John.
[13] This sentence has been crossed through.
[14] 'to tell you' through 'are well, and' has been crossed through.
[15] The initials have been crossed through.

Richardson to Elizabeth Leake Richardson[1]

Thursday 1 December 1748

MS: FM XV, 3, f. 9. Copy in SR's hand.[2]
Printed source: Facsimile in *The Times*, 4 July 1961, p. 11.

TO Mrs. RICHARDSON.

Dear BETT,

Do you know, that the beatified CLARISSA was often very uneasy at the Time her Story cost the Man whom you favour with your Love; and that chiefly on Your Account?

She was.

And altho' she made not a posthumous Apology to You, on that Account, as she did, on other Occasions, to several of those who far less deserved to be apologized to; I know so well her mind, that she would have greatly approved of This Acknowlegement; and of the Compliment I now make you, in Her Name, of the Volumes which contain her History.

May You, my dear Bett, May I, and all OURS, benefit by the Warnings and by the Examples given in them! – And may our Last Scenes be closed as happily, as HER Last Scene is represented to have done! – Are the Prayers of Yours most Affectionately, Whilst

S. Richardson.

Dec. 1. 1748.

[1] SR's second wife, Elizabeth Leake Richardson (1697–1773).
[2] SR originally inscribed this note in a copy of the first edition of *Clarissa*. He copied the inscription with late additions. We have preferred the facsimile of the original inscription as it was published in 1961. The location of the copy of *Clarissa* from which this facsimile was taken is unknown. MS endorsements on copy: 'With a Sett of Clarissa' (in SR's late hand); 'To my Wife, with a Set of Clarissa' (on the back of the letter in SR's hand).

Philip Yorke[1] to Richardson

Thursday 1 December 1748

MS: FM XV, 2, f. 14. Autograph letter sent (evidence of folding).
Endorsement: 'Letter 21' (in Martha Richardson's hand, on the first page of the letter); 'Dec. 1. 1748.' (in Gilbert Hill's hand, on the first page of the letter); 'Dec. 5. 1748. on Cl. Present. Clarissa' (in SR's hand, on the outside of the letter).

[1] Philip Yorke, second Earl of Hardwicke (1720–90), politician and writer (*ODNB*).

JOHN READ TO RICHARDSON, MONDAY 5 DECEMBER 1748

Sir

I think my self obliged to thank You for the agreable Present of Clarissa: I have not yet been able to look much into it, but I depend upon finding a great deal both of Instruction & Amusement in it. You write with so good a Design, & have so complete a Knowledge of human Nature, that Whoever is a Friend to Virtue & desires to understand the other, must likewise be your Wellwisher. —

As the last Volume is imperfect, I take the liberty <of> returning it,[2] & am Sir Your very humble Servant

P: Yorke

Decr the 1st 1748

---

[2] Presumably, the volume is missing one or more gatherings and Yorke is asking for a replacement.

John Read[1] to Richardson

Monday 5 December 1748

MS: FM XV, 2, ff. 28–9. Copy in Gilbert Hill's hand.
Endorsement: 'Letter 22' (in Martha Richardson's hand); 'M.ʳ John Read' (in SR's hand, crossed through).

Dec.r 5th 1748

Dear Sir

I can neither boast of in myself, nor should I much envy in any other Man, that bold Impartiality which enables him to discover too minutely the Imperfections of a Book, where he loves the Author. For which reason, was there no other, I should be very ill qualify'd for the Office your Candour has assign'd me – But 'tis necessary for me to say something, even out of gratitude, of a Work which has afforded me so many hours Elegant Entertainment.[2]

Who is there that does not flatter himself into an Opinion of his own Judgment in Subjects which regard common Life? This unhappy Mistake will create a thousand unletter'd[3] Critics on

---

[1] Probably John Read (d. 1760), clerk assistant to the House of Commons (1747–60); see also Read to SR, 2 February 1750, n. 1.
[2] I.e. *Clarissa*.
[3] 'Not instructed in letters; not possessed of book-learning' (*OED*).

185

JOHN READ TO RICHARDSON, MONDAY 5 DECEMBER 1748

Clarissa, who think they have an unlimited right of pronouncing on what seems so obvious to their Understanding – But in one particular You are fortunately secure from their Attacks – Your Plan is new, entirely your own, not thought of by the Antients, not treated of by Aristotle;[4] so that I know not by what Rules we shall go about to judge you, unless we condemn you by some Law made expost facto,[5] which will be a most arbitrary, most unprecedented manner of dealing with one who has deserved so well of the Publick. The chief Objection I hear made to your Book is to its length – The whole Business might have been carry'd on in a less Compass – Well then, What shall we strike off? Nothing, they say, can be spared but what we should lose with regret – This convinces me that the Complaint arises merely from a Boyish Impatience to arrive prematurely at the Event, without taking along with 'em some By-Circumstances, which trivial as they may appear at first sight, may be found upon a nearer Enquiry, to make a very essential, not to say a vital part of the whole. I declare frankly that I wou'd not prune a Tree whose Luxuriancies delighted me; even though its Health were concern'd in it. –

To tell you what I admire would take up too much of your Time; what gives me a little Offence, is comprized in very few words, which you'll hear with a good Nature peculiar to yourself. It must be own'd, that you have with uncommon Dexterity intermix'd the Narrative with the Drama without once losing sight of the Actors; that you have been very successful in hitting the Familiar without degenerating into Meanness; But is there not here & there a Nursery-Phrase, an ill-invented, uncouth Compound, a Parenthesis Which interrupts, not assists the Sense? — If I'm wrong, impute it to the rudeness of a College-Man, who has had too little Commerce with the World, to be a Judge of its Language.[6]

As to your poor suffering Heroine, There's a Cloud of Misfortune hangs over her from her first Appearance on the Stage, that attends her thro' every Scene, which you, who are the Arbiter of her Fate, cannot, consistently with Truth or Propriety, disperse. In excuse for those who out of an effeminate kind of Compassion are for saving her, because she is innocent & lovely, it might be

---

4   A reference to Aristotle's *Poetics*, the work that was supposed to govern neoclassical drama.
5   I.e. ex post facto, 'after the fact' (*OED*).
6   Marked by Barbauld in the manuscript. The lines beginning with 'But is there not' and running to the end of the paragraph are quoted in B: I, cxxxvi.

186

DAVID GARRICK TO RICHARDSON, THURSDAY 12 DECEMBER 1748

said, that 'twere to be wish'd indeed that Righteousness & Peace did always kiss each other;[7] but 'tis your Business to represent things, not as we wish 'em to be, but as, in the corrupted Currents of this World, they may be supposed to happen: for this reason we must bear to see that unmanly Villain, like the barb'rous North, Nip all her Buds from blowing[8] –

I should be in Pain to think how you will be able to acquit yourself to the Ladies, after having bared to publick Vie<w>[9] all the little Treacheries, Foibles, & Vices of the Female Hear<t> but that I know you are arrived at a Period of Life when you have not much to fear from the worst Effects of their Resentment: To the Wise & Virtuous of the Sex you have made ample Atton<e>ment – By them you must always be held dear, for shew<ing> to the World one complete Woman in the Character of Clarissa.

You were pleas'd to desire me to give you my thoughts on this Subject – I have obey'd you, at the expence perhaps of that kind opinion you have hitherto entertain'd in my favour; If I have forfeited any part of it, I am unlucky indeed, when the chief purpose of my writing was to assure you of the Sincerity with which I am, Dear Sir Your much Obliged most Affectionate Friend

J. Read[10]

[7] 'To touch or impinge upon lightly, as if in affection or greeting' (*OED*); here used in the sense of 'accompany each other'.
[8] I.e. 'blooming' (*OED*).
[9] The letter's right edge is here covered by the page onto which it has been pasted.
[10] Signature has been crossed out in SR's hand.

David Garrick[1] to Richardson

Thursday 12 December 1748

Printed source: Some Unpublished Correspondence of David Garrick, ed. George Pierce Baker (Boston: Houghton, Mifflin and Company, 1907), p. 23.[2]

Monday Dec.br 12th 1748

[1] David Garrick (1717–79), actor and playwright (*ODNB*).
[2] Baker saw and transcribed from a manuscript letter in the private collection of J. H. Leigh that now seems lost or not accessible.

187

ELIZABETH CARTER TO RICHARDSON, FRIDAY 16 DECEMBER 1748

Dear Sir.

Give me leave to return you my thanks for the three Vol.s of Clarissa,[3] & to confess to you how asham'd & sorry I am, that I have not seen you for so long a time.

I would not have you imagine, I am so sillily ceremonious, to insist upon seeing you first in King's Street:[4] I hate such formal doings; nor indeed am I so little Self interested to debar Myself the Pleasure of seeing You because You are too indolent[5] to come to Me –

The honour you have done Me (& I do most sincerely think it a great one) in your last Volume,[6] has flatter'd me extreamly; and had not a Visit from Me immedeately <on> the Receipt of Your present, appear'd m<ore> the Effect of your favours, than my Friendship I had seen you last Week; but as I ha<ve> now kept from you a decent time, I will wait upon you soon to thank you i<n> Person for your last good Offices to Me. I am Dear Sir Your most Obedient humble Serva<nt>

D. Garrick

[3] David Little and George Kahrl, *The Letters of David Garrick* (Cambridge, MA: Belknap Press, 1963), suggest that SR had sent Garrick vols. 5–7, which had just been published that autumn (p. 95, n. 2).
[4] Garrick's lodgings in King Street, Covent Garden.
[5] At best, 'Averse to toil or exertion'; at worst, 'slothful, lazy, idle' (*OED*).
[6] In the postscript to *Clarissa*, SR had written that Garrick 'deservedly engages the public favour in all he undertakes' (*Clarissa*, VII, p. 428).

Elizabeth Carter to Richardson

Friday 16 December 1748

MS: FM XV, 2, f. 11. Copy in Gilbert Hill's hand.
Endorsement: 'Letter 27' (in Martha Richardson's hand).
First printing: MM, no. 228 (1 July 1812), p. 535.

London, December 16. 1748.

Sir,

I am really quite ashamed, that I have not sooner made you my Acknowlegements of the very high Entertainment I have received from your Clarissa, for which I return you my most sincere

Thanks.[1] The Manner in which this Story is conducted, cannot fail of giving one the highest Opinion both of the Genius and Character of the Author. I congratulate you on the very judicious Conclusion of your Work, and heartily wish you that Success and Reputation, which you most truly deserve, and am with real Esteem, Sir Your most obliged, and very humble Servant,

E. Carter.[2]

[1] Also see the exchange between SR and Carter in December 1747.
[2] The signature has subsequently been crossed out.

Richardson to Elizabeth Carter

Saturday 17 December 1748

Printed source: MM, no. 228 (1 July 1812), p. 535.
First printing: MM (1812).

Dec. 17, 1748

Madam,

You have given me so much pleasure in signifying to me your approbation of my catastrophe, that I cannot forbear thanking you, as I most heartily do, for it. I have had infinite trouble and opposition to it, as well from persons (of both sexes) whom I know, as from others who wrote to me anonymously, and who professed so much love to Clarissa, as to deny her her triumph, and to grudge her her Heaven. What have I not suffered from an *affectation of a delicate concern for virtue.*[1] A great deal of this trouble I have had from publishing a work in Parts, which left every one at liberty to form a catastrophe of their own.

Miss C...'s approbation makes me amends for an hundred oppositions. And once more receive, for the signification of it to me, the grateful acknowledgments of, madam, your obliged and faithful humble servant,

S. Richardson.

[1] SR had used the same phrase in a letter to Edward Young, now lost, who then quoted it back to him in his extant reply; see Young to SR, 20 June 1744.

EDWARD MOORE TO RICHARDSON, FRIDAY 23 DECEMBER 1748

Edward Moore to Richardson

Friday 23 December 1748

MS: FM XV, 2, ff. 20–1. Copy in Gilbert Hill's hand.
Endorsement: 'Letter 13' (in Martha Richardson's hand, initially labeled as 'Letter 14' but later amended); 'Mr. Moore' (in SR's hand, on the letter's first and third pages, 'Moore' crossed out); 'Not read' (in Martha Richardson's hand, later crossed out).

Dear Sir
It is only now, after having read the last Pages of Clarissa,[1] that I can subscribe to the common opinion, and call her End an unhappy one. For had she lived thro' the last of these Volumes, I might have expected the Pleasure of a further Acquaintance with her, and so have promised myself an Entertainment that no other Story perhaps can give me.[2] – But even then it must have had an End – And so farewell Clarissa!

And now a Word or two for myself – I say, for myself, because the Praise I have to bestow will be more to gratify my own Vanity than to do you Justice. For to say that I have felt as you have felt, and have shed Tear for Tear with You thro' the Whole Story, is to tell you that I have your own Humanity; and that tho' I cannot write as you have written, I can read what you write with the Spirit of the Author. Upon the Whole, I have never been so interested, so entertained, or so instructed. I could have wished indeed that you had been a little more minute about the Death of Lovelace. He should have given Belford an Account of his own Remorses after the Duel; or if that had been improper (wounded as he was), Morden might have visited him privately, and have written the Account himself – In short, any one might have done it but a Servant.[3] The triumphant Death of Clarissa needed a more particular Contrast here than in the Deaths of Belton and Sinclair.

Your Postscript too is in my Opinion either improper or unnecessary: If the Death of Clarissa had wanted a Vindication, Mr. Addison and his Authorities should have slept in peace, while I had appealed to the Feeling of the Sensible Reader.[4] And here

[1] The final three volumes of *Clarissa* had been published at the beginning of the month.
[2] Moore may be alluding to SR's continuation of *Pamela* and many readers' hopes for a continuation of *Clarissa*, which the heroine's death precluded.
[3] Instead, Lovelace's death is described by his valet, F. J. de la Tour, in a letter to Belford.
[4] SR had defended Clarissa's death by appealing to *Spectator* no. 40, in which Joseph Addison justifies the death of 'virtuous or innocent' characters in tragedy.

190

EDWARD MOORE TO RICHARDSON, FRIDAY 23 DECEMBER 1748

I would have asked, who is there of such a Character, that wishes the Life of Clarissa after the Outrage she has suffered? – No Body perhaps. – But then the Outrage might have been omitted! – And so it might – if Clarissa had acted after it like a mere Woman; but her Mind was to be raised above the Level of her Sex; and nothing but the greatest of all Trials could have made her the most finished of all characters. If indeed she had been affraid of Death; if she had been desirous of Life, and had struggled for it in her last Moments, then might her End have been called an unhappy one, or if, after the Manner of Tragedy, in a mad fit of Despair she had laid violent Hands on herself, and by an Act of Guilt had finished a Life of Misery, then too might her End have been called unhappy. But where the Mind is raised by Calamity above the Pleasures of this World, and so prepared by it for the Happiness of Another; At the same time too, so totally excluded from all Hope of Comfort here, and so desirous of Death, both as a Relief and a Reward; it is then that I can see Clarissa in her shroud, and exult in the Loss of her.

That I have shed Tears thro' the whole Narrative of her Death, is an Argument in favour of what I have advanced. For whoever will take the Trouble to question his own Feelings, will learn that Joy has a much greater share in his Tears than Sorrow. The Distresses of a Lear, however undeserved or strongly painted, will affect an Audience with no other Passion than Terror;[5] And if Clarissa, innocent as she was, had lingered in Torments and died without Hope, the Reader had been frozen and not melted. It is her noble Forgiveness of Injuries, her Humanity, her Friendship, her Sweetness of Mind, and above all the Praises which are bestowed upon her, that compell Tears, and not that we have lost her.

I could be very wise upon this Subject, if Clarissa needed a Defence, or I had Time to write one; And besides, as I told You, I have more Inclination to praise myself than You. 'Tis enough for me that I can draw a Compliment from almost every Page to my own Heart; for I never knew how much I loved Virtue till Clarissa told me, nor how I hated Vice till instructed by a Lovelace. I am, Sir, Your Oblig'd & most faithful Servant

Dec.r 23. 1748.

[5] In the final act, Lear witnesses the death of Cordelia, the innocent daughter he had condemned, before dying himself. Samuel Johnson (1709–84), man of letters, famously refused to read this final act again until he was forced to do so as editor of *The Works of William Shakespeare*.

RICHARDSON TO EDWARD MOORE, <AFTER 23 DECEMBER 1748>

Richardson to Edward Moore

<After 23 December 1748>

MS: FM XV, 2, f. 21v. Copy in Gilbert Hill's hand; FM XIV, 2, ff. 76–7. Autograph draft.[1]

Endorsement: 'Letter 14' (in Martha Richardson's hand, above the first paragraph); 'Mine to Mr Moore' (in SR's hand, above the first paragraph).[2]

Dear Sir

You have done me great Honour, and given me high Pleasure, by yours of the 23rd and I should have acknowledged the Favour sooner, had I not been a good deal indisposed, and had I not Quarrelled with my Pen and Ink.[3] Indeed we are hardly Friends yet. But I thought myself oblig'd in Gratitude to You, to make the first Advances to the sullen Confederates,[4] who <xxxxered> till I <named> your Name determined to <stand> out against <me> whatsoever I called upon[5]

Methinks I would be above justifying a fault, merely because it is <past and> irretrievable. – But have not I dealt in Death & Terrors? Was it not time I should hasten to an end of my tedious work? Was not Story, Story Story the continual demand upon me? I did not desire that the *Reader* should pity Lovelace: But I would not punish more than were necessary in his *person*, a poor Wretch, whom I had tortured in Conscience (the punishment I always chose for my punishable Characters.)[6]

You say, Sir, that 'Lovelace should have given Belford an account of his own Remorses after the Duel, or, if that had been improper Morden might have visited him privately, and have written the

---

[1] SR's reply to Moore to SR, 23 December 1748, has been preserved in two separate sections. According to Anthony Amberg, Eaves believed that the second part of this letter was a copy in the hand of Anne Richardson (*The Foundling and the Gamester* (Newark: University of Delaware Press, 1996), p. 406, n. 30). However, we agree with Carroll that it appears to be SR's hurried hand.

[2] SR has later edited this to read, 'Mine in Answer'.

[3] 'and Ink' has been crossed out.

[4] 'Confederates' has been crossed out and 'Implement' inserted in SR's hand. The rest of this fragment of the letter has been rubbed out, though we have been able to restore most of it. '<xxxxered>' may be 'bickered', possibly used in its militaristic sense of 'To skirmish, exchange blows; to fight' (*OED*).

[5] FM XV, 2, f. 21v breaks off at this point. The remainder of the letter is in FM XIV, 2, ff. 76–7.

[6] The events that SR discusses in the rest of this letter are reported in de la Tour's letter to Belford, the final letter in the final volume of *Clarissa* (VII, pp. 412–15).

RICHARDSON TO EDWARD MOORE, <AFTER 23 DECEMBER 1748>

account himself.' – Run thro' the Body, delirious, vomiting Blood, the first was impossible: To the second I answer – Morden was wounded himself – They fought in the Austrian Dominions; It was concerted[7] that the Survivor to avoid public animadversions, should make off to the Venetian territories. De la Tour had actually some trouble from the majestrates on account of the Duel, tho' not the principal; and the principal out of their reach. – But suppose it had *not* been so – To whom must Morden have written? – To Belford? – Expatiating[8] upon the Death of *his* intimate friend? – Would it have been natural for Morden to have done this? – He was too brave to insult over the fallen Man – Must he have regretted the action and pitied him? – Would that have been right? Would not that have engaged for the unhappy Man general pity, which I was solicitous to prevent? – Had Morden written (to Whomsoever) he must in Modesty have been brief – cou'd not possibly have expatiated or triumphed. While every Praise of Morden from a Servant of Lovelace was praise indeed to Morden; and every half hint to the disadvantage of Lovelace a whole one.

You wish, Sir, that 'this account had been given by any but a Servant.' Shall we suppose that Mowbray or Tourville had been sent abroad with him (Belford was too much engaged) Mowbray would have given a Brutal or Farcical account if I had respected his Character, as he did of Lovelace's delirious behaviour on the first communication of Clarissa's Death – and if we judge by his behaviour in the Interview between Col. Morden & Lovelace at Lord M's, he cou'd not have been a patient spectator of the Exit of a Man of whose Skill & courage he had so high an opinion and whom he professed to Love; having also had high words with the Colonel which Lord M's mediation prevented at the time going farther. – Tourville was a coxcomb, and had beside Mowbray's partialities in Lovelace's favour – who then but a Servant cou'd give this account? – and was not de la Tour intrusted with the whole Management and Knowledge of the affair? Was he not a Servant who had Travelled with him before? A Servant whom he calls an ingenious & trusty fellow, and with whom he leaves all his orders in case he should fall?

---

[7] 'Jointly arranged or carried out; agreed upon, prearranged; planned, coordinated' (*OED*).
[8] 'To speak or write at some length; to enlarge; to be copious in description or discussion' (*OED*).

RICHARDSON TO EDWARD MOORE, <AFTER 23 DECEMBER 1748>

'The triumphant Death of Clarissa, (you say, Sir) needed a more particular contrast than in the Deaths of Belton & Sinclair.' – I have a few things to offer on this head, after I have observed that Lovelace's Remorses are so very strongly painted by himself in Letter CXI a *very few days before* the Duel, that there could not be a necessity for any persons giving an account of them after it was fought. I have shewn that there cou'd hardly *naturally* be *any* body by whom an account of the Duel cou'd be given, and of the behaviour of the two Gentlemen in it, but de la Tour, Lovelace's travelling valet. And if this be allowed me, let us observe whether that account be not given in *Character*, and tho' very brief, with Circumstances of *great Terror*, if duly attended to, and which carry in them the marks of *Signal* and *exemplary* punishment. – Did not Lovelace *wish to live* tho' *triumphed over*? was Clarissa so mean? did she wish for life after the infamous outrage? Indeed I was afraid that Lovelace would have been thought too mean in such his wishes after Morden had conquered him, by a skill superior to that on which he had valued himself. – I have made Belford say p. 399 'that he is confident that Col. Morden would not take his life at Lovelace's hand!' – Now what are Lovelace's words on receiving the mortal wound – 'The Luck is yours Sir' – Tho his characteristic Pride makes him call it *Luck*, here is a Superiority acknowledged – again when the Colonel takes leave of him – 'You have well revenged the Dear Creature!' – 'I have Sir says the heroic Colonel and perhaps shall be sorry &c' – again – the proud Lovelace yet succumbing 'There is a Fate in it – a *Cursed Fate* (see the Regret) or this had not been. Then more explicitly the acknowledged, (the however not ungenerously acknowledged) Inferiority – 'But be ye all Witnesses that I have provoked my Destiny and own that I fall by a man of Honour.' – now behold the visible Superiority in the Colonel's behaviour as related by de la Tour – 'Sir, I believe you have enough' – this said on giving the first wound – After the mortal wound, behold Morden throwing down his own sword, and running to Lovelace, 'Ah Monsieur, cries the Hero, You are a[9] dead man! – call to God for Mercy!' – See Morden represented by this Servant of Lovelace's 'as cool as if nothing so extraordinary had happened, and assisting the Surgeons, tho' his own wound bled much, and not suffering that to be dressed till he saw Lovelace put

---

9 'sword … You are a' has been written in pencil in a later hand on the paper frame that holds the letter and therefore covers the first line on this page.

RICHARDSON TO EDWARD MOORE, <AFTER 23 DECEMBER 1748>

into the Voiture[10] – giving a purse of Gold to Lovelace's Servant to pay the Surgeons, and to reward that Servant for his Care of his dying Master, and see him also bountiful to the very footman of Mr. Lovelace – What Circumstances of noble & generous triumph are these! – and over whom? – over the proud and doubly mortified Lovelace – 'Snatch these few fleeting Moments and commend yourself to God' – what further Generosity in these Words! Then for Lovelace's Remorses, even as represented by his Servant – at the moment he received his Death's wound (convinced that it *was* his death's wound) 'O my Beloved Clarissa, says he, – now art thou – inwardly speaking three or four words more' (his Sword dropping from his hand, his Victor hastening to support him) was not this more expressive than if those three or four words had been given? – Then may it not be seen that I have introduced a Ghost to terrify the departing Lovelace, tho' I had not intended any body but Lovelace shou'd see it – 'Take her away! – Take her away! but named nobody says de la Tour.' – I leave it to the Reader to suppose it the ghost of Miss Betterton, of his french Countess, or of whom he pleases, or to attribute it to his Delirium for the sake of horror & probability. – Hear Lovelace's *further Remorses* in de la Tour's account – 'And sometimes, says the honest valet, praised some Lady (that Clarissa I suppose, whom he called upon when he received his Death's wound) calling her Sweet Excellence! Divine Creature! Fair Sufferer! – And once he said – Look down, Blessed Spirit, look down. – and there stopt, his Lips however moving!' – what a Goddess does he make of the exalted Clarissa! – Yet how deplorably impious, hardly thinks of invoking the highest Assistance and mercy! –

Now for his *Sufferings* – 'The first wound followed by a great effusion of Blood' – after the mortal wound, see him represented as 'fainting away two or three times running and vomiting blood' – See him supposed Speechless, and struggling against his Fate, at times, in these words – 'The Colonel was concerned that my chevalier was between whiles (and when he *could* speak & struggle) *extremely outrageous.*' – Is not this a strong Contrast to the Death of Clarissa? 'poor Gentleman! add the pitying valet, behold Lovelace the object of his own Servant's pity! 'Poor Gentleman he had made quite sure of Victory!' – again – He little thought, poor Gentleman his end was so near!'

[10] I.e. carriage.

195

RICHARDSON TO EDWARD MOORE, <AFTER 23 DECEMBER 1748>

But farther as to his Sufferings – See the Voiture tho' moving slowly, by its motion setting his wounds bleeding afresh; and again with difficulty stopt. See him giving Directions afterward for his last Devoirs[11] to his Friend Belford. See him, contrary to all expectation, as de la Tour says, living over the night, but suffering much, as well from his *Impatience* and *Disappointment* as from his *wounds* – for, adds the honest valet, He seemed very unwilling to Die' – what a farther contrast this to the last Behaviour of the Divine Clarissa! – See him in his following Delerium Spectres before his Eyes! His Lips moving, tho' speechless – *wanting* therefore to Speak – 'See him in Convulsions, and fainting away at nine in the morning' – a Quarter of an hour in them; yet recovering to more Terror. The *Ultimate Composure* mentioned by de la Tour, rather mentioned to Comfort his Surviving Friends than appearing to have reason to suppose it to be so, from his Subsequent description of his last agonies: *Blessed*, his word – interrupted by another strong Convulsion – *Blessed* again repeated, when he recovered from it' rather to shew the Reader that he felt, than that he was so *Ultimately composed* – 'Then *Seeming* Ejaculation, – then speaking inwardly but so as not to be understood, – how affecting such a Circumstance in such a Man! – and at last with his wonted haughtiness of Spirit – *Let this Expiate*[12] all his apparent Invocation and address to the *Supreme*.

Have I not then given rather a dreadful than a hopeful Exit, with respect to Futurity, to the unhappy Lovelace! I protest I have been unable to reperuse the account of his Death, *with this great Circumstance* in my Head, and to think of the triumphant one of my Divine Clarissa, without pity – and I did hope that the contrast if attentively considered wou'd be very Striking.

[11] 'A dutiful act of civility or respect; usually in pl., dutiful respects, courteous attentions, addresses' (*OED*).

[12] 'To do away or extinguish the guilt of (one's sin); to offer or serve as a propitiation for', also 'To pay the penalty of' or 'make amends or reparation for' (*OED*).

Solomon Lowe to Richardson

Tuesday Morning 27 December 1748

MS: FM XV, 2, f. 103. Copy in Gilbert Hill's hand.
Endorsement: 'Letter 61' (in Martha Richardson's hand).

Tuesday Morn. 27. Dec. 1748.

Dear Sir,

I am, now, got near the middle of the last Volume of Clarissa;[1] throughout all which I find myself edified & affected, beyond any thing I ever felt afore: & therefore, though, at first setting out, I read with eagerness, through several volumes, still[2] amused & entertained with a variety of incidents most graphically[3] depicted; I, now begin to read, more abstemiously, with more frequent pauses; partly in pity to my swelling heart, & flowing eyes; &, partly, to prolong a repast I am loth should come to an end; the like of which I can never hope to enjoy, till (very much by your means) I overtake Clarissa, at her Father's house; where I anticipate, to myself, the joy of receiving you, at your triumphant entrance, with a multitude of Belford's in your train. Mean time, <xxxly xxxmer;>[4] Adieu.

Sol: Lowe.

[1] Volume VII, which SR had published on 8 December 1748.
[2] In the sense, now obsolete, of 'always' or 'continually' (*OED*).
[3] 'Producing by words the effect of a picture; vividly descriptive, life-like' (*OED*).
[4] Two words have been erased and replaced with 'Dear Sir,' in SR's hand.

Solomon Lowe to Richardson

Tuesday Evening 27 December 1748

MS: FM XV, 2, f. 105. Copy in Gilbert Hill's hand.
Endorsement: 'Letter 62' (in Martha Richardson's hand); 'Mr. Lowe' (in SR's late hand).

Tuesday Night. 27 Dec. 1748.

I had thought, when I begun to write to You in the Morning, only to tell you that (in compliance with your modest request) I had sent You a few petty observations on Your last performance: but –

However, as you are re-considering the whole, while the impressions are recent, with a view of improving it (a province fit only for Yourself) against[1] another edition:[2] as soon as I recover of the ecstasy you have given me, & find myself sunk into my (low) Self; I will send you, (as a token of respect to You, more than regard for myself) the poor animadversions I have been able to make upon You – You will, at least, reap this satisfaction from them, & from whatever you will receive from others, (if I am not greatly mistaken) on the same occasion; that neither the Pride of Criticism, nor the Envy of Rivalry (both of them very enterprizing passions) will be able to abate the lustre of your amazing superiority.

I am not (Yet) come enough to myself, to think of copying the poor hints I promis'd You: but I hope to give 'em you to-morrow morning; after some respite from the Ravishments of Clarissa. Mean while I am sensible that any body, but sweet Mr. Richardson[3] would be apt to think with himself

Quid dignum tanto feret Hic Promissor hiatu.[4]

S. L.[5]

---

[1] 'In anticipation of, in preparation for, in time for. *Obs.*' (*OED*).
[2] SR published a second, revised edition of volumes I–IV in June 1749.
[3] 'sweet' has been crossed out, and 'Mr. Richardson' crossed out and amended to 'Mr. R.' in SR's hand.
[4] Horace, *Ars Poetica*, l. 138: 'What will this boaster produce in keeping with such mouthing?' (Loeb, p. 194; said of a poet who overstates the scope or significance of his topic.)
[5] The initials have been supplied in SR's late hand.

Anonymous to Richardson

January 1749

MS: FM XV, 2, f. 36. Copy in Gilbert Hill's hand.
Endorsement: 'Letter *34*' (in Martha Richardson's hand); 'Clarissa Papers, No: II.' (in SR's hand, later crossed out); and 'Miss Clarissa' (in SR's late hand, 'Miss' later crossed out).

Jan.y 1748/9[1]

Sir

I am extremely concern'd that the once celebrated Author of Pamela, shou'd gain so little Applause in the Noble design he had

---

[1] Initially, SR added 'Received' to the date; in his late hand, added 'An unaccountable Letter' and wrote 'Dated' over 'Received'.

JOHN CHANNING TO RICHARDSON, <EARLY 1749>

of Libelling a private family. But, alas! this is a Misfortune; which
has sometimes attended the very best of Authors. You indeed can
boast the Glory of having murdered two Originals; yet in spight
of these advantages, poor Clarissa is condemn'd. No Art I fear
can e'er retrieve her Reputation, and one false step has intirely
damn'd her fame. For my part I can ascribe this to nothing but
ignorance; ignorance, I mean, of the real merit of the performance.
I flatter myself indeed with the hope, that I have it yet in my own
power, to contribute to that just applause, which is certainly due
to so elaborate & useful a Work: But what can the World think
at present, when they find Prior so stupidly condemn'd, & little
understood?[a] But that the Criticks & writers of our Age, are join'd
in a Confederacy to commend one another's blunders? I confess
that I have never seen your last 3 Vol: neither do I believe, that my
Curiosity will ever prompt me to read them; Therefore they may
equal Cicero's Works for ought I know.

> But no Artful ranging of the Alphabet
> No composition of vain empty sounds,
> Will e'er atone for adding wrongs, to wrongs.[2]

[a] Prior's Henry & Emma censured by a Lady in a Little Piece, she
published in Defence of the History of Clarissa.[3]

---

[2] Untraced; possibly of the letter-writer's own composition.
[3] A reference to *Remarks*. Footnote in SR's hand.

John Channing to Richardson

<Early 1749>[1]

MS: Boston Public Library, Index Lit MSS, 266. Copy in Gilbert Hill's hand.
Endorsement: 'Mr Channing to Richardson' (in Barbauld's hand); 'M.r Channing,
With the Ms. Copies of Brand's Letters.' (in SR's hand, later crossed out);
'Clarissa Papers. No. II.' (in SR's hand, later crossed out); and 'Letter *32*' (in
Martha Richardson's hand).
First printing: Barbauld, *Correspondence* (1804), II, 327–32.

1748/9

---

[1] Eaves and Kimpel believe that this letter followed Channing to SR, 28 November 1748,
because Channing had there regretted SR's decision to drop an Elias Brand letter from
Clarissa.

JOHN CHANNING TO RICHARDSON, <EARLY 1749>

Dear Sir[2]

Our good Friend Elias Brand, Master of Arts, of Brazen-Nose College, Oxford,[3] is a most admirable repository of the Wisdom of the Ancients. Happy in head & memory. But that you seem to be very well & intimately acquainted with him, I cou'd relate to you, innumerable presages of his future high Character, during his being my Schoolfellow. Not a Boy in the Class to which he belong'd, cou'd equal him in capping Verses,[4] as tis call'd! an X, or an R, were no more to him, than an O, or an I, to his other Schoolfellows. In short he twirl'd us all around his finger, whenever we pretended to contend with him. I have seen a Theme of his on those words O formose puer, nimium ne crede Colori.[5] which fill'd a whole Sheet of Paper backside and foreside,[6] margin and all: so deeply did he enter into his Subject; tho' some have imagin'd it a mighty superficial affair, his distinctions and contradistinctions were so fine, that ev'n Aquinas, Suarez or[7] Duns-Scotus,[8] might have been proud to have own'd them. To compare them to a Cobweb, or a hair, is to say nothing; they were pure Aether,[9] or if you please Entia Rationis.[10] My Master look'd on the Stripling[11] with the same eyes of joy and affection, as Hector look'd on his Son.[12] See here, says he, extending the Paper, a Pattern for you all. Where did you Steal all this, Elias? All my own, the fruits of last night's hard Study, replied the blushing

[2] Channing is writing this letter in the character of 'Orthodoxus Anglicanus', a fictional fellow collegian of SR's pedantic character, Elias Brand; see also Smith to SR, <Autumn 1747>.
[3] I.e. Brasenose College.
[4] 'to cap verses: to reply to one previously quoted with another, that begins with the final or initial letter of the first, or that rhymes or otherwise corresponds with it' (*OED*).
[5] Virgil, *Eclogues*, 2, lines 17–18: 'Ah, lovely boy, trust not too much to your bloom' (Loeb 63, pp. 32–3).
[6] 'backside and foreside' has been crossed out by Barbauld.
[4] 'or' has been replaced with an '&' by an undetermined hand.
[8] Thomas Aquinas (1225–74), an Italian Dominican priest; Francisco Suárez (1548–1617), a Spanish Jesuit priest; and John Duns Scotus (1266–1308), a Scottish Franciscan priest. All three were eminent scholastic philosophers and theologians in their time, but their system of philosophy was derided in eighteenth-century Britain.
[9] 'Air', but in this context probably also 'any of various extremely rarefied or intangible substances imagined or inferred to exist. Now *hist.*' (*OED*).
[10] *Ens rationis* (pl. *entia rationis*), in philosophy, 'an entity of reason, a being that has no existence outside the mind' (*OED*).
[11] 'A youth, one just passing from boyhood to manhood' (*OED*).
[12] In the *Iliad*, Book 6, Hector takes an emotional farewell from his wife Andromache and his infant son Astyanax before returning into battle and, unbeknownst to him, to his death.

JOHN CHANNING TO RICHARDSON, <EARLY 1749>

Youth. Macte virtute:[13] I prophesy, Elias, if you go on at this rate, you'll make one of the ablest Theologues in England. But one word in your Ear; when you become a Court Chaplain, Elias, as I know your Merit can no more be hid, than the Stars of a Sky-Rocket, be sure, Child, shorten as much as you can: for there, a discourse of five Minutes is excellent, of Ten scarce tolerable; but a quarter of an hour long, beyond all Patience; be the subject what it will.

Elias prosecuted his Studies with unusual Vigor; and amazing rapidity. At fourteen he was elected off to Brazen-Nose, where he soon became the envy of the Young, the Terror of the Fellows, and the delight of the Skulls.[14] At fifteen he wrote an elaborate Treatise against the famous John Locke,[15] a kind of a half Presbyterian, fill'd with much solid Learning. Next Year appear'd another anonymous treatise against Sir Isaac Newton, proving him to be an unsound Atheistical Writer, and shewing the evil Tendency of that so celebrated a performance.[16] And by the by, the Frenchman L'Abbe pluche is beholden to him, for all his objections to Sir Isaac, in the Histoire du Ciel, without naming him;[17] but a Frenchman & a plagiary[18] are, as you well know, synonymous terms. next year he betook himself to the Study of the Arabick Language, and the Year following, having made himself perfect Master of that Nice & difficult Dialect, he voluntarily went over to Tunis to convert the Moors, and to teach them the Art of Gunnery,[19] which at his leisure hours he had made himself well-acquainted with. The Dey[20] received him with the same ardor as Golius had experienc'd before

[13] 'Be blessed, blessing on you' (*Lat.*).
[14] 'Skulls' has been underlined in SR's late hand; slang for 'the head of an Oxford College or Hall' (*OED*).
[15] John Locke (1632–1704), philosopher (*ODNB*).
[16] Sir Isaac Newton (1642–1727), natural philosopher and mathematician (*ODNB*).
[17] Noël-Antoine Pluche (1688–1761), a French priest now best known for popularizing natural history in his *Spectacle de la nature* (9 vols., 1732–42). There and in his *Histoire du ciel* (1739), he had rejected the scientific and theological theories of Newton, Descartes, and others.
[18] A plagiarist.
[19] 'Moors' was a catch-all term for the Muslim inhabitants of North Africa and the Iberian Peninsula; converting them to Christianity had been one of the strategies in the centuries-long reconquest of Spain and remained a colonial fantasy throughout the eighteenth century. Here it may stand in for one of Brand's ridiculously useless or impossible projects, just like the idea of 'teach[ing] them the Art of Gunnery': the Ottoman Empire had developed the use of artillery by the end of the fourteenth century, long before any European nations.
[20] 'The titular appellation of the commanding officer of the Janissaries of Algiers, who, after having for some time shared the supreme power with the pasha or Turkish civil governor,

JOHN CHANNING TO RICHARDSON, ‹EARLY 1749›

him;[21] Entertain'd him in his own Palace; and treated him as his
Child; But his Love for his native Soil made him return to his
Alma Mater within the Year.

His Humility and Temperance were admirable. He was
esteemed to such a degree, that ev'n[22] his Relicks were[23] treasur'd in
the Archives of the University; one single instance let me give you.
'Tis his Tankard. Now tho' Wadham College[24] give it the name
of one of their own Members, believe me, Sir, the cunning Varlets
vilely stole it from Brazen-Nose. I have myself drank out of it
more than once to my inexpressible comfort. Never did Mr. Brand
contaminate his faculties with any other than Collegiate Liquor;
from whence in some measure no doubt did proceed his solidity
and weight in Argument.

When he was of Age, he enter'd[25] Holy Orders, and became
the most amazing Preacher of his Day. All grave, and Solid, and
Orthodox. A high admirer and quoter of the Fathers, quite down
to the thirteenth Century;[26] for all that follow'd he usually call'd
Children. He has been for some Years look'd upon, by my good
Lord Chamberlain,[27] for a Court Chaplain: Nay, has often been
importun'd to accept it. But he has constantly pleaded his Youth,
and want of experience. I hear, however, in confidence, and so I tell
it you, that he has been close shut up, & hard at Work, Night and
Day, these Ten Days past, employ'd by his worthy Patron Mr. John
Harlowe,[28] in Answering a Book of very dangerous Tendency as
'tis said by one M.[29] of Cambridge which said Book favours Popery
very much, & is intended to overthrow our Reformation, as by
Law established. I cou'd not help giving these scatter'd hints of my

---

in 1710 deposed the latter, and became sole ruler. There were also deys at Tunis in the 17th
c., and the title is found applied to the governor or pasha of Tripoli' (*OED*).

[21] Jacob van Gool (1596–1667), Orientalist and mathematician based at Leiden University in
the Netherlands, accompanied a Dutch diplomatic mission to Morocco in 1622–4.

[22] 'some of' inserted in SR's late hand.

[23] 'Relicks were' crossed out and replaced with 'common utensils are' in SR's late hand.

[24] 'Wadham College' crossed out and replaced with '——— ———' in SR's late hand.

[25] '[into]' inserted in Barbauld's hand.

[26] 'The Fathers' are influential scholars whose teachings established the theological founda-
tions of western Christianity. Their era is generally considered over by 700 CE.

[27] '(the title of) the senior officer of the British royal household' (*OED*). Charles FitzRoy,
second duke of Grafton (1683–1757), courtier and politician, was Lord Chamberlain in
1724–57 (*ODNB*).

[28] Some of the original text has been scratched out and 'Patron Mr. John Harlowe' inserted in
SR's late hand. John Harlowe is Clarissa's brother.

[29] The name has been scratched out and abbreviated to the initial by SR.

202

SARAH FIELDING TO RICHARDSON, SUNDAY 8 JANUARY 1749

old Friend & Schoolfellow, at the same time I return his Letter;
& thank you for it, as I most heartily do, for 'tis a most elaborate
& inimitable piece in its kind, as indeed all his are. I am, Sir, Your
most humble Servant &c &c

Orthodoxus Anglicanus.[30]

[30] On the back of the letter's final sheet, in Barbauld's hand:

'Note

By Richardson's Note indorsed on this letter (*Mr Channing with the copies of Brand's letters*) It seems probable that *he* was the friend who assisted him with the letters of the Pedant *Brand* in *Clarissa* & that this was intended to introduce his appearance. But Richardson might think the irony too apparent for his purpose ————'

('purpose' succeeds and substitutes for the crossed-out word 'work'). This was clearly an instruction for the compositor to insert the note in the *Correspondence*, where it appears verbatim (B: II, 332–3). Eaves and Kimpel have doubted Channing as SR's collaborator in creating Brand, identifying R. Smith as the most likely candidate instead; see Smith to SR, <Autumn 1747>.

Sarah Fielding to Richardson

Sunday 8 January 1749

Printed source: B: II, 59–61
First printing: Barbauld, *Correspondence* (1804).

Jan. 8th, 1748–9.

Sir,

You cannot imagine the pleasure Miss Collier and I enjoyed
at the receipt of your kind epistles.[1] We were at dinner with a *hic,
haec, hoc* man,[2] who said, well, I do wonder Mr. Richardson will be
troubled with such *silly women*; on which we thought to ourselves
(though we did not care to say it) if Mr Richardson will bear
us, and not think us impertinent in pursuing the pleasure of his
correspondence, we don't care in how many languages you fancy
you despise us; not but we know you do love and like us too, say
what you will to the contrary.

[1] These letters are now lost.
[2] 'hic', 'haec', and 'hoc' are the masculine, feminine, and neuter forms of the Latin demonstrative adjective, 'this', 'these'. Fielding is mocking her dinner companion's pretentions to learning. Battestin and Probyn suggest (p. 124, n. 2) that this may have been a reference to Arthur Collier, Jane Collier's brother and Sarah Fielding's tutor in Latin and Greek. However, this seems inconsistent with Arthur Collier's known character.

RICHARDSON TO THOMAS BIRCH, FRIDAY 13 JANUARY 1749

'Tis but a sham quarrel between you and your pen;[3] for had it been real, I flatter myself, that, knowing how delighted, how overjoyed, I should have been, with making your pen my master, you would have solicited him to have admitted me as his servant. Humble and faithful would I have been; I would have obeyed his call; his hours, though six, or even five, in the morning, should have been mine. Indeed, what is there I would not have done? Pleasantly surprised should I have been, suddenly to have found all my thoughts strengthened, and my words flow into an easy and nervous style: never did I so much wish for it as in this daring attempt of mentioning Clarissa:[4] but when I read of her, I am all sensation; my heart glows; I am overwhelmed; my only vent is tears; and unless tears could mark my thoughts as legibly as ink, I cannot speak half I feel. I become like the Harlowes' servant, when he spoke not; he could not speak; he looked, he bowed, and withdrew.[5] In short, Sir, no pen but your's can do justice to Clarissa. Often have I reflected on my own vanity in daring but to touch the hem of her garment; and your excuse for both what I have done, and what I have not done,[6] is all the hopes of, Sir, your ever faithful humble Servant,

S. Fielding.

[3] Reference unclear; Fielding seems to refer to previous correspondence with SR.
[4] A reference to her *Remarks*, which had been published the day before. Battestin and Probyn believe that this letter would have been accompanied by a presentation copy of the *Remarks*.
[5] This scene occurs in *Clarissa*, VII, p. 273.
[6] Probably an allusion to the General Confession in the Anglican Order for Morning Prayer (see Battestin and Probyn, p. 124, n. 5).

Richardson to Thomas Birch

Friday 13 January 1749

MS: BL Add. MS 4317, ff. 178–9. Autograph letter sent (evidence of black wax seal and folding).
Endorsement: 'To The Rev.^d Mr. Birch These' (in SR's hand).

Reverend Sir,
I find that I shall have Company with me at North-End, which will make my Return to Town on Monday Morning, time enough to attend you to St. James's Square, uncertain. If Tuesday

SOLOMON LOWE TO RICHARDSON, FRIDAY 13 JANUARY AND SUNDAY 15 JANUARY 1749

or Wednesday or Thursday Morning next week will be agreeable, instead of Monday, I will wait upon you at Mr. Millar's,[1] or elsewhere, at your Appointment. I am, Sir, Your most Obedient, and faithful Servant

S. Richardson.

Friday Night
[new line]January 13. 1748/9

---

[1] Andrew Millar (1705–68), bookseller, and Birch's publisher (*ODNB*).

Solomon Lowe to Richardson

Friday 13 January and Sunday 15 January 1749[1]

MS: FM XV, 2, f. 106r. Copy in SR's hand.
Endorsement: 'Letter 63' and 'Letter 64' (in Martha Richardson's hand); 'Mr. Lowe to Mr. R' (in SR's hand), 'with Mr. Cooper's Letter' (added in SR's late hand).

Sir,
Among the Objections, properly started and well answered in the Remarks on Clarissa,[2] I do not find any Traces of the Inclosed.
You will be pleased to consider it, at your Leisure; and give us your Thoughts of it, when it will be least inconvenient. I am, Sir, Your most Obedient Servant,

Sol. Lowe.

15 Jan. 1748/9.

Sol. Lowe. 13 Jan. 1748/9.

As Clarissa's inflexible Resolution not to marry Lovelace (notwithstanding the Importunities of his and her Friends) seems designed to establish this good Moral (in Defiance of a popular Prejudice) that 'It is extremely dangerous for a virtuous Woman to

---

[1] Lowe apparently first wrote on 13 January, failed to send it immediately, and then enclosed it in a second, much shorter letter. The letter of 13 January is thus not, as SR added in a late endorsement, from Thomas Cooper but from Lowe.
[2] Lowe here refers to Sarah Fielding's *Remarks*; see also Anonymous to SR, January 1749.

205

RICHARDSON TO SOLOMON LOWE, SATURDAY 21 JANUARY 1749

unite herself to a Libertine, however plausible his Pretences to a Reformation may be;[3]

Mr. Cooper [of Tokenhouse-yard,[4] a quondam[5] Scholar of mine][6] thinks that The Point would have been more effectually demonstrated, if she had been prevailed on to marry him.

Hereby, not only the Objection against her Character, as obstinate and unpersuadable, would have been prevented; but Experience would have added a considerable Force to the Theory. And this, he presumes, would have opened a large Field for such an Adept in Painting to have drawn a great many Scenes in matrimonial Life, both instructive and entertaining. – So excellent a Lady, disappointed in all her Endeavours to reclaim so sensible a Gentleman, would have been the strongest Proof how great a Mistake it is to suppose (as is commonly done) that A Reformed Rake is likely to make a good Husband.

And after a great Number of severer Trials, Clarissa might have died; an Object of greater Pity, and a Pattern of greater Perfection.

3 Not a quote from *Clarissa* but Lowe's way of presenting his distillation of SR's moral.
4 Thomas Cooper, not further identified (see Eaves and Kimpel, pp. 279, 307–8). Tokenhouse Yard is in the City of London, north-east of St Paul's Cathedral.
5 'former, one-time' (*OED*).
6 Square brackets in manuscript.

Richardson to Solomon Lowe

Saturday 21 January 1749

MS: FM XV, 2, ff. 106v–8. Copy in SR's hand.
Endorsement: 'Mr. R. <to Mr.> Lowe' (in SR's hand); 'Letter 65' (in Martha Richardson's hand).

Jan. 21. 1748–9.

Dear Sir,

In Answer to Yours of the 15th, I will acknowlege, that if Clarissa had been prevailed upon to marry Lovelace, and he had proved as profligate a Husband as he was a Man, a great many instructive and entertaining Scenes in the Matrimonial Life might have been drawn; and that one of my principal Morals, which is, to shew the Folly of trusting to the pernicious Notion, that a Reformed Rake makes the best Husband, would have been

RICHARDSON TO SOLOMON LOWE, SATURDAY 21 JANUARY 1749

experimentally[1] strengthened:[2] But then the Story would neither have answered my Design in other more material Points, nor been my Story.

Surely,[3] Sir, your worthy Friend has not well considered Clarissa's Letter to Miss Howe in Vol. VI. No. LXVI. (in which she gives her Reasons why she will not marry Mr. Lovelace); nor her Letter to Miss Montague, Vol. VI. No. XCIII. to the same Purpose; nor Mr. Lovelace's Letter, No. CIV. of the same Volume, so much to her Glory, and his Mortification; nor yet the following Paragraphs in her Letter to her Cousin Morden in Vol. VII. p. 122.

'Nor think me, my dear Cousin, blameable, *says she*, for refusing him. I had given Mr. Lovelace no Reason to think me a weak Creature. If I *had*, a *Man of his Character* might have thought himself warranted to endeavour to make an ungenerous Advantage of the Weakness he had been able' [by his Vows and Protestations of Love and Honour] 'to inspire. The Consciousness of *my own* Weakness, in this Case, might have brought me to a *Composition*[4] with *his* Wickedness.

'I can indeed FORGIVE HIM, *proceeds she*: But that is because I think his Crimes have set me *above him*! – Can I be *above the Man, Sir, to whom I shall give my Hand and my Vows*, and with them a SANCTION to the most *premeditated* Baseness? – No, Sir! Your Cousin Clarissa, were she likely to live *many Years*, and *that*, if she married not this Man, in *Penury and Want, despised* and *forsaken* by *all her Friends*' [as was then the Circumstance to which he had reduced her] 'puts not so high a Value upon the *Conveniences of Life*, nor upon *Life* itself, as to seek to *reobtain* the one, or to *preserve* the other, by giving such a SANCTION. A *Sanction*, which, *were she to perform her Duty*, would *reward* the Violator.'[5]

Shall we rob Clarissa, Sir, of a Triumph so glorious to her Virtue? – Her Sex of such an Example? – And deny to ourselves

---

[1] 'By experience; as the result of experience' (*OED*).
[2] See Lowe to SR, 13 and 15 January 1749; Lowe's former pupil, Thomas Cooper, who is referred to below as Mr C—r, had made many of the suggestions SR addresses here.
[3] The first part of 'Surely' has been crossed through in an undetermined hand.
[4] Most immediately, 'An agreement or arrangement involving surrender or sacrifice of some kind on one side or on both; a compromise' (*OED*).
[5] *Clarissa*, VII, pp. 122–3. The text quoted in this letter corresponds closely to the first and second editions of *Clarissa*, though SR introduces some variant spellings and punctuation. Some italics and other markers of emphasis correspond to those in *Clarissa*, but most are added in this letter.

RICHARDSON TO SOLOMON LOWE, SATURDAY 21 JANUARY 1749

the Opportunity of admiring the still more glorious Figure which she makes in her Interview with Lovelace, on her Recovery from her Delirium after the vile Outrage, and *down to*, and *in*, the Penknife-Scene?

But is there any *attentive* Reader, who can censure Clarissa as *obstinate* and *unpersuadable* for refusing her Hand to the Man, who had committed a *premeditated*, a *perfidious*, and even an *unmanly* Outrage upon her Honour? If so, who will deserve to be praised for *Firmness of Mind*? For *unshaken Virtue*? And for a *Conquest* over *her Passions*? – But surely the following Paragraph, and her Declaration, as above, that she could forgive, tho' she could not marry the Violator, will acquit her of such a Charge:

'Nor is it so much from PRIDE as from PRINCIPLE, *says she*, that I refuse him. What, Sir, when *Virtue*, when *Chastity*, is the *Crown of a Woman*, and particularly of a WIFE, shall your Cousin *stoop* to marry the Man, who could not form an Attempt upon *hers*, but upon a Presumption, that she was capable of receiving his *offered Hand*, when he had found himself mistaken in the vile Opinion he had conceived of her? – Hitherto, *says the noble Creature*, he has not had Reason to think me weak; nor will I give him an Instance so flagrant, that weak I am, in a point in which it would be *criminal* to be found weak.'

In the proud and haughty Mr. B. in Pamela, I had done something of what Mr. C—r would have had done in Clarissa. It is apparent by the whole Tenor of Mr. B.'s Behaviour to Pamela after Marriage,[6] that nothing but such an implicit Obedience, and slavish Submission, as Pamela shewed to all his Injunctions and Dictates, could have made her *tolerably* happy, even with a *Reformed* Rake. Who could be more miserable than she actually was in the Jealousy Scene,[7] and from thence till Lights[8] superior to those of mere Morality broke in upon him? – Let me observe, Sir, that Rakes and Free-livers, well as the Women generally love them, are jealous of their Prerogatives, and Tyrants of course.

Permit me, Sir, to refer you to Colonel Morden's Letter to Clarissa, at the latter End of Vol. III.[9] where you will find

6 The subject of *Pamela II*.
7 In *Pamela II*, esp. pp. 422ff.
8 'Pieces of information or instruction; facts, discoveries, or suggestions which explain a subject' as well as 'The opinions, information, and capacities, natural or acquired, of an individual intellect' (*OED*).
9 *Clarissa*, III, pp. 356–63.

RICHARDSON TO SOLOMON LOWE, SATURDAY 21 JANUARY 1749

Warnings given to the Sex of what sort of Husbands they may expect Rakes and Libertines will probably make them. Indeed I have every-where, as Occasion offered, touched upon this Subject as a Subject I had a principal View to enforce. Allow me to transcribe a few Passages out of a great many, which might be produced to this Purpose.

Clarissa, Vol. VI. p. 309.[10] wants not (as we shall see) to be actually married, to convince her, that Mr. Lovelace would have made her a very vile Husband.

'I cannot but reflect, *says she*, that I have had an Escape rather than a Loss in missing Mr. Lovelace for an Husband, even had he *not* committed the vilest of all Outrages.' [And shall she, thus convinced, marry him?]

'Let any one who knows my Story, collect his Character from his Behaviour to me *before* that Outrage, and then judge whether it was in the least probable, that such a Man should make me happy. But to collect his Character from his Principles with regard to the Sex in general, and from his Enterprizes upon many of them' [The Readers of Clarissa had still stronger Lights to judge by in his Letters to Belford, than Clarissa could have] 'and to consider the *Cruelty of his Nature*, and the *Sportiveness of his Invention*, together with the *high Opinion he has of himself*' [and which most Libertines have of themselves] 'it will not be doubted but a Wife of his must have been miserable, and more miserable if she loved him, than she could have been were she to be indifferent to him.'

But let me attend to a few of the many Lights that Mr. Lovelace helps me to, on the Point before us. In Vol. III. p. 275.[11] after accounting for a temporary Impulse that once he found in himself to enter into the *Life of Shackles*, as he always reverently calls the State of Matrimony, 'Wilt thou not think, *says he to Mr. Belford*, that my black Angel plays me booty,[12] and has taken it into his Head to urge me on to the *indissoluble Tie*, that he might be more sure of me (from the *complex Transgressions* to which he will *certainly stimulate me* when *wedded*) than perhaps he thought

---

[10] *Clarissa*, VI, p. 309.

[11] *Clarissa*, III, p. 275.

[12] 'To join with confederates in order to "spoil" or victimize another player; to play into the hands of confederates in order to share the "plunder" with them; hence to play or act falsely so as to gain a desired object; *esp.* to play badly intentionally in order to lose the game' (*OED*).

RICHARDSON TO SOLOMON LOWE, SATURDAY 21 JANUARY 1749

he could be from the *simple Sins*, in which I have so long allowed myself, that they seem to have the *Plea of Habit?*'

Vol. IV. p. 166, 167.[13] 'What Business have the Sex, whose principal Glory is *Meekness*, and *Patience*, and *Resignation*, to be in a Passion? Will not she who allows herself such Liberties as a Maiden, take greater when married?'

'And a Wife to be in a Passion! – Let me tell the Ladies, it is a damn'd *impudent* thing, begging their Pardons, and as *imprudent* as impudent, for a Wife to be in a Passion, if she mean not eternal Separation, or wicked Defiance, by it: For is it not rejecting at once all that *expostulatory Meekness*, and *gentle Reasoning*, mingled with *Sighs as gentle*, and graced with *bent Knees, supplicating Hands*, and *Eyes lifted up to your Imperial Countenance*, just *running over*, that should make a Reconciliation speedy, and as lasting as speedy? Even supposing the *Husband is in the Wrong*, will not his being so, give the greater Force to *her* Expostulation?

'Now I think of it, a Man *should be in the Wrong* now-and-then, *to make his Wife shine* — 'Tis a *generous Thing* in a Man to make his Wife shine at his own Expence: To give her Leave to triumph over him by *patient Reasoning*, &c. &c.'

In Vol. III. p. 281.[14] after having expressed himself afraid of Vapours in a Wife, to whom he would unquestionably give the Vapours; 'In this Case, *says he*, I should be *doubly* undone. Not that I shall be much at *home with her, perhaps, after the first Fortnight or so*: But when a Man has been ranging, like the painful[15] Bee, from *Flower* to *Flower*, for *a Month together*' [A blessed Husband!] 'and the Thoughts of Home and a Wife begin to have their Charms with him,' &c. &c.

A little lower, he describes the married Pair, as 'sitting dozing and nodding at each other in opposite Chimney-corners, in a *Winter Evening*, and over a *Wintry Love*.' Yet such a Woman as Clarissa, unpossessed, in his View.

In Vol. VII. p. 20.[16] on a Supposition that he is near Marriage, he is for compounding[17] for his future good Behaviour to Clarissa,

---

[13] *Clarissa*, IV, pp. 166–7.
[14] *Clarissa*, III, p. 281.
[15] 'Of a person: painstaking, assiduous, diligent. Now *rare*' (*OED*).
[16] *Clarissa*, VII, pp. 20–1.
[17] 'To agree, make terms, bargain, contract (with, for)', also 'To come to terms or settle a dispute, by compromise or mutual concession' (*OED*).

RICHARDSON TO SOLOMON LOWE, SATURDAY 21 JANUARY 1749

insinuating that when he is grown old, he will make her the best of Husbands, if she will bear till then with his broken Vows in Marriage. 'And if, my beloved Creature, *says he*, thou wilt but connive at[18] the Imperfections of thy Adorer, and not play the *Wife* upon me; if, while the *Charms of Novelty* have their Force with me, I should be drawn aside by the Intricacies of Intrigue, and of Plots that my Soul loves to form and pursue; and if thou wilt not be *open-eyed* to the *Follies of my Youth* (a *transitory State!*) every Excursion shall serve but the more to endear thee to me,' &c.

In Vol. IV. p. 192, 193.[19] he lets the Reader further know what may be expected from such a Husband, and what such a one will expect from his Wife.

'I would have the Woman whom I honour with my Name, *says he*, if ever I confer this Honour upon any one, forego even her *superior Duties* for me' [Clarissa, in her Letter, Vol. VI. No. LXVI. is apprehensive that her own Morals may be endangered by an Union with a Man, who will think himself intitled to her Obedience].[20] 'I would have her look after me, when I go out, as far as she can see me, as my Rosebud after her Johnny; and meet me at my Return with Rapture: I would be the Subject of her *Dreams*, as well as of her *waking Thoughts*: I would have her think every Moment lost, that is not passed with me' [Yet, as above, a Month abroad to a Fortnight at home!] – 'Sing to me, read to me, play to me, when I pleased – No Joy so great as in obeying me – When I should be inclined to Love, overwhelm me with it; when to be solitary, if *intrusive*, awfully so – Retiring at a Nod – Approaching me only if I *smiled Encouragement* – Steal into my Presence with *Silence*; out of it, if not noticed, *on Tiptoe* – Be a *Lady Easy*[21] to all my Pleasures; *valuing those most*, who *most contributed to them*; only sighing in private, that it was not *herself* at the time. – A *Tyrant Husband, adds he*, makes a *dutiful Wife.* And why do the Sex *love Rakes*, but because Rakes know how to direct their *uncertain* Wills, and *manage them?*'

It were endless to enumerate the Passages which shew what sort of an Husband a Libertine (continuing a Libertine, as Mr. C—r

---

[18] 'To shut one's eyes to a thing that one dislikes but cannot help, to pretend ignorance, to take no notice' (*OED*).

[19] *Clarissa*, IV, pp. 192–3.

[20] *Clarissa*, VI, pp. 236–43.

[21] The devoted wife who reforms her libertine husband in Colley Cibber's comedy, *The Careless Husband* (1704).

RICHARDSON TO SOLOMON LOWE, SATURDAY 21 JANUARY 1749

proposes) would make. If he reclaim from such Principles as should induce a virtuous Woman to give him her Hand, he cannot then make the vile Husband he is advised to be drawn.

How many unhappy Women are there, who give Examples of Patience and Resignation, their Spirits subdued by tyrannical Husbands, whose Outsettings[22] were not so threatening as those of declared Rakes and Libertines! And is a Clarissa to be reduced to bear so *common* a Lot? And let it also be considered, that if Lovelace had proved ever so cruel a Husband, he could not have been called to account for his Barbarity to his Wife, however excellent that Wife. And would not then the Warning and Example have been wanting, in his Punishment and Death?

And moreover, would not her *Duty* as a *Wife* have diminished, greatly diminished, the Merit of Clarissa's Patience, Forgivingness, and Resignation?

Permit me to say upon the Whole, that it would have been the highest Degree of Cruelty to keep longer out of the Heaven she aspired after, and was ripened for, in order to exercise with severe Trials, from the profligate and unrelenting Husband, the excellent Creature who had borne so many from the perfidious and ingrateful Lover.

A Woman of less Delicacy, of less Greatness of Mind; a Woman who had not *already* shewn herself to be above the World, and superior to Calamity – to be, as I may say, the genuine Daughter of divine Hope; might have married her Violator, at the Intreaties of all his Friends, and by the Advice of her own, and been a Subject for such After-Trials. But Clarissa could not.

Nor would it have been needful (to say the same thing in other Words) to have given Clarissa half her Sufferings, nor of consequence half her Merit, while a Single Woman, had I intended to make her principal Shining-time to be in the married State. And it will then follow, that the Story which at present is not defective in the Point recommended, must have been a quite different Story to that I have given the Public; and perhaps I should have had no more to do in that Case, than to have published the History of the late Lord and Lady <xxxxx *1 letter*>—n.[23]

---

[22] 'The action of setting something forth publicly; proclamation, publication, promotion. *Obs.*' (*OED*).

[23] The initial letter is perhaps purposely indistinct.

SOLOMON LOWE TO RICHARDSON, FEBRUARY 1749

You will be pleased, Sir, to make my Compliments to Mr. C—r, and to your own Ladies;[24] and to believe me to be Your affectionate and faithful Friend and Servant

S. Richardson.

If Mr. Lowe will be pleased to consider the great Length of this Letter as an Instance of my particular Attention to every-thing that comes from his Hand with the kind Appearance of an amicable Objection to the History of Clarissa, he will forgive that Length.[25]

[24] Presumably Lowe's wife and daughters; see Lowe to SR, <1 or 2> February 1749.
[25] 'that Length.' has been amended to 'the Length of this' in SR's late hand.

Solomon Lowe to Richardson

<Wednesday 1 or Thursday 2>[1] February 1749

MS: FM XV, 2, f. 109. Copy in SR's hand.
Endorsement: 'Mr. Lowe, To Mr. R.' (in SR's hand); 'Letter 66' (in Martha Richardson's hand).

Dear Sir,
By the Inclosed,[2] which I received this Evening, you will find, that, when (once) we are got into a Train of thinking, it is hard to get out of it; how much Deference soever we pay to those in a different way of thinking.

I read it (twice over) to my Daughters, to see what Effect it might have on their Minds: But, notwithstanding the Impression they had taken from your Letter,[3] was (in a great measure) effaced, and I gave all the Force I could to Mr. C—r's Representations; they were unpersuadably obstinate in their Belief, that, considering what Lovelace had done, and what plainly appeared (thro' the Whole of the History) to be the Bent of his Soul; it could have been an unreasonable Presumtion, and even a Crime, in a Lady of Clarissa's

[1] Lowe must have forwarded Cooper's letter to SR either on the day Cooper wrote it, 1 February (see below), or the day after, with enough time left for SR to forward it to his friend R. Smith and for Smith to react and write back to SR on 3 February (see Smith to SR, 3 February 1749).
[2] The letter from Lowe's former pupil, Thomas Cooper, to Lowe, transcribed below. Lowe, SR, and R. Smith discussed Cooper's thoughts regarding *Clarissa* between 15 January and 5 February 1749; see the relevant letters in this volume.
[3] SR to Lowe, 21 January 1749.

Character, to have ventured on the desperate Experiment of uniting herself to him – I have only to add, at present, that, when you return me the Inclosed, you would be pleased to let me know,
Whether you would choose an Index to each Volume?
Or, To the Whole only, at the End of the last?[4]

I am, Dear Sir, Your much obliged, and most obedient Servant,

Sol. Lowe.

If you have any Essay of Mr. Spence's,[5] and can spare it a few Days, I should be glad to peruse it, had I no other Opinion of the Writer's Worth, than what I conceive from his being one of the Beaux-Esprits[6] that you distinguish with your Regard.
If it will save you any Trouble, I will direct a Messenger to call on you about Eleven on Saturday next, to know your Pleasure.[7]

---

4 SR prefaced volume I of the second edition (June 1749) with a 'Table of Contents' summarizing the plot and guiding readers' evaluations of the main characters' actions.
5 'nce' has been crossed through. Joseph Spence, literary scholar, anecdotist, and SR's friend. SR had printed the second edition of Spence's *Essay on Mr. Pope's Odyssey* (1737) and would print the second edition of his *Crito: or, A Dialogue on Beauty* (1752) as well as the first edition of *Moralities: or, Essays, Letters, Fables; and Translations* (1753). Spence was also a contributor to the literary periodical, *The Museum* (1746–67), whose founder, Robert Dodsley, was Spence's erstwhile protégé and became one of the London booksellers for *Clarissa* as well as SR's friend.
6 Plural of 'bel-esprit', 'A clever genius, a brilliant wit' (*OED*).
7 This sentence has been crossed through.

Thomas Cooper to Solomon Lowe

Wednesday 1 February 1749

MS: FM XV, 2, ff. 110–11. Copy in SR's hand.
Endorsement: 'Mr. Cooper To Mr. Lowe' (in SR's hand); 'Letter 67' (in Martha Richardson's hand).

Febr. I. 1748/9

Sir,
I little thought the Objection I started against Clarissa after a *cursory* Reading would have been thought by you of any Weight; and can only say, It is an Instance of your kind Regard to my

THOMAS COOPER TO SOLOMON LOWE, WEDNESDAY I FEBRUARY 1749

Satisfaction even in the minutest Affairs: And Mr. Richardson's[1] obliging Pains to set me right deserve my best Acknowlegements. But as you both must have the meanest Opinion of me, if I did not either retract my Objection, or lay before you my Reasons, I shall need no other Apology for the Trouble I am now giving you.

Mr. R. allows, that *one* of his *principal* Morals is to shew the Folly of trusting to that pernicious Notion, that a Reformed Rake makes the best Husband. And does it not appear to the Readers of Clarissa? I must own it does to me, to be the *grand* Point of Instruction with respect at least to the younger Part of his fair Readers? Or give me leave to ask, What other there is of *greater* or even *equal* Importance?

Does Mr. R. say, he designed to shew the *infinite* Danger of a young Lady's *deserting* her Father's House, even under the *greatest Hardships*, and putting herself into the Arms of a Rake? And could *that* possibly have been shewn in a stronger Light than by the *Miseries* incident to *such* Conduct in the *most advantageous* View of it, viz. Marriage? Nor need this have prevented the Penknife-Scene, in which, as he justly observes, Clarissa has the most glorious Triumph, it being as finely imagined, and as delicately conducted, as any I ever read.

Mr. R. intimates, that her infinite Delicacy rendered Marriage impracticable (By the way, is not this the great Fault of all Novels, and that which renders them less useful, that the Characters are drawn too far beyond *real* Life? But allow *it not* to be the *present* Case) Could Mr. R.'s Genius be at a Loss, or would it have been inconsistent with the Character of *the* divine Clarissa to have doubted, Whether *Obedience* to her Parents Will, who might have then offered Reconciliation, together with the Hopes of reclaim<i>ng[2] a *Profligate*, and saving not his *Soul* alone, but many *others* too from *direful Mischief, ought* not to have outweighed that Delicacy? And when we see a Man who had in him, as I may say, the seed of sundry Virtues, and whose high Opinion of himself, the Sportiveness of whose Invention, and Cruelty of Disposition, made so very dangerous *while* unreformed, yet have, at the same time, an undaunted Resolution, good Un<d>erstanding,

---

[1] 'ichardso' has been crossed out by an undetermined hand.
[2] On two pages of the letter, the text on the top and outside margins is occasionally obscured by the paper frame on which the letter has been pasted.

215

THOMAS COOPER TO SOLOMON LOWE, WEDNESDAY I FEBRUARY 1749

and great Generosity apparent in his never aban<d>oning to
Poverty and Want the Unhappy he had once <d>eluded, and whose
Cruelty was only the *Result* of the wrong *Maxims* he had imbibed
with respect to a *particular Conduct*, and never indulged for its *own
Sake*, but only <t>o gratify a *favorite Passion*? had not Cl. much
greater Reason to hope his Reformation, than any young Lady
<c>an *possibly have* of the Reformation of those shallow Petit-
Maîtres,[3] and miserable Debauchees,[4] who too often <c>aptivate
their Hearts? And would not the Struggles of <C>l.'s Mind
between Obedience to her Parents, enforced with <th>e foregoing
Hope, and some small Sparks of Affection to her Profligate,
[have][5] afforded a Series of entertaining and <im>proving
Reflections? – Then the Reconciliation of the Families; the noble
Appearance she makes, while on one <S>ide stand her repenting,
but *now* – pleased Parents, an <a>bashed Brother, a humbled Sister;
on the other Lovelace in respectful Rapture, and all his Friends
in full Joy, <a>t the *so desired Match*, and she herself the grand
Blessing <w>hich unites the Whole! – In the Matrimonial State,
<a>s Mr. R. observes, he might have *experimentally* strength<e>ned
the Sentiments he would enforce, and made his charm<i>ng
Readers feel (And who could better make them feel?) the Distress
of such absurd Conduct; and thereby impressed it *infinitely more*
upon them, than all the Maxims of <t>heir Parents, nay, than the
many Strictures of that kind <t>o be found in Cl. itself. Sense
and Passion govern every Mind too much; but young Minds
especially feel their mighty <F>orce, and cool Reason has not
its *proper* Weight. Otherwise why write a Novel at all, but only
that Mankind might be impressed with *seeing* and *feeling that* in
Example, which would not be so much regarded in Precept? –

   As to Pamela; tho' the Jealousy-Scene is strong, yet what's
the Title of Pamela? Is it not *Virtue Rewarded*? What Pamela's
Marriage-State, but Happiness upon the Whole? Who was she?
Neither Mr. B.'s Equal in Birth, Fortune, or Education; but taken
to his Bed in Reward of her Virtue: And can Mr. R. think, that
Pamela's life with Mr. B. is sufficient to deter from marrying a Rake?

   Mr. R. asks, Is Cl. to be reduced to bear so common a Lot?
Why not, if her being the *divine* Cl. is *so far* from prejudicing the

---

[3] '*Derogatory.* An effeminate man; a dandy, a fop' (*OED*).
[4] 'One who is addicted to vicious indulgence in sensual pleasures' (*OED*).
[5] The square brackets are SR's.

THOMAS COOPER TO SOLOMON LOWE, WEDNESDAY 1 FEBRUARY 1749

Lesson she is designed to teach, that the *more divine* she is, the *more* Reason we have to expect she will work the desired *Reformation?* If *she* does not, What Hope can *others* have, who have neither *her* Virtue, Prudence, and exalted Understanding, nor her external Charms, nor yet a *Lovelace* for a Husband?

Would not this also have held out a striking Example to Parents themselves, that if they once by Hardships and Severities drive Children to Extremity, no *After*-reconciliation can be so circumstanced as to prevent their *Ruin*; for if a Reconciliation of the Harlowe Family with Mr. Lovelace, cemented by the Marriage of the Parties under all their *advantageous* Circumstances, could not prevent a Cl.'s Ruin, what *distant* Hope can *others* have?

Mr. R. will permit me to add, If the Story would then have been different from what it is, and he need not have given Cl. half her Sufferings in the Single State, if she was to have been tried in the Married one; it is agreed. But the Question is not, Whether the Story *would* stand just as it now does; but whether the *overthrowing* that pernicious Maxim, That a Reformed Rake, &c. is not the *most important* Lesson that Cl. *does* or *can* teach; and whether that Lesson is so *enforced* now, as it would *have been* by such an Alteration; or rather, Whether the *good Effect* of the *Whole* may not be *frustrated* when a brisk young Lady shall say, Cl. should have been married to L. and all would have been well. – I own the present Conduct of Cl. is more delicate; but the Inquiry is, whether it is more useful.

If the Generality of young Ladies have not Mr. R.'s great Delicacy, I cannot help it. It only shews the Necessity of Mr. R.'s condescending to instruct them as they *are*: Nor would Cl.'s Delicacy have *so much* suffered, as I apprehend, when her Conduct was owing to her *Duty* to her Parents, and her Regard to an immortal Soul.

Mr. R. adds, Had L. proved ever so cruel an Husband, he could not have been called to Account, &c. Admit it: But was there no way to punish him, but by her Cousin Morden's Sword? I am sure Mr. R. could have found no Difficulty here; and it would be Arrogance in me so much as to hint at one. And here I must observe, the Account of L.'s Death, the principal Actor in the Whole, is not *so* striking, as some Persons imagine it ought to have been; nor are the Tortures of the guilty Conscience, for which his good Understanding, and extreme Sensibility, laid the *properest* Foundation, so fully displayed as might have been wished. But when I am writing to you, my Pen flows on, and I forget I am at once remarking upon Cl. and detaining you from more important

R. SMITH TO RICHARDSON, FRIDAY 3 FEBRUARY 1749

Business. And therefore it is time to add my Compliments to Mr. R. and your Fire-side; and that I am, upon this account as well as others, Sir, Your obliged humble Servant,

Tho. Cooper.

Tokenhouse Yard, Feb. 1. 1748[–9].

R. Smith to Richardson

Friday 3 February 1749

MS: FM XV, 2, f. 112. Copy in SR's hand.
Endorsement: 'Letter 68' (in Martha Richardson's hand); 'Mr R. Smith's Thoughts on the preceding' (in SR's hand).[1]

Febr. 3. 1748–9.

Sir,

It is, I think, no small additional Unhappiness, now the *Flower of the World*[2] is withering in her Grave, to recall her to temporary Life, in order to inflict still greater Suffering upon her. It is like the Cruelty of Mezentius, who coupled the Quick and the Dead.[3] So, while some think she had sustained Injuries too many, others are for loading her with all that a savage-hearted Husband could devise, in wanton *Cruelty*, and wicked *Sportiveness* (p. 2).[4]

Whatever *Sparks of Affection* Cl. might have had before L.'s Designs appeared in their true Colours, they must have been intirely *quenched* by the *cold Water*, which, as he himself says, he *poured upon the rising Flame*.[5] Nor would it have been Cl. if this had not been so. It might have been the Character of Amanda the Wife of *Loveless*, but not of the exalted Conqueress of *Lovelace*.[6]

---

[1] This letter refers to Lowe to SR, <1 or 2> February 1749.
[2] I.e. Clarissa.
[3] An Etruscan king notorious in Roman mythology for his cruelty, Mezentius had living people ('the Quick') tied to dead bodies 'and, in the oozy slime and poison of that ghastly embrace, thus slay them by a lingering death' (Virgil, *Aeneid*, Book 8, lines 485–6; Loeb 64, pp. 94–5).
[4] Smith's page references are to Cooper's letter, from which he also quotes frequently – here 'Cruelty' and 'Sportiveness' – generally in italics.
[5] This is actually Clarissa's phrase when she encourages Lovelace in his (pretended) efforts to reform; see *Clarissa*, III, p. 138.
[6] Amanda is the virtuous wife of the rakish Loveless in Colley Cibber's comedy, *Love's Last Shift* (1696); Loveless reforms after Amanda proves her faithfulness to him by paradoxically posing as a prostitute and spending the night with him.

218

R. SMITH TO RICHARDSON, FRIDAY 3 FEBRUARY 1749

Could Cl. hope his Reformation after such repeated Violations of Oaths, and the Honour of a Gentleman? Was she not too well acquainted with those Violations? Could indeed any but the darkest Enthusiasts in Love as well as Religion expect such instantaneous Illumination? Especially when the *respectful Rapture* which the Gentleman[7] is pleased to suppose Mr. L. is to be acted with,[8] is so soon to give place to the most ungrateful Baseness, Neglect, if not Abhorrence of his virtuous Spouse? How inconsistent is this with the Supposition of a probable Reformation!

Motives of Religion therefore could not have exert themselves so probably as in Mr. B. He had more Humanity – and, not having so diabolical a Nature as L. was more easily wrought upon. When this is considered, and that every Man is not a Mr. B. any more than every Woman a Pamela, it may be a sufficient Caution to the weaker Sex how they trust themselves in any such hands. The Inequality of Station between the Lovers is also principally to be considered, before we can state this Question with tolerable Exactness. The Marriage with the superior Mr. B. made Pamela happy. The Marriage of Cl. with L. her Equal would have made her unhappy. And *Why so?* In Answer to the Gentleman's *Why not?* (p. 3) when she is more than enough unhappy already?

The Gentleman's Question, 'If a Reconciliation,' &c. may be thus retorted: 'If a Reflection on Cl.'s untainted Purity, admirable Oeconomy,[9] high Birth and Fortunes, *external Charms*, sincere Piety, uniform Evenness of Temper, solid Judgment, brilliant Wit, if the contrary on his own Ingratitude, &c. had no Effect upon L. to prevent Clarissa's Ruin,[10] what *distant* Hope can *others* of the Fair Sex have?' So that the Reconciliation is a vain Scheme, unessential to the Story itself, and ineffectual to any of the Purposes which are not already sufficiently provided for.

The Improbability of the Reformation of a Rake can never be the *most important* Doctrine to be deduced from so complex a History as that of Cl. The working out one's own Salvation with Fear and Trembling is a much more important one, and to be

---

[7] I.e. Cooper.

[8] 'acted with' is here probably used in the sense of 'actuated by': 'moved, stimulated, impelled' (*OED*).

[9] I.e. 'economy': 'The way in which something is managed; the management of resources; household management' (*OED*).

[10] SR originally wrote 'her' before striking out and clarifying as 'Clarissa'.

R. SMITH TO RICHARDSON, FRIDAY 3 FEBRUARY 1749

traced from a Comparison of the Deaths of L. and Cl. Belton, Sinclair, and Tomlinson: Not to mention other Passages of *most important* Consequence out of a Book that abounds with them.

Whatever a *brisk young Lady* may say, I think immaterial.[11] But I would have a solid Critic produce his strong Reasons for judging in the like manner. My Opinion runs the quite contrary way; viz. that the more delicate the Moral is, the more useful; the more indelicate, the more pernicious.

Why should Mr. R. *condescend* to the Indelicacy of the modern Ladies? Is it not his Design to teach them better Manners than they generally shew? And is this a Fault? Is it then an Excellency in a tragical Author to embellish his Piece with Fireworks and Capering,[12] becaus<e>[13] that is the indelicate Taste of the Age? Then is Dryden to be excused for his rythmical Tragedies, and Mallet to be condemned for his Eurydice.[14]

What Mr. R. can find Difficulty in, is above either the Gentleman's or my Comprehension. <Nor> is it necessary to the Point in question. The *Tortures of a guilty Conscience* (p. 4) are, I think, more nervous, expressed in few, than at large. Nor is it possible to express them as they are, any more than the Torments of the Damned, or the Joys of Heaven. Here would have been room for *Firework<s>* indeed – Tho' there is no *Peace* to the Wicked.[15]

Leaving therefore this melancholy Subject; since the Gentleman is so desirous of a Reconciliation, I am informed, that Mr. Brand (with whom I have some Acquaintance),[16] who wounded Clarissa's Fame, while living, with *auricular*[17] *Detraction*, repeated after her

---

[11] SR has erased something, now illegible, and over-written it with 'think immaterial'.

[12] 'Frolicsome dancing or leaping' (*OED*).

[13] Cropping of the letter's right edge here begins to result in a loss of text.

[14] The plays of John Dryden (1631–1700), poet, playwright, and critic (*ODNB*), had become unfashionable by the start of the eighteenth century primarily for their rhythmic, rhyming regularity. *Eurydice* (1731) was the first of several successful, popular tragedies by the Scottish playwright and poet David Mallet, with whom SR also corresponded; see Mallet to SR, <Between May and December 1741>; and Mallet to SR, <December 1741 or early 1742>.

[15] 'Peace' has been triply underlined.

[16] Probably a playful allusion to Smith's role in creating the character of Elias Brand; see also Smith to SR, <Autumn 1747>.

[17] 'Addressed to the ear; told privately in the ear', with the added implication of 'hearsay' (*OED*).

SOLOMON LOWE TO RICHARDSON, SUNDAY 5 FEBRUARY 1749

Death; turned his Resentment against her Defamers; and honoured her Memory (as he thought) with this Distick,[18] alluding to *Infelix Dido*, &c.[19]

> Infelix Virgo! Domibus depulsa duabus!
> Denegat hac vive, mortua ab illa locum.

> Bereft of both, O hapless Virgin! Roam;
> Alive, Thy Father's House; and, dead, thy Tomb.

[18] 'A couple of lines of verse' (*OED*).
[19] Upon encountering the ghost of his former lover, Queen Dido of Carthage, in the underworld, Aeneas addresses her as 'Unhappy Dido' (Virgil, *Aeneid*, Book 6, l. 456; Loeb 63, pp. 564–5).

Solomon Lowe to Richardson

Sunday 5 February 1749

MS: FM XV, 2, f. 114. Copy in Martha Richardson's hand.

Feb. 5 1748/9.

Cruel Mr. Richardson,
You have Captivated my Wife [one of the greatest conquests I ever read of!] Ravish'd my Daughters [an exploit beyond the reach of any other mortal!] and, (what is worst of all) You have put out my fire. – I had 3 or 4 Letters (of importance) to write, but, extinct, by your lustre (whether chatting or reading) I have no heart, (under my present self abusement) so much as to set about them. – Yet, under all these provocations I cannot help exposing myself, by unburthening my heart, to let you see, how much I am notwithstanding the mortification you have given me, Dear Sir, Your Admirer & Lover

Sol. Lowe.

Of business, when I am recover'd; to which the earnest looks, & the significant whispers of the meadows as passing-by (when You did me the honor of taking your leave at the gate)[1] have not a little contributed.

[1] I.e. SR walked Lowe out of the house.

Jane Collier to Richardson

Thursday 13 April 1749

Printed source: B: II, 65–8
First printing: Barbauld, *Correspondence* (1804).

Doctors Commons,[1] 13th April, 1749.

Dear Sir,

I return you my thanks for the play you sent me; and by what I have read of it, I think Mr. Garrick is very much obliged to the author for shewing the world how much he was in the right for refusing it.[2] I thought to have called upon you this morning, but cannot; nor do I believe that I shall see you, unless your kind intentions should lead you this way, before you go to North End. Mr. Harris[3] was telling me the other day, that he heard your sweet girl[4] most unmercifully condemned for not marrying Lovelace at St. Alban's. 'She should (said the lady who blamed her) have laid aside all delicacy; and if Lovelace had not asked her in the manner she wished, she ought to have asked him.' And more things of the same kind she ran on with; but, at last, closed all with saying, 'In short, Lovelace is a charming young fellow, and I own I like him excessively.'

You know I love to tell you every thing I hear concerning your Clarissa, or otherwise I should not furnish you with more instances of what you have reason to say you too often meet with; namely, the fondness most women have for the character of Lovelace. It vexes me so much when I hear of people talking in such a manner, that I cannot help attempting something like an answer;[5] but the best answer to the present criticism is, to give you the history and character of the lady who so ingenuously avowed her fondness for

---

[1] The address of Arthur Collier, Jane's brother, who was an advocate at the ecclesiastical court and had rooms there. Battestin and Probyn surmise that Jane may have lived there, too (p. xxviii).

[2] According to Alan Dugald McKillop, this was Tobias Smollett's tragedy, *The Regicide: or, James the First, of Scotland*, which he unsuccessfully tried to have staged throughout the 1740s and finally published by subscription in 1749; see McKillop, *Samuel Richardson, Printer and Novelist* (Chapel Hill: University of North Carolina Press, 1936), p. 180, n. 52.

[3] James Harris (1709–80), philosopher and musical patron, was a friend of Jane and Margaret Collier as well as of siblings Sarah and Henry Fielding (*ODNB*).

[4] I.e. Clarissa.

[5] She would eventually write, though not publish, such an answer; see Collier to SR, 19 September 1749.

SOLOMON LOWE TO RICHARDSON, THURSDAY 18 MAY 1749

Lovelace.[6] This lady is a person of very high rank, and therefore you must excuse my naming names. She lived as a mistress with a man for many years, and proved herself to have done so in a court of justice, in order to recover some money for a child she had by that very man. She then went into keeping with a noble lord (now her husband) and after having lived with him some years, she prevailed with him to marry her, by shewing him the *meekness* of her spirit, and the *gentleness* of her passions: for (besides being frequently in fits and sometimes in the most violent passions of rage) she once attempted to take laudanum to destroy herself; and, being prevented, she another time hanged herself, just as she knew he was coming up stairs; which last stratagem gained her ends: and now she is a woman of quality, and a woman of taste, and a perfect judge of delicacy, as appears by the before-mentioned criticism. I wonder whether her husband ever read your books, and whether he attended to your description of Belton, and his Thomasine![7]

If I should not have the pleasure of seeing you before you go out of town, I beg my compliments to Mrs. Richardson; and believe me, dear Sir, Your sincere Friend, And humble Servant,

J. Collier

---

[6] Tantalizingly unidentified.
[7] This description appears in *Clarissa*, IV, p. 93.

Solomon Lowe to Richardson

Thursday 18 May 1749

MS: FM XV, 2, ff. 116–17. Autograph letter sent (evidence of folding, seal, and fragment of postmark).
Address: 'To Mr Richardson Printer in Salisbury cou<rt>'[1] (in Lowe's hand).
Endorsement: '<Mr. Lowe>, 18 May, 1749' and 'Mr R. Smith's Translation at Sight' (in SR's hand); 'Greek Motto' and 'Clarissa' (in SR's late hand); 'Johnson' (in an undetermined hand).[2]

May 18 – 1749

---

[1] Address and endorsement are partially hidden by a strip of paper glued across the outside of the letter's central fold.
[2] The name 'Johnson' is accompanied by two notes in different hands: 'Dr. S. Johnson's own Signature; perhaps he called at Richardsons & wrote his name to shew that he had called. –' and 'Note by Mr. Upcott'. William Upcott bought much of SR's correspondence from Richard Phillips; see General Editor's Preface. The signature does not appear to be Johnson's. The entire letter has been crossed through.

SOLOMON LOWE TO RICHARDSON, THURSDAY 18 MAY 1749

Dear Sir,

Mottos (though a grotesque writer has lately taken-upon him to ridicule them)[3] I am apt to think, when well adapted, are very generally pleasing; as they have been very frequently used by the best writers, and appear to be instructively striking.

If you are in the same way of thinking, & and do not disapprove the inclosed; you will perhaps (unless you have your eye on a better) do it the honor to place it in the title-page of Clarissa,[4] if it come not too late: especially as it harmonizes with one part of your Advertisement; which I take to be well designed & well worded.[5]

Though I have not seen you this long long time, Believe me, Sir, I love to see & hear you: in want of which pleasure, I (every day) talk or think of you: and to this fondness for you, you owe this trouble from Sir Your most obedient Servant

Sol Lowe

18 May 1749

Τουσ ΜΗΘΟὺΣ ἀπεδέξαντο οὐχ οἱ Ποιηταὶ μόνον ἀλλὰ καὶ Πόλεις πολὺ πρότερον, καὶ ὁι Νομοθέται (τοῦ χρησίμοθ χάριν) Βλέψαντες ἐις τὸ Φυσικὸν Παθος τοῦ ΛΟΓΙΚ˜ΟΝ Ζ´ΩΟΝ. *Strab. geog* l. 1. p. 19 paris.[6]

which I interpret thus:

FICTIONS have been made-use-of, in preference to other compositions, not only by Poëts, but, long before, by States, & Law-giver<s>[7] (in regard to the usefulness advantage[8] of them) upon considering the natural disposition of a RATIONAL ANIMA<L>.

---

[3] This is probably a reference to Henry Fielding, *Tom Jones*, Book 9, ch. 1, which discusses the use of mottoes to differentiate between the learned and unlearned. SR was not himself proficient in Latin or Greek.

[4] SR did not include a motto in the title pages of either the second (1749) or third (1751) edition of *Clarissa*.

[5] In the Advertisement to the second edition, SR explained that a table of contents had been substituted for the first edition's prefatory materials and that *Clarissa* was a work 'in which ... Story is to be principally looked upon as a *Vehicle* to convey the proposed Instruction'.

[6] Strabo, *Geography*, Book I, C 19, 2:8: 'I remark that the poets were not alone in sanctioning myths, for long before the poets the states and the lawgivers had sanctioned them as a useful expedient, since they had an insight into the natural affections of the reasoning animal' (Loeb 49, pp. 66–7).

[7] Text is partly hidden by the page onto which the letter has been pasted.

[8] 'usefulness' is written above 'advantage'.

Mr. R. Smith's Translation, at Sight, without seeing Mr. Lowe's.

Not only the Poets, but also Republics long before, and Lawgivers (for Utility-Sake) encouraged Fables; in regard to the natural Affection of a reasonable Animal.[9]

[9] This note and translation written over the fold are in SR's hand.

R. Smith to Richardson

Saturday 20 May 1749

MS: FM XV, 2, f. 118. Copy in an undetermined hand.
Endorsement: 'Letter 71' (in Martha Richardson's hand); 'Clarissa' and 'Mr. R. Smith on Clarissa's Death' (in SR's late hand).[1]

May 20. 1749.

Sir,

As Mr. Lowe thinks Mottoes of such Importance,[2] and as that which you mentioned from Seneca[3] appears not in the Tragedian (but is probably in some part of the Philosopher's Works) tho' it occasion'd my looking over all the Tragedies, with a View to moral Sentences, in which the Author is too lavish, I there met with the following

O quam miserum est nescire mori! *Agam.*
How wretched is it not to learn to die![4]

Mors sola portus. – *Herc. Oet.*
Death is my only Haven. –[5]

In my Search after Morals, this Description struck me:

– Ipsa dejectos gerit
Vultus pudore; sed tamen fulgent genae,
Magisque solito splendet extremus decor.
Ut esse Phoebi dulcius lumen solet

[1] The entire letter has been crossed through.
[2] See Lowe to SR, 18 May 1749.
[3] Lucius Annaeus Seneca, also known as Seneca the Younger (4 BCE-65 CE), Roman Stoic philosopher, statesman, and dramatist.
[4] Seneca the Younger, *Agamemnon*, l. 610.
[5] Seneca the Younger, *Hercules on Oeta*, l. 1021.

225

Jam jam cadentis, astra cum repetunt vices,
Premiturque dubius nocte vicina dies.
Stupet omne vulgus: & fere cuncti magis
Peritura laudant. Hos movet formae decus,
Hos mollis aetas, hos vagae rerum vices.
Movet animus omnes fortis, & leto obvius.
Pyrrhum antecedit. Omnium mentes tremunt;
Miserentur, ac mirantur. — Troas.[6]

Down to the Ground her modest Eyes she casts:
Yet bloom her Cheeks; and Beauty, on the Verge
Of Life, with more than usual Lustre shines.
As when the Sun a milder Beam displays,
Just sinking, when the Stars resume their Turns,
And Twilight is by bord'ring Night expell'd.
Aghast the Vulgar stand: And all more prize
A Good near perishing. Her Beauty some,
Others her tender Age, or Fortune's Change,
All, her exalted Soul, prepar'd for Death,
Affects. *With hasty Steps she goes before
Her Murderer.* Then trembles every Mind,
By Admiration and by Pity sway'd.

This Speech is Part of the Description of *Polyxena* led to her Death to appease the Manes[7] of the inexorable *Achilles*.[8] What would the Critics have said,[9] if such a Scene of Horror had been represented in Clarissa; or if Lovelace's Revenge had not stopt short of the Violence offered to her Person; but he had ignominiously expelled her the House, as a *King's unworthy Son* once did;[10] or murdered her with his own Hands as a *more unworthy Judge* was said to have murdered his deluded Charge![11] The Circumstance of *going before the Murderer* is equally applicable to Clarissa, tho' in a more figurative Sense.

---

[6] Seneca the Younger, *Trojan Women*, lines 1137–48; the final line appears variably in Smith's version and inverted, as 'mirantur ac miserantur'.

[7] 'The spirit or shade of a dead person, considered as an object of homage or reverence or as demanding to be propitiated' (*OED*).

[8] The Trojan princess, Polyxena, is killed by Achilles's son, Pyrrhus; her murder finally ends the Trojan War.

[9] Smith probably aims this specifically at Lowe and his former pupil, Thomas Cooper, who had criticized some of SR's handling of Clarissa's fate; see the relevant letters in this volume.

[10] Reference to Amnon, Son of David, who raped Tamar and then banished her from the house in 2 Samuel 13.

[11] In Judges 11, Jephthah kills his only daughter to fulfil an oath to his Lord.

PHILIP SKELTON TO SAMUEL RICHARDSON, SATURDAY 27 MAY 1749

But if nothing less than a Greek Motto will please the Critic, and as the Motto propos'd only recommends Fable in general, I think I have hit upon one which more intimately concerns the specific Character of the Heroine. It is this:

– Φυὴν τ᾽ἐρατὴ καὶ εἶδος ἄνωμος. Hesiod. Theogon.
In equal Loveliness of Manners dress'd,
As her bright Form a faultless Grace express'd.[12]

I am, Sir, Your most obliged & obedient Servant

R: S.

[12] Hesiod, *Theogony*, l. 259: 'lovely in shape and blameless in form' (Loeb 57, pp. 24–5).

Philip Skelton[1] to Samuel Richardson

Saturday 27 May 1749

Printed source: B: V, 193–7
First printing: Barbauld, *Correspondence* (1804).

Monaghan,[2] *May 27, 1749.*

My Dear Friend

Should much sooner have heard from me, had any thing relating to him or me occurred, that was worthy of our friendship: but my whole time, since I left London, hath been spent in travelling from thence to Dublin, from Dublin to the north of Ireland, from the north to Dublin, and back again, in getting my books bound and delivered, in picking up my little pence for those books, and in an hundred other perplexing affairs;[3] together with about a thousand visits, which my long absence from my duty and my acquaintances unavoidably brought upon me. However, I have not, in the hurry of matters relating immediately to myself, been altogether unmindful of such as concerned my friend. I took a natural occasion of insinuating what I thought necessary to Dean Delany[4] about his

[1] Philip Skelton (1707–87), Church of Ireland clergyman and religious controversialist (*ODNB*).
[2] Town in County Monaghan, Ireland, where Skelton was a curate from 1732 to 1750.
[3] Skelton was in the process of publishing his attack on Deism, *Ophiomaches* (1749), which SR was printing for Andrew Millar.
[4] Patrick Delany (1685/6–1768), Church of Ireland dean of Down, and a writer (*ODNB*), and his second wife Mary, *née* Granville (1700–88), an artist and favourite at court (*ODNB*), were friends of SR; see also Barber to SR, 26 August 1741.

227

PHILIP SKELTON TO SAMUEL RICHARDSON, SATURDAY 27 MAY 1749

account; I don't mean that I mentioned that account to him, for that would have had the look of a complaint made by one of his friends to another; but that I prepared the way for the discharging that account, as soon as it shall be tendered by the creditor, from whom it will come with a better grace, than from any third person, who cannot speak of it without giving the Dean to understand that he is debtor, only because his performances were not sufficiently called for; and what is almost as bad, that Mr. Richardson had intimated as much to the Dean's friend.[5] The Dean and his lady are now at Bath, and will spend a year in England, chiefly about London.

As to Faulkner,[6] I had some chat with him about Clarissa, in which he complained of the public, and, to say the truth, I now believe with some reason; for that admirable work is pitched above the common taste; yet sure I am, he must have made pretty well by it, and ought to pay the very moderate sum that was promised, to which end I think the author ought, without ceremony, to demand it.

As to ———,[7] he is still in very good circumstances, if a man can be said so to be, who hath a great deal of other men's effects[8] in his hands. His privilege protects him in parliament time; and at all other times he skulks in the Isle of Mann, where nothing is to be come at, but such chattels as he may have with him in the island. Mr. Thompson[9] will run him to an outlawry; and, if it is thought expedient, I will make a trip to the island, and try what may be done through the bishop's[10] credit and authority there, as well as by other steps that may be taken when I am on the spot.

---

[5] SR had printed Delany's works since his *Revelation Examin'd With Candour* (1732), but at least some of the Dean's works had not been selling well, so that he owed SR money for printing.

[6] George Faulkner (1703?–75), Dublin printer and bookseller (*ODNB*), had published *Clarissa* in Ireland.

[7] Unidentified, but evidently a member of parliament escaping his creditors on the Isle of Man. MPs were safe from arrest in civil matters, which included arrests for debt, during parliamentary sessions as well as for forty days before and after. The Isle of Man became a haven for debtors after 1737, when lenient debt laws stipulated that 'foreign debt' incurred outside the island's limits could only be collected from the goods that debtors had with them in the island.

[8] 'movable property (originally: spec. merchandise)' (*OED*).

[9] Largely unidentified, though Samuel Burdy, Skelton's first biographer, notes in *The Life of the Rev. Philip Skelton, With Some Curious Anecdotes* (Dublin, 1792), p. 90, that 'a Mr. Thompson, a clergyman', accompanied Skelton to London in 1748–9 to publish his *Ophiomaches*. A Rev. Mr Thompson appears in the list of subscribers for the *Life*.

[10] Thomas Wilson (1663–1755), bishop of Sodor and Man from 1697 (*ODNB*).

PHILIP SKELTON TO RICHARDSON, SATURDAY 10 JUNE 1749

I know nothing in this world that could give me so much pleasure as causing justice to be done to the man who hath been so good a friend to me: but, whether we succeed or fail in our other endeavours, to serve our friends, there is one in which we cannot be disappointed; I mean that proposed by my dear friend, in soliciting Divine Providence for each other's happiness.

We may hurt our friends by the good we ignorantly attempt to do them ourselves; but, if we can by any means move the Almighty God, who delights in charity, to a longer continuance of his patience and pity towards them, in that case our friendship, conducted by a wisdom that cannot err, and supported by a power that cannot be assisted, must be secure of success without alloy. Let us therefore make religion the cement, and God the center, of our affection; and let us never forget to pray for each other.

Could I touch the heart like the author of Clarissa, I would tell him, in terms like his own, how much and how tenderly I am his,

Phil. Skelton.

Philip Skelton to Richardson

Saturday 10 June 1749

MS: FM XV, 2, ff. 47–8. Copy in Gilbert Hill's hand.
Endorsement: 'Letter 33' (in Martha Richardson's hand); 'Mr. Skelton' (in SR's hand).

Monaghan,[1] June 10.th 1749

Dear Sir,

I am almost blinded with gazing at the Sun in order to find out its Spots; and all that[2] I could discover (if they are not rather so many Motes in my own Eyes) are noted in the inclosed Paper.[3] The Lustre & Warmth of this Object often drew such Quantities of Moisture into my Eyes, as not only hinder'd me from seeing its Defects (if any it hath) but even hid from me the lovely Object itself. It is happy for the Readers of Clarissa, that its Author

---

[1] All but the first letter of 'Monaghan' has been crossed through and 'in Ireland' added in SR's late hand.
[2] 'that' has been crossed through.
[3] SR had asked that Skelton send him a list of faults in *Clarissa* and amendments for a second edition.

PHILIP SKELTON TO RICHARDSON, SATURDAY 10 JUNE 1749

proposed to himself so noble an End as that of rectifying the Heart
thro' its Passions; and not like other Novel-Writers, that only of
amusing its Corruptions; happy indeed! because he can do what
he will with the Heart. Is it because his Heart & mine are closely
united in Friendship, that every thing that comes from his, goes
directly, with all its Force, and Warmth, into mine? Or shall I for
this Reason have the Vanity to think my Heart is like his? No, his
excites Ardours in it, and forces Impressions on it, which it had not
before. And yet his tender Touches do not with more Power and
Expedition new-Model my Affections, than his just Sentiments,
and excellent Precepts, improve my Understanding. Some Writers
can move the Passions; others can inform the Mind; a very few
can do both. Some can Please and others Shock. But who, like this
Writer, can please and Shock, can fill us with Delight and Horror,
at once? Nay, what is still more, in the midst of this Tempest
(which, had it not first raged in his own Mind, could never have
been propagated into ours) can steadily keep his glorious End in
View; can so nicely take his Aim at our Corruptions; can with so
even an Hand, point[4] every violent Passion to his Purpose; and
while the Heart is deeply pierced, and powerfully stirr'd, and
laid open, as wide as it can stretch to him, can sedately form, and
plentifully pour in, the most useful, the most noble Lessons, of
Morality and Religion? It is an ordinary thing to see an Author,
who can raise, and ride in a Whirlwind; but give me the Man who
can direct the Storm?

In this little Sketch, may be seen, faintly represented, what
I think of Clarissa. And now give me leave, my dearest Friend,
Friend of my Soul, let me call you, to return you the Thanks of
an Heart, that is transported, and mended, by your Performance;
and at the same time to put you in Mind, that the Mob of your
Readers, wretchedly mistaking your Work for a mere Novel, and
having their Vices protected, by the Depravity of their Taste, lay it
aside, after having, with some Reluctance, hastily run over the first
and second Volumes. This is manifestly owing to their not being,
every Page, set agape at new Scenes, & surprizing Events. Hence
it is that they say it is too long, too tedious. Wou'd you have me
tell you how to shorten it for them? Keep every thing you have but

---

4   Here, 'To give a point or points; to work or fashion to a point or tapered end, to sharpen'
    (*OED*).

JAMES HARRIS TO RICHARDSON, TUESDAY 13 JUNE 1749

the Fire-Scene;[5] and add half the size of a Volume to the two first, consisting of Grotesque Characters, and Marvellous Adventures. This Addition (if it be large enough) will reduce your Work to half the Size it is at present, in the Eye of such a Reader, as wishes there were ten Folios, instead of one, in the Romance of Pharamond, or of Cassandra.[6] I am, dearest Sir, with inexpressible Tenderness, Yours

Phil. Skelton.[7]

My most Affectionate Respects to good Mrs. Richardson, my dear young Friends, particularly little Clarissa at N. End;[8] and to Mr. Millar, and the Ladies above Stairs.[9]

---

[5] At the time of this letter, SR defended the fire scene against the views of 'two particular divines' – one of whom may have been Skelton – in the short, privately circulated pamphlet, *An Answer to the Letter of a Very Reverend and Worthy Gentleman* (1749). Skelton may have voiced his objections to the fire scene in *Clarissa* at more length in another letter because Jane Collier refuted objections of 'your Friend in Ireland' at length in the following month; see Collier to SR, 9 July 1749.

[6] *Cassandre* (5 vols., 1642–50) and *Faramond, ou l'histoire de France* (12 vols., 1661–70) are both romances written by the French novelist and dramatist, Gauthier de Costes, seigneur de la Calprenède (1609/10–63).

[7] SR has crossed out and abbreviated the signature to read 'P. S.'

[8] SR's sickly third daughter, Anne (1737–1803), also called Nancy and, especially by Skelton, 'little Clarissa'; see Skelton to SR, 28 December 1752.

[9] The bookseller Andrew Millar and his wife and sister. This paragraph has been crossed through.

James Harris to Richardson

Tuesday 13 June 1749

Printed source: B: I, 161–2
First printing: Barbauld, *Correspondence* (1804).

Sarum,[1] *June* 13, 1749.

Dear Sir,

I am much obliged for your kind present;[2] yet, not so much for that, as for the very friendly and benevolent manner in which you make it. As to the work itself, I shall always value it, as having that stamp or character which alone can make any work valuable, to the

---

[1] 'Old Sarum': name of the ancient settlement of Salisbury. Continued to be used to refer to Salisbury.

[2] Probably *Clarissa*, possibly the second edition, which SR was publishing in June.

231

HENRIETTA ARABELLA CHURCHILL TO JANE COLLIER, JUNE 1749

liberal and disinterested; that is, I shall value it as the work not only of a sensible, but of an honest man.

My wife begs your acceptance of her compliments.[3] With her's I join my own to Mrs. Richardson, and your little family, for whose welfare you have our sincerest wishes. I am, Dear sir, Your most obedient servant,

James Harris.

[3] Elizabeth, *née* Clarke (1722–81).

<Henrietta Arabella Churchill[1] to Jane Collier?>[2]

Friday 30 June 1749

MS: FM XV, 2, ff. 22–3. Copy in Jane Collier's hand.
Endorsement: '<SC. on Cl.> [3] & T. Jones.' (in SR's hand, on the outside of the letter); 'L. 24.' (in Martha Richardson's hand, on the letter's first page).

Dalkeith[4] House June 30:th 1749

– I will now reply to your often repeated Request of my giving you my Sentiments on Clarissa Harlowe. I think take the Work

[1] Henrietta Arabella Churchill (1722?–56), daughter of Lieutenant-General George Churchill (*c.* 1690–1753), commander-in-chief of the land forces in Scotland. Henrietta Churchill was married to Captain James Stewart (d. 1762) of the 56th Regiment of Foot. Eaves and Kimpel attribute this letter to an otherwise unidentified 'Miss Churchill'.
[2] Eaves and Kimpel identify SR as the recipient, but internal evidence suggests that the letter was written *about* him rather than addressed *to* him. Instead, the letter was probably addressed to Jane Collier. Other possible addressees include Sarah Fielding or another of Collier and Fielding's friends in SR's circles. The letter was probably copied by Collier as of interest to the author of *Clarissa*. For a more extensive discussion of the letter's provenance and transmission, see 'Note on the Text' in this volume and Sören Hammerschmidt, 'Mysterious Miss Churchill: Jane Collier's Copy of a Letter in the Richardson Correspondence', *N&Q*, 67, no. 3 (September 2020), 415–21.
[3] The 'windowing in' method of mounting letters in the FM volumes has obliterated words in the endorsement. 'SC.' might refer to Susan Carr (d. 1808), friend of Jane and Margaret Collier and possible subscriber to Sarah Fielding's *Lives of Cleopatra and Octavia* (1757). An entry in SR's index for a volume of 'Letters, &c. Relating to Clarissa' reads 'Miss Carr to Miss Collier, on Clarissa' and might refer to this letter. If so, SR probably misremembered or guessed at the letter's sender when compiling his indexes: internal evidence shows that Carr cannot have been the letter's original sender (see Hammerschmidt, 'Mysterious Miss Churchill', 421).
[4] 'Dalkeith' has been crossed through and emended to 'D.—' in SR's late hand. Dalkeith House, near Edinburgh, was the primary residence of Francis Scott, second Duke of Buccleuch (1695–1751).

HENRIETTA ARABELLA CHURCHILL TO JANE COLLIER, JUNE 1749

altogether it is Contrary to most Books I ever read for it improves
in every Page. I admire the Author's being able to adapt his
language and keep up to the Spirit of each Character the whole
Way. Where there are many Actors even skillfull hands are
apt sometimes to let them run too much into their Neighbours
Provence: He really does not; and each thought word and Action
are natural Consequences of the Person whose Picture he has
at first presented you with. The fault I have heard most laid to
his Charge is the overstraining the Character of his principle
Heroine, for that it is impossible to meet with so much Self-Denyal
cloath'd in Mortality: I am afraid indeed there is no such perfect
Creature now existing, but I think it is no bad Compliment to Mr.
Richardson that He has given a Pattern which is censured for being
too good to imitate. I am not in the least <astonish'd> at your being
pleased with the Conversation of a Man who seems to understand
human Nature so well, which if not allow'd in Clarissa Harlowe
herself must be assented to in those other Characters He has drawn
so much to the Life, and which but too frequently occur every Day
we live. I am vastly diverted with a Book of Fieldings that is come
out lately, Tom Jones by Title. He has I believe a Fund of humour
which will never be exausted and I suppose his new proffession
of Justice of the Quorum[5] will furnish him with fresh Supplys of
Matter to set in an entertaining Light, if he has a mind to it. I like
nothing that has been wrote of late in the heroick Strain. I really
have been obliged to read Men more than Books for Sometime
past, and tho' not very old begin to grow heartily tired of the Study.
We live in a Constant Succession of Company and I could wish
Dalkeith[6] was a hundred Miles off Edinburgh if consistent with my
Fathers Business which the Week after next will call him more to
the North, having received Instructions to review some Dragoons
that are dispersed <u>p and down the Country[7] and I shall take
the Opportunity of accompanying Him, to see Perth Glasco<w>
Sterling Hamilton[8] &c: all which you shall have a<n> Account of at

---

5   Fielding had been commissioned as Justice of the Quorum, a select group of Justices of the
    Peace, on 25 October 1748. In this new role, and with the help of his half-brother, John
    (1721–80), he founded London's first professional police force, the Bow Street Runners.
6   'alkeith' has been crossed through, emended to 'D.'.
7   After the Jacobite Rising in 1745, garrisons had been established throughout Scotland; the
    dragoons, a 'species of cavalry soldier' (*OED*), would have been a part of the occupying
    British forces.
8   Perth, Glasgow, Stirling, and Hamilton, together with Edinburgh, were major urban and
    administrative centres of the Scottish Lowlands.

HENRY HOME TO RICHARDSON, FRIDAY 30 JUNE 1749

my Return in the mean Time let Me hear from you which will give
real Pleasure to you<r> most sincere and faithfull &c:

Henry Home[1] to Richardson

Friday 30 June 1749

**MS: Universiteitsbibliotheek, Universiteit van Amsterdam, No. 127Be.
Dictated letter in an undetermined hand, with autograph signature, sent
(evidence of folding and damage possibly from seal).**
Endorsement: On the outside of the letter: 'M\. Home from Edinburgh. June 30.
1749. Answ.\ July 11.' and 'Literary' (in SR's hand). On the letter's first page:
'*Subjects*', 'M\. Home on a Scheme of Education &c.' (in SR's hand; 'Subjects'
receives double underlining in SR's late hand); 'Letter 35' (in Martha Richardson's
hand).[2]

Edinburgh 30. June 1749

I write this according to promise that you may not entertain any
Suspicion of my cooling upon a favourite project; tho' I can do little
more than to recapitulate Shortly what we talk'd of at large.[3]

The education of Youth ought to be the principal object of
Government. This is a Sort of intuitive proposition, and yet how
shall we account for the Strange phænomenon that Education
is almost universally neglected in all Governments? Poison the
fountain, or let it but gather Mud, and the Stream can never be clear.

The Mind is compar'd to white Paper, equally Susceptible of any
Sort of writing. The Comparison is not accurate, because Youth is
more dispos'd to virtue than to vice. But it may well be admitted in
a looser Sense; because in a Course of perverse Education, a Saint
by nature may in practice be moulded into a Devil.

Education is abandon'd to Parents and Schoolmasters. It is hard
to Say whether the ignorance or partiality of the former has the
worst effect; and what can be expected of the latter who take to this
profession not by choice but for Bread?

---

[1] Henry Home (1696–1782), Lord Kames after 1752, judge and writer (*ODNB*).
[2] The letter's second and third page have been numbered '2.' and '3.' in the same hand as most
of the letter.
[3] No record remains of this earlier conversation.

HENRY HOME TO RICHARDSON, FRIDAY 30 JUNE 1749

In this Country, education is confined to the head to furnish out a Stock of knowlege; or rather confined to the means which lead to that end; that is to the acquiring of Languages. The Heart is totally neglected in every branch of Education. This is Strange. For if Action be of more importance than Speculation in the Commerce of Life, it must be of more importance to cultivate the Heart than the Head, and to make right impressions rather than accumulate knowlege.

Young Minds are fond of Life & action and of every representation of it. For this reason they are delighted with narration in all it's varieties. We may guess, but no man can certainly Say, who has not made an accurate experiment, what Strong impressions may be made upon the mind by artfully contrived Stories diversified and renewed at proper intervals. One experiment has been but too often made. To what do we owe, but to the tales of the Nursery the fantoms & Hobgoblins which many are pester'd with for life? If mere fancies can be thus in a great measure realis'd, one should imagine it not a more difficult task to confirm and Strengthen us in virtue, which is not a fancy or chimera, but a reality.

Therfor as a capital implement of education I desiderate a Collection of Stories of which I believe there is not one extant that is not greatly exceptionable. In making Such a Collection there are three aims. The first and principal is to discriminate the actions of Mankind, to put every action in it's true light, and to give to every action it's true weight. The second is to understand men as well as their actions. Such knowledge must be the result of Experience; but experience may be got by reading as well as by Conversing. A third aim is to form a correct taste in writing which Children gradually acquire by dealing in good Compositions.

Instruction by fable may be Successfully applied through every Stage of Life; therfor I would not have this undertaking confined to a narrow period. Education of one Sort or other commences more early than is generally thought. Nurses are our first Instructors and seldom fail of giving bad impressions. To preoccupy the tender Mind, and to prevent the poisonous effects of the common Nursery-Fables, I wou'd have a number of Stories compos'd of the greatest Simplicity both as to dress and composition yet so lively as to take the fancies of Nurses & Children. Nothing to distract or disturb the tender Mind ought to

HENRY HOME TO RICHARDSON, FRIDAY 30 JUNE 1749

get admittance. The Composition to be confined to human actions and so contrived as to convey nothing but just notions of things & right Sentiments. The language of the utmost Simplicity So as to bring the work down to the lowest Capacity.

When this, which I take to be the most difficult, tho' not the most shining part of the Undertaking, is over, the field opens and the road turns more pav'd. The second Book or Class may consist of Stories somewhat more varied & enlarged, told in the Simplicity of the antient Stile Such as is remarkable in the narrations of the Old Testament & in Xenophon.[4] We are too artificial in our manners to think of adopting Such a Stile in common practice. But we must admire it, and we ought to form our taste upon it. This second Class is calculated for giving true pictures of virtue and vice each painted in their proper colours to confirm the Mind in it's attachment to the one and aversion to the other; without necessity of much more Action than what may be indulg'd in Portrait painting.

In the 3rd Class may be put Stories from whence moral instruction may be drawn, that virtue tends to our happines and vice to our misery; that the best way to be Successful in life is to be honest and a thousand Such, which may be drawn from a well contriv'd fable as well as from true history. But these Stories in the 3rd Class ought to be Simple in their Composition and the moral instruction perspicuous, that it may not be lost to the Young Reader.

In the 4th & after Classes the Stories may be more complex and more diversified in the manner & composition, in the Stile & in the Moral to be drawn. And this according to the fancy or taste of the Compiler.

The last Class may be made up of Stories depending upon the nicer Springs of the heart in order to introduce young People into the knowlege of the more intricate parts of the human composition. And these Stories may be attended with proper illustrations and reflections, to make this work the more easy to the Reader. But we must not go too deep or too far in this attempt which is intended only as a Slight introduction to philosophy.

I would have the Work all along carried on with the utmost attention to correctness in the language. And particular care taken

---

4 Xenophon of Athens (*c.* 430–354 BCE), ancient Greek philosopher, historian, and soldier; student of Socrates.

HENRY HOME TO RICHARDSON, FRIDAY 30 JUNE 1749

not to load the narration with useless words. Exuberance of Stile is one of the great faults in our later Compositions. But I should esteem it a great beauty to have the Stile diversified according to the different natures of the Stories which are told.

Let not the Work be crowded with Love Stories; and let it be a law never to introduce one of them but what carries a useful moral instruction.

I by no means intend that you shou'd give yourself the trouble of the whole Composition. No Single man of however fertile a Genius would be equal to that task. I'm afraid you can have no help in the first Class, and perhaps not much in the 2nd. But as my notion is a Collection, I am for refusing no Story however common provided it be a good one. I propose to furnish you some few Specimens of the Stories I propose to enter into the last Class join'd with reflections explaining the intricacies of the Story and developing the human heart. And when you are ready for these, you have but to make a demand.[5] Wishing you all Success in a work which you undertake for the Good of your fellow Creatures, I am Dear Sir Your obedient humble Servant

Henry Home

I know you will pardon undigested hints thrown ou<t> in a hurry; for really I have extreme little time to Spare at this Season. My Complements to Mr. Millar and his Family: I reckon myself much obliged to him in particular for introducing me to Mr. Cay, who I esteem greatly.[6]

---

[5] This project finally came to fruition in *Home's Loose Hints on Education, Chiefly Concerning the Culture of Children* (1781).

[6] This may have been John Cay (1700–57), legal writer and classical antiquary, or his son, Henry Boult Cay (d. 1795), barrister (*ODNB*). The elder Cay had published an *Abridgment of the Publick Statutes, in Force and Use, from Magna Charta to the 11th Geo. II* (2 vols., 1739), which was continued in supplemental volumes by his son; and prepared the highly praised, posthumous *Statutes at Large, from Magna Charta to the 30th Geo. II* (6 vols., 1758), which received a 2nd edition in 1762, a supplemental volume in 1766, and was continued to 13 Geo. III in three more volumes (1769–73) by Owen Ruffhead (*c.* 1723–69), legal writer and author, at William Warburton's request and with his assistance, of the *Life of Alexander Pope, Esq. Compiled from Original Manuscripts* (1769).

Jane Collier to Richardson

Sunday 9 July 1749

MS: FM XV, 2, ff. 8–9. Autograph letter sent (evidence of folding).
Endorsement: 'Miss Collier.' July 9. Fire Scene, without P. S.'[2] (in SR's hand, on the outside of the letter); '<Axxxxx *1 word*>'[3] (in SR's hand, on the outside of the letter); 'xcvii.xc' (in SR's hand, on the letter's first page); 'L. 25' (in Martha Richardson's hand, on the letter's first page).

July 9:th 1749

Dear Sir,

I am not afraid to declare, that I have given your fire-Scene another Reading;[4] tho' I might be censured for it perhaps by Some who are (or fancy they are) extremely delicate: but give Me leave to say, and without Flattery, that whatsoever *you* publish, I'll read; and should any *I*mproper Ideas arise in my Mind, I shall always condemn myself, and know that it can proceed from no Reason but not keeping within the Bounds you intended to prescribe: but this is only judging for myself; and I pretend not to affirm what Deference Other People ought to pay to a Person who has shewn such an unbounded *k*nowlege of human Nature!

I believe it will be impossible for Me to say any thing that you have not said in the Letter I read at your House last Wednesday;[5] but the more I think of it, the more I admire that very Scene; nor can I conceive how it can raise in any Woman any Sensation but that of Pity for your divine Girl, and Indignation at the Insolent Villain; and if any Man can read it without having his Compassion greatly moved, He must be worse than even his Friend Lovelace.

---

[1] 'ollier' has been crossed through.

[2] Collier had probably included a more personal note on a separate sheet, which SR excluded. This note now appears lost.

[3] Possibly an abbreviation or signature.

[4] Several of SR's friends and readers, including Philip Skelton, had objected to this scene on grounds that readers might find it arousing and advised SR to excise it in future editions; see, e.g., Skelton to SR, 10 June 1749. Collier's letter sets out to refute these criticisms. For more, see Thomas Keymer, 'Jane Collier, Reader of Richardson, and the Fire Scene in *Clarissa*', in *New Essays on Samuel Richardson*, ed. Albert J. Rivero (New York: St Martin's Press, 1996), pp. 141–61.

[5] Probably SR's response to a critic like Skelton, either in a personal letter or in his privately circulated epistolary pamphlet, *An Answer to the Letter of a Very Reverend and Worthy Gentleman* (1749).

JANE COLLIER TO RICHARDSON, SUNDAY 9 JULY 1749

As you have, I think, fully proved that such a Scene was absolutely necessary, not only to exalt your Heroine, but as the Sole means He could think of to put Her to any sort of Trial (for She was too discreetly watchful to be liable to any Liberties but by some such Surprize) there could be no proper way of making it known, but by Lovelace's Account of it; for had Clarissa told it to Miss Howe, She must have express'd herself with such Resentment and Indignation, that I doubt, were the Generality of Women to judge of the Treatment She had met with by the Cause which They would have[6] sufficient to have incurr'd such Indignat<ion>[7] and Resentment, their own painting of this Scene would have be<en> much stronger than yours. I know you will be angry with Me for this general Reflection upon Women; but consider, Dear Sir, to whom I am speaking; and remember that I am not what you call publickly giving up the Cause in a place where I ought to defend it: nor can you justly blame Me for thinking as you yourself think; for what your Sentiments of Women (in some Cases) really are, appears pretty plain, tho', to puzzle the Case, you have put them into the mouth of a Lovelace. But to return to your Fire-Scene.[8] I most sincerely think it is so little exceptionable in the Light your too ingenius Friends seem to condemn it, that it is rather calculated (as Lovelace Himself says) to set bounds to the roving Imagination; and is so strong an Instance of the *power* of real and unfeign'd Purity of *h*eart over even a proffess'd Libertine, that it carries with it the most noble Instruction that can be taught; and I hope it is as natural as *I*nstructing. This Scene, I own, warms Me indeed; but 'tis in the Cause of injured Innocence; for I never could read her pathetic solemn Appeal to Him without Tears; and her Situation at that Time gave Me more shuddering Apprehensions for Her, than if you had placed her at the Entrance of <a> Lions Den in the most savage Desart of Africa: nor can I omit mentioning the Joy I felt when I heard her draw the other Bolt upon the Inhuman Return of the momentary generous Wretch (*generous* is too good a Word; but I cannot think of another): And, in short, what is this Scene, but the Same with many others? Namely, an Instance of your Power to alarm, to depress, to raise, and to carry where-ever you please,

[6] 'thought' has been inserted in SR's hand.
[7] Damage to one of the edges of the letter's first sheet occasionally obscures some of the text.
[8] This sentence appears to have been inserted over an erasure.

SOLOMON LOWE TO RICHARDSON, MONDAY 10 JULY 1749

the Heart of every Reader, that reads with the Heart, and not as a distant cool Spectator of Actions which are no ways Interesting.

You know that I have so good an Opinion of your Friend in Ireland,[9] that Any Objection of his (to any Work but a Clarissa &c:) would very much incline Me to acquiesce without even proper Examination (for I own myself a little too much inclined to Partiality, tho' not to Prejudice, I hope, against any One): But here in this Case, if He will consider with the Candour which generally attends such honest Hearts, as his, by his Writings, seems to be, I believe He will find, that the intended Censure He passes upon *Women* by supposing that they will be less likely to find *fault* with this Scene than the Men, is rather a Compliment to *Them*; and the Satyre lies against the *Men*: For to a female Reader there cannot possibly be any thing inviting or inflaming in the Idea of such a Scene, unless She should shamefully avow, that She condemn'd the Behaviour of Clarissa; and then indeed might She condemn the Scene: but the Reason of a Man's blaming it as being too highly painted must be from his dwelling more strongly on the Person of the lovely Sufferer, than on her Innocence and Distress. I seem as if I had not very clearly made out what I intended to say; but I know you'll excuse Me, and likewise this long Letter; and believe Me, Dear Sir, your very sincere and faithfull Friend,

J.C.[10]

[9] Probably Skelton.
[10] The signature has been crossed through.

Solomon Lowe to Richardson

Monday 10 July 1749

MS: FM XV, 2, f. 120. Autograph letter sent (evidence of folding).
Endorsement: '10 July 1749',[1] 'Cracker, T. Jones', and 'Clarissa' (in SR's hand).

July 10. 1749[2]

Sir

When I receivd your kind message last night, I had four gentlemen with me, nor was I at liberty till the dusk of the evening. –

[1] Date overlapped by album frame on which it is pasted as well as by paper used for damage repair.
[2] In SR's hand.

RICHARDSON TO HENRY HOME, TUESDAY II JULY 1749

Did you know how much I & my Daughters longd to be with you; you would pity us that were under a necessity of being very uneasy, out of pure regard to common decency – To make up this loss, I earnestly beg of you to favor us with your Company the first vacant hour you have; or to let us know, when it will be least inconvenient to you for us to wait on you at North-end.

Your answer to the Clergyman[3] shows that the more critically your performance is considerd, the more unexceptionable it appears, nay the brighter it shines – The fame of it (I find by Cave's magazine) is got into Holland;[4] & I do not doubt but all Europe will ring of it: when a Cracker, that was some thousand hours a-composing,[5] will no longer be heard, or talkt-of. Dear Sir, Adieu.

Sol Lowe

10 jul. 1749.

---

[3] Probably a reference to the Reverend Philip Skelton's suggestion that the fire scene in *Clarissa* be omitted in the second edition; see Skelton to SR, 10 June 1749, as well as Collier to SR, 9 July 1749. SR had rejected Skelton's suggestion but must have shared at least some of the exchange with Lowe; he also printed the pamphlet, *Answer to the Letter of a Very Reverend and Worthy Gentleman* (1749).

[4] Edward Cave (1691–1754) was editor of the *Gentleman's Magazine*, which had printed the first part of a translation of Albrecht von Haller's review of *Clarissa* in June 1749 (see *Gentleman's Magazine*, XIX, 245–6). Haller (1708–77), a Swiss physician and writer, had originally published his review in the Amsterdam-based French-language periodical, *Bibliothèque raisonnée des ouvrages des savans de l'Europe*. A modern edition of the full review appears in *Samuel Richardson's Published Commentary on 'Clarissa', 1747–65*, ed. Thomas Keymer (London: Pickering & Chatto, 1998), I, pp. 121–39.

[5] Henry Fielding's *History of Tom Jones: A Foundling* (1749), which the narrator claims 'hath employed some Thousands of Hours in the composing' (Book XI, ch. 1). A 'cracker', in the sense of a firework, is here used metaphorically to indicate Lowe's sense that *Tom Jones*, which had been published to much acclaim in February, would fizzle out soon.

Richardson to Henry Home

Tuesday 11 July 1749

MS: Universiteitsbibliotheek, Universiteit van Amsterdam, No. 128Dl. Autograph draft or copy not sent (evidence of space left in address for Home's first name, folding not consistent with patterns used for sent letters).
Endorsement: On the outside: 'of Edinburgh, In Answer to his of July 11. 1749' (in SR's hand), and 'Literary' (in SR's late hand, heavily smudged); on the letter's first page: 'Letter 36' and 'July 11_1749' (in Martha Richardson's hand).

RICHARDSON TO HENRY HOME, TUESDAY 11 JULY 1749

To   Home, Esqr
I received Yours, good Sir, and perused it with a great deal of Pleasure.

May I presume to request, that you will, at your Leisure, oblige me with slight Heads in each of the Classes you recommend? And particularly with Copies of what you have by you? – This last Favour under what Restrictions you please.

You are so much Master of the Subject, and I am so diffident of my Abilities, that such a Direction and Communication, will be a great Ease to my Mind; and enable me, if I shall think my self likely to answer, in any tolerable Manner, your Expectations, to enter into the Plan with that Warmth which is necessary to a successful Execution.[1]

Excuse, Sir, the Freedom of this Request, and believe me to be, as I am, with great Respect, Your faithful and obedient Servant

S.R.

Mr. Millar, and his Spouse and Sister, desire their Compliments to you. He will make yours to Mr. Kay; and is very glad he was the Means of bringing together Two Gentlemen, whose Esteem of each other he now knows to be mutual.[2]

---

[1] Only a few months later, SR had abandoned Home's project to begin work on *Grandison*; see SR to Lady Bradshaigh, <late November> 1749.
[2] For the relationships among Millar, Home, and Cay, see Home to SR, 30 June 1749.

WILLIAM STRAHAN TO RICHARDSON, THURSDAY 17 AUGUST 1749

Richardson to the Countess Dowager of Pembroke[1]

Friday 11 August 1749

MS: FM XV, 2, f. 37. Copy in Gilbert Hill's hand.
Endorsement: 'Letter 38' (in Martha Richardson's hand); 'Clarissa' (in SR's hand).[2]

> Salisbury Court, Fleet Street, Aug. 11.
> 1749

Should your Ladiship refuse to the Author of the History of Clarissa, the Honour of your Acceptance of it[3] from his Hands, it wou'd be a great Mortification to Your Ladiships Most obliged and faithful humble Servant

> S. Richardson.

To the Right Honorable The Countess Dowager of Pembroke These.[4]

---

[1] Mary Howe (d. 1749), Countess Dowager of Pembroke, daughter of Scrope Howe (first Viscount Howe (1648–1713), Whig politician (*ODNB*)) and widow of Thomas Herbert (eighth Earl of Pembroke and fifth Earl of Montgomery (1656/7–1733), politician and government official (*ODNB*)). In her youth, the Countess Dowager had been a maid of honour to Caroline as princess of Wales and a lady of the bedchamber to her as queen. After marrying the Honourable John Mordaunt (1709?–67), army officer and politician, the Countess Dowager lobbied and engaged her family connections in Nottinghamshire on behalf of her husband's political ambitions. She resided at Peterborough House at Parson's Green in Fulham, near the Richardsons' suburban house, from 1735 until her death on 12 September 1749, a month after this letter. It is unclear exactly how SR came to know the countess.
[2] The entire letter has been crossed through.
[3] I.e. a copy of *Clarissa*, probably the second edition, which had been published on 15 June.
[4] Written in the same hand as the rest of the letter, erased.

William Strahan to Richardson

Thursday 17 August 1749

Printed source: B: I, 136–9.
First printing: Barbauld, *Correspondence* (1804).

> Edinburgh, Aug. 17, 1749.

Dear Sir,

After an agreeable, though somewhat fatiguing, journey of five days, we arrived safely at this place, where we found all friends as well as we expected. The alterations in persons, places, and

243

WILLIAM STRAHAN TO RICHARDSON, THURSDAY 17 AUGUST 1749

things, since I was here last, struck me exceedingly, and afforded me the most convincing proof imaginable of the mutability of human affairs. Many people are strangely altered, many have disappeared, and many are now no more, which it is impossible to think of without concern, and a degree of seriousness not to be suddenly checked. Nay, so natural is it to be prejudiced in favour of the appearances things had when we were young, that even the alterations for the better please me not; at least, not till I have reasoned myself into the utility and propriety of the change.

I am like to be very well entertained while I stay here. There are sensible men in plenty; though such as Mr. R. are rarely found any where. I assure you the most valuable folks here like your writings best. You may, with great propriety, say, *exegi monumentum*.[1]

There is nothing in this place worth writing you, only that there seems to be a great spirit of industry gone forth, which I am sure will turn to the advantage of both parts of the united kingdom.[2]

I hope this will find you in perfect health, and happy in every sense. None merits every good thing better than you do; nor is there any person better qualified for the enjoyment of every rational pleasure. I hope your little girl is somewhat better,[3] and that the rest continue perfect models of what young ladies should be. You will be so good to give my best respects to the valuable Mrs. Richardson; and to Mrs. Poole and Miss Dutton,[4] whom, you know, you and I both love.

I remember your long-continued friendship for me with pleasure and gratitude. I admire your generosity, your benevolence, your sagacity, your penetration, your knowledge of human nature, and your good heart; I esteem you as my friend, my adviser, my pattern, and my benefactor; I love you as my father; and let me, even me also, call you my Nestor.[5]

---

[1] Horace, 'The Poet's Monument' (*Odes*, Book 3, 30, line 1): 'I have finished a monument', a statement on the immortality of poetry and of the poet (Loeb 33, pp. 216–17).

[2] The United Kingdom was created when England and Scotland signed the Act of Union in 1707. Scotland and England retained separate legal systems, educational systems, and state religions, and were seen as distinct in culture and economic development.

[3] SR's third daughter, Anne (1737–1803), was suffering through one of her sickly spells; see also Skelton to SR, 10 June 1749.

[4] Mary (bap. 1716) and Margaret (*c.* 1718–56), the orphaned daughters of SR's neighbour, Thomas Dutton (d. 1741); Mary married John Poole in 1742.

[5] In the *Iliad*, the elderly Nestor, King of Pylos, dispenses advice to the younger warriors, though he also tends to boast about his past achievements before giving such advice.

244

WILLIAM STRAHAN TO RICHARDSON, THURSDAY 24 AUGUST 1749

My wife and her mother[6] bid me say every thing that is kind and respectful to you and Mrs. Richardson: shall we have the pleasure of hearing from you? – Mr. Hamilton will, no doubt, have occasion to trouble you now and then.[7] I know you will not grudge giving him your best advice; whose every long day is filled with acts of benevolence to every body you know. I am, dear Sir, Your most obliged humble servant.

W. Strahan.

[6] Strahan married Margaret Penelope Elphinston (1719–85) on 20 July 1738; her mother was Rachel Honeyman (d. 1750), niece of the bishop of Orkney (*ODNB*).

[7] Probably Archibald Hamilton (1719–93), printer and publisher (*ODNB*), who moved from Edinburgh to London in 1736 to serve out his apprenticeship there and was made free of the Stationers' Company on 6 June 1749. *ODNB* records Hamilton as working as Strahan's principal manager by 1752, but this letter indicates that Strahan was mentoring, if not already employing, Hamilton immediately after the latter had completed his apprenticeship. Hamilton certainly was in charge of Strahan's business by 27 July 1751, when Strahan was travelling in Scotland again; see *William Strahan to David Hall*, 27 July 1751, in J. E. Pomfret, 'Notes and Documents: Some Further Letters of William Strahan, Printer', *The Pennsylvania Magazine of History and Biography*, 60, no. 4 (Oct. 1936), 460–1.

William Strahan to Richardson

Thursday 24 August 1749

Printed source: B: I, 136–9.
First printing: Barbauld, *Correspondence* (1804).

Edinburgh, Aug. 24, 1749.

Dear Sir,
  If I were to be long at a distance from you, I fancy I should become as troublesome in writing, as you have experienced, to your cost, I have often been in talking to you, as every thing I see puts me in mind of you. – What would Mr. Richardson think of this? – Here is room for his praise; – and here for his censure: – this would raise his compassion; this his indignation; this would touch his benevolent heart with joy; and here he would exercise his charity; this man's solid sense would delight him; the ladies would, in general, charm him; and the honest prejudices of many, in favour of their native country,[1] would make him smile. These,

[1] In Strahan's case, Scotland.

and many other such-like thoughts often occur to me, so that I am oftener in your company than you imagine. The civilities I daily meet with, and the hospitality with which I am entertained, are not to be expressed. I have nothing to do but go from feast to feast, the manners of the better part of this country bearing a very near resemblance to those of North End. I am overwhelmed with their kindness, so that I must really make my stay here as short as possible, lest living thus riotously should prejudice my health. But no more of this till I see you – a pleasure I truly long for.

At intervals, as I am now almost become a stranger to this country, and am possibly now taking my leave of it, I visit what is ancient or curious. Yesterday I paid my compliments to the remains of King James the Fifth,[2] and shook Lord Darnley by the hand; he was Queen Mary's husband, you well know, and was seven foot eight inches in stature: a portly personage once, and now – what we all must be.[3] O what a pleasing melancholy filled me on beholding their venerable remains. To see the very bodies of two such great men, who existed two centuries ago, is a curiosity indeed. They are in the chapel of Holyrood House, a very noble structure, but almost entirely demolished at the revolution, and since utterly neglected.[4] Here monuments of men, like men, decay! But, however, the outside is firm, so that it may easily be repaired, when the government thinks proper.

What else I have seen, with my observations on every thing that occurs, will afford me matter of conversation with you, when my tongue, perhaps, would be more impertinently employed. I shall therefore say no more now. Suffer me only to take every occasion of making my sincere acknowledgments for your continued and uninterrupted kindness and friendship to me. When I think of

[2] James V (1512–42), of Scotland (*ODNB*). Buried in the royal vault of Holyrood Abbey in Edinburgh, his body and the bodies of others buried there were a tourist attraction for eighteenth-century travellers.

[3] Henry Stewart, Duke of Albany (1545/6–67), known as Lord Darnley, his father's subsidiary title, second consort of Mary, Queen of Scots (1542–87) (*ODNB*). Darnley seems to have been over six feet tall, which was remarkable for the period and close to Mary's own six feet. He was buried in the royal vault.

[4] The Palace of Holyroodhouse, a blend of sixteenth- and seventeenth-century architecture, has served as the principal residence of the kings and queens of Scotland since James IV ordered it built in 1501–5. The adjacent Holyrood Abbey, founded in 1128 and site of the royal burial vault since 1370, was first looted and burned by an English invasion force in 1544, further damaged in 1559 during the Scottish Reformation, and largely demolished in 1570.

WILLIAM STRAHAN TO RICHARDSON, SATURDAY 2 SEPTEMBER 1749

particular instances of your goodness to me, all I can say to you upon that subject comes so very short of what I feel, that I do myself great injustice in endeavouring to say any thing at all. I am, Dear Sir, Your most obliged servant,

W. Strahan.

William Strahan to Richardson

Saturday 2 September 1749

Printed source: B: I, 143–6.
First printing: Barbauld, *Correspondence* (1804).

Sept. 2, 1749.

Dear Sir,

Could you communicate to me a very small portion of your lively and creating fancy, my letters would be much more worthy of your perusal. The Israelites, who were obliged to make bricks without straw,[1] were, in my opinion, in a much more tolerable situation than the man who is obliged to write without genius, because, though they had, indeed, no allowance of straw delivered out to them, they had the whole land of Egypt to glean it in; and as that, like Clarissa, was notoriously a most fruitful country, in which there were doubtless many delicious spots, they unquestionably found very pretty pickings in it.

Since my last, I have been at Glasgow, a town greatly altered for the better, in point of trade, since I was there last.[2] Several large manufactories are set on foot, in which the poor of all ages, and both sexes, are usefully employed. From thence I went to Paisley, where Mr. Millar's father is minister,[3] a venerable old man, who,

---

[1] In Exodus 5.1–9, after Moses and Aaron have requested three days' relief from labour so the Israelites can celebrate and sacrifice to their god, Pharaoh orders that delivery of straw to them be halted while requiring the same quota of bricks as before. Straw was necessary as binding material in the production of mudbricks.

[2] At mid-century, Glasgow's growth was accelerating as the city was beginning to benefit from access after the Union (1707) to English colonial territories and markets as well as to the slave and tobacco trade. In 1747, this position was further enhanced by the French monarchy granting the city a monopoly on the importation of tobacco into French territories. The fourth edition of Defoe's *Tour* (1748), printed by SR, states: '*Glasgow* is a City of Business, and has the Face of Foreign and well as Domestic Trade; ... 'tis the only City in *Scotland*, at this Time, that apparently increases in both' (4.124).

[3] The Reverend Robert Millar (1672–1752) of Port Glasgow and, after 1709, of Paisley (*ODNB*).

247

like the church he preaches in, is nodding to his dissolution, but beautiful even in ruins. The town is almost entirely composed of manufacturers, and is in so exceeding thriving a way, that it is, they tell me, considerably increased even since last year when Mr. Millar was there. I returned thence to Stirling, and visited the castle, and went over the noble monuments of the amazing grandeur of our kings before the union of the crowns that are crumbling into dust.[4] Here is a fine palace built by King James the Fifth,[5] and a parliament-house, infinitely superior to that of Westminster. Here is a chapel also, purposely erected for the christening of Prince Henry, King Charles the First's eldest brother.[6] Had he been preserved, who knows how things might now have been altered from what they are. – All these are hastening to decay, as no care is taken of any thing here except the fortifications. I had forgot to tell you, that the great church at Glasgow, and that noble structure at Paisley,[7] are about 600 years old, and are most authentic proofs of the power of the church, or rather churchmen, in those days, who were able, in times of poverty and rudeness,[8] to erect a variety of piles,[9] any one of which would sensibly distress the whole kingdom, now, in its improved and flourishing state, to finish. On my return to Edinburgh, I passed by the ruins of the abbacy of Culross, part of which is now turned into a stable.[10] The remains of gentlemen's houses, of long standing, occur every where; in which the builders have visibly studied strength and security, preferably to pleasure and conveniency. During this excursion, I was continually comparing past times with the present; the ancient glory of a prince, and a few noble families, supported at the expence of the lives of some, and the liberties of all the rest of the people, (who,

---

[4] A centre of royal administration by 1110, the castle that Strahan would have seen and that survives today was built in the fourteenth through sixteenth centuries. The union of the Scottish and English crowns occurred on 24 March 1603, when James VI of Scotland (1566–1625) succeeded Elizabeth I to also become James I of England (*ODNB*).

[5] James V (1512–42), of Scotland (*ODNB*); he grew up at Stirling Castle and added the central Royal Palace.

[6] James VI had the Chapel Royal constructed for the baptism of his firstborn son, Henry Frederick, prince of Wales (1594–1612), in 1594; when the prince died of typhoid fever, his younger brother Charles (1600–49) became crown prince (*ODNB*).

[7] Glasgow Cathedral and Paisley Abbey were both founded in the twelfth century.

[8] 'Lack of knowledge or education; want of learning; ignorance' as well as 'Lack of culture or refinement; roughness of life or habits; uncouthness' (*OED*).

[9] 'A large building or edifice' (*OED*).

[10] Culross Abbey, founded in 1217, had largely been abandoned and fallen into decay by 1500 and was not restored until 1823.

the clergy excepted, laboured under the last degree[11] of poverty, slavery, and ignorance) with the present economy of things, when our merchants are princes, and tradesmen enjoy the good things of the earth; when property may be acquired and safely enjoyed by the meanest labourer; and when superstition and ignorance can hardly find shelter in our meanest cottages. And yet, comfortable as this comparison is, the ruin of these ancient badges of our slavery, by reason of their splendour and magnificence, impresses me with a very deep concern.

I have insensibly spun out a long letter, without saying hardly any thing; and, least I tire you too much at once, I shall only add, at present, the assurances of my most perfect gratitude and esteem, being always, Dear Sir, Your's, &c.

W. Strahan.

[11] 'the utmost measure' (*OED*).

Richardson to John Conybeare[1]

Tuesday 12 September 1749

MS: FM XV, 2, f. 38. Copy in Gilbert Hill's hand.
Endorsement: 'Letter 37' (in Martha Richardson's hand); 'Clarissa' and 'To Dr. Conybeare' (in SR's late hand).[2]

12, Sept. 1749

Reverend Sir,

In revising the History of Clarissa, while the Subject is warm in my Mind, in order to lay it by, as a Copy ready for the Press, if the Public Favour shou'd bring it to a 3rd Edition; I consider'd your Advice, and what you thought defective in the Piece, as to the Knowlege you wou'd have the Harlowe-Family be known to have of the Excellencies of their Daughter, in order to give a sharper Point to an Anguish they deserved to feel.[3]

You will permit me, Sir, to lay before you for your Correction, what I have done. A Letter written on Purpose I thought wou'd be too great an Alteration from the former Edition, and possibly

[1] For Conybeare's early admiration for SR, see Swinton to SR, 19 January 1742.
[2] The entire letter has been crossed through.
[3] Conybeare's letter is now lost.

249

JANE COLLIER TO RICHARDSON, <TUESDAY 19 SEPTEMBER 1749>

alter the Thread of the Story. I therefore propose, according to
the Places in which it might be proper to insert it,[4] to put it in the
Conclusion, which is supposed to be written by Mr. Belford, p 416.
Vol. VII. immediately after this Paragraph,

'*Temporary Alleviation*, we, repeat – for they were far from being
happy or easy in their Reflections upon their own Conduct
– And still the less –'

As you have given this Piece the Honour of repeated Perusals I
shou'd think myself greatly obliged to you, Sir, for the Correction
of the above;[5] and for any other Corrections that may occur to your
Thoughts. For I know not the Gentleman to whose Judgment I
wou'd so readily submit in every Point that tends to the Cultivation
of the Principles designed to be inculcated in this Story.

Be pleased, Reverend, and good Sir, to forgive the Freedom of
the Address from, Your most obliged and faithful humble Servant

S. R.

[4] 'alter the Thread ... therefore propose' has been crossed through, and 'interrupt the Thread
of the Story. I therefore propose' has been inserted at this point, in SR's hand.

[5] I.e. the suggestions SR makes here. A passage beginning 'And still the less' was indeed
added, as proposed, to Belford's conclusion in the third edition (1750).

Jane Collier to Richardson

<Tuesday 19 September 1749>[1]

MS: FM XV, 2, f. 49. Autograph letter sent (evidence of folding).
Endorsement: On fragment of outside of letter: 'Miss Collier <Clarissa>'[2] (in SR's
hand); on first page of letter: 'L. 28' (in Martha Richardson's hand); 'xcv' and
'June 1749' (in SR's late hand).

Dear Sir,
I had wrote the Inclosed Letter to send to Mr. Cave[3] for I
was quite vex'd to see a Man who seem'd so capable of entering
into your designs in some places and so sensible of many of the

[1] Though dated 'June 1749' in another hand, Collier is referring to both parts of Haller's
review of *Clarissa* as published in the *Gentleman's Magazine*, the second of which appeared
in August (see below). Eaves and Kimpel surmise that the enclosure Collier mentions in
this letter is the one included here, dated 19 September.

[2] The part of the sheet that would have formed the outside of the letter has been torn away
almost entirely.

[3] Edward Cave (1691–1754), printer and proprietor of the *Gentleman's Magazine* (*ODNB*).

250

JANE COLLIER TO EDWARD CAVE, TUESDAY 19 SEPTEMBER 1749

Excellencys of Clarissa in others make such foolish Objections.⁴ He has pleased Me so much in some things that He says that I will not take Notice of some Passages even in the first Part of his Criticism where I think him a little wrong. I love Pamela extremely, nay I admire her, and will not suffer any Body to say they love her better than I do, and yet will you forgive Me that I cannot love to hear Clarissa call'd her *younger* Sister. This Appellation in real Life may be deem'd a Compliment, but in this Case it seems a Sort of a Lessening, and I cannot admit that Clarissa should stand as Inferior or give Place to Pamela; and if not to Her not to any one upon Earth. But I began this with an Intention to tell you that as soon as I had wrote the Inclosed I grew dissatisfied with it, and could not send it to Mr. Cave so do as you please and you will please your sincere Friend and Humble Servant

J: C:

⁴ Collier responds to the two-part translation of a review of *Clarissa* by the Swiss physician and writer Albrecht von Haller (1708–77) – originally published in French in the Amsterdam-based *Bibliothèque raisonnée* – that had appeared in the *Gentleman's Magazine* in June (XIX, 245–6) and August 1749 (XIX, 345–9); see also Lowe to SR, 10 July 1749. The second instalment included a response to the critic, possibly by SR himself. A modern edition appears in *'Clarissa': The Eighteenth-Century Response*, ed. Lois E. Bueler (New York: AMS Press, 2010), I, pp. 18-27.

Jane Collier to Edward Cave

Tuesday 19 September 1749

MS: FM XV, 2, f. 33. Copy in Gilbert Hill's hand (originally sent to SR as enclosure with preceding letter).
Endorsement: 'Miss C. Design'd for Gentlemans Magazine' (in SR's hand); 'xcvi' (in SR's late hand); 'L. 27' (in Martha Richardson's hand).

Sept. 19.th 1749

Sir,

On seeing some Remarks on Clarissa by a French Author in your Magazine of June,¹ I was quite impatient to see the Conclusion; as the Remarker shew'd a Candour very uncommonly shewn to Works of a different Nation, and to a Contemporary Writer. But on reading the End of the French Critic's Remarks in

¹ Collier mistakes Haller's nationality.

251

your Month of August, I was surprized to find that a Man who in some Parts seems to enter so much into the Design of the Author of Clarissa, cou'd make such strange & trifling Objections; most of which I think perfectly well answer'd. But if what occurr'd to me upon reading the Objections and Answers, shou'd appear worth publishing, you may, if you please, give it a Place in your next Magazine. I am, Sir, Your very humble Servant.

Objection V.[2] The Answer to this very proper. And if the Letters from Lovelace to Belford were attended to, tis impossible any such Objection cou'd be made. But even the candid Remarker, who cou'd in one Place say that Clarissa was by Artifice compell'd to go away with Lovelace almost in spite of herself, can here say, that She *suffer'd herself* to be carried off! Is not this a strange Inattention? Her going off was in truth no more Voluntary, than in that Case where Shakespeare says in King Lear

> . . . . Thou'dst shun a Bear;
> But if thy Flight lay toward the roaring Sea
> Thou'dst meet the Bear i'th' Mouth.[3]

And this Restraint was enough to have justified even more Reserve to *such* a *Man*, than her generous Heart, ever willing to believe and hope the best, could shew.

Objection VI.[4] Surely this required no Answer; and 'tis rather Matter of Astonishment to me, how any one could forbear praising the Author of Clarissa for avoiding all Coarseness of Expression in describing some Scenes necessary towards the History; and for preserving a Decency and Delicacy which no Writer but Himself upon such Occasions ever did preserve.

Objection VII.[5] This has too little Force in it to want an Answer; and it must be want of Attention to the great Care that is taken to preserve Probability, that cou'd produce such an

---

[2] Collier's own responses are keyed to the numbering of Haller's points of critique introduced by the *Gentleman's Magazine* to identify 'some critical annotations, in answer to what he has objected' (p. 347). Haller's objection had been that 'she shews too scrupulous a delicacy after she has suffered herself to be carried off by *Lovelace*' (p. 348).

[3] *King Lear* II.9–11.

[4] Haller had complained that SR 'has dispersed, in some parts of his book, the particulars of freedoms taken by *Lovelace*, which exceed the bounds of decency' (p. 348).

[5] Building on 'Objection VI.', Haller had asked: 'Can it be thought that *Lovelace*, who was not deficient in understanding, and who expected to be a peer of the realm, would expose himself to the persecution of a powerful family, exasperated against him, beyond the possibility of reconciliation?' (p. 348).

WILLIAM STRAHAN TO RICHARDSON, THURSDAY 21 SEPTEMBER 1749

Objection. Or else it may indeed be owing to the Difference of the French and English Customs; & therefore proper, as the Remarker Himself says to be answer'd by a Native of England. Nor could it ever have been supposed that she was kept at Mother Sinclair's knowingly against Will, had a Letter been left in, which gave an Account of her going out by herself in a Hackney Coach to make the Tryal. But that with many more much to be regretted was omitted on Account of the foolish Objection made by some against the Length of a Work, which, to those who have a true Taste for it, has no other Fault but its not continuing as long as the Faculty is left for Reading.

The Objection between Number VII. and VIII.[6] I see has no Answer; and you may very properly tell the World, it deserves none. Yet Indignation prompts me to say, That to those who are not affected with the Pathetic Incoherence of those Scatter'd Pieces of Paper, they *may perhaps* appear Trifling; nor can any other Answer be given to any Objections that might be raised to those Passages which are addressed intirely to the Heart and not to the Head. Of the same Kind is Clarissa's signing her Hand in that particular Manner to the Will, and her last Letter to Miss Howe. And if the Author understood Human Nature well enough to know that there were some Hearts capable of being touched by such uncommon and surprizingly pathetic Passages, is it not hard that by the UNFEELING He shou'd be accused of Affectation?

[6] Collier means an unnumbered paragraph between points 8 and 9 (rather than between 7 and 8) in which Haller had suggested that there was 'something trifling in the incoherences, which *Clarissa* writes in her delirium' (p. 349).

William Strahan to Richardson

Thursday 21 September 1749

Printed source: B: I, 151–5.
First printing: Barbauld, *Correspondence* (1804).

September 21, 1749.

Dear Sir,

I think it is an observation of your own, that people cannot be at a loss for a subject when they write to those they esteem and love.[1] I own I am entirely of your opinion, and therefore when I sit down to write to you, I am not at all puzzled to say enough, but only to say something that may in some degree deserve your reading. If this was not the case, you might expect to be overpowered with my letters, as you have often been with my talking, when, from a sincere desire to please and divert you, (however short I came of my intention) I have opened the sluices of every folly in my brain, and overwhelmed you with nonsense.

Since I wrote last I have been in the north, seeing an old and a dear comrade, the parting from whom pierced me to the very soul. In my way I visited the ancient city of St. Andrew's, a most august monument of the splendour of the Scots episcopal church in former times. It is a most awful heap of ruins, to which I could wish all high-churchmen in Britain would take a visit once a-year, in pilgrimage, where they will behold a tremendous and amazing instance to what a deplorable degree of contempt and ruin they may reduce themselves, by their excessive arrogance, pride, and oppression.[2]

On my return I had the pleasure to receive your letter.[3] I shall set out for London in about eight days, and hope to have the pleasure to see you ten days after that.[4]

This recess from the hurry of business has been no disagreeable pause to me: it has, I may venture to say, afforded me both amusement and instruction. It is like turning over another leaf in the book of life, which, though not so crowded with the most useful matter, is nevertheless much fairer to the eye, more legible and pleasant in the reading. In traversing the country I have had occasion to see several pictures of life, which, though not entirely new to me, were yet nearly so. I have seen (a rare sight in London) indolence, inactivity, poverty, tranquillity, and happiness, dwelling under one roof. I have seen the several gradations from that to

---

[1] No specific source traced, but similar sentiments appear in several places in *Clarissa* as well as throughout SR's correspondence.

[2] The largest church to have been built in Scotland, St Andrews Cathedral was founded in 1158 and had been abandoned and was falling into ruin by 1561, following the Scottish Reformation. The High Church was 'A division or tradition within the Anglican communion emphasizing ritual, priestly authority, the Sacraments, and historical continuity with Catholicism' (*OED*).

[3] Now lost.

[4] Ten days was about the time it took a mid-century stagecoach to travel from Edinburgh to London, barring any accidents or delays.

WILLIAM STRAHAN TO RICHARDSON, THURSDAY 21 SEPTEMBER 1749

the busy moiling[5] trader, and from him again to those who were born to every earthly enjoyment. How seemingly different their situations, how nearly equal their pretences to real happiness! What an amazing variety in one little island. Here the poor reaper issues from his homely cot,[6] in the bleak regions of the everlasting mountains, contented if after the weeks of harvest are over in the more fertile plains, he can return home with a few shillings to subsist him till the return of that season. This is the utmost his most laborious employment of cutting down the corn, can procure him. There, the merchant thirsts after a princely inheritance; or the ambitious statesman labours to lord it not only over all his fellow-subjects, but even over his prince. But I will tire you no longer than till I tell you, that I have seen Captain C—,[7] who is a very pretty[8] gentleman, and lives in the finest house in Scotland, which he is exceedingly fond of, and is indeed particularly pleased with this country. I am really greatly affected, and my wife more so, with the loss of my pretty little Anne,[9] and could delineate the pangs I felt on that occasion, but that I write to one who is too susceptible of the most tender impressions, and who has had too many occasions (may he never find another) to exercise the most difficult of all christian duties, resignation to the will of heaven.

I hope you will believe, that I remember not only you, but your's, with very great respect and affection. I wish to find health even in that part of your family where you seem least to expect it; and my wife and her mother join me in every good wish to you all. I am, &c.

W. Strahan.

---

[5] Here: 'labouring, toiling; fatiguing, toilsome' (*OED*).
[6] 'cot' is short for 'cottage'.
[7] Unidentified.
[8] In this context, 'clever, skilful, able' (*OED*), but also cf. his use of 'pretty' in the next sentence, which is (probably) more in line with the word's modern meaning.
[9] Anne Strahan (1748–9) died on 12 September.

William Strahan to Richardson

Sunday 1 October 1749

Printed source: B: I, 156–7.
First printing: Barbauld, *Correspondence* (1804).

Answick,[1] Oct. 1, 1749.

Dear Sir,

I am thus far on my road to you, and long to finish my journey; but as I travel with women and a child,[2] we make but a slow progress.

Had I a tolerable pen, I could describe to you, I think, in lively colours, what I felt at parting with dear friends, some of whom I am sure I shall see no more. I could tell you how exquisitely pleasing the sight of my native country has been to me; and how easily, how naturally, how cordially, I have renewed old friendships. I could tire you with descriptions of the different states of my mind, as I was differently affected with joy, sorrow, surprise, &c. I could paint to you the analogy between an excursion of this kind, and the journey of life itself. But these things I must defer for a few days longer, and am, meanwhile, Dear Sir, Your most obedient humble servant,

W. Strahan.

P.S. There is a very pretty lady in company, much resembling your Clarissa.

---

[1] An 'Answick' does not exist in Britain; may be a transcription or printer's error for Alnwick, a prominent market town on the Great North Road from Edinburgh to London, about halfway between Newcastle-upon-Tyne and the border town of Berwick-upon-Tweed.

[2] Strahan's wife, Margaret, and possibly his daughter, Rachael (1742–65); another daughter, Anne, had just died (see Strahan to SR, 21 September 1749). However, the letter also makes clear that there was at least one other passenger in the stagecoach.

William Strahan to Richardson

Thursday 5 October 1749

Printed source: B: I, 157–60.
First printing: Barbauld, *Correspondence* (1804).

York, October 5, 1749.

Dear Sir,

Once more – I am now half way,[1] and shall have the pleasure of seeing you two days after you receive this: as nothing has occurred during our journey worth mentioning, I have nothing to say on that subject. The lady in my last postscript is one after your own heart;[2] she has true simplicity of manners, attended at the same time with a most becoming and easy dignity. Her person is well proportioned and stately, and commands respect; her deportment, her unaffected and engaging affability and constitutional good-nature, commands your affection; she discovers a fund of good sense, and knowledge of life and manners, accompanied with a solidity of judgment rarely to be found with so few years, and so much beauty: her sweet temper is most engaging, whilst her conversation is most instructive. Having seen much of the world, she seems to have made a very proper use of it, and made a just estimate of human life. Thus qualified, I prophesy you will be very fond of her. I have not done her half justice; your penetrating judgment will soon discover a thousand beauties which I have not sagacity enough to find out: But from what I have said, you may easily perceive my wife has no small cause of jealousy; but I am open and above-board with it, and freely own I cannot help admiring beauty and loving virtue, wherever I find it; and she has good sense enough not to be offended, and is indeed as fond of her as I am.

While I am writing, I cannot help looking back with some astonishment on my manner of life for these two months. Instead of plodding in business; hunting after pleasure, roving from place to place, from company to company, with a degree of unconcern about my most material affairs, which I did not believe myself capable of. These scenes have, however, been interspersed with others of a distressful kind, which gave me pause; and while they melted my heart with grief, and stirred up all that was friendly and

---

[1] York was halfway between Edinburgh and London on the Great North Road.
[2] See Strahan to SR, 1 October 1749.

affectionate in me, at the same time afforded proper motives for recollection, and gave occasion for many serious, and, I hope, not unuseful reflections.

Your goodness and your known friendship for me, will, I hope, excuse me for troubling you, upon all occasions, with whatever is uppermost in my heart. You, yourself, will answer for me, that I mean well; for you know how much I am, Dear Sir, Your most obliged and affectionate humble servant,

Wm. Strahan.

Richardson to Joseph Spence

Monday 30 October 1749

MS: Yale (Osborn). Autograph letter sent (evidence of folding and seal).
Endorsement: 'To The Rev:ᵈ Mr Spence in Stratton-Street Picadilly' (in Gilbert Hill's hand, on the outside of the letter); 'To Mr Spence.' and 'Oct 30 – 1749' (in Gilbert Hill's hand, on the letter's first page); 'Particular' (in SR's hand, on the letter's first page).

How wrong was it in my dear Mr. Spence, to forbid me coming to him, for some undetermined time in September, if he desired my Attendance? – Yet never to give me a Line to acquaint me when that time was over? – Surely, thought I, my *gentle* Friend intends to be in Town; and then will stretch to this smoaky Part of it: Or, who knows but he will, knowing my Days, and knowing my Family, make North-End his Town-house, not only now, but whenever he shall come to Town?

Thus, my dear Friend, have you puzzled me, till the Season is come in which no Invalid can travel.[1] Did you design it? – If not, why did you not make a Call upon me before now?

But, indeed, I should hardly have waited for this Call; having actually settled on my Return from Wellwyn, with my poor Friend Mr. Grover, the Visit to be made you. But inexorable Death, that cuts us off in the midst of our Designs and Views, interposed, and

---

[1] Eaves and Kimpel note (pp. 155–7) that SR's overall health had improved over the course of the 1740s but that his tremors had become much worse in late 1748 and early 1749.

RICHARDSON TO JOSEPH SPENCE, MONDAY 30 OCTOBER 1749

took my Friend, and left me embarrassed with his Affairs, yet but little able to grapple with my own.[2]

Hearing nothing from you, I thought it incumbent upon me to ask the Reason: And how you do? And how the Ladies do? And how the New Habitation, and the New Air, agrees with them and with you?[3] And at the same time to tell you, that I am, slight me as you will, as much as ever, Dear and Reverend Sir Your faithful Friend, and Humble Servant,

S. Richardson

London, Oct. 30. 1749.

---

[2] John Grover, an assistant to the chief Clerk of the House of Commons, Nicholas Hardinge, had died in September 1749. Welwyn was the place of residence of the writer Edward Young (bap. 1683, d. 1765), who was also rector there, and had been the site of baths since at least the third century.

[3] Though he evidently retained an address in London, Spence had in May 1749 moved to a thirty-acre estate in Byfleet, Surrey, and proceeded to redesign the gardens of his own and of his neighbours' houses; his 'forbidding' SR to visit in September may have had to do with the recent move and settling into a new home. The 'Ladies' were Spence's mother, Mirabella Spence, née Collier (1670–1755), and his cousin, a Mrs Collier (d. 1753), who both lived with him; Spence never married.

APPENDIX

ORDERS AND RECEIPTS OF PAYMENT

Richardson's surviving documents include an order of payment for printing government documents as well as a number of receipts for annuities he was collecting. Some of these documents, especially the receipts for annuities, largely consist of a printed form into which specific amounts, endorsements, and signatures have been entered by hand, while others are entirely drawn up by hand. These documents are dispersed across archives in Europe and North America; since they offer valuable insights into Richardson's business and financial dealings, we have collected them in this appendix.

Receipt of interest to Richardson for annuities

Wednesday 13 July and Tuesday 19 July 1715

MS: Houghton Library, MS Hyde 81 (9). Printed form with autograph insertions.
Endorsement: 'RG' in the left margin; large checkmark in the bottom-right quarter of the receipt. On the back, the receipt has been crossed through with a large, looping s-shape.

> *BANKERS Annuities.*
> Record' 13th July 1715[1]
>
> The 19th Day of July – 1715[2]
> R*Eceived by me* Sam:el Richardson for two Bankers Annuities
> ass\<ignee\> of Rooks, & Scot[3] *Of the Right Honourable* John *Lord*

---

[1] '13th July 1715' is an insertion in an undetermined hand.
[2] '19th', 'July–', and '15' are insertions in the same undetermined hand.
[3] 'Sam:el Richardson for two Bankers Annuities ass\<ignee\> of Rooks, & Scot' is an insertion in the same undetermined hand. The receipt carries the following calculations, also in the undetermined hand, in the margin following the printed word 'Number':
Scot 1830 – 2:5:0
Rooks 1803 – 7:0:4½
£9:5: 4½
Rooks and Scot are unidentified. We also do not know how SR acquired these annuities.

APPENDIX ORDERS AND RECEIPTS OF PAYMENT

De la Warr,[4] *One of the Four Tellers of the Receipt of His Majesty's* Exchequer, *the Sum of* Nine Pounds Five Shillings & 4½d[5] *being for* Eighteen– *Months Annuity, due the* 27th *Day of* June 1715[6] *by Vertue and in Pursuance of a late Act of Parliament, (Entituled,* An Act for the Better and more Regular Paying and Assigning the Annuities, after the Rate of Three Pounds *per Cent. per Annum,* payable to several Bankers, and other Patentees, or those claiming under them;)[7] *And in Lieu of* Fifty pounds & One Hundred & Fifty pounds one Shilling & 8d ——[8] *Principal Money: And to be paid Quarterly out of certain entire Weekly Payments of Three thousand seven hundred Pounds, arising and issuing out of the Hereditary Rates and Duties of Excise upon Beer, Ale,* &c. *as by the said Order does more fully appear. I say Received by me* ————— Sam:el Richardson[9]

[4] John West, sixth Baron De La Warr (1663–1723), courtier, and Teller of the Exchequer (1714–15).
[5] The entire amount is an insertion in the same undetermined hand. The 'd' stands for 'pence'.
[6] 'Eighteen–', '27th', 'June', and '15' are all insertions in the same undetermined hand.
[7] Signed into law by Queen Anne in 1704 and effective from 25 December 1705, this act regulated the payment of certain government annuities originally granted by Charles II.
[8] The entire set of numbers is an insertion in the same undetermined hand.
[9] SR's autograph signature.

Order and receipt of payment to Richardson for parliamentary printing

Tuesday 5, Saturday 16, and Monday 18 February 1734

MS: Huntington Library HM 3167. Printed form with autograph insertions.
Endorsement: 'order Saml. Richardson 124[£]:10[S]:__[1] Record 16 Feb 1733[2] En<tered>' (in an undetermined hand).

> Saml. Richardson ... ..
> Order is taken this vth day of February 1733 By virtue of his Majesty's General Letters Patent Dormant bearing the date the 22nd day of June 1727 That you deliver and pay of such his Majesty's Treasure as remains in your charge unto Samuel[3] Richardson or his Assigns the Sum of One hundred twenty four pounds and ten shillings without Account in Satisfaction and

[1] Sums of money were in this period often written as: [x] pounds:[y] shillings:[z] pence. One pound was twenty shillings, one shilling was twelve pence.
[2] Prior to 1752, the new year began on 25 March.
[3] 'Samuel' is inserted in a different hand from the rest of this passage, though it does not look like SR's hand.

261

APPENDIX ORDERS AND RECEIPTS OF PAYMENT

Discharge of a bill for printing several bills and reports for his Majesty's Service in the House of Commons. And those together with his or his assigns acquittance shall be your discharge herein.[4]

My Lord Onslow Pray pay this order out of Hereditary & Temporary Excise[5] 16th February 1733

Examiner Recorder 16 February 1733 Cxxiiij[£] X[S] Onslow[6]
Examiner: G: Halifax[7]
February 18 1733
Received the Contents of this Order by me, Saml. Richardson[8]

[9]3.18

——————

1:17.6

1:10:0

7

124.10.0 .   .   .   .   .   1.17.6 fees
                                                         3:2:3 poundage[10]

                                              ————————

Rst – 100 £   4.19.9
C . . 19.10   119:10.3

---

[4] The entire paragraph has been crossed through. In the margin, this section also restates the sum, 'Cxxiiij[£]:x[S]___', and carries the following autograph signatures: 'R Walpole' – Robert Walpole (1676–1745), first Earl of Orford (from 1742), prime minister (1721–42) (*ODNB*); 'Wm: Clayton' – William Clayton (1671–1752), first Baron Sundon (from 1735), MP and, at the time of signing this order, a lord of the Treasury; and 'Will: Yonge' – Sir William Yonge, fourth Baronet (*c.* 1693–1755), MP and, at the time of signing this order, a lord of the Treasury (*ODNB*).

[5] In 1660, two Acts created separate revenue streams to meet the expenses of the Crown by taxing domestic and imported beer, ale, cider, and other drinking alcohol as well as coffee, drinking chocolate, sherbet, and tea: Temporary Excise was granted to the king during his lifetime; Hereditary Excise was granted to the king, his heirs, and successors in perpetuity. A year later, another Act added a tax on hearths and stoves in every house to the Hereditary Excise.

[6] Autograph endorsement and signature of Arthur Onslow (1691–1768), speaker of the House of Commons (1727–61) (*ODNB*).

[7] Autograph signature of George Montagu (*c.* 1684–1739), Earl of Halifax (from 1715), Auditor of the Exchequer (1714–39).

[8] SR's autograph signature. The rest is in an undetermined hand.

[9] The following are calculations on the inside of the folded sheet of the order, not part of the main text, that detail costs, fees, and duties to arrive at the total amount owed to SR.

[10] Probably '*gen*. A payment of so much per pound sterling, or so much per cent in other currencies, upon the amount of any transaction in which money passes; a commission, or fee, of so much a pound or so much per cent' though it could also be more specifically 'A duty or tax of so much per pound sterling on merchandise' (*OED*). Some of the other abbreviations remain unidentified.

262

APPENDIX ORDERS AND RECEIPTS OF PAYMENT

Order and receipt of payment to Richardson for parliamentary printing

Tuesday 9 November 1736

MS: location unknown (sold in the 1990s by bookseller Stuart Bennett). Autograph letter sent.
Printed source: Stuart Bennett, *Catalogue 18: A Mill Valley Miscellany* (September 1993), item 172.

Order <xxxxx *unknown number of words*> for One hundred and thirteen pounds, twelve shillings and sixpence without Account in full Satisfaction and Discharge of a Bill for Printing, Folding and Stitching several Bills and Reports during this last Sessions of Parliament <xxxxx *unknown number of words*>.[1]

9 Nov. 1736
Received the Contents of the within Order[2]

---

[1] Ellipses in catalogue entry.
[2] Signed by SR. The order also bears the autograph signatures of Robert Walpole, Halifax, 'and other officials' (Bennett, *Catalogue 18*, item 172).

Receipt of interest to Richardson for annuities

Friday 2 January and Sunday 4 January 1741

MS: Haverford College Library, Charles Roberts Autograph Letters Collection 145. Printed form with autograph insertions.
Endorsement: 'l. d.' (in an undetermined hand).

Annuities, 14 per Cent.
Record' the 2d of January 1740[1]

---

[1] 'the 2d of January 1740' is an insertion in John Poumies's hand. Poumies (d. 1769) was a Huguenot army agent; in the 1760s, he was listed at Bolton-Street in London. For a detailed study of the role of regimental agents, see Alan J. Guy, 'Regimental Agency in the English Standing Army, 1715–1763: A Study of Georgian Military Administration: I', *Bulletin of the John Rylands Library*, 62, no. 2 (1980), 423–53, and 'Regimental Agency in the English Standing Army, 1715–1763: A Study of Georgian Military Administration: II', *Bulletin of the John Rylands Library*, 63, no. 1 (1980), 31–57. Guy points out that regimental agents often doubled as government officials and clerks.

APPENDIX ORDERS AND RECEIPTS OF PAYMENT

The 4th Day of January 1740[2]
R*Eceived by me* Samuel Richardson Assignee of Charles
Godfrey and Hugh Chudleigh Esqrs[3] *Of the Honourable* Thomas
Townshend, *Esq;*[4] *one of the Four Tellers of His Majesty's Receipt
of* Exchequer, *the Sum of* Twenty Eight pounds fifteen Shillings
————[5] *in full of all former Directions, and for* Three *Months
Annuity, due at* Christmas – *last past, of* one hundred and fifteen
Pounds per Annum,[6] *by Virtue of an Act of Parliament, (Entitled,* An
Act for Granting to their Majesties certain Rates and Duties upon
Beer, Ale, and other Liquors, for securing certain Recompences
and Advantages mentioned in the said Act, or other subsequent
Act or Acts, for purchasing the Reversions of the said Annuities;)[7]
I say Received by me ———— Saml. Richardson[8]
Witness

John Poumies[9]

[2] '4th', 'January', and 'o' are insertions in Poumies's hand.
[3] 'Samuel Richardson Assignee of Charles Godfrey and Hugh Chudleigh Esqrs' is an insertion in Poumies's hand. The receipt carries the following calculations in its margin, also in Poumies's hand, following the printed word 'Number':
£. S. d
157–17:10.0
5686–1:15:0
6131–9:10:0
£28:15:0
Charles Godfrey (c. 1648–1715), courtier and politician, was also brother-in-law to John Churchill, first Duke of Marlborough (1650–1722), and his younger brother, George Churchill (bap. 1654, d. 1710), naval officer and politician.
Hugh Chudleigh (c. 1642–c. 1707), Clerk to the Tellers of the Exchequer and, by 1704, Comptroller of the Treasurer's Accompts.
We do not know how SR acquired these annuities.
The receipt also, on the bottom of the sheet, carries the notes '530' (in Poumies's hand); 'BW 25' (in SR's hand, in a secretary hand, with 'BW' crossed through); and the calculation (also in SR's hand):
14
28.15
————
42:15
[4] Thomas Townshend (1701–80), politician (*ODNB*).
[5] The entire amount is an insertion in Poumies's hand.
[6] 'Three', 'Christmas–', and 'one Hundred and fifteen' are insertions in Poumies's hand.
[7] This act, passed in 1692, levied an excise tax on beer, ale, and other forms of drinking alcohol to help fund England's Nine Years' War with France.
[8] SR's autograph signature.
[9] 'Witness' is an addition in Poumies's hand, followed by his autograph signature.

264

APPENDIX ORDERS AND RECEIPTS OF PAYMENT

Receipt of interest to Richardson for annuities

Monday 5 October and Tuesday 13 October 1741

MS: Fitzwilliam Museum, Cambridge. Ashcombe Collection V.3. Printed form with autograph insertions.
Endorsement: 'JS' (in an undetermined hand); and '38' (in an undetermined hand). On the back, the receipt has been crossed through diagonally.

> *Annuities*, 14 per Cent.
> Record' 5th of October 1741[1]
>
> The 13th Day of October 1741.[2]
> R*Eceived by me* Samuel Richardson Assignee of Charles Godfrey and Hugh Chudleigh Esqrs–[3] *Of the Honourable* Thomas Townshend, *Esq*; *one of the Four Tellers of His Majesty's Receipt of* Exchequer, *the Sum of* Twenty Eight pounds f<ifteen> Shillings[4] *in full of all former Directions, and for* Three——— *Months Annuity, due at* Michaelmas *last past, of* one Hundred and fifteen *Pounds* per Annum,[5] *by Virtue of an Act of Parliament, (Entituled,* An Act for Granting to their Majesties certain Rates and Duties upon Beer, Ale, and other Liquors, for securing certain Recompences and Advantages mentioned in the said Act, or other subsequent Act or Acts, for purchasing the Reversion of the said Annuities;) *I say Received by me* —— Saml. Richardson.[6]
> Witness
>
> John Poumies[7]

[1] '5th of October 1741' is an insertion in Poumies's hand.
[2] '13th', 'October', and '1' are insertions in Poumies's hand.
[3] 'Samuel Richardson Assignee of Charles Godfrey and Hugh Chudleigh Esqrs' is an insertion in Poumies's hand; 'and Hugh Chudleigh Esqrs' has been crossed through. The receipt carries the following calculation, also in Poumies's hand, in the margin following the printed word 'Number':
£. S. d
157 Godfrey 17:10:00
5686 Godfrey 1:15:00
6131 Churchill 9:10:00.
28:15:00
'Churchill' has been crossed through.
[4] The entire amount is an insertion in Poumies's hand.
[5] 'Three', 'Michaelmas', and 'one Hundred and fifteen' are insertions in Poumies's hand.
[6] SR's autograph signature.
[7] 'Witness' is an addition in Poumies's hand, followed by his autograph signature.

265

APPENDIX ORDERS AND RECEIPTS OF PAYMENT

Receipt of interest to Richardson for annuities

Tuesday 5 October and Thursday 14 October 1742

MS: National Library of Scotland, MS.582, no.656. Printed form with autograph insertions.

Endorsement: '322' (in Poumies's hand, on bottom right of receipt). On the back, the receipt has been crossed through diagonally.

Annuities, 14 per Cent.
Record' the 5th of October 1742[1]

The 14th Day of October 1742[2]
R*Eceived by me* Samuel Richardson Assignee as per Margent[3] *Of the Honourable* Thomas Townshend, *Esq*; *one of the Four Tellers of His Majesty's Receipt of* Exchequer, *the Sum of* Twenty Eight pounds fifteen Shillings ————[4] *in full of all former Directions, and for* Three *Months Annuity, due at* Michaelmas – *last past, of* one hundred and fifteen *Pounds* per Annum,[5] *by Virtue of an Act of Parliament, (Entitled,* An Act for Granting to their Majesties certain Rates and Duties upon Beer, Ale, and other Liquors, for securing certain Recompences and Advantages mentioned in the said Act, or other subsequent Act or Acts, for purchasing the Reversion of the said Annuities;)[6] *I say Received by me* ————
Saml. Richardson[7]
Witness

John Poumies[8]

---

[1] 'the 5th of October 1742' is an insertion in Poumies's hand.
[2] '14th', 'October', and '2' are insertions in Poumies's hand.
[3] I.e. 'margin'. 'Samuel Richardson Assignee as per Margent' is an insertion in Poumies's hand. The receipt carries the following calculation, also in Poumies's hand, in the margin following the printed 'Number':
£. S. d
157. Cha. Godfrey – 17:10.0
5686. Geo. Churchill and Hugh Chudleigh 1:15:0
6131. Cha. Godfrey – 9:10:0
£28:15:0
[4] The entire amount is an insertion in Poumies's hand.
[5] 'Three', 'Michaelmas–', and 'one Hundred and fifteen' are insertions in Poumies's hand.
[6] This act, passed in 1692, levied an excise tax on beer, ale, and other forms of drinking alcohol to help fund England's Nine Years' War with France.
[7] SR's autograph signature.
[8] 'Witness' is an addition in Poumies's hand, followed by his autograph signature.

266

APPENDIX ORDERS AND RECEIPTS OF PAYMENT

Receipt of interest to Richardson for annuities

Thursday 2 January and Thursday 9 January 1746

MS: Wisbech & Fenland Museum, 2003.35.2.77.5. Printed form with autograph insertions.
Endorsement: 'J' (in an undetermined hand); and '556' (in an undetermined hand). On the back, the receipt has been crossed through diagonally.

> *Annuities*, 14 per Cent.
> Record' the 2nd of January 1745[1]
>
> The 9th Day of January 1745[2]
> R*Eceived by me* Samuel Richardson. Assignee as per Margent[3] *Of the Honourable* Thomas Townshend, *Esq*; *One of the Four Tellers of His Majesty's Receipt of* Exchequer, *the Sum of* Twenty Eight pounds fifteen Shillings ————[4] *in full of all former Directions and for* Three *Months Annuity, due at* Christmas *last past, of* One Hundred and <fif>teen *Pounds* per Annum,[5] *by Virtue of an Act of Parliament, (Entitled,* An Act for Granting to their Majesties certain Rates and Duties upon Beer, Ale, and other Liquors, for securing certain Recompences and Advantages men<ti>oned[6] in the said Act, or other subsequent Act or Acts, for purchasing the Reversions of the said Annuities;)[7] *I say Received by me* ——— Saml. Richardson[8]
> Witness
> John Poumies[9]

[1] 'the 2nd of January 1745' is an insertion in Poumies's hand.
[2] '9th', 'January', and '5' are insertions in Poumies's hand.
[3] I.e. 'margin'. 'Samuel Richardson. Assignee as per Margent' is an insertion in Poumies's hand. The receipt carries the following calculation, also in Poumies's hand, in the margin following the printed 'Number':
£. S. d
157. Cha. Godfrey – 17:10.0
5686. Geo. Churchill and Hugh Chudleigh 1:15:0
6131. Cha. Godfrey – 9:10:0
£28:15:0
[4] The entire number is an insertion in Poumies's hand.
[5] 'Three', 'Christmas', and 'One Hundred and <fif>teen' are insertions in Poumies's hand.
[6] A printer's error has dropped two letters and left an empty space in the middle of the word.
[7] This act, passed in 1692, levied an excise tax on beer, ale, and other forms of drinking alcohol to help fund England's Nine Years' War with France.
[8] SR's autograph signature.
[9] 'Witness' is an addition in Poumies's hand, followed by his autograph signature.

APPENDIX ORDERS AND RECEIPTS OF PAYMENT

Receipt of interest to Richardson for annuities

Thursday 5 January and Tuesday 10 January 1749

MS: Houghton Library, MS Hyde 81 (9). Printed form with autograph insertions.

> *Annuities* 14 per Cent.
> Record' the 5. January 1748[1]

> The 10th Day of January 1748[2]
> R*Eceived by me* Samuel Richardson Assignee as per Margent[3] *Of the Honourable* Thomas Townshend, *Esq*; *One of the Four Tellers of His Majesty's Receipt of* Exchequer, *the Sum of* Twenty Eight pounds fifteen Shillings ————[4] *in full of all former Directions and for* Three *Months Annuity, due at* Christmas – *last past, of* One Hundred and Fifteen *Pounds* per Annum,[5] *by Virtue of an Act of Parliament, (Entitled,* An Act for Granting to their Majesties certain Rates and Duties upon Beer, Ale, and other Liquors, for securing certain Recompences and Advantages mentioned in the said Act, or other subsequent Act

---

[1] 'the 5. January 1748' is an insertion in Poumies's hand.

[2] '10th', 'January', and '8' are insertions in Poumies's hand.

[3] I.e. 'margin'. 'Samuel Richardson Assignee as per Margent' is an insertion in Poumies's hand. The receipt carries the following calculations, also in Poumies's hand, in the margin following the printed word 'Number':
£. S. d
157. Cha. Godfrey – 17:10.0
5686. Geo. Churchill and H. Chudleigh 1:15:0
6131. Cha. Godfrey – 9:10:0
£28:15:0
The receipt also, in the right margin, carries (in SR's hand) the calculation:
21
28.15
‾‾‾‾‾
49.15

[4] The entire amount is an insertion in Poumies's hand.

[5] 'Three', 'Christmas–', and 'One Hundred and Fifteen' are insertions in Poumies's hand.

268

APPENDIX ORDERS AND RECEIPTS OF PAYMENT

or Acts, for purchasing the Reversions of the said Annuities;)[6] *I say Received by me* —— Saml. Richardson[7]
Wit<ness>

<John Po>umies[8]

---

[6] This act, passed in 1692, levied an excise tax on beer, ale, and other forms of drinking alcohol to help fund England's Nine Years' War with France.
[7] SR's autograph signature.
[8] Poumies's addition of 'Wit<ness>' and autograph signature largely obscured by badly damaged manuscript, full text and name supplied from Receipt of interest to SR for annuities, 2 and 9 January 1746, and Receipt of interest to SR for annuities, 2 and 9 October 1749.

Receipt of interest to Richardson for annuities

Thursday 5 January and Tuesday 10 January 1749

MS: Universitätsbibliothek Basel: Autogr Geigy-Hagenbach 1504. Printed form with autograph insertions.
Endorsement: 'P' (in an undetermined hand, in secretary hand, in two places on front); 'Tonnage', 'Paid 10 January 1748', and '£130 / Set off at Interest' (in Poumies's hand on the back of the receipt; most of the receipt's back has been crossed through).

Tonnage, 1694. &c.
Record' the 5th January 1748[1]

The 10th Day of January 1748.[2]
R*Eceived by me* Samuel Richardson Assignee of Geo. Churchill and Hugh Chudleigh[3] *Of the Honourable* Horatio Walpole, *Esq*;[4] *One of the Four Tellers of His Majesty's Receipt of* Exchequer, *the Sum of* Six pounds five Shillings[5] *in full of all former Directions of the said Order, and for* Six ——*Months Annuity, due at* Christmas *last past, of* Twenty five *Pounds* per Annum,[6] *by Virtue of an Act*

---

[1] 'the 5th January 1748' is an insertion in Poumies's hand.
[2] '10th', 'January', and '8.' are insertions in Poumies's hand.
[3] 'Samuel Richardson Assignee of Geo. Churchill and Hugh Chudleigh' is an insertion in Poumies's hand. The receipt carries the following note, also in Poumies's hand, in the margin following the printed word 'Number': '472. – £6:5:0'.
[4] Horatio Walpole (1678–1757), first Baron Walpole of Wolterton (from 1756), diplomatist and politician, Teller of the Exchequer (from 1741), younger brother of Prime Minister Sir Robert Walpole (1676–1745) (*ODNB*).
[5] The entire amount is an insertion in Poumies's hand.
[6] 'Six————', 'Christmas', and 'Twenty five' are insertions in Poumies's hand.

APPENDIX ORDERS AND RECEIPTS OF PAYMENT

of Parliament, (Entituled, An Act for Granting to their Majesties certain Rates <a>nd Duties upon Tonnage of Ships and Vessels, and upon Beer, Ale, and other Liquors, for securing certain Recompences and Advantages in the said Act mentioned, to such <Per>sons as shall voluntarily advance the Sum of Fifteen <hun>dred thousand Pounds towards carrying on a vigorous <War> against *France;)[7] I say Received by me* ——— Saml. Richardson[8]
<Witness>

<Joh>n Poumies[9]

[7] Also called the Bank of England Act, passed in 1694, this act levied an excise tax on the tonnage of ships as well as on beer, ale, and other forms of drinking alcohol to help fund England's Nine Years' War with France. Damage to the receipt has obliterated some of the text.
[8] SR's autograph signature.
[9] Poumies's usual addition of '<Witness>' missing and autograph signature largely obscured by badly damaged manuscript, full text and name supplied from Receipt of interest to SR for annuities, 2 and 9 January 1746, and Receipt of interest to SR for annuities, 2 and 9 October 1749.

Receipt of interest to Richardson for annuities

Monday 2 October and Monday 9 October 1749

MS: Houghton Library, MS Hyde 81 (9). Printed form with autograph insertions.
Endorsement: 'J' (in an undetermined hand).

Annuities 14 per Cent.
Record' 2d October 1749[1]

The 9th Day of Ditto 1749[2]
R*Eceived by me* Samuel Richardson Assignee as per Margent[3]
Of the Honourable Thomas Townshend, *Esq; One of the Four Tellers*

[1] '2d October 1749' is an insertion in Poumies's hand.
[2] '9th', 'Ditto', and '9' are insertions in Poumies's hand.
[3] I.e. 'margin'. 'Samuel Richardson Assignee as per Margent' is an insertion in Poumies's hand. The receipt carries the following calculations, also in Poumies's hand, in the margin following the printed word 'Number':
£. S. d
157. Cha. Godfrey – 17:10.0
5686. Geo. Churchill and H. Chudleigh 1:15:0
6131. Cha. Godfrey – 9:10:0
£28:15:0

APPENDIX ORDERS AND RECEIPTS OF PAYMENT

of His Majesty's Receipt of Exchequer, *the Sum of* Twenty Eight
pounds fifteen Shillings ————[4] *in full of all former Directions
and for* Three *Months Annuity, due at* Michaelmas– *last past, of*
one Hundred and fifteen *Pounds* per Annum,[5] *by Virtue of an Act
of Parliament, (Entitled,* An Act for Granting to their Majesties
certain Rates and Duties upon Beer, Ale, and other Liquors, for
securing certain Recompences and Advantages mentioned in the
said Act, or other subsequent Act or Acts, for purchasing the
Reversions of the said Annuities;)[6] *I say Received by me* ————
Saml. Richardson[7]
Witness

John Poumies[8]

[4] The entire amount is an insertion in Poumies's hand.
[5] 'Three', 'Michaelmas–', and 'one Hundred and fifteen' are insertions in Poumies's hand.
[6] This act, passed in 1692, levied an excise tax on beer, ale, and other forms of drinking alcohol to help fund England's Nine Years' War with France.
[7] SR's autograph signature.
[8] 'Witness' is an addition in Poumies's hand, followed by his autograph signature.

Receipt of interest to Richardson for annuities

Thursday 11 April 1751

MS: Bodleian Ms. Autogr. B. 4. P. 28. Printed form with autograph insertions.
Endorsement: 'Bk25 J' (at bottom of sheet, in an undetermined hand).

> *Annuities,* 14 per Cent.
> Record' the 11th April 1751–[1]
>
> The 11th Day of April 1751. –[2]
> R*eceived by me* Samuel Richardson Assignee as per Margent[3] *Of
> the Honourable* Thomas Townshend, *Esq; One of the Four Tellers of*

[1] 'the 11th April 1751' is an insertion in Poumies's hand.
[2] '11th', 'April, and '1' are insertions in Poumies's hand.
[3] I.e. 'margin'. 'Samuel Richardson Assignee as per Margent' is an insertion in Poumies's hand. The receipt carries the following calculations, also in Poumies's hand, in the margin following the printed word 'Number':
157. Charles Godfrey £17:10.0
5686. Geo. Churchill, and Hugh Chudleigh 1:15:0
6131. Charles Godfrey – 9:10.0
£28:15:0

APPENDIX ORDERS AND RECEIPTS OF PAYMENT

His Majesty's Receipt of Exchequer, *the Sum of* Twenty Eight pounds
fifteen Shillings ————[4] *in full of all former Directions and for*
Three *Months Annuity, due at* Lady Day– *last past, of* one Hundred
and Fifteen *Pounds* per Annum,[5] *by Virtue of an Act of Parliament,
(Entituled,* An Act for Granting to their Majesties certain Rates
and Duties upon Beer, Ale, and other Liquors, for securing certain
Recompences and Advantages mentioned in the said Act, or other
subsequent Act or Acts, for purchasing the Reversions of the said
Annuities;)[6] *I say Received by me* ——— Saml. Richardson[7]
   Witness

John Poumies[8]

[4] The entire amount is an insertion in Poumies's hand.
[5] 'Three', 'Lady Day–', and 'one Hundred and Fifteen' are insertions in Poumies's hand.
[6] This act, passed in 1692, levied an excise tax on beer, ale, and other forms of drinking alcohol to help fund England's Nine Years' War with France.
[7] SR's autograph signature.
[8] Poumies's autograph signature.

INDEX

Ackers (Acres), Charles (1702/3–82) xxxix, l, 106
Addison, Joseph (1672–1719) 119, 159, 190
Allen, Elizabeth neé Buckeridge (d. 1736) 99, 148
Allen, Ralph (bap. 1693, d. 1764) xliii, xlviii–xlix, 15, 60–1, 93, 96, 98–9, 111, 147, 154, 155
Alston, Philip 138
Amberg, Anthony: *The Foundling and the Gamester* 192
Anderson, James (bap. 1679, d. 1739) 19
Aquinas, Thomas (1225–74) 200
Aristotle (384–322 BCE) 92
    Poetics 186

Balfour, George (1711–51) 104
Barbauld, Anna Laetitia neé Aikin (1743–1825) xxxix, xlviii, l, liii–lv, 83–8, 93–4, 98, 103, 143, 149–50, 156, 164, 186, 199–200, 202–3
    The Correspondence of Samuel Richardson (1804) xxxix, xlviii, l–li, liii–lv, 83–6, 93–4, 98, 103, 128, 138, 143, 145–6, 148–50, 156, 164, 171, 179, 186, 199, 203, 222, 227, 231, 243, 245, 247, 253, 256–7
Barber, Constantine (1714–83) 59
Barber, Mary (c. 1685–1755) xliii, 53–4, 57–9
Barber, Rupert (1719–72) 53, 54, 57
Barber, Rupert (d. 1777?) 59
Baskett, John (d. 1742) 117
Baskett, Robert (d. 1767?) 117
Baskett, Thomas (d. 1761) 117
Bath General Hospital 15, 19–20
'Bennet, Mr' 119–20
Bertrand, Paul (fl. 1732–48) 51–2, 56–7, 96
Bettenham, James (1683?–1774) 16
Birch, Thomas (1705–66) xl, lvi, 18–19, 101, 102–3, 107–9, 204–5
booksellers xl
Bowyer, William the younger (1699–1777) 94
Brady, Nicholas (1659–1726) 165
Brand, Elias xlv, xlvii, 128, 164, 181–2, 199–203, 220–1
Buckley, Samuel (1674?–1741) 117
Bueler, Lois. E.: *'Clarissa': The Eighteenth-Century Response* 251
Burney, Frances: *Evelina* (1778) xxxvii
Burroughs, Samuel (d. 1761) 21

Campbell, Archibald: *The Necessity of Revelation* (1739) 16
Cant, Andrew (1584/90–1663) 90
Cant, Andrew (d. 1685) 90
Carew, Thomas (c. 1702–66) 19
Carr, Susan (d. 1808) lviii, lix, 232
Carr, Timothy (d. 1771) lviii
Carte, Thomas (bap. 1686, d. 1754) 19, 21
Carter, Elizabeth (1717–1806) xi, xiv, xvii, xxxvii, xlii, lii, liv, 120, 132, 133–4, 135–6, 188–9
Cave, Edward (1691–1754) xxxvii, 136, 241, 250–3
Cay, Henry Boult (d. 1795) 237, 242
Cay, John (1700–57) 237, 242
Cervantes: *Don Quixote* (1615) 45
Chambers, Ephraim: *Cyclopaedia: or, An Universal Dictionary of Arts and Sciences* (1738) 12
Champion, The (1739–45) 47
Chandler, Richard (c. 1713–44) 40, 48, 54
Channing, John (c. 1703–75) liii, 164–6, 177–83, 199–203
Channing, John (d. 1725) 180
Channing, Wingate 180
Chapone, Hester, neé Mulso (1727–1801) li
Charles, Prince of Wales (1600–49) 248
Cheale, John (bap. 1699, d. 1751) 144–5
Chetwode, Knightley (1679–1752) 35–6
Chetwood, Knightly (bap. 1650, d. 1720) 35–6
Cheyne, George (1672–1743) xlviii, liv, 23, 51, 52, 56, 93, 96, 97, 142, 155
Chudleigh, Hugh (c. 1642–c. 1707) 264, 265, 266, 267, 268, 269, 270, 271
Churchill, Awnsham (1658–1728) lviii
Churchill, Charles (1679–1745) lvii
Churchill, General Charles (1656–1714) lvii
Churchill, George (bap. 1654, d. 1710) lvii, lviii, 264, 266, 267, 268, 270, 271, 272
Churchill, Henrietta Arabella ('Miss Churchill') (1722?–56) lvi, lvii, 232–4
Churchill, John, first Duke of Marlborough (1650–1722) lvii, 264, 266, 270
Churchill, Lieutenant-General George (c. 1690–1753) lvii, 232
Cibber, Colley (1671–1757) xlv, 119, 125, 150–1, 211, 218

273

INDEX

Cicero, Marcus Tullius (106–43 BCE) 65, 128, 199
   De Natura Deorum 91
Clarke, John 117
Clayton, William, (1671–1752) first Baron
   Sundon 262
Collier, Arthur (d. 1777) 203, 222
Collier, Jane (bap. 1715, d. 1755) xxxvii, xxxviii,
   xlii–xliii, xlv, lii, lvi–lviii, lix, 171–2, 203,
   222–3, 231–4, 238–40, 241, 250–3
   The Cry: A New Dramatic Fable (1754) (with
     Sarah Fielding) lvii
Collier, Margaret (1719–94) lix, 172, 222, 232
Conybeare, John (1692–1755) 73, 249–50
Cooper, Anthony Ashley, third Earl of
   Shafterbury (1671–1713) lviii
Cooper, Thomas xlvii, 206, 207, 213, 214–18
Costes, Gauthier de seigneur de la Calprenède
   (1609/10–63)
   Cassandre (1642–50) 231
   *The Correspondence of Henry and Sarah
     Fielding*, ed. Martin C. Battestin and
     Clive T. Probyn (1993) 203, 204, 222
   Faramond, ou l'histoire de France (1661) 231
Courteville, Raphael (Ralph) (fl. 1720–72) 35–6,
   39–40
Coxeter, Thomas (1689–1747) 11
Curll, Edmund (1683–1747) xxxvi–xxxvii
Curran, Louise x, lii

Daily Advertizer (1731–96) 20
Daily Gazetteer (1735–97) xxxix–xl, 15, 19–20, 33,
   35, 71, 106
Darnley, Lord, see Stewart, Henry, Duke of
   Albany, Lord Darnley 246
Defoe, Daniel (1660?–1731) xxxviii
   Robinson Crusoe (1719) 31–32
   A Tour Thro' the Whole Island of Great Britain
     (1724–7) 39, 247
Delany, Margaret (d. 1742) 54, 58
Delany, Mary *née* Granville (1700–88) xvii, 227
Delany, Patrick (1685/6–1768) 53, 54, 58, 227–8
Descartes, René (1596–1650) 164, 201
Dodsley, Robert (1704–64) 11, 38, 214
Dryden John (1631–1700) 220
Duck, Stephen (1705?–56) xliv, 38, 66–8
Duns Scotus, John (1266–1308) 200
Dutton, Margaret (c. 1718–56) 244
Dutton, Mary (bap. 1716) 244
Dutton, Thomas (d. 1741) 244

Eaves, T. C. Duncan, and Ben D. Kimpel:
   Samuel Richardson: A Biography x, xi,
     xvii, xviii, liv–lviii, 3, 11, 28, 38, 62, 71–2,
     82, 84–6, 95, 98, 103, 107–8, 115, 119, 124,
     126, 133, 136, 164, 199, 203, 206, 232,
     250, 258
Elizabeth I (1533–1603) 248
Elphinston, Margaret Penelope (1719–85) 104, 245

Evelyn, John (1620–1706) 21
Evelyn, Sir John, 1st Baronet, of Wotton
   (1682–1763) 21

Faulkner, George (1703?–75) 53, 69, 228
Fielding, Edmund (1680–1741) lvii
Fielding, Harriet (1743–66) 176
Fielding, Henry (1707–54) xxxvii–xxxviii, xlii, li,
   liv, lvii, lviii, 15, 41, 47, 98, 169, 172–7,
   222, 233
   The Jacobite's Journal (1747–8) 169, 173
   Joseph Andrews (1742) xxxvii
   Shamela (1741) xxxvii, xlii
   Tom Jones (1749) 15, 169, 172, 224, 233, 241
Fielding, John (1721–80) 233
Fielding, Sarah (1710–68) xxxvii, xxxviii, xlii, liv,
   lvii, lviii, 171–2, 203–5, 222, 232
   The Cry: A New Dramatic Fable (1754) (with
     Jane Collier) lvii
   The Governess; or, Little Female Academy (1749)
     171
   Lives of Cleopatra and Octavia (1757) 232
   Remarks on Clarissa (1749) 204–5
FitzRoy, Charles (1683–1757) 202
Fortunate Country Maid, The (1741) 84
Frederick, William (d. 1776) 96
Freval, Jean Baptiste de (fl. 1737–51) 28–30
Fulford, Anthony (c. 1714–54) 76

Garrick, David (1717–79) xlv, l, liv, 183, 187–8,
   222
Gay, John: *Polly* (1728/77) 33
General Evening Post (1733–1822) 20
Gentleman's Magazine (1731–1922) xxxvii, 136, 241,
   250–1, 252
Gerrard, Christine xlix, li, 22
Gilmore, Robert 100
Godfrey, Charles (c. 1648–1715) 264, 265, 266, 267,
   268, 270–1
Gool, Jacob van (1596–1667) 202
Gordon, Alexander (c. 1692–1754?) 16–19, 22, 45–7
Gosling, Francis (1719–68) 51
Gravelot, Hubert-François (1699–1773) 61
Green, James (bap. 1692) 165
Green, John (bap. 1677) 165
Grover, John (d. 1749) lvi, 107, 258–9

Hall, Elizabeth (m. 1760, d. 1774?) 132
Haller, Albrecht von (1708–77) 241, 250–3
Hamilton, Archibald (1719–93) 245
Hamilton, Gavin (1704–67) 104
Hammerschmidt, Sören 'Mysterious Miss
   Churchill' lvi, 232
Hardinge, Nicholas (1699–1758) 107, 259
Harris, James (1709–80) lviii, 222, 231–2
Hartley, David (bap. 1705, d. 1757) 96
Hayman, Francis (1707/8–76) 61
Hazard, Joseph (d. 1750) 34

274

INDEX

Henry Frederick, prince of Wales (1594–1612) 248
Hervey, James (1714–58) 120–1, 122–3, 128–30, 145–6
Hesilrige, Lady, *née* Hannah Sturges (1710–65) 83
Hesilrige, Sir Arthur, 7th Baronet (1705–63) 83
Hesiod (fl. between 750 and 650 BCE) 227
Heylyn, Edward (1695–1765) 131
Heylyn, Elizabeth (d. 1759) 131
Heylyn, Elizabeth, *née* Ebbutt (d. 1747) 131
Heylyn, Jane, *née* Slaughter 131
Heylyn, John (1684/5–1759) 130, 131
Heylyn, John (1712–68?) 131
'Heylyn, Mary' 131–2
Heywood, John: *Dialogue of Proverbs* (1546) 153
Highmore, Joseph (1692–1780) xlv, 124–5, 126, 178
Hill, Aaron (1685–1750) xlix, li, 12, 22, 23, 71, 84, 92, 118, 125, 178
Hill, Gilbert (fl. 1694–1750) xxiii, xlix, li–lii, 28, 30, 33, 35, 36, 38, 39, 44, 47, 51, 53, 55, 56, 57, 60, 61, 66–7, 69, 71–3, 74, 76, 77, 80, 82, 84, 85, 86, 89, 93, 102, 107, 119, 124, 126, 130, 131, 135, 144, 151, 153, 157, 158, 161, 163, 166, 169, 177, 178, 181, 184, 185, 188, 190, 192, 197, 198, 199, 229, 243, 249, 251, 258
Hoblyn, Robert (bap. 1710, d. 1756) 107
Holder, Elizabeth (d. 1766) 99
Home, Henry (1696–1782) 234–7, 241–2
Homer (c. 8th century BCE) 66, 91, 92, 159
Honeyman, Rachel (d. 1750) 104, 245
Hooke, Nathaniel (1687–1763) 31
Hooker, Richard see Webster, William (1689–1758)
Horace (Quintus Horatius Flaccus) (65–8 BCE)
Ars Poetica 91, 128, 198
Odes 177, 244
House of Commons
Importation Act of 1738 xl, lvi, 107–8
Journals xl, liv, lv, 103
SR printing for liv–lv, 261–2, 263
Howe, Mary, Countess Dowager of Pembroke (d. 1749) 243
Howe, Scrope, first Viscount Howe (1648–1713) 243
Hudson, John (1662–1719) 11

James V of Scotland (1512–42) 246, 248
James VI of Scotland & I of England (1566–1625) 248
Jekyll, Sir Joseph (bap. 1662, d. 1738) 12–13
Johnson, Samuel (1709–84) xxxvi, xxxvii, liv, 191, 223

Kelly, John: *Pamela's Conduct in High Life* (1741) 44, 48, 69
Keymer, Thomas, and Peter Sabor: *'Pamela' in the Marketplace* xliii, 48, 70, 83–4, 119

Le Bas, Stephen (fl. 1738–41) 20–1
Leake, Amelia (da. of James Leake Sr) 55
Leake, Ann (da. of James Leake Sr) 55
Leake, Elizabeth (da. of James Leake Sr) 55
Leake, Elizabeth (SR's second wife), see Richardson, Elizabeth, *née* Leake
Leake, Hannah Hammond (bap. 1699, d. 1751) 15, 55, 56, 96, 99, 148
Leake, James (1686–1764) xli, xlviii, liii, 15, 34, 47–51, 55, 56, 61, 93, 96, 99, 110, 129, 148
Leake, James, Jr (1724–91) 55, 95–7
Lennox, Charles (1701–50) 144–5
Lesage, Alain-René: *Gil Blas* (1715–35) 33
Lintot, Henry (bap. 1703, d. 1758) 11–13
Little, David, and George Kahrl: *The Letters of David Garrick* 188
Lloyd, William (1627–1717) 115–16
Lobb, Joseph (1743–1811) 98, 110, 112, 148, 149
Lobb, Samuel (1690–1761) xl, xlv, xlviii, 19, 97–100, 109–14, 115, 137–8, 146–9
The Benevolence Incumbent on Us, as Men and Christians, Considered (1746) xl, 109, 112, 137, 146
Lobb, Stephen (d. 1699) 116
Lobb, Susanna, *née* Shipley (1700–77) 98, 111, 149
Lobb, William (c. 1736–65) xlviii, 98, 111, 113, 115–16, 149
Locke, John (1632–1704) 201
London Evening Post (1727–1806) 15, 20
London Magazine (1732–85) xxxvi, xxxix, 106
Long, Elizabeth 133
Longinus: *On the Sublime* (c. 1st century CE) 92
Lowe, Solomon (d. 1750) xlv, xlvii, xlix, li, lii, liii, 69–70, 158–61, 197–8, 205–18, 221, 223–5, 226, 240–1, 251
Lyttelton, George (1709–73) 107

Mallet, David (formerly Malloch) (1701/2–65) 71, 220
Marsh, Charles (fl. 1734–67) lii, 22–3
Mary, Queen of Scots (1542–87) 246
McCarthy, William l, liii
McKillop, Alan Dugald: *Samuel Richardson, Printer and Novelist* 222
Meston, William: *The Knight* (1723) 90
Middleton, John (1710?–60) 96
Midwinter, Edward (d. 1736) 51
Midwinter, Elizabeth (1724–1806) 51
Millar, Andrew (1705–68) xli, 15, 173, 205, 227, 231, 237, 242, 247, 248
Millar, Rev. Robert (1672–1752) 247
Milton, John (1608–74) 19, 41, 42–4, 91, 143
Montagu, George, Earl of Halifax (c. 1684–1739) 262
Montesquieu: *Persian Letters* (1721) 95
Monthly Magazine (1796–1825) l, liv

INDEX

Moore, Edward (1712–57) xliv, xlv, xlvii, l, li, liii, liv, 166–8, 169–70, 190–6
   Fables for the Female Sex (1744) 169
   The Foundling (1748) 169
   Gil Blas (1751) 169
   Trial of Selim the Persian (1748) 169
Moore, Reverend John (1708–74) 168
Mordaunt, John (1709?–67) 243
Morgan, H. 161–3
'Morley, Reverend' 72–3
Mulso, Hester, see Chapone, Hester, *née* Mulso

Nash, Richard 'Beau' (1674–1761) 15
Negotiations of Sir Thomas Roe, in his Embassy to the Ottoman Porte, The (1740) 14, 18–19, 20–1, 22
Newton, Richard (1676–1753) 39, 73
Newton, Sir Isaac (1642–1704) 201
Nichols, John (1745–1826) 11, 16
Noel, Baptist, fourth Earl of Gainsborough (1708–51) 83
Noel, Elizabeth *née* Chapman, Countess of Gainsborough (1708–71) 83
Norris, John (1657–1712) 133

Oliver, Dr William (1695–1764) 19, 99, 148
Onslow, Arthur (1691–1768) 118, 262
opera 33, 46–7, 68
order of payment liv, 260, 261–3
Osborn, John (d. 1739) bookseller 49, 58
Osborne, John, Sr (d. 1745) xli, 93

Palmer, Ashley (d. 1792) 168, 169
Palmer, Sarah (1721?–1801) 168
Palmer, Susanna (1736?–1829) 168
Pamela Censured (1741) 30
Pamela in High Life (1741) 44
Parker, Thomas, first Earl of Macclesfield (1667–1732) 117
Pennington, Montagu (1762–1849)
   Memoirs of the Life of Mrs. Elizabeth Carter (1807) 133
   A Series of Letters Between Mrs. Elizabeth Carter and Miss Catherine Talbot, from the Year 1741 to 1770 (1809) 132, 135
'Philaretes' xv, xlii, xlvi, 40–4, 136–7, 179
Philips, Ambrose: *The Distrest Mother* (1712) 162
Phillips, Richard (1767–1840) liii–liv, 223
'Philo-Paideias' xli–xlii, 36–7
Philopamela 89–90
Pluche, Noël-Antoine (1688–1761) 28, 201
Poole, John (m. 1742) 244
Pope, Alexander (1688–1744) xxxv, 22, 40, 93, 100–1
   correspondence xxxvi–xxxvii
   critique of his Homer translations 159
   Dunciad (1728) xxxviii
   on *Pamela* 93–5

Porteous, John (*c.* 1695–1736) 12
Poumies, John (d. 1769) 263–73
Psalmanazar, George (1679–1763) 62

Ramsay, Andrew Michael: *The Travels of Cyrus* (1727) 31
Read, John (d. 1760) 185–7
receipt 20–1
   of payment xlix, liv–lv, 137–8, 260–73
Reni, Guido (1575–1642) 141
Rich, John (1692–1761) 100–1
Richardson, Anne (bap. 1737, d. 1783) xlviii, lii, 58, 133, 192, 231, 244
Richardson, Elizabeth, *née* Leake (1697–1773) xlviii, 13, 46, 47, 51, 56, 59, 98, 99, 105, 111, 124, 133, 183, 184, 223, 231, 232, 244–5
Richardson, Jonathan the elder (1667–1745) 100
Richardson, Martha ('Patty') (bap. 1736, d. 1785) (SR's daughter) xlviii, xlix, lii, 22, 58, 119, 124, 126, 131, 135, 136, 144, 151, 153, 157, 158, 161, 163, 166, 169, 172, 177, 178, 181, 184, 185, 188, 190, 192, 197, 198, 199, 205, 206, 213, 214, 218, 221, 225, 229, 232, 234, 238, 241, 243, 249, 250, 251
Richardson, Martha (m. 1721, d. 1731) 34
Richardson, Mary (bap. 1735, d. 1783) xlviii, 58
Richardson, Samuel (1689–1761)
   I. *Life and Professional Activities*
     as letter-writer 113–14
     handwriting xix
     use of copyists xvi, lii–liii
     as mentor and promoter of authors and letter-writers 115–16
     as trade colleague xiv, xl
     anonymity 59
     copyright 22
     correspondence xxxv–xxxviii
      familiar correspondence xlvii–xlix
      a novelist's correspondence xli–xlvii
      printing correspondence xxxviii–xli
      text xlix–lix
     duty to God 10
     health of 50, 58
      advice about health 23–4
     nephew as apprentice 3–10
     newspapers (advertising in) 19–20, 24–8, 33–4, 39, 47
     North End, house at 110–11, 159
     printing costs 16–18, 121, 122–3, 137–8
     printing-house xl–xli, 7, 9, 114
     printing projects 101, 102, 102–3, 106, 107, 108–9, 109–10, 112, 121, 122–3, 129, 146, 171–2
     Salisbury Court, house and shop at xxvi, xxviii, xxix, xxxi, 15, 23, 82, 107, 134, 145, 243
     soliciting correspondence 33–4, 57, 93–4
     women readers xlii–xliii

276

INDEX

II. *The Novels*:

Clarissa (1747–8) xxxv–xxxviii, xxxix,
  xli–xlviii, xlix, 120, 124, 224, 251
  3rd and 4th editions of xxix, xlv, 128, 182
  commentary on xxxvii–xxxviii, xlii, xliv,
    xlv, 125–7, 139, 140, 151–3, 158–63, 173–83,
    185, 188, 190–1, 192–9, 250–1
  composition of 110, 128
  discussion of characters in 194–6,
    206–12
  ending of 40, 137, 156, 179–80, 189, 190–1
  index to 14, 159, 213
  Irish publication of 69, 228
  lack of index in 159
  neologisms 160–1
  paintings 123
  postscript to 182, 188, 190–1
  preface xlvi, 125
  prefatory material to xlvi, 125, 153–5, 156–7,
    224
  publication of 163
  reader response to 119–20, 124–5, 126–8,
    131–2, 135, 136–7, 139–44, 144–5, 146,
    150–1, 151–3, 157–8, 158–61, 161–3, 166–8,
    173–7, 177–8, 179–81, 181–3, 185–7, 188–9,
    190–1, 197–8, 198–9, 200–3, 204, 205,
    213–14, 214–17, 218–21, 222–3, 225–7,
    229–31, 232, 238–40, 250–1
  responses to reviews of 251–3
  revisions to 110, 182, 198, 249–50
  rumoured ending of 40
  SR on reader response to 169–70,
    192–6
  table of contents to 14, 138
  title of 130
  translation of xii
Pamela (1740) xxxv, xxxvi, xxxviii, xli–xlvi,
  xlix, l–li, 69
  advertisement of 34, 39
  commentary on xlii, xliii, 22, 24–37, 38–45,
    53–4, 89, 190
  discussion of characters in 208
  ending of 136
  factual basis of 29, 40, 82–4, 85
  French translation (1741) 93
  index to manuscript of 38
  introductory materials 15
  prefatory materials to 15, 24–8, 28–30, 44,
    60–1, 76, 92
  publication of 39–40
  reader response to 22, 24–37, 38, 39–40,
    40–2, 44–5, 53–4, 77–9, 89–92, 190, 216,
    219, 251
  references to xlix
  SR on reader response to, 80–1
  translation of 30, 93
  unauthorized continuations 30,
    44, 70

Pamela II (*Pamela in Her Exalted Condition*)
  (1741) xxxv, xli, xliii–xlvi, xlix, l, 15, 38,
    40, 46, 47–51, 55, 60, 61, 66–7, 69, 71, 72,
    75, 79, 82–4, 89, 90, 92, 95, 208
  advertisement of 71
  factual basis of 82–4, 85
  'Letter from Lady Davers' 61–6
  reader response to 15, 38, 50–1, 51–2, 53–4,
    55, 56–7, 58–9, 60–1, 66–7, 67–8, 69, 70,
    71, 72, 73–4, 74–6, 89–92, 94–5
II. *Other Works*
  *Answer to the Letter of a Very Reverend and
    Worthy Gentleman, An* (1749) 231, 238,
    241
  Apprentice's Vade Mecum, The (1734) xxxvi, 3
  Clarissa (1751) xxix, xl
  Familiar Letters (1741) xli
  *Letters and Passages Restored from the
    Original Manuscripts of the History of
    Sir Charles Grandison* (1753–4) xxxv,
    xxxvi, xxxviii, xliv, xlvi, 69, 100, 112, 124,
    159, 242

Richardson, Sarah (bap. 1740, d. 1773) xlviii,
  46, 58
Richardson, Thomas Verren (bap. 1717–32) (SR's
  nephew) xxxvi, 3–10
Richardson, William (SR's brother) lii, 3
Richardson, William (SR's nephew) xlix, lii, 136
Rivington, Charles (1688–1742) xl–xli, xliv, xlix,
  li, 30–3, 34
Rivington, James (1724–1802) 129, 146
Rivington, John (1720–92) 129, 146
Roberts, James (fl. 1714–54) 38, 107–8
Roe, Sir Thomas (1581–1644) 14, 21, 22
Rowe, Nicholas: *The Ambitious Step-Mother*
  (1700) 93
Ruffhead, Owen (c. 1723–69) 237

Sacheverell, Henry (bap. 1674, d. 1724) 117
Scott, Francis, second Duke of Buccleuch
  (1695–1751) lvi, 232
Seneca the Younger (5 BCE–65 CE) 225–6
Shakespeare, William (1564–1616) 93, 143
  Henry VI, Part 3 (1591) 153
  King Lear (1606) 191, 252
  Troilus and Cressida (1609) 92
Sharpe, John (1700?–56) 116–17
Sherburn, George, ed: *The Correspondence of
  Alexander Pope* 100
Sidney, Philip (1554–86)
  Arcadia (1581/1590/1593) xli
  Defence of Poesie (1595) 65
'Six Ladies' lii, 82–8
Skelton, Philip (1707–87) xlv, 58, 227–31, 238, 240,
  241, 244
'Smith, R.' xlv, xlvi, 125, 126–8, 164, 200, 203, 213,
  218–21, 223, 225–7
Smollett, Tobias: *The Regicide* (1749) 222

277

INDEX

Society for the Encouragement of Learning (1735–49) xxxvi, 14–15, 16, 18, 19, 20, 21, 45
Solon (*c.* 630-560 BCE) 156
Spectator, The (1711–12) 119, 159, 162, 190
Spence, Joseph (1699–1768) xliv, xlvi, 138–42, 145, 214, 258–9
Spirit Duties Act, The ('Gin Act,' 1735) 12–13
Stationers' Company xxv–xxx, xxxix, xli, 34, 117, 245
Statute of Anne, The (1710) 22
Staunton, Elizabeth (1723–?) 131
Steele, Richard (1672–1729)
    essays 159
    The Funeral, or Grief à-la-Mode (1735) 32
Stewart, Captain James (d. 1762) 232
Stewart, Henry, Duke of Albany, Lord Darnley (1545/6–67) 246
Strabo (*c.* 64 BCE–*c.* 24 CE) 224
Strahan, Anne (1748–9) 105, 244, 255
Strahan, David (1754–5) 105
Strahan, Margaret, *née* Elphinston (1719–85) 104, 245, 255–7
Strahan, Rachael (1742–65) 256
Strahan, Samuel (1745–7) lv–lvi, 103, 105
Strahan, William (1715–85) xxxix, liv, lv, 103–5, 243–9, 253–8
Sturges, Hannah see Hesilrige, Lady, *née* Hannah Sturges
Suárez, Francisco (1548–1617) 200
Swift, Jonathan (1667–1745) xxxvii, 35, 53
Swinton, John (1703–77) 73–4, 249

Talbot, Catherine (1721–70) 132, 135
Tate, Nahum (*c.* 1652–1715) 165
Tatler, The (1709–11) 159
Tenison, Richard (d. 1725) 54
Tonson, Jacob I (1655/6–1736) 33, 117
Townshend, Etheldreda, Viscountess (*c.* 1708–88) 106
Townshend, Thomas (1701–80) 264–8, 270–2
Tucker, Gertrude (d. 1796) 155

Upcott, Wiliam 223

Vanderplank, Samuel (d. 1750) 84–5
Virgil (70–19 BCE) 92
    Aeneid 218, 221
    Eclogues 200
    Georgics 128

Walpole, Horatio (1678–1757), first Baron Walpole of Wolterton 269
Walpole, Robert (1676–1745), first Earl of Orford 35, 262, 263, 269
Warburton, Elizabeth, *née* Hobman (d. 1748?) 154
Warburton, William (1698–1779) xxxvii, xliv, xlv, xlvi–xlvii, 40, 93–5, 100, 153–5, 156–7, 237
Ward, John (1678/9–1758) 16, 21–2
Watt, Ian: *Rise of the Novel* xli
Webster, William (1689–1758) xliii, 24–8
Weekly Miscellany (1732–41) xliii, 24
West, James (1703–72) 107
West, John, sixth Baron De La Warr (1663–1723) 260–1
Weston, James (1688?–1748) 117
Wilde, Allington (1700–70) 34
Wilde, John (d. 1720) 34
Wilson, Bridget (m. 1742) 53
Wilson, Thomas (1663–1755) 228
Windus, John (fl. 1720–25?) 23–4
Winnington, Thomas (1696–1746) 106
Woodward, Thomas (fl. 1726–43) 93
Wotton, William (1666–1727) 115–16

Xenophon of Anthens (*c.* 430–354 BCE) 236

Yonge, Sir William, fourth baronet (*c.* 1693–1755) 262
Yorke, Charles (1722–70) 103, 107, 108–9
    Some Considerations on the Law of Forfeiture, for High Treason (1746) xl, lvi, 107–8
Yorke, Philip, second Earl of Hardwicke (1720–90) xxxix, 184–5
Young, Edward (bap. 1683, d. 1765) xli, xliv, xlvi, lii, liv, 189, 259
    Conjectures on Original Composition (1759) xli, xliv, xlvi